MENLO SCHOOL
MENLO COLLEGE
founded 1915

Gift of

MENLO FACULTY WIVES CLUB

July 1968

THE FOUR BRONTËS

THE FOUR BRONTËS

EMILY, CHARLOTTE, BRANWELL, AND ANNE

THE
FOUR BRONTËS

THE LIVES AND WORKS
of
CHARLOTTE, BRANWELL, EMILY,
and ANNE BRONTË

by

LAWRENCE and ELISABETH HANSON

WITH A NEW PREFACE BY THE AUTHORS

ARCHON BOOKS
1967

FIRST PUBLISHED 1949
OXFORD UNIVERSITY PRESS

FOURTH IMPRESSION 1967
CORRECTED AND WITH A NEW PREFACE BY THE AUTHORS

LIBRARY OF CONGRESS CATALOG CARD NUMBER: 67–11475
PRINTED IN THE UNITED STATES OF AMERICA

PREFACE TO THE 1967 EDITION

WHEN a reprint of this book was suggested to us, our first impulse was to wait until we had time to rewrite the entire work. Then we had second thoughts. Innumerable examples from the work of writers far more important than ourselves show that a drastically revised text, though it corrects errors of fact and judgment and, as prose, is often vastly superior to the original draft, fails in one vital particular, to preserve the spontaneity of the book as first written. This creative spur which leads to composition is the heart of any work; take it away and life goes too. So we agreed to a reprint of the first impression of *The Four Brontës* (there have been three to date) with errata. These errata consist in the main of corrections of style and psychological judgments which we made to the second and third impressions and listed for a few months after the appearance of the third impression with a view to a further impression. Some, therefore, are new to the present impression. A few factual corrections have also been made but these mercifully were never numerous. New material was also added.

We also include here an outline of what we believe to be the book's chief faults.

Background   We ought to have given more space to a full exposition of the heritage and home life of the Brontës. It is not possible to understand the Brontë children or their work unless the biographer has made abundantly clear that they were wholly Celtic and that they lived in one of the crudest, most violent and most bigoted parts of England. Mrs. Gaskell, whose biography, with all its omissions and weaknesses, remains the best so far written, understood this very well. Unfortunately, she wrote under the heavy handicap of having prominent characters in the Brontë story still alive. Hence her picture is necessarily incomplete and at times even false. We corrected the falsities; we should have filled the gaps more comprehensively than we did.

Mr. Brontë   Before his death the father of the Brontës said that, whatever might be thought and written about him, had he not been what he was his children would not have been as they

were. We saw this truth but neglected to profit by it. We succumbed to the temptation of treating Mr. Brontë ironically. We
thereby missed the opportunity of establishing him in his right-
ful place, as the most vital human factor in the lives and work
of his children. If we had our time again we should entitle our
book *The Five Brontës* and should give much closer attention
to Mr. Brontë's life prior to settling at Haworth, to a serious
analysis of his life there, including the reasons for his retirement
and heavy drinking at a comparatively early age, and the degree
to which he influenced his boy and girls by his words, his attitude and, finally, by his withdrawal from them.

Juvenilia We did not sufficiently emphasize the correspondence between the juvenilia and the mature works of the
Brontës. The effect of the one on the other was immense; not,
we still feel, as immense as Miss Fannie E. Ratchford would
have us believe, but nevertheless much more considerable than
one would suppose from reading our book.

The Novels We underrated Anne's novels as we tended to
underrate Anne herself (Mrs. Gaskell, we feel, allowed herself
in this instance, even more than with Emily, to be governed by
outward appearance and manner)—and particularly did we
underrate the devastatingly truthful picture of life as it was
lived in *Agnes Grey*. In the reverse direction we overpraised
Wuthering Heights, The Professor, Jane Eyre and *Shirley*, particularly the last.

Psychology Most of the faults of psychology in our book
arise from that common failing in the biographer, an uncritical
acceptance of the popular view. There are two outstanding
examples:

1. We associated ourselves with the general condemnation
of Charlotte's picture of local society in *Jane Eyre*. In fact her
characters were accurate delineations, in manner and even in
the apparently incredible stilted speech, of the people she and
Anne had heard and seen at Stonegappe, Rawdon, Blake Hall
and Thorp Green. And as a matter of interest we know that even
today in these regions behavior and conversation is almost un-
believably bookish and old fashioned.

2. We likewise followed the popular view that Heger's
complete disinterest in Charlotte was proven by his use of her

letters; we even echoed the general indignation at this base treatment of such precious material. Yet little discernment is needed to see that if Heger had been as disinterested in Charlotte as had been generally assumed, or as untouched by her appeals, he would have destroyed her letters as soon as read. As it was, he carried them in his pocket for years, risking discovery by the formidable Mme. Heger. And his use of them is so typical of his thrifty countrymen—whom we have since come to know well—as to bear no stigma whatever, quite the contrary.

Since *The Four Brontës* was first published a number of books on the subject have appeared: excellent studies of Charlotte (by a distinguished Methodist), Branwell and Anne; a painstaking and most valuable source book on Mr. Brontë; a competent and well written general biography, marred only by an attempt on somewhat flimsy grounds (set school essays) to present Emily an as orthodox believer—a view that surely does very much less than justice to that fine and essentially pagan spirit and renders much of her poetry meaningless; and finally we have seen the inevitable novel on the Brontës, a form that seems to arrive every decade or so.

All this and more. But what has not appeared is a modern Mrs. Gaskell supported by all the resources of twentieth-century scholarship. And until such a work is written we feel that, with all its faults, *The Four Brontës* has a value that is unaffected by the passing of time. Our reasons for so thinking are simple; the book was written *con amore* by people who had loved the Brontës since childhood and had lived with them in spirit all the years after. In consequence we believe that our portraits of the immortal family, both singly and in their effect one on another, remain in general as valid as they were when first set down more than twenty years ago.

E. H.
L. H.

1966

PREFACE

THIS book has had a long history. I began to collect materials for it as far back as 1931, and, a year or two later, had a draft on paper. By that time, however, several Brontë scholars were at work—Mr. Wise and Mr. Symington in this country, and Mr. Hatfield and Miss Ratchford in the United States, for instance—and I decided to await the publication of their works before proceeding with my own. There were also at that time some existing Brontë manuscripts that I had not been able to trace, and I did not wish to publish my book until I had seen all of them or had had them examined.

Eventually, I finished the final draft in 1940, and the typescript was sent to the United States for safe keeping during the war. When it was returned, after the war, the book no longer satisfied me as it stood. My wife and I therefore decided to rewrite it—and it is this version that is now published.

The original plan of the book, and the main idea behind it, remain. Its purpose is, first, to provide a full and accurate one-volume life of the Brontës, using all existing material. Beyond this, the aim of the book is to study in detail the effect of the Brontës on each other.

It seems to me that there has been in the past a tendency—understandable, certainly, but susceptible to error—to give undue prominence to one or more of the Brontë children at the expense of the others; and at the expense, also, of the truth about this family so far as it can now be known.

Thus we have had Lives in plenty of Charlotte; many of Emily; some of Charlotte and Emily together; a few of the three sisters; and one or two of Branwell; but none dealing fully with all four Brontës. It can be said that every Brontë biography necessarily mentions all the children. None could, of course, be omitted; but the fact is that, in biographies of Charlotte, the portrait of Emily is often subordinated to the central figure, while those of Anne and Branwell are frequently mere sketches. Likewise in biographies of Emily. This leads inevitably to a distortion of truth. Such treatment, however natural it may seem, is unnecessary, and defeats its own ends. In any considered study of the Brontës, the predominance of the two greater figures will assert itself; but this in no way detracts from the part played in their lives by the two lesser figures; nor are these lesser figures without intrinsic interest in themselves. But the fact that Anne and Branwell here receive what may be described (with a possible exception in the case of Branwell) as their first full-length study, matters less than the fact that an attempt has now been made to consider and appraise their true contribution to the lives and works of the two major figures. For this reason, I am glad that this book is likely to appear in the centenary year of the death of Anne.

The four Brontës lived the greater part of their lives in a seclusion that is particularly difficult to imagine to-day. They were doubly secluded. They lived in a remote village, to which the coming of a stranger was an event; to which the news of the outside world had a fabulous, unreal quality, as if from another planet. They lived among people whose violence of thought, language, feeling, and action was intensified by hard living, by a hard, sombre country setting, and, above all, by the propinquity none could escape. Yet, though they absorbed this atmosphere, and were profoundly affected by it, the four Brontës were secluded even from the restricted life of the village. They did not mix with the village people. They lived in a small house in which, at most, they had the use of one living room, the kitchen, and two bedrooms. All these rooms were small, and, in winter, so cold that the children were confined to the two downstairs rooms. The weather was so hard that for days at a time they could not leave the house; and when they did leave it, they left it together. Under such conditions they could not have withdrawn from each other's company, even had they wished. In fact, they did not wish it. They lived together, day after day, month after month, year after year, without a break, secluded within, secluded without, rarely parted, rarely interrupted, virtually uncontrolled. Scarcely a movement of one could escape the eyes of the other three. Scarcely a word could be said that was not heard by all. Scarcely a thought could pass through the mind of one that was not known to the others. They were as near one person as could well be imagined.

And yet they were not one person, but four very different

people. And that is why in the present book—as its title suggests —each Brontë is given full consideration; is given, in fact, the kind of attention that each one was given by the other three. And although the actual space devoted to one necessarily exceeds that given to another, I have tried to indicate with greater precision than hitherto the interplay of character and action between the four Brontës, since the influence of one upon another was always profound and often decisive.

This, then, beyond the correction of detail now made possible by reference to the manuscripts, is the main object of the present study. And I hope that it succeeds in some measure in defining and clarifying the nature and scope of these influences, and so in making known a little more about all four Brontës.

I am indebted to the work of the editors of the *Shakespeare Head Brontë*; and in particular to the late Thomas James Wise, who allowed me to spend much time in his Ashley Library, and gave me freedom to examine and use his Brontë manuscripts. I must also acknowledge the similar kindness and generosity of the late Mr. Henry H. Bonnell, Mr. C. W. Hatfield, and Sir Alfred Law. I much appreciate the willing help given to me, or to those who worked for me when I was engaged in war duties, by the Municipal Authorities and Librarians at Bradford, Keighley, and Halifax, and in the University of Leeds, in this country; and by the Librarians of Harvard University Library and the Henry E. Huntington Library in the United States.

To Mrs. Henry H. Bonnell I wish to express my great appreciation of her kind interest in my work, and of her permission to examine manuscripts of Emily's poems, and drawings by the Brontës, and to print or reproduce them in this volume. My thanks are also due to the President and Chairman of The Brontë Society for their kindness in giving me facilities to examine the Bonnell Collection and other manuscripts at Haworth, and for their permission to print and reproduce them here; and to Mr. W. T. Oliver, Mrs. A. Weir and Mr. H. G. Mitchell for their help in this connexion.

I am most grateful to Mrs. Doris Long and Messrs. Hodder & Stoughton Ltd., for permission to quote from Mr. Clement K. Shorter's *The Brontës: Life and Letters*: and *The Complete Works of Emily Brontë: Volume One—Poems*; and I should like to take this opportunity of paying my tribute to the pioneer work of the late Mr. Shorter—work on which all succeeding Brontë studies have depended almost entirely.

I am much obliged to Miss Fannie E. Ratchford for her interest and helpfulness, and also for the assistance that her own work on the Brontës has been to me. My thanks also go to Mr. John D. Gordan, Curator of the Henry W. and Albert A. Berg Collection in the New York Public Library, for his courteous assistance, and to the authorities in charge of the Berg Collection for their permission to examine and publish manuscripts in their possession. To the Director of the British Museum I must express my gratitude for permission to print and reproduce manuscripts in his custody; and to the staff in the Manuscript Room, the Reading Room, and the North Library for their helpfulness on many occasions. I also acknowledge with thanks the permission of Mr. Basil Blackwell to quote from *The Shakespeare Head Brontë*; of the Editor of *The Times* to reprint letters from Charlotte which first appeared in his newspaper; and of the Director of The National Portrait Gallery to reproduce a portrait in his collection.

I am indebted to Professor D. R. MacCalman for his views on the psychology of the Brontës; and to the comments of Dr. Catherine C. Maclean, who read twice through my manuscript and typescript—once under conditions of great difficulty.

Finally, I want to make clear that, if this book succeeds at all in its object, the credit must go very largely to my wife. She came late to the collaboration, and had to work against time, but she has managed to make the joint version a great deal better than its predecessors, and very much closer to my original but always unfulfilled aims.

L. H.

Evesham 1940—*London* 1948

CONTENTS

ILLUSTRATIONS

CORRECTIONS TO THE FIRST IMPRESSIONS OF
THE FOUR BRONTËS

Page

1, *l.* 3 up *for* ". . . article show that. . . ." *read* ". . . article express conventional ideas clearly."

2, *l.* 2 down *delete* "or early the next year"

5, *l.* 7 up *for* "violent" *read* "determined"

5, *l.* 7 up *delete* "even"

6, *l.* 2 down *for* ". . . it appealed to a . . . integrity" *read* ". . . it appealed to his love of violence—though he had little of Grimshaw's integrity."

6, *l.* 15 down *for* "Mr. Brontë was able . . . dark" *read* "Mr. Brontë spent long quiet hours every day in the parlour; his wife was occupied by the baby and five other children, all confined to the living room or kitchen because their father disliked noise, and by what to her was a cold and unlovely house in a dark. . . ."

6, *l.* 5 up *delete* "warm"

7, *l.* 5 down *delete* "in fact"

8, *l.* 11 up *read* "Mary Burder's reply was chilling. She pointed out that she was no longer the. . . ."

9, *l.* 8 down *read* "Miss Burder had by no means finished with her old lover and the bitterness of her letter chiefly illuminates the uncommon vanity of a suitor who could believe that shabby behavior would be forgotten in the joy of recapture."

9, *l.* 23 down *delete* "Baffled"

9, *l.* 10 up *read* "While these negotiations were going on, the children. . . ."

10, *l.* 5 down *for* "He had little love . . . children;" *read* "He loved children little and understood them less;"

10, *l.* 12 up *for* "he sank . . . parish." *read* "he drew steadily into a premature retirement at home and in the parish."

11, *l.* 22 down *delete* "to be"

11, *l.* 11 up *read* ". . . education at a low fee for daughters of poor clergy."

12, *l.* 4 down *for* ". . . Charlotte, in her savage . . ." read ". . . Charlotte's savage. . . ."

13, *l.* 18 down *for* ". . . imagination fastened . . . challenge," *read* ". . . imagination fed on the atmosphere of early death and even earlier resentment. To Emily death and resentment alike took the form of a challenge. . . ."

13, *l.* 21 down *delete* "And even"

13, *l.* 9 up *for* "She also introduced . . . Methodism." *read* "More important, she introduced the children to the Methodism in which she had been brought up in Cornwall and which she opposed fiercely to their father's more conventional brand of religion."

13, *l.* 6 up *for* "extravagant" *read* "uninhibited"

13, *l.* 2 up *for* ". . . damned, was to . . . exciting." *read* ". . . damned struck them as fearful and exciting."

14, *l.* 2 down *read* ". . . words quickly became part of their vocabulary."

14, *l.* 4 down *for* "violent" *read* "crude and even brutal"

14, *l.* 5 down *delete* "very"

14, *l.* 9 down *read* "Mr. Brontë's withdrawal from family life and parish duties became, like his huge white cravat, more pronounced every year, but one significant exception was the Greek and Latin lessons he gave to Branwell. In Mr. Brontë's world women were created to minister to men and sons were allowed many liberties denied to daughters. Like all would-be heavy fathers, when he discriminated he leaned over backwards; as an only son Branwell had a particularly generous ration of freedom of action unknown to his sisters and, naturally enough, promptly took more. He successfully evaded his father's ban on friendship. . . ."

14, *l.* 15 down *for* "His charm, wit . . . soon" *read* "His charm, quick mind and distinctive looks stood out in a village where such advantages were a rarity and soon . . ."

14, *l.* 18 up *read* ". . . to whom her sisters and the supposedly superior brother all looked for a lead. Charlotte. . . ."

14, *l.* 16 up *for* ". . . great doings had fired her . . ." *read* ". . . great deeds fired her. . . ."

14, *l.* 15 up *for* ". . . something of herself . . . drive. *read* ". . . something of the family. She was no stoic like Emily, had no trace of Anne's humility, and despised Branwell's airy optimism which, she knew, disguised too often merely a dislike of hard work. She had made up her mind to advance them all and advance they should. She was well dowered for the task. She had some of her father's egotism and a touch of his subtlety, she inherited her mother's passionate family feeling, and she possessed what both parents conspicuously lacked, energy, drive, and vision."

14, *l.* 7 up *for* ". . . even Emily . . ." *read* ". . . even that stout individualist Emily. . . ."

14, *l.* 4 up *for* "so" *read* "as"

14, *l.* 3 up *for* "Anne, who was . . . loving" *read* "Anne, in childhood apparently little more than a loving. . . ."

15, *l.* 5 down *read* ". . . in the kitchen which was not only the one tolerably warm room in the house (the inaccessible parlour excepted) but contained the stimulating personality of Tabitha Aykroyd, the nearest to a mother they were ever to know. Tabby, as she quickly became to all, had come to the parsonage as cook and maid of all work soon after the return of Charlotte and Emily from Cowan Bridge the previous year, and her typical Yorkshire blend of sharp, rough tongue and warm heart soon endeared her to the children. It . . . subject."

17, *l.* 9 down *read* "Each of the twelve Young Men soon acquired a. . . ."

17, *l.* 14 up *read* "Then the young Brontës carried the game a stage further; they began to lead a double existence in it."

17, *l.* 9 up *read* "In this way they enjoyed the best of both worlds, the exciting but uncertain . . . gods."

17, *l.* 2 up *for* "As" *read* "When"

18, *l.* 16 up *for* "called" *read* "named"

21, *last line read* ". . . a rival saga later to be invented. . . ."

23, *l.* 2 up *for* "gives" *read* "gave"

23, *last line read* ". . . distinction as it was to give their novels greatness."

24, *l.* 4 down *continue* after "birthday" "The future had to be thought of and this, for a girl of that time and social standing, meant a post as governess. Her schooling had been short and her official home tuition had long since come to an end; neither her father nor aunt could teach her more. In some directions she was already educated far beyond most adults, her reading wide, her knowledge of history and politics exceptional for a woman, let alone a girl in her mid-teens. And in sheer common sense born of early responsibility and a keen mind she could have few rivals in any walk of life. But a masculine intellect would no more help her to get a post as governess than a passionate and wholly feminine heart, so the powers that be decided that she must be finished off in the approved conventional style. Arrangements. . . ."

24, *l.* 10 down *for* "Charlotte's" *read* "her"

24, *l.* 6 up *for* "strong-minded *read* "self-confident"

24, *l.* 4 up *continue* after "imagination" "There are traces of these changes of thought in their early Gondal writings."

25, *first line delete* "Meanwhile"

25, *l.* 15 up *delete* ", in the arts,"

26, *l.* 10 down *for* "Her reasons for . . . eldest" *read* "She had made her reasons clear; she had not wanted to come to school—she expected nothing but unhappiness away from Haworth—but as the eldest. . . ."

26, *l.* 19 down *continue* after "games" "It is a measure of Charlotte's strong and sincere personality and of a charm that percolated even through such outward dowdiness that her stand was accepted, not only by Mary Taylor and Ellen Nussey, but by every girl in the school. In the final reckoning her diminutive figure, her queer accent, her outmoded appearance, her superficial priggishness could not weigh against such passionate eagerness to forward her family's interests, such formidable mental powers and moral superiority. So she was left unhindered to make her own way, and she set out, resolute in restrained sorrow, to cultivate her tastes. . . ."

27, *l.* 9 down *for* ". . . her own, an outlook . . . remained" *read* ". . . own and as she was as self-willed and independent as Charlotte the friendship soon revealed its limitations.
In spite of her two friends, Charlotte remained. . . ."

28, *l.* 2 down *for* ". . . seeing, not ruined . . . gory" *read* ". . . seeing, not deserted mills peacefully surrounded by fields but gory. . . ."

29, *l.* 14 down *delete* "her"

32, *l.* 13 down *read* "Branwell did not fulfill his early promise. He lacked application and was casting his net too widely. Drawing, painting, music, writing—he threw himself into one after the other with immense enthusiasm, tried to do too much too quickly and became discouraged. He was unlucky, with such a temperament, to be an only son; he needed criticism and. . . ."

32, *l.* 20 down *continue* after "all" "Only Charlotte spoke her mind from time to time. Whatever Roe Head may have done for her in the way of learning the social graces—and it did not do much—it had not eradicated a naturally pungent tongue. Yorkshire country people in the first half of the nineteenth century were brutishly plain-spoken and Charlotte, eager, impatient, hot tempered, proved a good pupil, improving on her masters. The Haworth people were crude and could get no further than plain abuse; Charlotte had brains and a gift of expression and, when angry, her words stung. But one of the few people they affected least was the brother who most needed them. Branwell could always choose to read envy behind her anger, possibly not always without cause. Besides, he had been taught by experience to rely successfully on his considerable charm; in the end he could usually smile or talk everybody round, even a cantankerous sister."

32, *l.* 17 up *read* "No serious control was put upon. . . ."

37, *l.* 22 down *for* "brilliant" *read* "smart"

37, *l.* 11 up *for* ". . . tender but conventional . . . freedom." *read* ". . . tender religious conscience of Anne. She valued her younger sister's unquestioning affection, and admired and envied . . . freedom."

38, *l.* 11 up *delete* "sharp-tongued, almost always"

39, *l.* 8 up *for* ". . . to endure it—and her affection for . . . intolerable." *read* ". . . endure it, and she raged. To her, yearning to make a place for herself and her sisters in the world, domestic work at home, for which she had no gift, a badly paid and humiliating post as governess, years of waiting for an unlikely offer of marriage, seemed equally intolerable."

40, *l.* 4 down *read* "... darling of aunt and preferred by her father."

42, *l.* 11 up *for* "... and she was afraid that ... Haworth." *read* "... and was afraid that she was going into a rapid decline. She felt that Emily would die if she did not go home, and could not rest until she was sent back to Haworth."

43, *l.* 13 up *for "is" read* "is"

43, *l.* 7 up *read* "... reality and which one entering into manhood would look back on as a glorious dream. I speak so sir because while a child 'Blackwood' formed my cheif delight, and I feel certain that no child before enjoyed reading as I did, because none ever had such works as "Noctes," "Christmas Dreams," "Christopher in his Sporting Jacket" to read.'"

44, *first line read* "'Long long ago seems the time when we danced hand in hand with our golden-haired sister whom all that looked on loved, long long long ago, the day on which she died. That hour so far more dreadful than any hour that now can darken us on this earth—When her coffin and that velvet pall descended—and descended—slowly—slowly—into the horrid clay and we were borne deathlike and wishing to die out of the churchyard. . . .'"

44, *l.* 9 down *for* "sir" *read* "Sir"

44, *l.* 11 down *read* "'... remembered now afford feelings which I repeat—I cannot describe.'"

44, *l.* 15 down *for* "... Noctes", when I was a child, laid" *read* "Noctes, when I was a child laid a hold."

44, *l.* 18 down *for* "... Hogg, and ..." *read* "... Hogg and ...'"

44, *l.* 21 down *continue* after "He ends" " 'But don't think Sir that I write nothing but miseries. My day is far too much in the morning for such continued shadow—Nor think either (and this I entreat) that I wish to deluge you with poetry. I send it because it is soonest read and comes from the heart—If it goes *to* yours print it and write to me on the subject of *contribution*. Then I will send prose —But if what I send *now* is worthless what I have said has only been conceit and folly—yet CONDEMN NOT UNHEARD."

46, *l.* 5 down *for* "life" *read* "future"

46, *l.* 9 down *read* "... and a lifetime of boredom."

46, *l.* 8 up *delete* "Charlotte writes"

47, *l.* 17 down *delete* "Charlotte scribbles in her diary"

49, *l.* 3 down *for* "excesses" *read* "flights"

49, *l.* 6 down *for* "... indication of how much ... her." *read* "indication of her sufferings. At last she confided in Ellen, trying with typical intensity to set up her mild friend and her equally mild religious faith as example and guide, and during the next two years she was to make one attempt after another to ease her mind in letters that Ellen must have found strange to the point of embarrassment."

53, *l.* 14 down *delete* "already"

60, *l.* 18 up *for* ". . . in Elizabeth Patchett's school . . . Halifax." *read* ". . . in Law Hill school, Southowram, near Halifax."

60, *l.* 12 up *read* "Of Emily's short stay at Southrowram little is known. Law Hill had been opened some years earlier by the sisters Maria and Elizabeth Patchett but by the time Emily arrived there Maria had married and gone to live in Dewsbury and Elizabeth, a stately and austere woman, managed the school. The building, with a three-story main wing, was old (the schoolrooms in the west wing had once been a weakers workroom) but set high and healthy on its hill, unlike Heald's House, which was soon to make Anne ill. The air, then, did not account for Emily's second collapse away from home; this was due to her inability to accommodate herself to life outside her home, a matter as always with her of the mind. Her "extreme reserve" with strangers was remembered at the school and so too was her "generous considerateness" towards those she liked. These are the only comments that have survived. Charlotte drew a gloomy. . . ."

60, *l.* 14 down *read* "During the months away from home Emily wrote lyrics which more than her Gondal poems gave her the. . . ."

61, *l.* 13 down *for* ". . . wreck."[18] *read* ". . . wreck. Roe Head had done nothing for her and from Law Hill she took only a name, but a name she was to make famous. One of the servants at the school was a Mrs. Earnshaw."[18]

66, *l.* 11 up *read* "But the youngest Brontë, whose mildness concealed considerable strength of character, was prim, and, after considerable. . . ."

69, *l.* 3 down *continue* after "speech" "What Charlotte could not know was that Anne was minimizing her sufferings in this deplorable situation; the truth was only to come out when she read the plainspoken account in *Agnes Grey.*"

71, *l.* 16 down *delete* "It was . . . she wrote."

73, *l.* 2 down *read* ". . . unexpected compliment—unexpected to her, that is, for she had no conception of her attractiveness to men. At the beginning. . . ."

75, *l.* 14 up *delete* "or deep"

78, *l.* 2 up *for* ". . . yet not happily." *read* ". . . but wretchedly."

87, *l.* 11 up *read* ". . . effect." (*delete* "the emotional . . . clear action.")

88, *l.* 5 down *for* ". . . by the pretty tyranny . . . employers."[1] *read* "by the tyranny of her charges, and their parents' fatuous child worship."

88, *l.* 10 up *read* "Charlotte." (*delete* "who despised . . . of purpose.")

88, *l.* 2 up *read* ". . . this moment she finally lost faith in him, and began to see and treat him, not as the family hope but its disgrace and positive obstacle to the future of herself and her sisters. When an ambitious and impatient young woman confesses that she has put her hopes on the wrong shoulders, she does not always consider how much her own attitude has contributed to weakening those shoulders, she is too busy feeling resentful at being taken in. In her novels Charlotte was to show herself a first rate psychologist. Nearer home she failed signally, she did not understand Emily, underrated Anne and did not read Branwell aright until too late. Whatever the provocations she suffered from him, and they were many, she was savagely unjust to the brother she had made so much of. He needed the loving discipline she alone could have given him. Her contempt and abuse made sure that he would go to pieces."

89, *l.* 14 down *read* "life." (*delete* "and clamoured for relief.")

96, *l.* 3 down *read* ". . . did she dream of happiness with. . . ."

96, *l.* 8 down *delete* "She could . . . of her state."

96, *l.* 14 up *read* "For the Brontë children, gifted with an intensity. . . ."

99, *l.* 2 down *delete* "game, a"

99, *l.* 3 down *continue* after "saga;" "they developed into a vital substitute for emotional fulfilment when the young authors reached physical maturity without a corresponding growth of experience or contact with reality. Anne, indeed, had seen a horrifying brand of reality at close hand but this had only enhanced the escape value of the Gondal world. Emily knew reality of a kind, the reality of an efficient girl about the house, but in knowledge of the world outside the parsonage she remained a child, obstinately refusing to grow up; everything had to be romanticised. Her love of violence, inherited from her father, and Anne's increasing morbidity both satisfied themselves in the unblushing melodrama of so many of the Gondal poems they were writing; both could try to sublimate, through their Gondal characters, longings and aspirations, feelings sensed rather than felt, they were inhibited from expressing in their more obviously personal poetry.

Every Gondal poem. . . ."

100, *l.* 6 down *delete* "for long"

100, *l.* 5 up *read* ". . . the work as such, she fretted under the discipline of people she could not respect."

101, *first line read* ". . . it had to be earned in such a way as to satisfy both pride and ambition."

101, *l.* 13 up *read* ". . . work, a weakness Charlotte, eager for independence, relegated to the back of her mind, their own education. . . ."

101, *l.* 7 up *delete* "her"

102, *l.* 11 down *read* "Soon after this, Anne and Emily agreed to write and seal papers describing what the writer was doing and thinking at the time, the papers to be opened four years later. This seems to have been an extension of an old habit of the sisters, of making special diary entries on their own, Charlotte's and Branwell's birthdays. This time, they wrote on Emily's birthday, and Anne, not long back with the Robinsons after her holiday at home, speculates on the school scheme Charlotte had outlined to her by letter:
July the 30th, A.D. 1841"

103, *l.* 4 up *read* "Emily filled her days with housework, studying, looking after her pets, wandering over. . . ."

104, *l.* 5 up *for* ". . . was ended, and . . . clearly:" *read* ". . . was ended. Emily was left alone with a Charlotte grimly determined to foist independence on her sisters whether they wanted it or not. Emily, already rich in another sort of independence, did not take kindly to Charlotte's emphasis on material benefits, and her poems, faithful index to her feelings, began to image the stoic:"

109, *l.* 19 down *read* "Emily's consent to the Dewsbury scheme had been won only after a struggle; she was dismayed and angry to learn that Dewsbury had been dropped without a word to her and that she was now expected to accept as a pleasurable and complimentary alternative a plan for her to go to school again and in a foreign country. It says much for her strength of will that, appreciating Charlott'e sincerity, she eventually submitted to a course that promised her little but wretchedness."

111, *l.* 5 down *delete* lines 5 through 12.

116, *l.* 13 down *read* ". . . again at Law Hill attacked her in. . . ."

119, *l.* 17 down *continue* after "woman." "—a view that the few essays which have been preserved, conventional in subject though they are, help to bear out."[20]

119, *l.* 2 up *for* "very" *read* "more than"

120, *l.* 10 up *for* "contented" *read* "triumphant"

122, *l.* 4 down *delete* "they"

124, *l.* 6 up *read* " '. . . great desire for activity.' And he was active, to the point of sending more verses to Blackwood "emboldened by the kind advice and encouragement of Mrs. Southey." He explained "They endeavour—feebly enough, I fear—to describe the harsh contrast between a mind, changed by long absence from home, and the feelings still alive in those who have never wandered; and who vainly expect the absent to return with a heart as warm as when they bade him farewell."—an undisguised reference to Charlotte, still his beacon. Again he received no reply from Blackwood and was driven back on drink and drugs to drown his disappointment."[7]

126, *l*. 5 up *for* "had" *read* "felt"

126, *l*. 4 up *for* "upon" *read* "on"

129, *l*. 2 down *continue* after "personality" ". . . , a man she had already thought of too warmly to be lightly given up. On both counts she was fiercely anxious to return. Emily was equally determined not to leave Haworth; her French was now good. . . ."

129, *l*. 9 down *for* "Tabby had emerged . . . Emily" *read* "Tabby had insisted on coming back to the parsonage, but although heartily welcomed, especially by Emily,

129, *l*. 18 up *for* "Mr. Brontë, who . . . attention."[22] *read* "Branwell took his liking for drink from his father, and Mr. Brontë was showing signs of needing watchful attention."[22]

129, *l*. 13 up *for* ". . . the single-mindedness of her desire." *read* ". . . her single-mindedness."

129, *l*. 8 up *for* "a cordial" *read* "an exceptionally cordial"

129, *l*. 6 up *for* ". . . finally decided Charlotte . . ." *read* ". . . gave Charlotte's conscience precisely the sanction it was looking for. . . ."

132, *l*. 9 up *continue* after "Branwell," "who had been temporarily forgiven when he took the post with Anne, "I can discern. . . ."

136, *l*. 20 up *delete* "yet"

136, *l*. 13 up *delete* "as"

137, *l*. 3 up *for* "probably" *read* "certainly"

144, *l*. 5 down *for* ". . . before; and she was . . . Charlotte. . . ." *read* ". . . before; and it was a torment to think that she had disappointed Heger by leaving. She. . . ."

144, *l*. 19 up *delete* "steadily"

144, *l*. 6 up *for* "Charlotte" *read* "she"

144, *l*. 4 up *delete* ". . . though remaining . . . to Charlotte. . . ."

144, *l*. 3 up *for* ". . . plane; and Charlotte's . . . girls." *read* ". . . plane; the relationship with Heger, not to be talked of except in general terms, effectively weakened the intimacy between the two young women."

145, *l*. 6 down *for* "They loved one . . . intimacy." *read* "Charlotte tended to turn to Emily as Branwell lost his hold on her affections, but the wish was not mutual, the feeling much more on the side of the elder. Emily had always regarded Charlotte as a kind of work and progress addict, relying on her early mother-relationship with the rest of the children to quash objection; she was wary and not to be caught again. Besides, Charlotte could not be frank about

Brussels, fearing her sister's condemnation, and without complete frankness one was lost with Emily."

145, *l.* 15 down *read* ". . . than a tolerably patient listener. Emily had no wish. . . ."

145, *l.* 15 up *for* "Emily's liking for . . . frailties. . . ." *read* "Emily's feeling for animals was characteristic of the solitary, passionate, reserved person. Wild, difficult, inarticulate, helpless—all these versions of animal life found favour in her eyes. A true solitary, she saw in animals none of the frailties. . . ."

145, *l.* 8 up *delete* "The wildness . . . and helpless."

146, *l.* 14 down *for* ". . . fear, and telling . . . them;"[19] *read* ". . . fear, murmuring endearments;[19]. . . ."

150, *l.* 7 down *continue* after "verses." "Charlotte knew that her sisters wrote poems but was not shown them—a sidelight on the relationships in the parsonage which speaks for itself. Emily locked her books in her desk, Anne took hers with her to Thorp Green.[28]

Charlotte was made of stern stuff; the check at Brussels had left her guilty, discontented, restless, but had done nothing to tame her spirit. Far from it; the contrast, emphasised daily, between the stagnation of Haworth and the intellectual animation of Heger soon became so intolerable that she began to form another plan. She broached this plan when Branwell and Anne came home in June for their summer holiday and Ellen paid a visit to see the reunited family at the parsonage. The school, Charlotte suggested, might. . . ."

151, *l.* 15 down *for* "accept" *read* "tolerate"

151, *l.* 16 down *for* ". . . weakling—. . . affection." *read* ". . . weakling."

153, *last line for* ". . . half-blind father. . . ." *read* "half-blind heavy-drinking father. . . ."

154, *first line delete* "as . . . them."

154, *l.* 8 down *read* "who became more remote the more Charlotte tried to win her confidence."[40]

154, *l.* 16 down *for* ". . . time." *read* ". . . time."[42]

154–158 *for* notes 42 through 49 *read* notes 43 through 50.

158, *l.* 4 down *read* "Whatever the truth about Branwell and. . . ."

158, *l.* 6 down *for* ". . . love with her. She . . . but he. . . ." *read* ". . . love. To her he was simply a welcome and amusing diversion in a boring life with an elderly and ailing husband. According to the family medical adviser, Dr. Ryott of Thirsk, who saw much of them together, she led him on. This is what one would expect. Branwell's letters on the subject are morbid, extravagant and skirt the edge of paranoia, but he. . . ."

159, *l.* 6 up *read* ". . . all her scathing comments on men, were so many affirmations of what she was so busy denying. She despised the husband-hunter, but she knew what she was missing. . . ."

163, *l.* 6 down *delete* "clinging"

168, *l.* 21 up *delete* "of ill"

169, *l.* 15 down *for* "could" *read* "would"

170, *l.* 15 down *delete* "ghastly"

170, *l.* 6 up *begin new paragraph* "The Brontë sisters watched this slide. . . ."

204, *l.* 3 down *delete* "That Mrs. Robinson . . . not be supposed." *continue* "Yet it was true enough that Mrs. Robinson tolerated when she. . . ."[23]

204, *l.* 6 down *for* "passion" *read* "feelings"

204, *l.* 13 down *delete* "Mrs. Robinson cannot . . . this." *continue* "Now Mrs. Robinson had become aware. . . ."

209, *l.* 17 up *continue* after "book." "Some of the stories Branwell had heard at Luddenden Foot and repeated in the parsonage were being used by her in what was to be *Wuthering Heights*. There is even much to be said for the theory that the often-discussed first chapter of Branwell's novel was to become the opening chapter of *Wuthering Heights*. But whether indebted to Branwell and building on his beginnings or merely feeling sorry for him, Emily could not admit him into the circle. . . ."

209, *l.* 14 up begin new paragraph, *read* "And though Branwell would surely have welcomed such an inclusion, it was the daily silence of Charlotte . . . depressed him.[38] There was just a . . . not to try."

209, *l.* 8 up *for* "Branwell" *read* "he"

209, *l.* 3 up *for* "Branwell" *read* "he"

209, *l.* 2 up *delete* "She had good . . . must remain."

213, *l.* 18 down *delete* "even"

213, *l.* 9 up *delete* "any"

214, *l.* 8 down *delete* "of"

216, *l.* 7 down *delete* "Self indulgence . . . finer faculties."

218, *l.* 6 down *delete* "one"

218, *l.* 7 up *delete* "Yet all this . . . in the end."

222, *l.* 17 down *read* ". . . most unusual novel, with a gripping story, good characterization and, for its time, some remarkably plain speaking on the relations between men and women. In it Anne succeeded in conveying the true passion of a man for a woman— a rare feat, this, for a woman novelist and one which neither of her famous sisters was able to achieve—and had it not been for a fault in construction *The Tenant of Wildfell Hall* might now enjoy a life that has been denied it. The transfer of the action to the heroine's diary half way through the book is a major error. *The Professor*, which had. . . ."

222, *last line for* "had sent" *read* "sent"

223, *first line continue* after "Elder." "George Smith, then owner of the publishing house, read the long manuscript in a single day. He said afterwards that he simply could not put it down. He accepted it almost immediately, it was published on. . . ."

223, *l.* 5 up *for* ". . . remarkably . . . lay down." *read* ". . . and remarkably easy to read."

231, *l.* 7 down *for* ". . . set out simply . . . governess." *read* "set out the life of a governess with deceptive simplicity and much charm."

231, *l.* 10 down *delete* "mild and"

231, *l.* 11 up *continue* after "experience." "That is why *Agnes Grey* has been and will continue to be persistently underrated, for what it loses in art it more than makes up for in truthfulness and—at such a time—courage. It is a grim piece of social history and an equally grim piece of first rate psychology."

256, *l.* 2 down *for* "so interesting to" *read* "so absorbing.[21] If Huntingdon is . . . and abandon."

256, *l.* 7 down *delete* "Nevertheless *The* . . . deserve remembrance."

257, *l.* 12 up *delete* "As the Brontës . . . they were not."

257, *l.* 12 up *read,* paragraph: "Smith found Anne "a gentle, quiet, rather subdued person, by no means pretty yet of a pleasing appearance." As she left the talking to Charlotte he was never able to go beyond this conventional summing up. Charlotte interested him in spite of her more obvious physical imperfections—"She was very small and had a quaint old-fashioned look, her head seemed too big for her body and her fine eyes were marred by the shape of the mouth and the want of complexion"—and his wish to fete them was in consequence more genuine than that of most publishers faced with embarrassingly countrified authors. Charlotte, however, gave what she would have called a decided negative to this plan, which did her no harm at all with Smith. They wanted to remain anonymous, she said, and quiet. He agreed that they should be introduced as the Misses Brown but was less amenable on the second count."[25]

258–262 *for* notes 25 through 35 *read* notes 26 through 36.

266, *l.* 8 up *delete* "disgust and"

266, *l.* 6 up *for* "her grief" *read* "grief"

273, *l.* 5 up *delete* ", she loved Charlotte, and"

277, *l.* 11 down *delete* ", never strong,"

277, *l.* 10 up *delete* "needed"

280, *l.* 9 down *read* "failed." (*delete* "another . . . cut off.")

282, *l.* 6 up *for* ". . . eagerness, her hope, . . . Charlotte." *read* ". . . eagerness, her hopefulness, her joy at the thought of Scarborough, were harrowing to her sister's feelings, and her silent wonder at Charlotte's unresponsiveness was an additional reproach."

286, *l.* 17 up *read* "The picture that emerges from the youngest Bronte's words, from. . . ."

286, *l.* 9 up *continue* after "all." "An unbreakable shyness misled everyone, at home and outside the home, into thinking her weak or at the least pliant. In fact she possessed moral strength and perseverance in high degree. Of all the Bronte children she alone stuck to an unpleasant job year after year, and she did so not through feebleness but strength, because she believed herself to be best helping the family by staying where she was. Everyone liked her because, unlike her sisters, she had a sweet and good nature and gave it out as freely as true modesty permitted. Even on a wordly man such as George Smith she left an impression of her own mild radiance which the years could not dim. Her manner was. . . ."

290, *l.* 13 down *continue* after "people." "Besides, and perhaps most poignant of all, as that rare combination, a passionate and intellectual woman, she paid too heavily for the delights, as they were, of her few visits to London for her to dare to repeat them often. The attraction George Smith came to have for her, for instance, was not wholly physical; he symbolised in her eyes civilization, high culture, life itself, the personality fully expanded—everything that Haworth with its silent, self-absorbed father was not. So, though she was to have moments of excitement, of hope, and even of happiness, by far the greater part of the. . . ."

292, *l.* 2 down *read* "rebellion against stagnation; and a. . . ."

297, *l.* 13 down *continue* after "gravely." "Smith confirmed this account, with an important exception. She was a difficult guest, he said, never perfectly at ease. She "remained very quiet and self-absorbed, and gave the impression that she was always engaged in observing and analysing the people she met." She could, however, become "eloquent when excited."[19]

300, *l.* 6 up *continue* after "sought it." "Lewes, tasteless and tactless, distinguished himself at lunch by saying to Charlotte across the table "There ought to be a bond of sympathy between us, Miss Bronte, for we have both written naughty books." Smith observed Charlotte's reaction with mingled amusement and alarm: "This fired the train with a vengeance, and an explosion followed." His guest's "indignant eloquence" stilled all conversation for several minutes.[44]

Yet "I could not feel otherwise to him than half sadly, half tenderly—a queer word the last—but I use it because the aspect of *Lewes's face* almost moves me to. . . ."

301, *l.* 10 down *delete* "She was very . . . by the complexion."

308, *l.* 7 up *continue* after "beliefs." "Records of their conversation are scanty. When the talk moved to mesmerism, then all the rage, Harriet Martineau questioned the account of Jane Eyre hearing Rochester crying out when she was far from him, but Charlotte declared "It was true or I should not have put it." If her hostess is to be believed, Charlotte spoke harshly of Catholics: "All their good works are disease. They are always doing evil that good may come, or good that evil may come." During her stay Charlotte tried, for the second time, to read Jane Austen, "but could not get on." By the time the visit was ended Charlotte believed that she and Harriet Martineau had become good friends, surely with some assistance from her hostess; yet after her death Harriet Martineau denied it: "That word was never attained."[90]

311, *l.* 12 down *continue* after "rage." "After his lecture the impenitent Thackeray introduced Charlotte to his mother as Jane Eyre. His voice was loud, everyone looked around and Charlotte was confused and annoyed. The next afternoon Thackeray called on Charlotte, and Smith, coming into the drawing room, saw "Thackeray standing on the hearthrug looking anything but happy. Charlotte Brontë stood close to him, with head thrown back and face white with anger. The first words I heard were 'No, Sir! If *you* had come to our part of the country in Yorkshire, what would you have thought of me if I had introduced you to my father before a mixed company of strangers . . .?' "[102]

All in all, Charlotte had little time to herself."

326, *l.* 14 down *read* ". . . published. Some, commenting on the author's preoccupation with love, displeased Charlotte and she wrote for sympathy to, of all people, Harriet Martineau. She begged for candour, for honest judgment, for the whole truth. This Harriet Martineau found hard to give and for the best of reasons, that, unknown to Charlotte, she was one of the offenders. Reviewing the book in the Daily News, she had objected to the fact that "all the female characters, in all their thoughts and lives, are full of one thing only—love", and had criticised "the assumption that events and characters are to be regarded through the medium of one passion only." She described the review (though not to Charlotte) as "Quite gentle" and added a revealing "Must help the governesses who were furious."[172]

She tried to avoid a direct reply, but Charlotte was the last person in the world to be fobbed off in a matter that meant so much to her; she insisted in her most rhetorical style: "I worship truth. Here is the right cheek, Smite!—strike hard! The tears may spring, but never mind! here is the left . . . I trust you to treat me as a near and dear friend and spare me no pain."[173] Harriet Martineau liked neither the language nor the claim to close friendship, which was, indeed, mere verbiage, and finally wrote a letter in stronger terms than her review: "I have but one thing to say . . . they offered.[174]

Like most authors put to the test, Charlotte immediately discovered the unbridgeable gap between theory and practice. She was deeply hurt; she could forgive any amount . . . truth and disinterestedness.'[175]

Harriet Martineau tried appeasement but Charlotte would have none of it.[176]

330, *l.* 13 down *continue* after "father." "Mrs. Gaskell showed what she really thought of Mr. Brontë's contumacy when, after this visit, she began to arrange with Monckton Milnes how the marriage could be made possible. They thought of collecting among their friends to give Nicholls either a pension or an outright sum sufficient for him to marry on. Mrs. Gaskell knew Charlotte's fiery pride well enough to keep silent with her: "She never for one instant suspected anything—or my head would not have been safe on my shoulders!"[186]

Before the plan could be carried further than a first interview between Milnes and a Nicholls puzzled to understand this sudden interest in an obscure curate, Charlotte had taken the matter into her own hands and forced the issue. At first she had not felt able to act until her mind was clearer.[187] But early in the New Year Nicholls again asked Mr. Brontë for permission to visit the parsonage. Mr. Brontë refused brusquely. When, the next month, Nicholls appealed to Charlotte direct, his persistence and her father's lack of manners had had their effect; she decided to have it out.

There was some plain speaking. "Father," she said, "I am not a young girl, not a young woman even. I never was pretty. I now am ugly. At your death I shall have £300 besides the little I have earned myself—do you think there are many men who would wait seven years for me?" Mr. Brontë harped on Nicholls' lowly position; would she, the famous novelist, marry a curate? "Yes," replied Charlotte. "I must marry a curate if I marry at all; and not merely a curate but *your* curate; and not merely *your* curate but he must live in the house with you, for I cannot leave you." At this her father stood up and said solemnly "Never. I will never have another man in this house."

For a week he did not speak to her. Then Tabby, who could not bear such dissention in the house, took an impartial hand in the struggle; she demanded of Mr. Brontë "if he wished to kill his daughter?" and afterwards went into Charlotte's room and abused Nicholls for not having "more brass."[188]

Mr. Brontë weakened, but without grace. He was proud of his distinguished daughter and did not wish her to throw herself away, he was no doubt jealous, but he had also discovered how excellent a curate he lost in Nicholls. He gave way. "It was very hard and rough work at the time," Charlotte reported in March, "but the issue after a few days was. . . ."

332, *l.* 8 down *continue* after "think" "Her father, too, was now conciliatory, anxious, it seemed, to make up for his injustice, and so kind that Charlotte felt "she could cry that she had not been able more to gratify his natural pride."[204] All things appeared to be for the best. "I have not a minute. . . ."

332, *l.* 19 up *continue* after "implications." "There is no sign that Nicholls had at heart put aside his "cold and disapproving"[211] view of Charlotte's work; his idea of a married woman's purpose in life was wholly Victorian-Irish. And there is every sign that he did not approve his wife's friendships. His treatment of Ellen Nussey is known. For the rest, Mrs. Gaskell put the matter in a nutshell when she said before the marriage "I am terribly afraid he won't let her go on being as intimate with us heretics. I see she is too, a little."[212] And that in fact is what happened.

Yet for the short time left to her, the change. . . ."

332, *for* notes 211 through 219 *read* notes 213 through 221.

332, *last line continue* "So ends the story of the Four Brontës. All four led unusually frustrated lives, Charlotte most of all because she felt the most. She was pursued throughout her life by the cruellest of fates, irony. Her manner, which had been adopted in self-defence, and her appearance, which she could not alter, consistently deceived almost everyone she met and effectually belied her true self. She appeared and was accepted as austere, blunt, censorious, ungracious, gauche; in truth she was passionate, intelligent, sensitive, charming and gay. She went to Brussels to find a fuller life, only to endure an appalling loneliness. She deeply loved an Emily and Heger who existed only in her romantic imagination and was bitterly hurt because, being themselves, they could not return her feeling. In London her noble conception of love in *Jane Eyre* was mistaken for indecency and she herself, the most feminine of women, for a man. Her fame, so long awaited, delayed until she could no longer enjoy it fully; instead of the triumph she had so long imagined, first for them all, then for herself and her sisters, she suffered torments because it came too late. She probed the depths of solitary satisfaction. Of all the Brontës she was least fitted to endure solitude and indifference, yet she was left alone and unloved for years.

And she was dogged by irony beyond life. Of the two men she left behind, the father for whom she had sacrificed herself lived tranquilly on after her death, and Nicholls, who appeared equally dependent on her and who exhibited such sorrow at her deathbed, was so little conscious of the treasure he had won and lost that he married again happily, had a large family, and lived to a ripe age. She who craved for love was forced for lack of it to seek compensation in her books; and, final irony, she has been loved and admired by so many millions because of these books which, had she been free to chose, she would gladly have left unwritten in exchange for one man who understood her intellectually and loved her with passion."

335 to follow Poems by Emily Brontë

Essays by Emily Brontë. The Bonnell Collection, Haworth Museum (2); The Henry W. and Alfred A. Berg Collection, New York Public Library (2); The Stark Collection, University of Texas (1).

354, *n.* 6 *read* "Blackwood Papers, National Library of Scotland, *Dowden.*"

356, *n.* 17 *continue* "*A New Identification of Wuthering Heights* by T(homas) Keyworth, The Bookman, March 1893."

356, *n.* 18 *continue* "Cf. Keyworth, *op. cit.*"

363, *n.* 16 *continue* "The manuscript of an autobiographical note by Emily and Anne written on Branwell's birthday is in the Haworth Museum."

364, *n.* 20 *continue* "See Bibliography for the five extant essays by Emily."

365, *n.* 7 *continue* "Letter of 6 September, 1842, Blackwood Papers, N.L.S."

369, *n.* 50 *continue* "Cf. Blackwood Papers, N.L.S."

376, *n.* 6 *read* "*George Smith B.* Cf. *A Memoir* and *Some Pages of Autobiography* by the same author; *Shorter* I, 358; *S.H.* II 139."

378, *n.* 9 *continue* "Cf. *George Smith, op.cit.*"

380, *n.* 21 *read* ". . . *Agnes Grey;* Cf. *Conversations in Ebury Street* by George Moore, London 1924; Note 28 below."

380, *new note* 25 "*George Smith, op.cit.*"

380–81 *for* notes 25 through 35 *read* notes 26 through 36.

386, *n.* 19 *for* "*George Smith C*" *read* "*George Smith, op.cit.*"

387, *n.* 44 *continue* "*George Smith B.*"

387, *n.* 45 *continue* "Harriet Martineau's comment on this was "Baboon, most hideous!" T.L.S. 9.6.50."

389, *n.* 90 *continue* "See Harriet Martineau's annotations to the Gaskell biography, T.L.S. 9.6.50."

390, *n.* 102 *continue* "*George Smith, op.cit.*"

392, *n.* 172, 173 *continue* "See T.L.S. 9.6.50."

393, *n.* 181 *read* "Letters of 15 July 1850 and 5, 21 May 1854 from Charlotte to Ellen; *S.H.* III, 214, 231, 236; *Shorter* II 207; Letter of 18 May 1854 from Mrs. Gaskell to John Forster; MS 2262 N.L.S."

393, *n.* 186 *continue* "Mrs. Gaskell to John Forster 18.5.54 MS 2262 N.L.S."

393, *n.* 18 *read* "Letter of 18 May 1854 from Mrs. Gaskell to John Forster MS 2262 N.L.S. and of 23 April 1854, B.M. Add 38794. Cf. Note 182 above."

393, *n.* 195 *read* ". . . John Forster, B.M. Add 38974; . . . ."

394, *n.* 204 *continue:* "Mrs. Gaskell to John Forster 23 April 1854, B.M. Add 38974."

394, *new note* 211 "Letter of 23 April 1854 from Mrs. Gaskell to John Forster, B.M. Add 38974."

394, *new note* 212 "Ibid."

394 *for* notes 211 through 219 *read* notes 213 through 221.

THE FOUR BRONTËS

EDITH

I

THEIR BEGINNINGS

Marriage of Patrick Brontë and Maria Branwell. Birth of the Brontë children. Move to Haworth. The Parsonage.

EARLY in 1812 Maria Branwell[1] came up from her home in Penzance to stay with her cousin Jane Fennell near Leeds,[2] where Jane's father, John Fennell,[3] was Governor of Woodhouse Grove Wesleyan Academy. Here Maria met and became engaged to Patrick Brontë,[4] then curate of Hartshead near Dewsbury. On 29 December they were married in Guiseley Church[5] by William Morgan, formerly fellow curate with Brontë at Wellington, Shropshire. It was a double wedding, for Brontë on the same day married Morgan to Jane Fennell.

Patrick Brontë, who was thirty-five, had then been curate of Hartshead for rather more than a year—his fourth curacy since he took orders at Cambridge in 1806.[6] He was a self-made man, the only one of a large Irish family to achieve any notable measure of advancement. Even in the name by which he was finally known can be seen something of his determination to rise above humble birth. His family name was commonly known as Brunty (a probable corruption of the original O'Prunty); but he adopted the name of Brontë soon after Nelson, for whom he had a great admiration, was made Duke of Brontë in 1799.[7]

Patrick Brontë was a handsome, high-spirited man, a great raconteur, and something of a ladies' man,[8] but narrow-minded and egotistical.

Maria, six years his junior, was quiet, serious, gentle, and pious. It seems probable that, of the two, her affection, though less demonstrative, was deeper and more unselfish. She and her husband enjoyed writing, and showed a certain aptitude for it. Patrick Brontë published a few volumes of religious verses and prose—all undistinguished.[9] His wife's letters and an unpublished religious article show that, although conventional in thought, she was able to express herself clearly.[10]

After their marriage in 1812 the Brontës settled in a house at the top of Clough Lane, Hightown. There Maria was born, late in 1813 or early the next year, and Elizabeth, in February of 1815,[11] but before Elizabeth was christened, her father had arranged an exchange with Thomas Atkinson,[12] incumbent of the perpetual curacy of Thornton. To this place, only four miles from the Morgans, now at the vicarage of Christ Church, Bradford, the Brontës moved on 19 May 1815.[13] Thornton, in common with much of the surrounding manufacturing district, was a stronghold of the nonconformists, and Patrick Brontë's church —the Old Bell Chapel—had fierce but friendly competition from the Independents. In this church, in August, Elizabeth was christened after her godmothers—her aunt, Elizabeth Branwell, who had come from Penzance to help the family move and had stayed on, and Elizabeth Firth.

Elizabeth Firth and her father of Kipping House, both staunch church people, were the first friends the Brontës made in Thornton. Elizabeth Firth stood as godmother, not only to Elizabeth, but to two other little Brontës also. Visits between the two households became regular and prolonged. When Miss Branwell left her sister for Penzance, fourteen months after the arrival of the Brontës in Thornton, there was a sad leave-taking at Kipping House, and when Mrs. Brontë was brought to bed, her children spent the time at Kipping House until she was delivered.[14]

Maria bore several children in the cottage in Market Street known as the parsonage. A third daughter, Charlotte, was born on 21 April 1816; three more children followed in quick succession—Patrick Branwell, the only son, on 26 June 1817; Emily Jane on 30 July of the next year; and Anne on 17 January 1820.[15]

Mrs. Brontë, never strong, was now an invalid. A further move was decided upon—to the higher and healthier town of Haworth, between Bradford and Keighley. Mr. Brontë obtained his licence with some difficulty a few weeks after Anne's birth, and walked over the moors from Thornton to Haworth every Sunday until he was able to take his family to Haworth parsonage two months later.[16]

One day in April seven carts left Thornton for Haworth, loaded with the Brontës' furniture[17] and probably with the Brontës themselves.[18] When the little convoy had climbed as far as Cullingworth Moor, Mrs. Brontë and her children were able for the first time to see Haworth.[19] Below them, from left to right, ran the trough of a deep valley. Keighley, at the mouth of this valley, to the right, and Oxenhope, at its head, to the left, were out of sight, although the smoke from the factory chimneys of Keighley darkened the distant air. Opposite to the travelling party and forming the farther wall of the valley, rose a yet higher line of moorland hills. In April, as in most months of the year, these moors, though not colourless to the accustomed eye, appeared sullen, unlovely, and even formidable to the newcomer. They spread in a series of harsh undulations to the Lancashire border, an occasional farm breaking the solitude of wind, cloud, and heather.

The Brontës could see, on these moors, only one sign of man. This was their destination, the village of Haworth, which clung about a single track from the valley almost to the top of the moor. Above the grey roofs and dark walls a church tower looked down on the straggling line of houses. Beyond the church, and hidden by it from the Brontës, stood the last and highest house in the village. This house was the parsonage. But to reach the parsonage the seven carts had first to descend steeply into the valley, crossing the stream that flowed down to Keighley, and about which were grouped the Haworth mills. There they joined the road from Keighley, and began to climb Haworth high street.

At the top of this hill, paved then as now with horizontal stone setts to provide a foothold, the carts came into a small square. To their left was a public-house, the Black Bull. Facing them was an entrance to the church and the lower end of the churchyard. A lane led out of the square alongside the churchyard wall. Ahead, the lane dwindled to a rough track across the moors, which stretched unbroken into the distance. To the right were a cottage or two and a large open space for funeral gatherings. To the left, beyond the churchyard wall, was a solitary house, the parsonage.

The parsonage and its garden were bounded by the high churchyard walls, but separated from the churchyard itself by a low wall, above which rose the crowded heads of gravestones. A path through this garden led to the front door of the parsonage. The garden was a small rectangle about sixty by forty feet sloping down and away from the house. In the time of the Brontës it remained bare and unattractive, the rough grass broken only by a few stunted thorns, shrubs, and currant bushes.[20] At the end of it a small gate in the wall opened on to a path leading straight to the church, but the path was rarely used.

The house was two-storied, built, like the rest of the village, in the local grey stone, with a slate roof. In front, were two windows on either side of the door and four above them, with a fifth over the front door. When the Brontës entered the parsonage they found themselves in a stone-flagged passage ending in a short flight of stone stairs and a small landing with a window seat. The right-hand front room became 'the parlour', soon appropriated by Mr. Brontë as his study; to the left, facing the parlour was the family dining- and living-room. Behind the parlour were the kitchen and back kitchen; behind the dining-room, a room used for storing peat. Above the parlour was Mr. Brontë's bedroom; above the kitchen, the servant's bedroom; above the dining- and store-rooms, bedrooms for Mrs. Brontë and the children. And the little room between the two front bedrooms was used at first as the children's playroom. All the floors of the parsonage were stone-flagged; the Brontës only carpeted two rooms. The parlour possessed a few bookshelves, the dining-room a couch; and a mahogany table and some horsehair chairs in both rooms completed the furniture, which was correspondingly simple throughout the house. The windows—in deference to Mr. Brontë's fear of fire—were uncurtained. All the walls were distempered or lime-washed. Every room overlooked the churchyard, except the kitchen and the servant's bedroom; these faced the moors at the back, where sheep grazed right up to the house.

To this place, in April 1820, came Patrick Brontë, his wife, and their six children; the eldest, Maria, was then six years old.[21]

II

COWAN BRIDGE

The people of Haworth. Mr. Brontë's predecessors. Illness and death of Mrs. Brontë.
Mr. Brontë's attempts to remarry. Miss Branwell agrees to live at the parsonage. Four
of the children sent to school at Cowan Bridge. Illness and death of the two eldest. Effect
on the others. Their life at the parsonage. They begin to write.

THE people of Haworth—as of all the moorland region—corresponded to their surroundings in their manner of life. Haworth village was isolated, except for the one poor road to Keighley four miles down the valley; from Keighley the railway ran to London and the northern cities. Although the villagers' brutality has been exaggerated, they were ignorant, uncouth, full of stubborn pride, and easily roused to violence.

To some extent this roughness persists to-day, although counterbalanced now—as then—by an underlying kindliness; the people must still know and like a man before he is accepted. Such folk proved magnificent material for the early nonconformist preachers. John Wesley, the first and most famous of them, had stayed at the old Haworth parsonage,[1] and had preached in Haworth Church.[2] One of his staunchest disciples, William Grimshaw, was occupying Haworth pulpit when Wesley came. Grimshaw had been vicar of Haworth for more than twenty years[3] and although his incumbency had ended long before the Brontës arrived, he was still vividly remembered for miles around.[4] His long, impassioned, often embarrassingly personal harangues from the pulpit were still the boast of Mr. Brontë's older parishioners.[5] Stories were still told of his forcible conversions, whip in hand, prayer on lip, and of his violent pursuit of the devil even to the very death-bed of a local sinner.

With such a man the moor and factory people of Haworth had much in common; they were bound to respect a parson who could hit as hard as the next man, who did not mince his words, and who spared no one, not even himself. His church was thronged; his memory revered; and he had set a high standard for his successors. Patrick Brontë admired Grimshaw's fanaticism—it appealed to a cruel streak in him—though it is doubtful whether he was capable of Grimshaw's integrity. He had written a poem in honour of Jabez Bunting,[6] Wesleyan founder of the Woodhouse Grove School, and many of his verses show a strong Wesleyan influence which dated back to his childhood.[7]

Haworth knew nothing of his Wesleyan leanings. He and his family would in any event have been coolly received as foreigners, and had considerable prejudice to overcome because of the still inevitable comparison with the great Grimshaw; but in addition, he had been appointed to Haworth pulpit over the heads of the church council. This caused much resentment, and the Brontës were virtually ostracized until the matter had been thrashed out.[8] The burden of this isolation fell mainly upon Mrs. Brontë. Mr. Brontë was able to withdraw into the parlour to spend long quiet hours there. His wife had not this privilege; she had six small children to tend, a house to look after—to her, a cold and unlovely house—in a dark, bleak village, a far cry from warm, friendly Penzance. The roads were so bad, the chances to use a vehicle so few, that her friends at Thornton might almost as well have been a hundred instead of ten miles away. And she was ill.

Mrs. Brontë was indeed very ill. She had not long to live. Less than a year after her removal to Haworth, she was found to be suffering from an incurable cancer. Elizabeth Branwell came up from Penzance to look after her—a visit that lasted for the rest of her life. To her husband, watching, the state of Mrs. Brontë's mind during the course of the illness left something to be desired. Her mind, he observed, was not always with God.[9] Nevertheless, after his wife's death in September 1821, Mr. Brontë was able to assure his former vicar: 'She died calmly and with a holy yet humble confidence that Christ was her Saviour and Heaven her eternal home.'[10] He regretted only that her death lacked triumph.[11]

Mrs. Brontë's pain was not always confined to her body. She looked back with longing to warm, homely Cornwall and its hearty ways. She would beg the woman who looked after her to raise her in bed so that she could see the grate being cleaned: 'because she did it as it was done in Cornwall'.[12] But her mind was set more upon her children, whose future she regarded with terrified anxiety. For some time before she died she could not bear to have them in her room; she did not want them to see her in pain, and the sight of them revived her dread for their future. 'Oh God, my poor children—Oh God, my poor children!' were in fact her dying words.[13]

Mr. Brontë shared this anxiety; but his fears were not for his children alone. After a suitable interval, and when the prolonged stay of Miss Branwell seemed likely to call for definition, he approached Elizabeth Firth with an offer of marriage. He was refused but the friendship continued.[14]

Undaunted, Mr. Brontë next addressed a letter to the mother of Mary Burder, at Wethersfield in Essex, whose hand he had sought unsuccessfully during his first curacy. Picking up, with considerable adroitness, the threads of an acquaintance that might well have been considered many years dead, he gave Mrs. Burder particulars of his career since leaving Wethersfield. He mentioned his marriage with a very amiable and respectable lady, who had been dead for nearly two years. He explained that the perpetual curacy at Haworth was his for life, that no one could take it from him. He pointed out that the only difference between the curacy and a vicarage was that in the latter instance the salary is derived from tithes, and in the former, from the rent of freehold estates—which, he added, he liked much better. The amount of his salary—about £200—was given; and, in extenuation of this somewhat unimpressive figure, the fact that he had in addition a good house rent free for life. He added that no one had anything to do with the church but himself, and that the congregation was large. Then, with these inducements fairly spoken, he passed on to the primary object of his letter. How were all his old friends at Wethersfield? he wondered. Did Mrs. Burder's children remain unmarried? And were they doing well, both as respects this life, and that which is to come? For, as he went on to explain, it is sometimes good to lay up treasure on earth, but it is always far better to lay up treasure in Heaven, where moths do not corrupt and where thieves do not break through nor steal. He hoped his old friends would favour him with a call if ever near Haworth, and he expressed an intention of passing through Wethersfield that summer, and of renewing acquaintance with them. He did not mention his children.[15]

After a few months of suspense, Mr. Brontë ran his quarry

to earth; and forthwith addressed himself direct to Mary Burder at Finchingfield Park, near Braintree. He did not waste much time. He had, he said, experienced a very agreeable sensation in his heart on reflecting that she was *still* single. 'For', he reminded her, '*you* were the *first* whose hand I solicited, and no doubt I was the *first* to whom *you promised to give that hand.*' 'I am sure', he continued, 'you once loved me with an unaffected innocent love.' Turning for a moment to himself, he observes, '*You* cannot doubt my love for you.' Almost fifteen years had passed since he had set eyes on her. They had, he confessed, left him looking something older. Nevertheless, he gave it as his opinion that he had gained more than he had lost. 'I hope', he wrote, 'I may venture to say that I am *wiser* and better. I have found this world to be but vanity. . . .' He has, he tells her, a *small* but sweet little family, and, despite past sorrows, needs but *one* addition to his comforts this side eternity. Can Miss Burder guess the nature of this addition? Mr. Brontë wishes to see a dearly Beloved Friend, kind as he *once* saw her, and as *much* disposed to promote his happiness. 'If', he adds finally, 'that dear Friend should have doubt respecting the veracity of any of my statements, I would beg leave to refer her to the Rev. John Buckworth, Vicar of Dewsbury, an excellent and respectable man.'

He then reaches the real purpose of his letter. Will Mary Burder tell him candidly whether she and Mrs. Burder would have any objection to seeing him at Finchingfield Park, as an *old friend.* And he cannot resist ending his letter with an admission that, 'I must say *my* ancient love is rekindled, and I have a *longing* desire to see you.'[16]

But Mary Burder, as she herself pointed out in her reply, was no longer the young, inexperienced, unsuspecting, ignorant girl of Wethersfield days. She was neither impressed nor deceived by the protestations of her former lover. But she wished first to relieve her mind of certain grievances that fifteen years had not obliterated. She had recently been reading over, she said, a number of letters from Mr. Brontë in the years 1808, 1809, and 1810. The result of this reperusal was to excite in her bosom increased gratitude and thankfulness to that wise, that indulgent Providence which withheld her from forming in very early life an indissoluble engagement with one whom she could not think was altogether clear of duplicity. Nor was this all; for she went on to remark, not without irony, that she was thankful to discover that, despite the statements in Mr. Brontë's letters to her when she had brought their engagement to an end, she had not after all been the cause of hindering his promotion, of preventing a brilliant alliance, or of causing his great and affluent friends to withhold their patronage on her account.

But Miss Burder had by no means finished with her old lover. She deals first with his request. Does he think it possible, she asks, that she or her dear Parent could give him a cordial welcome to the Park as an *old friend?* She answers the question herself. 'I must', she continued, 'give a *decided* negative to the proposed visit.' She then dispatched him neatly with his own weapon. 'I truly sympathize with you and the poor little innocents in your bereavement,' she wrote. 'But', she added, 'the Lord can supply all your and their needs.' She could not resist giving the knife a twist: 'It gives me great pleasure', she says, 'always to hear the work of the Lord prospering. May he enable you to be as faithful, as zealous, and as successful a labourer in His vineyard as was one of your predecessors, the good old Mr. Grimshaw, who occupied the pulpit at Haworth more than half a century ago.'[17]

Baffled, Mr. Brontë was not minded to accept defeat readily. He appealed again for an audience, choosing for his letter the first day of the new year, 1823, that he might soften—or chasten—the hard-hearted with well chosen New Year greetings.[18] But the battle was already lost, as a less egotistical man would have known. He had to accept the less romantic solution to his difficulty, and after some persuasion Miss Branwell agreed to take permanent charge of the household.

Meanwhile, the children had been left to themselves; from the moment their mother's illness had first become serious they had seen little of her.[19] Some of them slept with the servant, some in the little room over the passage. They had to steal about the house in case their feet clattered on the stone floors. They had to speak softly in case their voices echoed in the curtainless, half-furnished rooms. For affection, apart from the brusque but kindly words of a busy servant, they were dependent on one another. Yet, mothered by untidy, loving little Maria, they played contentedly enough on the moors in summer and, in winter, made out stories in the house that lost nothing in excitement because of the whispers in which they had to be told. After Mrs. Brontë died, this solitary life continued, for Mr. Brontë appeared almost as reluctant to see them as his dying wife had been. He had little love and less understanding of children; the only meal, and the only long period of the day that he spent with them was breakfast-time, when he told blood-curdling tales—of his Irish days, his Methodist heroes, and the cotton riots.[20] However, his pride, vanity and sense of duty made him try to mould them into his conception of right-thinkers. Their recorded answers to various questions he put to them show them as sententious as he. All replied from behind a mask to the questions so that shyness should not prevent a frank answer. Maria, asked what was the best way to spend time, replied: 'By laying it out in preparation for a happy eternity.' Elizabeth was asked what was the best kind of education for a woman; she replied: 'That which would make her rule her house well.' Charlotte, asked for the name of the best book in the world, said 'The Bible', and, asked for the next best, said 'The Book of Nature.' Branwell was asked the best way to tell the difference between the minds of men and women. He answered: 'By considering the difference between them as to their bodies.' Emily, asked what was best to do with Branwell when he was naughty, said: 'Reason with him, and when he won't listen to reason whip him.' And Anne, asked what she most wanted, replied: 'Age and Experience.'[21]

For the rest, the children's innocent prattle distressed him, Mr. Brontë said, and reminded him of his lost wife.[22] And after the failure of his attempts to remarry he sank steadily into a retirement, both at home and in the parish. He preached regularly—he had at this time no curate—and he visited when he believed a visit to be essential, but social activities ceased. Visitors were not encouraged. Life in the parsonage pursued a rigid, an inflexible routine.

The death of their mother seems unlikely to have caused the children obvious sorrow, except for Maria and Elizabeth, who were eight and seven. The others were too young, they had seen too little of her in the year before her death. For a time their days were pleasantly free from regulation indoors, and quite uncontrolled outdoors, so long as their father's injunction not to mix with the village children was obeyed. They were thrown back upon themselves, but there were six of them, and while Maria and Elizabeth remained to look after the younger ones, the children's life was fairly enjoyable.[23]

When Miss Branwell finally took charge, early in 1824, there was more discipline in the house but little more affection. Her preference for gentle, violet-eyed Anne, and for perky, red-haired Branwell, was not then obvious enough to cause more than occasional ill-feeling. Though strict after her fashion—particularly in the ordering of the household—Miss Branwell was not unkind. Like her brother-in-law, she became increasingly self-centred, but at first, before the bleak and forbidding setting of the parsonage had caused her to withdraw into herself, she brought a brisker atmosphere into her new home. She talked often about her sacrifice in leaving Cornwall to care for her sister's children, and her consciousness of this, her financial independence, and her sharp and obstinate nature, kept her on terms with Mr. Brontë. She was able to meet both his silence and his dogmatism unflinchingly, and at times with positive anticipation.[24]

The influence of Miss Branwell upon the lives of the Brontë children was soon to be seen. A few months after she took over the household, all the children except Branwell and Anne were sent to school for the first time—Maria and Elizabeth on 1 July; Charlotte on 10 August; and Emily, just past her sixth birthday, on 26 November.[25]

The school was the newly-opened Clergy Daughters' School at Cowan Bridge, a few miles from Haworth, on the main road from Leeds to Kendal. Its purpose was good—the provision of an adequate education for the daughters of poor clergy at a low fee. The staff included women of integrity and kindliness. But this is about all that can be said in its favour.

The school was situated in a low, damp, unhealthy valley. The girls worked and slept in a cold, badly ventilated building. They were rarely given enough food, and the cooking was deplorable. The school had been founded by William Carus Wilson, a narrow evangelical, vain, bigoted, and covering his sadism and love of power with scriptural quotations and appeals to the Deity. Carus Wilson, while the Brontës were there, was absolute master. The rigorous discipline and harsh teaching—intended to mortify the flesh and subdue the spirit (the only suitable training, in Mr. Wilson's opinion, for poor girls with a humble future)—compared unfavourably even with the normal school of the time. His own writings testify that Charlotte, in her savage indictment of him in *Jane Eyre*, 'exaggerated nothing'.[26]

Maria and Elizabeth had barely recovered from measles and whooping cough when they were sent to school. In fact, the school authorities hesitated about admitting them, but, in an unhappy moment, decided to stretch the point. Maria, in particular, was unable to accommodate herself to the harsh, impersonal discipline of Cowan Bridge and the loveless travesty of Christianity she met there. Her untidiness became a sin, her lack of method a heinous offence, her inability to learn quickly a crime; and her meek acceptance of punishment only antagonized the teachers still further. It seems she made no complaint to her father; but if she did, he took no notice, because first Charlotte and then Emily were sent to join their sisters.

By the time Emily arrived, Maria had developed tuberculosis. She grew steadily worse, and on 14 February 1825, six months after her arrival at Cowan Bridge, she was sent home. The doctor knew too little about the disease to help her; and by this time it had obtained too firm a hold. She was nursed by Miss Branwell and a servant; but they, though kind, could not take the place of her mother. Branwell and Anne were too young to keep her company, and the other children, who could have cheered her, were at the school which held such unhappy memories for her.

Maria died on 6 May; she was twelve years of age. How much Mr. Brontë was affected it is difficult to say—at that period an early death was not uncommon in large families. His only recorded comment was that she exhibited during her illness many symptoms of a heart under Divine influence.[27]

Meanwhile, the conditions at Cowan Bridge had produced their inevitable results. An epidemic broke out; and Elizabeth, who had never recovered strength after her illness of the previous year, was one of the first victims. On the last day of May, less than a month after Maria had died, Elizabeth was brought home in a similar condition. Mr. Brontë, roused at last, fetched home Charlotte and Emily the next day. Neither of the younger girls appeared to have suffered in health. They were only at the school for a few months, they were in good health when they went there, and they were both popular—Charlotte because she was clever and Emily because she was one of the youngest and so was made something of a pet. But Elizabeth was in an even worse state than Maria, and by 15 June, only two weeks after she had been brought home, she was dead.[28] Hers was the third death in the Brontë family since they had come to Haworth five years before.

So, at nine years of age, Charlotte suddenly found herself the eldest child of the family. She had to take Maria's place as mother to the other three. But, unlike Mr. Brontë, Charlotte was by no means resigned; her hot little heart burned with resentment. She brooded especially on Maria's death and what had caused it; and gradually her imagination built up two strongly-contrasted ideas—one, of Maria as the epitome of goodness; the other, of Cowan Bridge as the epitome of evil.

Nor did the other children entirely escape. Branwell was spared the school, but his already extravagant imagination fastened upon the new, disturbing atmosphere. To Emily, the atmosphere was a challenge—posing questions that she could not answer.[29] And even Anne, already inclined to be a melancholy child, became quieter and more reserved.

For some years there was no further talk of the children going to school. Aunt Branwell, as the children called her, spent the greater part of the day upstairs in her bedroom, bemoaning the cold and draughty parsonage, and harping on the pleasures and warmth of Penzance. When she did come down she clicked about the stone floors on pattens, a small, fussy woman, dressed in old-fashioned clothes with a large cap set on auburn curls piled high. In her bedroom she gave the three girls simple lessons and taught them sewing and home management.[30] She also introduced the children to Methodism. She made them learn many of the hymns, read out passages from magazines which she had sent to her, and taught them Methodist prayers. All these, with their extravagant appeal to the emotions, were eagerly absorbed by the young Brontës, already accustomed to violence of thought and feeling by their father's breakfast-time stories. The Methodist doctrine, reeking of hell-fire, of glorious saints, and sinners eternally damned, was to them both fearful and exciting. The children understood little of the mystical meaning of all they heard, but the passionate words themselves quickly became part of their lives.[31]

Mr. Brontë was accustomed to hold forth on politics over breakfast. His extreme Tory views and his violent expression of them were very much to the taste of his young audience. He also continued to tell his weird Celtic stories, and, as he came to know Haworth, he added true stories that he had heard from his parishioners of village riots, family tragedies, suicides, and even murder. Mr. Brontë, whose retirement from family and parish life became, like his huge white cravat, more pronounced every year, gave Greek and Latin lessons to Branwell. The boy, although his father's especial pride, and, in comparison with his sisters, allowed many liberties, was already taking many more. He defied his father's ban on friendship with the village boys, and was always slipping out to meet them. His charm, wit, and good looks soon made him a local favourite.

All three girls were expected to take their share of work in the house and kitchen as well as caring for their own clothes. Emily soon showed that she not only liked household work, but had a real talent for it. In time, she was able to relieve her aunt of much of the responsibility of running the house. The heavier responsibility—the children—was gradually assumed by Charlotte, to whom her brother and sisters looked for a lead. For Charlotte was a domineering and ambitious child. Her father's stories of great men and great doings had fired her with a determination to make something of herself and of the others. She was no stoic like Emily; she had none of Anne's humility; and she had little use for Branwell's optimistic vanity. She had made up her mind to advance them all, and she was well fitted to do so. Egotistic like her father, and not without some of his subtlety, absorbed in the family like her mother, she had what both parents lacked—energy and drive.

Charlotte's single-mindedness gave her an advantage over the others which even Emily was unable to resist. All three, in their various ways, responded to her leadership. Branwell gladly allowed Charlotte to make his decisions and shield him from trouble so long as she did not interfere with his village friendships. Anne, who was in many ways a loving if imperfectly comprehending shadow of Emily, followed her favourite sister in this as in everything else. So, in 1826, they were a happy and united group under the direction of Charlotte. They worked together, played together, were soon to write together. For it was not long before the children's first writings began to take shape. Although they had the run of the dining-room, they spent most of their free time in the kitchen—the attraction there, apart from its comfortable warmth, being Tabitha Aykroyd—their Tabby—who had come as servant to the parsonage soon after Charlotte and Emily's return from Cowan Bridge a year before. Her sharp Yorkshire tongue and warm heart were very much to the children's liking. And it was in her kitchen, on the wooden table before the fire, that Charlotte wrote the explanation of their games which has served ever since as an introduction to the subject.[32]

III

ANGRIA AND GONDAL

Origins of the stories. The children begin to write. Development of Angrian and Gondal chronicles. Analysis of the Brontë genius.

ON 5 June 1826 Mr. Brontë returned from a visit to Leeds with a box of wooden soldiers for Branwell. There were twelve of these English soldiers, writes Charlotte, and they made a brave show in their high black caps, light scarlet jackets and pantaloons, and the solitary shoe like a round flat cake, into which each pair of gaily coloured legs was inserted. With them Mr. Brontë brought home that evening a set of small dark ninepins.

The next morning Branwell took the box of soldiers into the little room over the hall where Charlotte and Emily now slept. The girls were 'as delighted as he with the gift, and, jumping out of bed, each seized upon a soldier and claimed it for her own'. 'This is the Duke of Wellington! This shall be the Duke!' cried Charlotte; for Mr. Brontë's readings from the *Leeds Intelligencer* and *John Bull*, and his reminiscences of the wars against Napoleon, had given her a passionate reverence for this man of blood and iron—a hero who provided at once an antidote to her feeling of inferiority at being plain and small, a protector in place of her mother and elder sisters, and a prototype of almost all the chief male characters in her writings. 'Mine', Charlotte declared, 'is the prettiest of the whole, and the tallest, and the most perfect in every part.' Emily chose 'a grave looking fellow' who was called Gravey. Anne, too, wanted a soldier when she came downstairs from her aunt's bedroom. Her choice was, thought Charlotte, a queer little thing, much like herself. He was nicknamed 'Waiting boy'. Branwell had already chosen his soldier.

The next stage was to find a game to play with them. The newspapers had a good deal to say about the Ashanti Wars on the Gold Coast—only two years earlier, at Insamankow, the English had been routed by the Ashanti Confederacy, and their

Governor, Sir Charles McCarthy, had been killed. It was not surprising therefore that West Africa (soon to be renamed Angria) was the place fixed on for the adventures of the twelve soldiers.[1] They were sent there to conquer it; and the dark little ninepins were cast for the thankless role of the Ashantees, whose bloody but ineffectual efforts to repel the invasion were to occupy so large a place in the children's thoughts during the next few years.[2]

Each one of the twelve Young Men acquired a distinctive personality which reflected the characteristics of the child who named it. Charlotte's Duke, for instance (soon translated into his son, Arthur Wellesley) 'was a bold and brave young lad, ardent for all military glory and fame, and though only twelve years old would have shamed many older men than himself in his patience under fatigue and coolness in the hour of danger'. Alexander Sneaky, alias Bonaparte, Branwell's choice, was 'ingenious, artful, deceitful, but courageous'. Emily's Edward Gravey was 'naturally grave and melancholy, and his temper was still further soured by the sneers and laughter which the rest raised against him, but like the rest he was daring and brave'. William Edward Parry (a rechristened version of Gravey) was 'a brave sailor-like young man, differing from mariners in general in one respect only, that of being a little too fond of subterfuge'. The John Ross, or 'Waiting boy', of Anne differed again—for he was 'frank, open, honest, and of a bravery when in battle sometimes approaching to madness'.[3]

The young Brontës now began to lead a double existence in their games. They lived in the persons of Wellesley, Sneaky, Gravey, Ross, and the rest of the Young Men; they also took immortal shape as the genii Brannii, Tallii, Emmii and Annii, guardians of the protagonists (an echo of Branwell's reading of Homer).[4] So they possessed at once the exciting and uncertain life of men, and the omniscience of gods.[5]

The adventures of the twelve Young Men began, as would be expected, with the miming of the parts. At first the game had rivals—Charlotte and Emily, for instance, played secret games in bed. But, as the possibilities of the twelve Young Men became clearer, as the characters they had created began to possess the children's imaginations, all other games were dropped. As the game developed and new characters were brought into it, the children went a stage further; to live the adventures more fully and make them permanent, they began to write them down.

These prose tales had already begun when Charlotte sat down at the kitchen table on the morning of 12 March 1829 to write what she called the *History of the Year*.[6] Tabby was washing up the breakfast things, Anne was kneeling on a chair looking at some cakes just baked, Emily was in the parlour brushing the carpet, Miss Branwell was in her room, Mr. Brontë and Branwell on their way to Keighley to fetch the *Leeds Intelligencer*. Charlotte explains that the family take in both this paper—'a most excellent Tory newspaper'—and the *Leeds Mercury*. They are lent *John Bull*, high Tory, very violent, and *Blackwood's Magazine*, 'the most able periodical there is'. She then passes to the games—*Young Men's Play*, established June 1826; *Our Fellows*, July 1827; the *Islanders*, December 1827; and the secret bed plays. 'All these plays', she wrote, 'are very strange ones.' Then follows a short description of the origins of the games— the first originated in Branwell's wooden soldiers; the second, in a reading of *Aesop's Fables*; the third, in 'several events which happened'. Charlotte is explaining how the *Young Men's Play* began when, unfortunately, the manuscript breaks off.[7]

It is not until two years later[8] that the explanation is fully set out, when Branwell finished his *History of the Young Men*. This tells how the Young Men, after settling in the land of the Ashantees, founded the Twelve's town, to be called successively Glass-town, Verreopolis and Verdopolis. The kingdom they established was named Angria; its capital, Adrianopolis.[9] In the game of *Our Fellows*, which succeeded but did not supplant the *Young Men's Play*, each child took as his own a country peopled by giants; and again each child named his own head-man.[10]

Of the next game, *Islanders*, more is known from a preface to an early story, *Tales of the Islanders*,[11] written by Charlotte in 1827. She takes the reader into the Brontë kitchen between six and seven o'clock on a November evening. All the children, with Tabby, were sitting in the firelight, Tabby having refused to light a candle. After a long pause, Branwell said, 'I don't know what to do.' This was echoed by Emily and Anne, and Tabby said, 'Wha, you may go t' bed.' 'I'd rather do anything than that,' exclaimed Branwell. Then

Charlotte remarked how wonderful it would be if each of them possessed an island. This appealed to them all, and each child at once chose an island and began to populate it. Branwell chose the Isle of Man, his three leading citizens being John Bull, Astley Cooper, and Leigh Hunt. The Isle of Wight was Charlotte's choice, and on it she put, in addition to the inevitable Duke of Wellington and his sons, Christopher North and Co., and Mr. Abernethy. Emily peopled the Isle of Arran with Walter Scott, J. G. Lockhart, and his son Johnny; whilst Anne chose Michael Sadler, Lord William Bentinck, and Sir Henry Halford for her Guernsey.[12] This fascinating theme was quickly developed; and by the next day the population had been increased so rapidly that most of the leading statesmen, soldiers, and writers of Great Britain were living in one or other of the four islands. By the following summer, one of them contained a school for a thousand children, and the next year Charlotte began to write down the adventures on the islands. In the *Tales of the Islanders* occurs Charlotte's now famous paragraph on the passing of the Catholic Emancipation Bill—a paragraph which shows a descriptive power, dramatic sense and feeling for words remarkable in a child of eleven.

'Oh, those six months, from the time of the King's Speech to the end! Nobody could write, think or speak on any subject but the Catholic question, and the Duke of Wellington and Mr. Peel. I remember the day when the Intelligence Extraordinary came with Mr. Peel's speech in it, containing the terms on which the Catholics were to be let in! With what eagerness papa tore off the cover, and how we all gathered round him, and with what breathless anxiety we listened, as one by one they were disclosed, and explained, and argued upon so ably, and so well! and then when it was all out, how aunt said that she thought it was excellent, and that the Catholics could do no harm with such good security! I remember also the doubts as to whether it would pass the House of Lords, and the prophecies that it would not; and when the paper came which was to decide the question, the anxiety was almost dreadful with which we listened to the whole affair; the opening of the doors; the hush; the royal dukes in their robes, and the great Duke in green sash and waistcoat; the rising of all the peeresses when he rose; the reading of his speech—the paper saying that his words were like precious gold; and lastly, the majority of four to one in favour of the Bill.'[13]

With these *Tales of the Islanders* the prose record of the most serious rival to the Angrian plays comes to an end. The Angrian story was still developing, and, as the masterful Charlotte took over much of its direction from Branwell, it is hardly surprising that Arthur Wellesley, though no more than a trumpeter when the Young Men left for Africa, quickly followed his admiring creator in assuming control. For when the mighty deeds of the Young Men reached England, and an ambassador from Pitt and the Ministry had begged the twelve adventurers to spare one of their number to lead the English army against Napoleon, Arthur Wellesley was the choice of the Genii. And when, having defeated Napoleon, he returned to Angria with his victorious troops, Wellesley (by that time Duke of Wellington) was crowned King and ruler of the Twelve's town.[14]

Then, the Angrian kingdom established and its setting defined, Charlotte and Branwell produced a magazine and newspaper written and edited by their Young Men. These formed the starting point of the Angrian writings.[15]

Branwell began the series in January 1829, with a tiny four-leaved periodical measuring two by one inches—proportionate, as he reckoned, to the size of the twelve soldiers. And, to give this and its successors the appearance of real books and magazines, he and Charlotte printed them laboriously in capital letters so minute that the naked eye often cannot read them.[16]

In June of the same year, Charlotte began to take a hand in the work; and so congenial was it to her, that after the next month's issue of the magazine she persuaded Branwell to abandon the editorship in her favour and to found, instead, a Glass-Town newspaper.

Brother and sister soon began to follow their own bent: Charlotte, writing in the name of Captain Tree, developed the more romantic aspects of Angrian life, consisting more often than not of the loves and triumphant progress of the Wellesley family; whilst Branwell, writing in the name of Sergeant Bud, stirred up revolutions, revolts, and invasions whenever Angria settled into a period of calm which his restless mind found unbearable. This gratuitous enlivenment of Angrian affairs was usually undertaken by Branwell in the person of his favourite, the ex-pirate Alexander Rogue, Viscount Ellrington, alias Colonel the Honourable Alexander Augustus Percy, who turned eventually into that unscrupulous Prime Minister and poet, the Earl of Northangerland.

Page after page of these little books flew from their busy hands, until the bedroom and dining-room of the parsonage were thick with records of Angria. The two children were to be seen at all hours, carefully folding and stitching the tiny sheets, their pens scratching out the printed characters that had to serve for type; Charlotte's head almost touching the paper, her short-sighted eyes closely following every letter; Branwell, tightly holding his nose between thumb and forefinger, speaking rapidly, and writing down the resultant sounds, which he had christened the Young Men's language.[17] Day after day, month after month, year after year, they wrote on, their imaginations spilling out endlessly into the Angrian world. And when, their hands too tired to hold the pen, they walked over the moors to their secret waterfall, to some lonely farm in its fold of the hills, to the village shop for fresh supplies of paper, to the library at Keighley or Ponden House for *Ossian* or some other exciting discovery, they sauntered in a delightful dream, weaving fresh romances or bloody battles as they went; treading, not Yorkshire earth, but the hard, sun-baked soil of Angria; seeing, not a Haworth shepherd or mill hand, but gorgeously apparelled Angrian nobles and their ladies—Wellesley, Northangerland, Lady Zenobia Ellrington, the Duchess of Zamorna, and the whole brilliant band of the Glass-Town aristocracy.

More than a hundred of these little manuscript books still exist. The smallest is just an inch and a half long. Most of them are stitched and covered in coarse wrapping paper, usually blue or brown, from Haworth shops. Inside some of them the name of the tradesman is still to be seen. Hundreds of little manuscript pages, made up of folded notepaper, were left loose. Some of these tiny pages contain as many as fifteen hundred words, the last word printed as carefully, clearly, and minutely as the first. Yet the millions of words still in existence represent only a part of their total output—a prodigious feat for any child. Almost all of these books are by Charlotte and Branwell, and almost all deal with Angria.[18]

Of the prose writings of Gondal, a rival saga invented by

Emily and Anne, little remains, though it is possible to gather something of the story from the poems written some years later. The action takes place on two islands, Gondal in the north Pacific, and Gaaldine, in the south Pacific, which probably developed from Emily's Arran and Anne's Guernsey of the *Islanders*.[19] The islands are rent from time to time by civil strife —prince against prince and, later, royalist against republican. The inhabitants love greatly, hate deeply, fight bravely—and none more so than the two chief figures, King Julius Brenzaida, Prince of Angora, who moves through the Gondal saga in romantic splendour at the side of his love, Rosina, Princess of Alcona; and his daughter, the dark-haired, passionate but treacherous Augusta Geraldine Almeda. The fighting is fierce and merciless, sparing neither woman nor child. Fortunes fluctuate wildly—the chain-bound victim of one moment is the victorious warrior of the next. Almost without exception love bows before patriotism or principle. Most of the leading characters die—sometimes in the heat of the battle, sometimes assassinated by an unscrupulous rival, sometimes lingeringly, in dark dungeons, but more often when, mortally wounded, they have dragged themselves aside from the fighting. Their passing is invariably noble, whether they are plighting their love for the last time, pleading for a final glimpse of their homeland, or facing death with heroic indifference. Nobility is, in fact, the key-note of the Gondal saga. Both the Gondal and Angrian chronicles are, superficially, blood and thunder, concerned with savage struggles for love and power; but while the Angrian tales are amoral, even when they are no longer told by children, the Gondal poems, even at their most bloodthirsty, show a clear sense of right and wrong.[20]

The thoughts of the Brontë children were dominated more and more by these fantasies. Their life was exceptionally secluded. They had no friends—indeed, with the exception of Branwell, they never mixed with other children—and their contact with adults was restricted to their father and aunt, and to Mr. Brontë's infrequent visitors—for Miss Branwell saw no one. They liked being with Tabby in the kitchen, but she was unable to give their lively young minds the stimulus they needed. So, increasingly, Angria and Gondal became their true life. The loves and hates, the desperate fights, the deaths, imprisonments, triumphs, and agonizings of Wellesley, Julius, Augusta, and the rest—this was their escape from the monotonous parsonage existence.

The earlier Angrian stories are on the whole well-constructed, and, although full of the expected clichés, cloudy rhetoric, and wild extravagance of phrase and thought, they are unlike the stories that children usually write. At quite an early stage there is more than a suggestion of character development in Charlotte's heroes and heroines, and both children—Branwell in particular—often handle their material with adult ease, whether it be political procedure, social etiquette, or the complicated relationships of large families.

These stories and poems show that the newspapers and quarterlies of the parsonage were not the only source of the children's writings. The *Arabian Nights, Pilgrim's Progress,* Scott, Shakespeare, Homer, Greek history, *Ossian,* the *Imitation of Christ,* and, of course, the Bible, can all be traced there.[21] But perhaps the most vital influence was their aunt,[22] with her hymns, prayers, Ladies' Magazines, and, in Charlotte's words, 'the mad Methodist magazines, full of miracles and apparitions of preternatural warnings, ominous dreams and frenzied fanaticism, and the equally mad *Letters of Mrs. Elizabeth Rowe from the Dead to the Living*'; and their father, with his Wesleyan, Irish and local tales.[23]

We can account in this way for the main sources of the stories and poems, and for the manner in which they were written. But we must look elsewhere for the original and co-ordinative element which distinguishes them from the writings of other children. This is to be found in the Brontë imagination—compact of Irish father, Cornish mother, and Yorkshire environment. And it is this creative imagination, bold, impassioned, richly and unfailingly inventive, which gives their early writings distinction and their novels greatness.

IV

ROE HEAD

Charlotte goes to school. Reactions of Branwell, Emily, and Anne. Charlotte's friends and school life. The Luddite Riots.

THIS period of hard work about the house, of walks on the moors, of cosy evenings in the kitchen, and of blissful hours in bedroom and dining-room making out Angrian stories, came to an end for Charlotte a few months before her fifteenth birthday. Arrangements were made for her to go as a boarder to Miss Margaret Wooler's[1] school at Roe Head near Huddersfield.

One January morning in 1831, Charlotte drove away sadly in the local covered cart, leaving her brother and sisters to adjust themselves to life in the parsonage without her purposeful leadership. One of the first consequences of Charlotte's leaving home was that Emily and Anne broke away from the Angrian game. They did not take kindly to Branwell as leader, and invented a rival saga, the Gondal, leaving their brother to write the Angrian chronicles alone. He, deprived of Charlotte's moral support, began to seek distraction more and more with the village lads, and in the Black Bull, where he was regarded as the Haworth prodigy and welcomed as entertainer of the guests.

Another consequence of Charlotte's absence was that Emily and Anne once more came directly under their aunt's surveillance. Emily began to realize, with increasing disdain, the self-righteousness that played so large a part in Miss Branwell's religious outlook; and at the same time she began to understand the mystical meaning of the words that her aunt repeated so glibly. The effect of Miss Branwell's religous teachings on Anne was more disastrous. The younger girl, less critical and less strong-minded than her sister, was unable to resist the Wesleyan doctrine of predestination, which began to take a firm hold on her imagination. Neither girl was able, nor indeed wished, to talk about these changes of thought, which were in any case nebulous, but there are signs of them in their early Gondal writings.

Meanwhile, at Roe Head, one of the pupils, Mary Taylor, had seen Charlotte arrive, in very old-fashioned clothes, and looking cold and miserable. When she came into the schoolroom she had changed her dress, but it was just as unfashionable as the other. To Mary, she looked a little, old woman, so short-sighted that she always appeared to be seeking something, and moving her head from side to side to catch sight of it. She was very shy and nervous, and spoke with a strong Irish accent.[2]

Another picture of Charlotte in her first days at the school is given by a new girl, Ellen Nussey, who arrived a few days later. Charlotte's soft brown hair, writes Ellen, was then screwed up unbecomingly· into tight little curls; she was very short, painfully thin, and sallow-complexioned. Her old-fashioned dark, rusty green stuff dress made her look even more unattractive.

Ellen first came across Charlotte in the schoolroom, alone and in tears. She, like Ellen, was homesick; and the two girls comforted each other.[3] For a time, Charlotte appealed to the kind-hearted Ellen because she seemed such an unhappy little thing; but Ellen's pity turned to respect when she discovered the strength behind Charlotte's odd appearance; and the friendship was not very old before Ellen found herself leaning on Charlotte in almost everthing. Mary Taylor was made of different stuff. She came of sturdy Radical stock, was plain-spoken and possessed a will of her own. Yet she, too, came to respect her friend's views even when she could not share them, and, in the arts, to rely on them long after she and Charlotte were separated.

In the arts and in political and general knowledge Charlotte more than held her own in the school. At first the other girls thought her ignorant because her grounding in the routine subjects was poor,[4] but their feeling of superiority did not last long. Charlotte confounded them by revealing knowledge quite out of their range. She knew most of the poetry they had to learn; was able to tell them the authors and titles of the poems from which the extracts were taken, and would sometimes recite a page or two and explain the plot of the complete poem.[5] And although some girls, Mary Taylor in particular, were 'furious politicians', the shy, dowdy Brontë girl, who had been encouraged to discuss politics ever since she was five years old, for whom the Radical and Tory newspaper reports were adventure stories and the rival party leaders heroes and villains, gained easy dialectical victories and the prestige that went with them, whenever politics were raised.[6]

She would not play games, partly because she was short-sighted, but mainly because of her prematurely strong sense of duty.[7] She had come to the school to learn, and learn she would. And it says much for her that the other girls accepted and respected this reason for Charlotte's aloofness. Both her friends were impressed by this responsible attitude, which, together with a passion for self-improvement, determined Charlotte's behaviour. Her reasons for it were clear. She had not wished to come to school. She had no hope of happiness away from Haworth. But as the eldest Brontë child, with a living to make, the step had been inevitable. So she set herself to make the result worth the sacrifice.[8]

She told Mary Taylor: 'There is enough of hard practicality and useful knowledge forced on us by necessity, and the thing most needed is to soften and refine our minds.' With such an aim no time could be spent on games. So she began, unhappily but resolutely, to cultivate her tastes, and store her mind with knowledge. She picked up every scrap of information about painting, sculpture, poetry, music, as though it were gold. Her time at the school was filled with urgency. A year or two at Roe Head was the longest period Mr. Brontë could afford for her, and the future of the other children at home might well be determined by her efforts there.[9] For Charlotte would not face, either for herself or for her brother and sisters, the life of a nonentity, bounded by what she called 'the little wild moorland village where we reside'. She was determined that a mark should be made in the world by the Brontës. But if her friends came up against this formidable side of Charlotte, they shared also in the fiercely protective affection that was dragged out of her unwillingly, so fearful was she of rebuff, so sensitive to her own supposed unworthiness.

To both Ellen and Mary she talked much of Maria and Elizabeth. She dwelt, said Mary, on Maria's sufferings at Cowan Bridge—how she suffered with the sensibility of a grown-up person, and endured with a patience and fortitude that were Christ-like; and she brooded incessantly on Maria's miserable and untimely death, and on the injustice of the fact that those responsible for it went unpunished.[10] Charlotte spoke of this to both her friends, but more fully to Ellen,[11] and it became plain after a time that, of the two, Ellen was to occupy the foremost place in Charlotte's affections, if not in her respect. Not only was Ellen the more sympathetic and understanding, but she came gradually to accept and even to take pride in Charlotte's domination, and this, to a strong character, is temptation indeed. Mary, on the other hand, looked askance at any view of life that differed from her own, an outlook as biased in its way as Charlotte's—and as she was just as self-willed and independent, she would accept no friendship in which she did not play an equal part.

Despite Mary and Ellen's companionship, however, Charlotte remained resigned rather than contented at Roe Head. By devoting almost all her spare time to improving herself, she rose quickly to the head of her class and then of the school. Her disinclination for games persisted, but she became popular in another way— the girls discovered her ability to tell long, mysterious stories; and for a time the dormitory in which Charlotte slept was the scene of many a horrifying tale, until a surpassing imaginative effort reduced one of the girls to hysterics. After that, she was forbidden to tell any more stories after lights were out.[12]

The head mistress, Miss Wooler, was also a good storyteller—but hers were stories of real life. She thrilled the girls with eyewitness accounts of the Luddite riots—the long struggle in the early part of the century between cotton workers and millowners. Many of the places she described were close to the school. A mill that Charlotte could see from the dormitory window had been attacked by rioters twenty years earlier. On Crossland moor, near by, a manufacturer had been murdered. At Heckmondwike, two miles away, a Tory clergyman, Hammond Roberson, had organized parties to fight the workers;[13] and Mr. Brontë, who had succeeded Roberson in one of his curacies, used to tell his children lurid stories about this eccentric man.[14]

Miss Wooler's accounts of the riots awakened all Charlotte's memories of her father's tales. She was greatly excited by the thought that she actually lived in the midst of the once-troubled district. She asked many questions, and could not rest until she had seen the places described by the headmistress. Sometimes, during school walks, the girls passed the scenes of clashes between hungry cotton workers and Tory bands, and Charlotte would stare, fascinated—seeing, not ruined, deserted mills and peaceful fields, but gory battlegrounds where desperate men fought and bled.[15]

She did not forget what she saw and imagined. The pictures stored up in her mind remained until, many years later, she brought them to life in her third novel, *Shirley*.[16]

Charlotte wrote home regularly. She addressed most of her letters to Branwell, for to him she found most to say. A few months after she went to Roe Head, Branwell walked over to the school to see her. They had much to tell each other. The defeat of the Reform Bill of that year in the House of Lords had aroused all Charlotte's delight in politics. She heard with joy that Miss Branwell had agreed to take in regularly *Fraser's Magazine*—which, although unlikely to unseat the beloved *Blackwood's* in Charlotte's estimation, was, she realized, a great deal better than nothing. And, of course, she was eager to hear what Branwell was making of the Angrians—for they were never far from her thoughts.[17]

V

HOME STUDIES

Charlotte leaves Roe Head. Effect of school life. She teaches Emily and Anne. Drawing and Music masters at the Parsonage. Branwell's character.

CHARLOTTE stayed at Roe Head for just over a year. When she came home for good, after the spring term of 1832, one of the first things she did was to ask Branwell how he had developed the Angrian chronicles while she had been away. He was as enthusiastic as ever, and had been very active devising new battles, insurrections, and other bloody scenes. As for Charlotte, her enthusiasm was all the greater for her enforced absence from the Angrian world. She flung herself into new tales of love and intrigue in the Angrian court. These new stories differ little from those written before she went to school, except that one of them—a story about industrial disturbances in Glass-Town—is based on the Luddite riots. Apart from this, the stories are, if anything, even more wildly romantic.

But if her life at school had encouraged Charlotte's extreme romanticism, it had at the same time greatly strengthened the very practical and realistic side of her. The social atmosphere at Roe Head was very different from Cowan Bridge, the only other place where she had met girls of her own age. At Roe Head, the girls all came from well-to-do families and were assured of an established place in life, unlike Charlotte, who knew that when she grew up she must either marry or earn her living by teaching. To her indignation she saw that these girls, far from taking advantage of their good fortune, were actually unaware of it; they accepted their schooling, like the rest of their comfortable life, as a matter of course. And, galling thought, they were all intellectually inferior to her.

All this roused Charlotte's ready sense of injustice, and made her contemptuous and bitter—feelings which appear in many female portraits in her novels. But it did more than this. It made her more determined than ever to get on, and it showed her that, lacking the social advantages of the other girls, the only way to do it was by educating herself and the others. She had made the fullest possible use of her time at Roe Head. She had learned all that the school could teach her. She had made great strides in her general education, particularly French and drawing, and had developed her appreciation of the arts. Roe Head had given her a good start—but the rest she would have to do for herself, and for her brother and sisters.

So the account of Charlotte's day given to Ellen soon after settling down at Haworth showed that she had taken her lesson to heart. She wasted no time. 'In the morning from nine o'clock till half-past twelve', she writes, 'I instruct my sisters and draw, then we walk till dinner, after dinner I sew till tea time, and after tea I either read, write, do a little fancy work or draw, as I please.'[1] She said nothing about Angria. This was still a secret.

Of these activities, only the sewing was not included in the plan of life which Charlotte had now set herself. Miss Branwell made her reluctant nieces sew charity clothing day after day in her bedroom. It was proper for them to do it, she said when they protested, and was for their own good.[2] This view was not shared by the three girls, least of all by Charlotte. None of them took pleasure in sewing; but to Charlotte, this hindrance to her plans for everybody's advancement was peculiarly unwelcome; and she worked all the harder when she was free to teach her sisters. It is doubtful whether Emily and Anne always accepted the necessity for this unrelenting self-improvement. They had the Gondal stories, which offered a fascinating escape from monotony and discipline, and they had spent their time happily enough together on the moors and in the house while Charlotte was away. But they were only fourteen and twelve years old, and no match for a Charlotte, backed by her father, and determined to pass on what she had learned at school. Charlotte had her way.

However, one thing all four of them enjoyed. Among the many enthusiasms Charlotte brought back from Roe Head drawing was pre-eminent. She spent hours copying prints and engravings as she had done at school, and she had no difficulty in persuading Emily and Anne to join her.[3] But her ambitious mind was not content with this rough-and-ready way of improving their technique, and she asked her father if he would let them have a drawing-master. Mr. Brontë, who regarded their studies with benevolence, and who occasionally took a hand in them himself, was easily prevailed upon, and a drawing master, William Robinson, came over from Leeds.[4] They all welcomed his lessons,[5] particularly Charlotte and Branwell, who had been illustrating their Angrian books for many years.[6] Branwell, eager to excel in this new distraction, worked with zest.[7] The teacher and Mr. Brontë and Miss Branwell soon thought they saw promise in his work, and he began a course of portrait painting in Robinson's studio in Leeds.[8] A career for him as a portrait painter in London was discussed in the family as more than a possibility. By the time Ellen Nussey visited the parsonage, in the autumn of 1833, Branwell was already painting in oils.[9]

The girls were, in their way, almost as enthusiastic as Branwell about his brilliant prospects. Although they teased him about his bumptiousness, and the rosy view he took of his own future, they never seriously questioned his right to be considered first. But for a time Charlotte thought that she and her sisters, though unlikely to become famous, might also earn money by drawing.[10]

For months she kept all three of them hard at work copying engravings. She and Branwell became completely absorbed in the study of art; they admired the work of the local sculptor, J. B. Leyland of Halifax, who was just then gaining notice, and probably visited his exhibition in Leeds; and they read every book on art and artists that they could lay their hands on.

Charlotte took tremendous pains to improve herself. She spent six months copying a single engraving. But she was forced to stop because of her eyesight, which had already been weakened by the strain of printing the minute Angrian books. So, when the course of lessons ended, Charlotte gave up any hope of the girls earning money in this way, because it was already clear that neither Emily nor Anne had her talent. For the future, they did no more than illustrate the Angrian and Gondal stories and make occasional sketches of the people and the pets in the parsonage. But Charlotte never lost her keen interest.[11]

Another regular visitor to the parsonage at this time was A. S. Sunderland, the organist at Keighley, who came to give pianoforte lessons to everyone but Charlotte, who possessed no gift for music.[12] Branwell, as usual, showed brilliant facility, and developed a passion for the organ when he heard John Greenwood, who came over from Leeds to play on the new organ in Haworth church. Branwell went to Leeds to hear Greenwood play, began to learn the instrument himself, and was often to be seen playing the organ in the church. He was also fascinated by the flute, and one of his manuscript books contains many airs for it composed by him. But he liked all instrumental music.[13] And when Ellen Nussey visited London for a few days, she was asked by Charlotte on Branwell's behalf if she could find out how many performers there were in the King's Military Band.[14]

But Branwell did not fulfil any of his early promise. He lacked concentration, and his interest in these arts, though intense, was shallow and egotistic. Besides, he was casting his net too widely. Drawing, painting, music, writing—he devoted himself to them all and excelled in none. His father, aunt, and sisters did nothing to help him. He needed criticism and guidance—instead, his natural conceit and wild optimism were fed by the immoderate admiration given him by all. Charlotte, it is true, spoke frankly enough at times. But Branwell was accustomed to her sharp tongue, and must have been tempted to attribute her unfavourable comments to envy.

Nor was any serious control put upon the amount of time he wasted in the village, especially at the Black Bull. His father complained occasionally when asked for money, but almost always gave it. Miss Branwell seems to have made no attempt to restrain him, and even Charlotte, whose moral sense was fanatical, only made caustic remarks when he left unfinished an Angrian story, an illustration, or a painting. For Charlotte accepted the prevalent idea of one law for men, another for women. To her, there was something romantic in a young man having his fling. It seems never to have occurred to her that Branwell would lack sufficient strength of character to grow out of his youthful excesses. She detested weakness, especially in men, and when she at last realized, beyond a shadow of doubt, that Branwell was weak, she was quite unable to make allowances.

Although Branwell showed the most promise in music, Emily and Anne were not without ability, and Emily became quite an accomplished pianist. Anne played the piano and sang and composed a few songs. Her voice, says Ellen Nussey, was weak, but very sweet.[15] But in spite of their talent, neither of them at this time shared Charlotte and Branwell's fervour for education. In fact, far from being earnest students, they were reluctant to do the most elementary task that kept them indoors —as Emily's diary[16] candidly declares:

'It is past twelve o'clock Anne and I have not tided ourselves, done our bed work, or done our lessons and we want to go out to play We are going to have for dinner Boiled Beef, Turnips, potatoes and apple pudding The kitchin is in a very untidy state Anne and I have not done our music exercise which consists of b major Taby said on my putting a pen in her face Ya pither pottering there instead of pilling a potate. I answered O Dear, O Dear, O Dear I will derectly With that I get up, take a knife and begin pilling. Finished pilling the potatoes Papa going to walk Mr. Sunderland expected.'[17]

VI

PLANNING A CAREER

Charlotte writes to her friends. Visits Ellen's home. Ellen returns the visit. Her description of the Brontës. Effect of secluded life on the four children. The books they read. Three of them prepare to leave home.

CHARLOTTE wrote regularly to Ellen Nussey, and, less often, to Mary Taylor. Both her father and aunt had always impressed on the children that they must be cautious in their dealings with the outside world. This combined with Charlotte's own pride to make her early letters stiff and formal, but when she realized that both girls were really fond of her, her manner changed. The cynicism she affected dropped away, she began to use endearments and even some of the extravagances common to most schoolgirls. Her style varied; in the letters to Ellen she was inclined to adopt a didactic tone. But she wrote to Mary in quite another strain—as she herself told Ellen in words that smack of the eighteenth century. 'Being in one of my sentimental humours I sat down and wrote to you such a note as I ought to have written to none but M. Taylor who is nearly as mad as myself.'[1] And, as this extract shows, her style also varied according to what she was reading at the time.

In September 1832, a few months after she had left school, Charlotte, who had never stayed with anyone in her life before, now accepted with dignity an invitation to visit Ellen, excusing the acceptance on the grounds that she thinks their friendship is 'destined to form an exception to the general rule regarding school friendships'.[2] Escorted by Branwell, she was driven over in the Haworth gig to Ellen's home, The Rydings—a fine battlemented house in its own grounds near Birstall.[3] Brother and sister were both in high spirits and delighted to be together. Branwell was in ecstasy over everything. He walked round the garden, full of praise for the old turret-roofed house, the fine chestnut trees on the lawn, and the large rookery, which gave the house a good background. He told his sister he was leaving her in Paradise, and if she were not intensely happy she never would be. Charlotte was not intensely happy; her pride and her feeling of inferiority made her silent and shy. One day, on being led in to dinner by a stranger, she trembled and nearly burst into tears; but despite her shyness, which was often painful to others as well as to herself, she was liked and respected when she spoke her mind.[4]

Not until the summer of the next year did Ellen pay a return visit to Haworth—Miss Branwell considering the moorland winter and spring too cold for a visitor.[5] When Ellen did arrive, her visit proved a distinct success.[6] Miss Branwell talked much, and regretfully, of her younger days; recalling the balmy air and gay social life of her dear Penzance, and implying that she had been quite a belle. She took snuff, presenting the box to Ellen with a little laugh, enjoying the astonished look on her young guest's face. She spent part of the afternoons reading aloud to Mr. Brontë; and Ellen heard discussions on the reading when the family met for tea. Miss Branwell was stirred to unusual liveliness by having a visitor in the house, and boldly tilted against Mr. Brontë in argument. At the meal Mr. Brontë repeated strange stories, which had been told to him by some of the oldest inhabitants, of the extraordinary lives and doings of people near and far—stories which made Ellen shiver, but which she could see were full of grim humour and interest to the family. In these recitals of Celtic horrors and bloodcurdling Yorkshire memories, all the Brontës—Anne possibly excepted —met on common ground.

Already Mr. Brontë had begun to go early to bed. At eight o'clock the household gathered for prayers. An hour later, he would lock and bar the front door, then look into the dining-room on his way upstairs, to say, 'Don't be up late, children'; half-way up the stairs he would pause to wind up the grand-father clock. Every morning Ellen heard him firing a pistol from his bedroom window. This habit of making sure that the pistol would fire, which seems to have been a legacy from Ludite days, was continued by Mr. Brontë because of his fear of marauders, and because, as Ellen discovered, he had a delight in anything connected with fighting.

Ellen describes Emily and Anne. Emily, she says, had by this time acquired a lithe, graceful figure. She was the tallest person in the house, except her father. She wore her hair, which was naturally as beautiful as Charlotte's, in the same unbecoming tight curl and frizz, and she had a similar lack of complexion. She had very beautiful eyes—kind, kindling, and liquid, at times dark grey, at other times dark blue, but she did not often look at visitors. She talked very little. She and Anne were inseparable. Anne—dear, gentle Anne—says Ellen, was quite different in appearance from the others. Her hair was a very pretty light brown, and fell on her neck in graceful curls. She had lovely violet-blue eyes, fine pencilled eyebrows, and a clear, almost transparent complexion. She was Miss Branwell's favourite niece, and still did her lessons and sewing under the guidance of her aunt.

Ellen had hard work to make friends with the shy Anne and the reserved Emily. She succeeded—but only for a time—when they walked across the hills behind the house, and into the glens and ravines that here and there broke what, to Ellen, seemed the monotonous line of moorland. Once out of the house and on the moors, where the heather was beginning to turn purple, Ellen saw with astonishment how happy and carefree all three Brontë girls became. The change in Emily was particularly marked.

Emily, Anne, and Branwell (when he came with the party) usually went ahead, fording streams and often placing stepping-stones for Charlotte and Ellen. They all lingered by the streams, picking wild flowers, throwing stones into the water, laughing, and talking—and of them all, Emily showed the greatest pleasure. One long ramble was made over the moors to a spot which Emily and Anne called The Meeting of the Waters—a small oasis of green turf in a deep wooded glen. Here, they sat on large stones overhanging a clear, rushing stream, hidden from the world, with nothing in sight except miles of heather, blue sky, and bright sun. The four girls made fun of each other, and called themselves the quartette. Emily, half-lying on a slab of stone, played like a young child with the tadpoles in the water, making them swim about, and, as she chased them with her hand, moralized on the strong and the weak, the brave and the cowardly.[7]

Once, when Charlotte felt too unwell to go for a walk, Emily was left to play hostess to Ellen; and Charlotte waited with some trepidation for the pair to return. But she need not have

MR. BRONTË

from a photograph taken towards the end of his life

HAWORTH PARSONAGE
as it was in the time of the Brontës

feared; Emily, in her element on the moors, was good company when she liked her companion; and she liked Ellen.[8] After Ellen had gone home, Charlotte repeated the remark of Emily and Anne that 'They never saw anyone they liked so well as Miss Nussey.' Mr. Brontë and Miss Branwell both held up Ellen to Charlotte as a model of correct behaviour, and even Tabby seemed fascinated by this rare guest.[9]

With Ellen gone, the parsonage family sank back into its dull and uneventful routine. But what the children's lives lacked in outward incident, they made up generously in mental adventures. And it was precisely the disciplined simplicity of the parsonage routine that allowed their imaginations to expand. Mrs. Gaskell, wise in this as in so many things, says rightly that 'it was positive repose to have learnt implicit obedience to outward laws'.[10]

Nevertheless, living the secluded life they did, some kind of repression was inevitable, and none of them entirely escaped.[11] Charlotte relieved herself to some extent in her letters to Ellen and Mary, and in her Angrian writings. Branwell, least repressed of all, flung off superfluous energy and feeling in many ways— his Angrian tales, his painting, writing, drawing, music, his brilliant monologues at the Black Bull, and his visits to cronies of the artistic, hard-drinking set at Keighley and Bradford.

Emily had most difficulty in finding an outlet for strong feelings that were more intense and unworldly in her than in any of them. She was uncompromising, inarticulate, and troubled by many impulses she did not understand except to feel that they were being restrained. She looked with mingled contempt and pity upon the struggles which were beginning to convulse the tender but conventional religious conscience of Anne.[12] She valued her younger sister's unquestioning affection, though its limitations must have been obvious to her. She admired and envied Branwell's freedom. She looked sympathetically but with impatience on Charlotte's efforts to achieve greatness for them all. She became increasingly uncommunicative, living the Gondal life, doing housework, and spending more and more time by herself on the moors.

Anne, still a pupil of her aunt and father, was on the whole the least perturbed, the most contented of all four. She loved, admired, and clung to Emily, loved and perhaps a little feared

Charlotte, and regarded the mercurial Branwell with pride. Her day was busy with lessons, practice, helping in the kitchen, walking on the moors, dreaming her gentle, sentimental dreams, enjoying the long delicious hours of making out stories with her Gondal partner. Yet even she was not without spiritual conflict. The doctrines of Calvinism in their most cruel and literal form were torturing her mind. Anne, most like her mother in character, began to show a distressing propensity for self-immolation, and she lacked the necessary common sense and humour to reduce it to reasonable proportions.[13]

The four Brontës had never been encouraged to express their emotions. On the contrary, their father and aunt had told them that they should try not to show their feelings in front of people. Branwell, who was more spontaneous than his sisters, paid little attention to their advice, though even he was most himself outside the parsonage. His feelings for Charlotte and Emily were already being tempered by respect, not unmingled with fear.

The three sisters, naturally reserved, and denied normal emotional outlets, believed it right and proper to conceal emotion, and turned more and more to the loves and adventures of the Angrian and Gondal characters and to their hopes for their brilliant brother. In this, girls, aunt, and father were at one, and Branwell, persuaded easily that he felt an impulse towards greatness, accepted this concentration on his future with customary *bonhomie*. In his careless, haphazard way, he appreciated his sisters' attitude; many faults were appearing in him, but lack of generosity was not one of them. Of all four Brontës, the boy alone was undeniably charming. Charlotte was already a little bitter, sharp-tongued, almost always on the defensive; Emily's forbidding reserve turned often enough into plain obstinacy and rudeness; Anne's shyness made her almost incoherent whenever a stranger appeared; and it is no wonder, when set against these unpromising exteriors, that the talkative, perky, and readily affectionate Branwell impressed most people with his potential brilliance.

Charlotte, in an introduction to an Angrian tale of October 1834, describes Branwell, not without friendly malice, as she sees him: '. . . a low slightly built man attired in a black coat and raven grey trousers, his hat placed nearly at the back of his head, revealing a bush of carroty hair so arranged that at the sides it projected almost like two spread hands, a pair of spectacles placed across a prominent Roman nose, black neckerchief arranged with no great attention to precision, and, to complete the picture, a little black rattan flourished in the hand. His bearing as he walked was tolerably upright and marked with that indescribable swing always assumed by those who pride themselves on being good pedestrians. . . . As a Musician he was greater than Bach, as a Poet he surpassed Byron, as a Painter, Claude Loraine yielded to him, as a Rebel he snatched the palm from Alexander Rogue, as a Merchant, Edward Percy was his inferior, as a Mill Owner, Granville came not near him, as a Traveller, De Humbolt, Ledyard, Mungo Park, etc. etc. never braved half his dangers or overcame half his difficulties.'[14]

Branwell describes his sisters at this time—in a story written by Charlotte. In the story, he is asked if his sisters are as queer as he. 'Oh,' he replies, 'they are miserable silly creatures not worth talking about. Charlotte's eighteen years old, a broad dumpy thing, whose head does not come higher than my elbow. Emily's sixteen, lean and scant, with a face about the size of a penny, and Anne is nothing, absolutely nothing.' 'What! Is she an idiot?' he is asked. 'Next door to it,' is Branwell's curt reply. And when an explanation is required of his ambition to leave Haworth, which Charlotte describes as 'a miserable little village, buried in dreary moors and moss-hags and marshes'—he answers that he is 'not satisfied with being a sign-painter in the village as Charlotte and them things were with being sempstresses'.[15]

Here Charlotte put her finger on the truth of their situation. She knew well enough that she and her sisters were stagnating. She was equally alive to Branwell's blithe, cocksure determination to escape from home and obscurity, and to his opinion of his sisters for appearing to endure it—and her affection for Branwell could not save her from bitterness. Sempstresses under the direction of their aunt at home, or badly-paid, ill-treated governesses away—these appeared as the alternatives before the girls. To Charlotte, burning to carve out a place for herself and her sisters in the world, a lifetime at home, or years of waiting for an improbable offer of marriage, seemed intolerable. To Emily, antagonistic to all authority and already dependent for health and spirits on the freedom of the moors, working under strangers was unthinkable. Anne alone regarded such a career with pleasure, for she alone possessed any real affection for children; yet of the three sisters she, darling of aunt and father, was least likely to be sent away.[16]

One outlet, apart from their writing, all four Brontës possessed in common; for all were reading steadily—the girls being now old enough to walk the eight miles to Keighley and back to fetch an armful of books from the Mechanics' Institute library. The periodicals they read included, in addition to the inevitable *Blackwood's* and *Fraser's*, the *British Essayists*, *The Rambler*, *The Mirror*, and *The Lounger*.[17] Charlotte gives some idea of the books they read, when she writes to Ellen a year after her friend's visit to Haworth. Ellen had asked her what course of reading she recommended. Charlotte leaped at the opportunity. 'If you like poetry,' she wrote, 'let it be first rate, Milton, Shakespeare, Thomson, Goldsmith, Pope (if you will, though I don't admire him) Scott, Byron, Campbell, Wordsworth and Southey.' At this point Charlotte thought a word of reassurance necessary: 'Now Ellen don't be startled at the names of Shakespeare and Byron. Both these were great men and their works are like themselves. You will know how to choose the good and avoid the evil, the finest passages are always the purest, the bad are invariably revolting, you will never wish to read them over twice. Omit the Comedies of Shakespeare and the Don Juan, perhaps the Cain of Byron, though the latter is a magnificent Poem, and read the rest fearlessly. That must indeed be a depraved mind which can gather evil from Henry the 8th, from Richard 3rd, from Macbeth and Hamlet and Julius Caesar, Scott's sweet, wild, romantic Poetry can do you no harm, nor can Wordsworth's nor Campbell's nor Southey's, the greater part at least of his, some is certainly exceptionable. For History read Hume, Rollin, and the Universal History if you can—*I* never did. For fiction—read Scott alone; all novels after his are worthless. For biography, read Johnson's Lives of the Poets, Boswell's Life of Johnson, Southey's Life of Nelson, Lockhart's Life of Burns, Moore's Life of Sheridan, Moore's Life of Byron, Wolfe's Remains. For Natural History, read Bewick and Audubon, and Goldsmith and White—of Selborne.'[18]

Early the following year Charlotte paid a second visit to

Ellen, but she did not tell her friend of the plans being discussed in the parsonage. William Robinson thought well of Branwell's progress in portrait-painting; and this was quite enough for Branwell to see himself at the Royal Academy. The family, eager to see and forward greatness in him, were just as enthusiastic, and, a few months before he had finished his lessons with Robinson, Branwell was asking the secretary of the Academy if he might join as a student in the autumn of 1835.[19] Nor was Branwell the only one to be leaving the parsonage. Mr. Brontë and Miss Branwell decided that Emily, who had become rather more than Charlotte could deal with, should prepare herself to be a governess or teacher by going to school.[20] And this in turn decided Charlotte to help replace the money to be spent on Branwell and her sister. So, she tells Ellen in a letter written on the second day of July: 'We are about to divide, break up, separate, Emily is going to school, Branwell is going to London and I am going to be a Governess. This last determination I formed myself, knowing that I should have to take the step sometime . . . and knowing also that Papa would have enough to do with his limited income should Branwell be placed at the Royal Academy, and Emily at Roe Head. Where am I going to reside? you will ask—within four miles of yourself, dearest, at a place neither of us are wholly unacquainted with, being no other than the identical Roe Head mentioned above. Yes I am going to teach in the very school where I was myself taught— Miss Wooler made me the offer and I preferred it to one or two proposals of Private Governess-ship which I had before received. I am sad, very sad at the thoughts of leaving home but Duty— Necessity—these are stern mistresses who will not be disobeyed.'[21]

VII

ROE HEAD AGAIN

Failure of Charlotte's expectations. Emily is sent home. Anne takes her place. Branwell fails to enter the Academy. Charlotte's depression and Angrian dreams. Improves during holidays but relapses on return to school. The effect of Cowper.

ON 29 July 1835, Charlotte returned to Roe Head; this time as teacher and with Emily for companion. Both Ellen Nussey and Mary Taylor came to see her, and Mary, with customary bluntness, asked her friend how she could give so much for so little money when she could live without it. Charlotte owned that, after clothing herself and her sister, there was nothing left, though she had hoped to be able to save something. She confessed it was not brilliant, but what could she do?[1]

Even more disappointing to Charlotte was Emily's reaction to school life. She had chosen to return to Roe Head rather than to accept more money as private governess because of Emily's companionship, but this expectation, like Charlotte's hope of saving from her salary, proved vain. Within three months Emily was back again at the parsonage. She missed the moors, and, still more, what they stood for—the freedom of mind and action she had been winning steadily at home. She would not tell Charlotte what was the matter; she pined in silence; and her sister watched the effects of this mental struggle with dismay. She saw Emily's strength failing, her face becoming whiter every week, her body thinner, and she was afraid that her sister was going into a rapid decline. She felt that Emily would die if she did not go home, and she could not rest until her sister was sent back to Haworth. Her place was taken by Anne.[2]

But the cruellest blow to Charlotte's hopes was her brother's failure to carry out his part of the plan. What actually happened in London is not clear. Branwell certainly went there, having memorized the names and positions of all the city streets so that before he even left Haworth he could give points to a Londoner.[3] All that is known for certain of his movements in London is that he visited, amongst other famous buildings,

Westminster Abbey, which he was later to sketch with accuracy from memory;[4] and that he frequented the then famous Castle Tavern in Holborn, run by the former prize-fighter Tom Spring. Prize-fighting was a sport dear to Branwell—he was an ardent reader of *Bell's Life in London*—and at the Castle Tavern he soon attracted attention by his knowledge of the sport and by his racy conversation. He met there a man called Woolven, with whom he was later to become friendly.[5] Apart from this, all is mystery. There is no indication that Branwell even took the preliminary examination at the Academy. It is possible that he was discouraged by the sight of so many great pictures. At all events, he went no further in the matter.

The one hint that Branwell has left about his movements in London is to be found in an Angrian story written by him soon afterwards. In this, the hero, who in some respects is a glorified Branwell, visits London to study art, but does not enter the big art galleries or present his letters of introduction to those in charge of them. This, writes Branwell, is because the hero has 'an instinctive fear of ending his pleasure by approaching reality'.[6]

Even the date of Branwell's visit to London is uncertain. He had asked the secretary of the Academy if he might join in August or September of 1835, but by December of this year he had already written three times to the editor of *Blackwood's Magazine* asking, in letters which are an unpleasant mixture of cocksureness and self-abasement, for an opportunity to become a contributor. 'The idea of my striving to aid another periodical', he told the editor, '*is horribly repulsive.*' He speaks of John Wilson: 'I cannot express, though you can understand, the heavenliness of associations connected with such articles as Professor Wilson's, read and re-read while a little child, with all their poetry of language and divine flights into that visionary region of imagination which one very young would believe reality, and which one entering into manhood would look back on as a glorious dream. I speak so, sir, because while a child 'Blackwood' formed my chief delight, and I feel certain that no child before enjoyed reading as I did, because none ever had such works as "The Noctes", "Christmas Dreams", "Christopher in his Sporting Jacket" to read.' He quotes a number of passages he had read, ending with:

'Long, long ago seems the time when we danced hand in hand with our golden-haired sister, whom all that looked on loved. Long, long ago, the day on which she died. That hour so far more dreadful than any hour which can now darken us on earth, when she, her coffin and that velvet pall descended—and descended—slowly—slowly—into the horrid clay, and we were borne death-like, and wishing to die, out of the churchyard that from that moment we thought we could never enter more.'

And he comments: 'Passages like these, sir (and when that last was written my sister died)—passages like these, read then and remembered now, afford feelings which, I repeat, I cannot describe.'

Branwell also mentions James Hogg: 'The writings of that man in your numbers,' he tells the editor, ' his speeches in your "Noctes", when I was a child, laid a hold on my mind which succeeding years have consecrated into a most sacred feeling.' And he ends this letter: 'You have lost an able writer in James Hogg, and God grant you may gain one in PATRICK BRANWELL BRONTË.'[7]

Branwell sent yet another letter the following April, together with a poem entitled 'Misery'. He ends: 'But don't think, sir, that I write nothing but Miseries. My day is far too much in the morning for such continual shadow. Nor think either (and this I entreat) that I wish to deluge you with poetry. I send it because it is soonest read and comes from the heart. If it goes *to* yours, print it, and write to me on the subject of *contribution*. Then I will send prose. But if what I now send is worthless, what I have said has only been conceit and folly, yet CONDEMN NOT UNHEARD.'[8]

But he had no answers to his letters, and, left without Charlotte's drive and encouragement, he alternated between bouts of melancholy and high spirits. The Black Bull saw much of him, and so did the set of young artists and writers in Bradford. At home, he made a few desultory attempts at painting, and he wrote more Angrian adventures. But he could settle to nothing.

Thus Charlotte's sacrifice had proved vain. And the position at Roe Head for which she was in no way suited (for she was not at her ease with children) was made a great deal worse by her extreme sense of duty which, with rare exceptions, forbade her to see Ellen and Mary, even though both lived close to the school, and both urged her frequently to stay with them. When she did go to Ellen's home, Charlotte found peace. She also, though she did not know it, attracted the attention of Ellen's brother Henry. Another brother, George, acted more than once as a go-between in carrying letters and packets between the girls.[9]

At the home of Mary and her lively sister Martha, Charlotte's Tory principles were rudely handled. Joshua Taylor, a cultured and kindly Yorkshireman, whose pleasure it was to drop into the rough local mannerisms, professed the most Radical views in politics and religion; and his daughter's guest, heavily out-numbered, was sometimes reduced to tears, though she put up a good fight when roused, and freely defended her opinions. But although Charlotte's sense of humour was often unequal to these occasions, she enjoyed herself more often than not, and looked back on her visits to Mary's home with great pleasure. Mr. Taylor spoke and read French almost like a native, and with his help she began to study the language seriously. This interest was to play a considerable part in her future plans and in the development of her life.[10]

As time passed, Charlotte sank into melancholy. She saw little either of Anne or of Miss Wooler. Her neurotic mind fed on loneliness. She sat alone in the dark, brooding, until the fearfulness of the images conjured up by her imagination haunted her and drove her elsewhere. She could neither sleep at night nor attend to her work in the day.[11]

The uncongeniality of this work; the sense of failure as teacher; the realization that her sacrifice in leaving home had been useless; the knowledge that her salary was barely paying for herself and Anne; all this made Charlotte more unhappy. Her health, never robust, was weakened by lack of exercise, by unwise diet, and by the constant pressure of an extravagant imagination. This poor health depressed her spirits, invited melancholia.[12] And now, at an age when few girls escape physical and mental stress, she was assailed by an over-sensitive conscience, and a craving for romantic love.

In fact, the main reason for her unhappiness at Roe Head was the gulf between life as it was and life as she would like it to be. For years she had been using the Angrian game as a shield to hide the drabness of reality. Many a child has acted the same way, but few with Charlotte's intensity. So much the greater, then, became her disillusionment when, at Roe Head, with little time or heart for writing, she could not avoid facing the apparent hopelessness of her life. The monotony of her long days, the dreary round of distasteful teaching and uneasy sleep, proved too much for her. All hope of a romantic and colourful life retreated. She seemed doomed to mediocrity, frustration, and boredom.

Charlotte did not give up her imaginative world; she tried hard to keep it, but it began to lose the power to protect her from the world's coldness, and from her insignificance. As a result, she fluctuated between secret outpourings in her diary of Angrian hopes and fears, and outbursts of penitence in a style much like her aunt's Methodist magazines.

First, her diary. She writes: 'It is seven o'clock at night; the young ladies are all at their lessons; the schoolroom is quiet, the fire is low; a stormy day is at this moment passing off in a murmuring and bleak night. I now assume my own thoughts; my mind relaxes from the stretch on which it has been for the last twelve hours, and falls back onto the rest which nobody in this house knows of but myself. I now, after a day of weary wandering, return to the ark which for me floats alone on the billows of this world's desolate and boundless deluge. It is strange I cannot get used to the ongoings that surround me. I fulfil my duties strictly and well . . . if the illustration be not profane,— as God was not in the fire, nor the wind, nor the earthquake, so neither is my heart in the task, the theme, or the exercise. It is the still small voice always that comes to me at eventide, that . . . takes up my spirit and engrosses all my living feelings, all my energies which are not merely mechanical. . . . Haworth and home awake sensations which lie dormant elsewhere.'[13]

Later, Charlotte writes: 'And now once more on a dull Saturday afternoon I sit down to try to summon around me the dim shadows, not of coming events, but of incidents long departed, of feelings, of pleasures, whose exquisite relish I sometimes fear it will never be my lot again to taste . . . . Pen cannot portray the deep interest of the scenes, of the continued train of events, I have witnessed in that little room with the low, narrow bed and bare white-washed walls twenty miles away . . . . There have I sat on the low bedstead, my eyes fixed on the window, through which appeared no other landscape than a monotonous stretch of moorland and a grey church tower rising from the centre of a church-yard so filled with graves that the rank weeds and coarse grass scarce had room to shoot up between the monuments . . . . A long tale was perhaps then evolving itself in my mind, the history of an ancient and aristocratic family . . . . My dream shifted to some distant city, some huge imperial metropolis, where the descendants of the last noblemen, the young lords and ladies, shine in gay circles . . . faces looking up, eyes smiling, and lips moving in audible speeches that I knew better almost than my brother and sister . . . there they are before me; in throngs, in crowds they come, they go, they speak, they beckon, and that not like airy phantoms, but as noblemen and ladies of flesh and blood . . . . I cannot write of them; except in total solitude, I scarce dare think of them.'[14]

Again Charlotte scribbles in her diary: 'All this day I have been in a dream, half miserable, half ecstatic . . . . I had been toiling for nearly an hour with Miss Lister, Miss Marriot, and Ellen Cook, striving to teach them the distinction between an article and a substantive. The parsing lesson was completed; a dead silence had succeeded it in the schoolroom, and I sat sinking from irritation and weariness into a kind of lethargy. The thought came over me; Am I to spend all the best part of my life in this wretched bondage, forcibly suppressing my rage at the idleness, the apathy, and the hyperbolical and most asinine stupidity of these fat-headed oafs, and of compulsion assuming an air of kindness, patience and assiduity? Must I from day to day sit chained to this chair, prisoned within these four bare walls, while these glorious summer suns are burning in heaven and the year is revolving in its richest glow? Stung to the heart with this reflection, I started up and mechanically walked to the window. A sweet August morning was smiling without. The dew was not yet dried off the field, the early shadows were stretching cool and dim from the hay-stacks and the roots of the grand old oaks and thorns scattered along the sunk fence. All was still except the murmur of the scribes about me over their tasks. I flung up the sash. An uncertain sound of inexpressible sweetness came on a dying gale from the south. I looked in that direction . . . I listened—the sound sailed full and liquid down

the descent: it was the bells of Huddersfield Parish Church. I
shut the window and went back to my seat. Then came on me,
rushing impetuously, all the mighty phantasm that this had
conjured from nothing . . . I felt as if I could have written
gloriously. The spirit of all Verdopolis . . . came crowding into
my mind. If I had had time to indulge it I felt that the vague
suggestions of that moment would have settled down into some
narrative better at least than anything I ever produced before.
But just then a dolt came up with a lesson . . . .'[15]

Branwell was still weaving story after story of Angria; and
his accounts of them were at once Charlotte's chief solace and
a source of grief that she was not free to write likewise. In
October 1836 she notes in her diary: 'About a week since I got
a letter from Branwell containing a most exquisitely characteristic epistle from Northangerland to his daughter. It is
astonishing what a soothing and delightful tone that letter
seemed to speak. I lived on its contents for days.'[16]

Branwell later writes to announce the burning of Adrianopolis; and his sister's imagination needed no further bidding: 'Last
night I did indeed lean upon the thunder-waking wings of such
a stormy blast as I have seldom heard blow, and it whirled me
away like heath in the wilderness for five seconds of ecstasy;
and as I sat by myself in the dining-room while all the rest
were at tea, the trance seemed to descend on a sudden, and
verily this foot trod the war-shaken shores of the Calabar, and
these eyes saw the defiled and violated Adrianopolis shedding
its lights on the river.'[17]

She sees the couch of the Queen of Angria, 'where she had
lain imperially robed and decked with pearls, every waft of her
garments as she moved diffusing perfume, her beauty slumbering and still glowing as dreams of him for whom she kept herself in such hallowed and shrine-like separation, wandered over
her soul,' while on the couch lay 'a swart and sinewy Moor,
intoxicated to ferocious insensibility'. Charlotte goes on, her
sense of humour, never very strong, now entirely absent:
'While he was full before her eyes, lying in his black dress on
the disordered couch, his sable hair dishevelled on his forehead,
his tusk-like teeth gleaming vindictively through his parted
lips, his brown complexion flushed with wine and his broad
chest heaving wildly . . . the dining-room door opened, and

Miss Wooler came in with a plate of butter in her hand. "A stormy night, my dear!" said she.'[18]

Those imaginative excesses led, inevitably, to painful reactions. In her diary Charlotte confessed that she had been a stranger to agreeable thoughts for many weeks. This, for Charlotte, is moderation indeed, and gives no indication of how much she suffered. Ellen now knew something of her friend's mental state, and it was in letters to her during the next two years that Charlotte tried to ease her mind. She comforted herself with thoughts of Ellen, and looked forward to a life with her.

When Ellen attempted reassurance, Charlotte would have none of it. 'I won't play the hypocrite, I won't answer your kind, gentle friendly question in the way you wish me to. Don't deceive yourself by imagining that I have a bit of real goodness about me. My darling, if I were like you I should have my face Zionward though prejudice and error might occasionally fling a mist over the glorious vision before me, for with all your single-hearted sincerity you have your faults, but I am *not like you*. If you knew my thoughts; the dreams that absorb me; and the fiery imagination that at times eats me up and makes me feel Society as it is, wretchedly insipid, you would pity and I dare say despise me. But Ellen I know the treasures of the Bible, I love and adore them, I can *see* the Well of Life in all its clearness and brightness; but when I stoop down to drink of the pure waters they fly from my lips as if I were Tantalus.'[19]

Then ashamed of her weakness, her pride rising again, she bursts out angrily: 'I have written like a *fool*. Don't think me mad, this is a silly letter.'[20] But she is soon driven back to her confessional: 'It is a stormy evening, and the wind is uttering a continual moaning sound that makes me feel very melancholy. At such times, in such moods as these, Ellen, it is my nature to seek repose in some calm, tranquil idea, and I have now summoned up your image to give me rest. There you sit upright and still in your black dress and white scarf, your pale, marble-like face looking so serene and kind—just like reality. I wish you would speak to me . . . . What am I compared to you? I feel my own utter worthlessness when I make the comparison. I am a very coarse, commonplace wretch, Ellen. I have some qualities which make me very miserable, some feelings that you can have no participation in, that few, very few people in the world can at all understand. I don't pride myself on these peculiarities, I strive to conceal and suppress them as much as I can, but they burst out sometimes, and then those who see the explosion despise me, and I hate myself for days afterwards.'[21]

And again she turns on herself: 'We are going to have prayers,' she finishes abruptly, 'so I can write no more of this trash, yet it is too true.'[22]

The battle went on in Charlotte's mind, between the safe and placid, and the romantic and unknown. She felt the existence of a barrier between Ellen, serene and peaceful, and herself. She tried repeatedly to break it down and relieve her troubled mind. The true difference between them she did not suspect. 'I will no longer shrink from your questions,' she tells her friend. 'I *do* wish to be better than I am. I pray fervently sometimes to be made so. I have stings of conscience—visitings of remorse—glimpses of Holy, inexpressible things, which formerly I used to be a stranger to.'[23] Then, thinking this may suggest that she considers herself one of the elect, Charlotte hurriedly breaks out: 'Do not mistake me, Ellen, do not think I am good, I only wish to be so, I only hate my former flippancy and forwardness. O! I am no better than I ever was. I am in that state of horrid, gloomy uncertainty, that at this moment I would submit to be old, grey-haired, to have passed all my youthful days of enjoyment and be tottering on the verge of the grave, if I could only thereby ensure the prospect of reconcilement to God, and Redemption through His Son's merits. I never was exactly careless of these matters, but I have always taken a clouded and repulsive view of them; and now, if possible, the clouds are gathering darker, and a more oppressive despondency weighs continually on my spirits. You have cheered me, my darling; for one moment, for an atom of time, I thought I might call you my own sister, in the spirit, but the excitement is past, and I am now as wretched as ever. This very night I will pray as you wish me. May the Almighty hear me compassionately! and I humbly trust He will—for you will strengthen my polluted petition with your own pure requests.'[24]

Ellen, moved by this uncritical admiration, and eager, like most young women, to improve others, did her gentle best to draw her friend to the light. On rare occasions she appeared on the point of succeeding: 'I will not tell you all I think and feel about you, Ellen,' wrote Charlotte in one of her softer moments. 'I will preserve unbroken that reserve which alone enables me to maintain a decent character for judgment; but for that, I should long ago have been set down by all who know me as a Frenchified fool. You have been very kind to me of late, and gentle, and you have spared me those little sallies of ridicule which, owing to my miserable and wretched touchiness of character, used formerly to make me wince as if I had been touched with a hot iron: things that nobody else cares for enter into my mind and rankle there like venom. I know these feelings are absurd and therefore I try to hide them but they only sting the deeper for concealment. I'm an idiot!'[25]

And she concludes: 'Ellen, I wish I could live with you always, I begin to cling to you more fondly than ever I did. If we had but a cottage and a competency of our own I do think we might live and love on till Death, without being dependent on any third person for happiness.—Farewell my own dear Ellen.'[26]

When Charlotte went home for the holidays, many of her doubts and torments fell away; and in the summer of 1836, when Ellen and the four Brontës were all at Haworth, she regained much of her common sense and cheerfulness. The young people, sometimes four, sometimes five of them, spent happy weeks together. The Brontës were beginning to feel conscious of their powers, they laughed at Branwell's witticisms and verbal battles with Charlotte, played the piano, sang, analysed books and articles and their writers, talked freely in the house, and walked over the moors day after day with much high spirits and good companionship. The evening march in the dining-room, a habit learned at school, was in keeping with their holiday mood; they walked round the table in pairs, Emily and Anne, Charlotte and Ellen, with arms linked or round each other's waist, except when Charlotte, in a spurt of high spirits, broke away for a moment and made a pirouette before returning to her companion.[27]

But when she went back to Roe Head, Charlotte quickly relapsed into depression. She began once more to analyse her feelings; 'I feel in a strange state of mind,' she told Ellen, 'still gloomy but not despairing. I keep trying to do right, checking wrong feelings, repressing wrong thoughts—but still—every instant I find myself going astray. I have a constant tendency to scorn people who are far better than I am—a horror at the idea of becoming one of a certain set—a dread lest if I made the slightest profession I should sink at once into Phariseeism, merge wholly into the ranks of the self-righteous. In writing at this moment I feel an irksome disgust at the idea of using a single phrase that sounds like religious cant—I abhor myself— I despise myself—if the Doctrine of Calvin be true I am already an outcast. You cannot imagine how hard, rebellious and intractable all my feelings are. When I begin to study on the subject I almost grow blasphemous, atheistical in my sentiments. . . .'[28]

After this confession Charlotte becomes fearful that even the loyal and devoted Ellen may become too shocked. 'Don't desert me, don't be horrified at me—you know what I am—I wish I could see you my darling, I have lavished the warmest affections of a very hot, tenacious heart upon you. If you grow cold—it's over.'[29]

These letters to Ellen show that Charlotte, in her morbid state, had fallen a temporary victim to the bleak threat of Calvinism embodied in her aunt's teaching. She dissected the motives behind every action, and imagined unforgivable sins. Nor was her aunt alone responsible for Charlotte's pessimism. The Brontës had known and loved Cowper's poems since they were children, and his *Castaway* became a favourite with them all. This poem, with much of Cowper's other writings, reinforced Miss Branwell's Methodist teaching and literature, and presented the impressionable, introspective children with the possibility of eternal damnation.[30]

Emily alone, accepting no guidance—least of all that of her aunt—in her religion, rejected the doctrine of predestination. Branwell, unstable, and inclined to fits of melancholy, for a time read little else but Cowper, and practically appropriated his *Castaway*; and often suffered bad attacks of conscience.[31] Anne, who had quickly developed a morbidly delicate religious conscience, read and loved the poet; and when she thought about Cowper's dreadful conviction that he was damned—this man, so much greater and more worthy of a heaven than her-

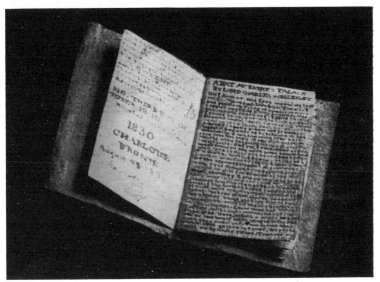

TWO NUMBERS OF THE YOUNG MEN'S MAGAZINE

written by Charlotte
(exact size)

ROE HEAD SCHOOL

self—she began in her solitary moments to suffer terrible distress of mind. Charlotte, in good health and spirits, had too robust a common sense to succumb to such a doctrine; but at Roe Head, low health and depression gave these fears insidious force. 'I know not how to pray,' she told Ellen, 'I cannot bind my life to the grand end of doing good. I go on constantly seeking my own pleasure, pursuing the gratification of my own desires, I forget God and will not God forget me?'[32]

She saw little of Anne at Roe Head—for the same extreme sense of duty that stopped Charlotte from taking advantage of her friends' hospitality forbade her also to spend much spare time with her sister. Yet the constant society of Anne would have proved a mixed blessing; for although she was only sixteen, her pensiveness had already begun to resolve itself into a deep melancholy.

Charlotte may well have had Anne as well as her aunt in mind when she told Ellen of 'the melancholy state I now live in, uncertain that I have ever felt true contrition, wandering in thought and deed, longing for holiness which I shall *never, never* attain —smitten at times to the heart with the conviction that ——'s ghastly Calvinistic doctrines are true—darkened in short by the very shadows of Spiritual Death!'[33]

This was just before Christmas 1836, and Charlotte was able to turn to more cheerful, if not more healthy, thoughts. She wrote: 'I trust ere another three weeks elapse I shall again have my comforter beside me, under the roof of my own dear quiet home. If I could always live with you and daily read the Bible with you, if your lips and mine could at the same time drink the same draught from the same pure fountain of mercy, I hope, I trust, I might one day become better, far better, than my evil wandering thoughts, my corrupt heart, cold to the spirit and warm to the flesh, will now permit me to be.'[34]

VIII

THE END OF ROE HEAD

Charlotte and Branwell seek advice about their writings. Southey's reply. Emily and Branwell go to work. Emily's first poems. Anne, Emily and Branwell all return home. Charlotte leaves Miss Wooler. Visit of the Taylors.

AT home this Christmas, Charlotte, anxious to escape from Roe Head and a life of teaching, decided to seek the opinion of some eminent author about her writings. Branwell was also eager to have an opinion on his work, so they agreed that he should write to Wordsworth, and Charlotte to Southey, the Poet Laureate. They both enclosed some verses with their letters.

Southey thought Charlotte's letter 'flighty',[1] and did not reply to it until the spring, when she was back at Roe Head. His advice was not encouraging; he described it to a friend as 'a dose of cooling admonition'.[2]

'You evidently possess', he wrote, 'and to no inconsiderable degree, what Wordsworth calls the faculty of verse. I am not depreciating it when I say that in these times it is not rare. Many volumes of poems are now published every year without attracting public attention, any one of which, if it had appeared half a century ago, would have obtained a high reputation for its author. Whoever, therefore, is ambitious of distinction in this way ought to be prepared for disappointment. But it is not with a view to distinction that you should cultivate this talent, if you consult your own happiness. I, who have made literature my profession and devoted my life to it, and have never for a moment repented of the deliberate choice, think myself, nevertheless, bound in duty to caution every young man who applies as an aspirant to me for encouragement and advice against taking so perilous a course. You will say that a woman has no need of such a caution; there can be no peril in it for her. In a certain sense this is true; but there is a danger of which I would, with all kindness and all earnestness, warn you. The day dreams in which you habitually indulge are likely to induce a distempered state of mind; and, in proportion as all the ordinary uses of the world seem to you flat and unprofitable, you will be unfitted for them without becoming fitted for anything else. Literature cannot be the business of a woman's life, and it ought not to be. The more she is engaged in her proper duties, the less leisure will she have for it, even as an accomplishment and a recreation. To these duties you have not been called, and when you are you will be less eager for celebrity. You will not seek in imagination for excitement, of which the vicissitudes of this life, and the anxieties from which you must not hope to be exempted, be your state what it may, will bring with them but too much. But do not suppose that I disparage the gift which you possess, nor that I would discourage you from exercising it. I only exhort you so to think of it, and so to use it, as to render it conducive to your own permanent good. Write poetry for its own sake; not in a spirit of emulation, and not with a view to celebrity; the less you aim at that the more likely you will be to deserve and finally to obtain it. So written, it is wholesome both for the heart and soul; it may be made the surest means, next to religion, of soothing the mind, and elevating it. You may embody in it your best thoughts and your wisest feelings, and in so doing discipline and strengthen them. Farewell, madam. It is not because I have forgotten that I was once young myself, that I write to you in this strain; but because I remember it. You will neither doubt my sincerity, nor my goodwill; and, however ill what has here been said may accord with your present views and temper, the longer you live the more reasonable it will appear to you. Though I may be an ungracious adviser, you will allow me, therefore, to subscribe myself, with the best wishes for your happiness here and hereafter, your true friend.'[3]

Charlotte, who had long since given up hope of a reply, was not unduly depressed by Southey's letter. She wrote of it: 'Southey's advice to be kept for ever. My twenty-first birthday, Roe Head, April 21, 1837.'[4] She also replied, gratefully, but with a touch of asperity.

'I cannot rest till I have answered your letter,' she wrote, 'even though by addressing you a second time I should appear a little intrusive; but I must thank you for the kind and wise advice you have condescended to give me. I had not ventured to hope for such a reply; so considerate in its tone, so noble in its spirit. I must suppress what I feel, or you will think me foolishly enthusiastic. At the first perusal of your letter I felt only shame and regret that I had ever ventured to trouble you with my crude rhapsody; I felt a painful heat rise to my face when I thought of the quires of paper I had covered with what once gave me so much delight, but which now was only a source of confusion; but after I had thought a little, and read it again and again, the prospect seemed to clear. You do not forbid me to write; you do not say that what I write is utterly destitute of merit. You only warn me against the folly of neglecting real duties for the sake of imaginative pleasures; of writing for the love of fame; for the selfish excitement of emulation. You kindly allow me to write poetry for its own sake, providing I leave undone nothing which I ought to do, in order to pursue that single, absorbing exquisite gratification. I am afraid, sir, you think me very foolish. I know the first letter I wrote to you was all senseless trash from beginning to end; but I am not altogether the idle, dreaming being it would seem to denote. My father is a clergyman of limited though competent income, and I am the eldest of his children. He expended quite as much in my education as he could afford in justice to the rest. I thought it therefore my duty, when I left school, to become a governess. In that capacity I find enough to occupy my thoughts all day long, and my head and hands too, without having a moment's time for one dream of the imagination. In the evenings, I confess, I do think, but I never trouble any one else with my thoughts. I carefully avoid any appearance of preoccupation and eccentricity, which might lead those I live amongst to suspect the nature of my pursuits. Following my father's advice—who from my childhood has counselled me, just in the wise and friendly tone of your letter—I have endeavoured not only attentively to observe all the duties a woman ought to fulfill, but to feel deeply interested in them. I don't always succeed, for sometimes when I'm teaching or sewing I would rather be reading or writing; but I try to deny myself; and my father's approbation amply rewarded me for the privation. Once more allow me to thank you with sincere gratitude. I trust I shall never more feel ambitious to see my name in print; if the wish should rise, I'll look at Southey's letter and suppress it. It is honour enough for me that I have written to him, and received an answer. That letter is consecrated; no one shall ever see it but papa and my brothers and sisters . . . your advice shall not be wasted, however sorrowfully and reluctantly it may at first be followed.'[5]

Southey replied within a few days: 'Your letter has given me great pleasure,' he wrote, 'and I should not forgive myself if I did not tell you so. You have received admonition as considerately and as kindly as it was given. Let me now request that, if you ever should come to these Lakes while I am living here, you will let me see you. You would then think of me afterwards with the more good-will, because you would then perceive that there is neither severity nor moroseness in the state of mind to which years and observation have brought me. It is, by God's mercy, in our power to attain a degree of self-government, which is essential to our own happiness, and contributes greatly to that of those around us. Take care of over-excitement, and endeavour to keep a quiet mind (even for your health it is the best advice that can be given you): your moral and spiritual improvement will then keep pace with the culture of your intellectual powers.'[6]

Southey believed that Charlotte would think kindly of him as long as she lived;[7] and it is certainly true that, even though she did not follow his advice, she was grateful for the interest he had shown in her. Branwell had not even this consolation; but he had only himself to blame. The verses he enclosed in his letter to Wordsworth closely resembled the poet's *Intimations of Immortality*. This was not tactful, nor was the form of the letter likely to please.

'I most earnestly entreat you to read and pass your judgment upon what I have sent you,' he wrote, 'because from the day of my birth to this nineteenth year of my life I have lived among secluded hills, where I could neither know what I was or what I could do. I read for the same reason that I ate or drank, because it was a real craving of nature. I wrote on the same principle as I spoke—out of the impulse and feelings of the mind; nor could I help it, for what came, came out, and there was an end of it. For as to self-conceit, that could not receive food from flattery, since to this hour not half-a-dozen people in the world know that I have ever penned a line. But a change has taken place now, sir; and I am arrived at an age wherein I must do something for myself; the powers I possess must be exercised to a definite end, and as I don't know them myself I must ask of others what they are worth. Yet there is not one here to tell me; and still, if they are worthless, time will henceforth be too precious to be wasted on them. Do pardon me, sir, that I have ventured to come before one whose works I have most loved in our literature, and who most has been with me a divinity of the mind, laying before him one of my writings, and asking of him a judgment of its contents. I must come before one from whose sentence there is no appeal; and such a one is he who has developed the theory of poetry as well as its practice, and both in such a way as to claim a place in the memory of a thousand years to come. My aim, sir, is to push out into the open world, and for this I trust not poetry alone; that might launch the vessel, but could not bear her on. Sensible and scientific prose, bold and vigorous efforts in my walk in life, would give further title to the notice of the world; and then again poetry ought to brighten and crown that name with glory. But nothing of all this can be even begun without means, and as I don't possess these, I must in every shape strive to gain them. Surely, in this day, when there is not a *writing* poet worth a sixpence, the field must be open, if a better man can step forward. What I send you is the Prefatory Scene of a much longer subject, in which I have striven to develop strong passions and weak principles struggling with a high imagination and acute feelings, till, as youth hardens towards age, evil deeds and short enjoyments end in mental misery and bodily ruin. Now, to send you the whole of this would be a mock upon your patience; what you see does not even pretend to be more than the description of an imaginative child. But read it, sir; and, as you would hold a light to one in utter darkness—as you value your own kind-heartedness—*return* me an *answer*, if but one word, telling me whether I should 'write on, or write no more. Forgive undue warmth, because my feelings in this matter cannot be cool; and believe me, sir, with deep respect, your really humble servant.'[8]

This letter disgusted Wordsworth, who thought it grossly flattering to himself and abusive of other poets, including Southey.[9]

So Charlotte, hoping that she would never again feel the wish to see her work in print, and Branwell, cast down by yet another unanswered letter, took up once more their accustomed round. Charlotte was handicapped by her work at Roe Head, but she continued to write her Angrian tales, while, at the Parsonage, Branwell wrote more furiously than ever. He had recently joined the Masonic Lodge of the Three Graces, as Secretary, Organist, and Junior Warden; and as the Lodge held its meetings at the Black Bull, he now had an official excuse for frequent calls at the inn. He also continued to visit Bradford and Halifax whenever he could persuade his father to give him money.[10] He still read a great deal at home and in the libraries of the Mechanics' Institutes then coming into favour in town and village. He also played the organ in Haworth church when the mood took him, and dabbled with his painting in the little room he had converted into a studio on the parsonage first floor;[11] and, as relaxation from Angria, he wrote poems, mostly sombre and bizarre, but showing promise.[12]

Charlotte was without her brother's distractions. She had to endure as well as she could the routine, loneliness, and uncongeniality of school life. She did not in fact endure these things very well. No sooner had she returned with Anne than she learned that Ellen was to spend several months away, in London and Bath: 'Why are we to be divided?' she asked herself as much as her friend. 'Surely, Ellen, it must be because we are in danger of loving each other too well—of losing sight of the *Creator* in idolatry of the *creature*. At first I could not say "Thy will be done." I felt rebellious; but I know it was wrong to feel so. Being left a moment alone this morning, I prayed so fervently to be enabled to resign myself to *every* decree of God's will—though it should be dealt forth with a far severer hand than the present disappointment. Since then, I have felt calmer and humbler—and consequently happier. Last Sunday I took up my Bible in a gloomy frame of mind; I began to read; a feeling stole over me such as I have not known for many long years—a sweet, placid sensation like those that I remember used to visit me when I was a little child, and on Sunday evenings in summer stood by the open window reading the life of a certain French nobleman who attained a purer and higher degree of sanctity than has been known since the days of the early Martyrs. I thought of my own Ellen—I wished she had been near me that I might have told her how happy I was, how bright and glorious the pages of God's holy word seemed to me. But the "foretaste" passed away and sin returned.'[13]

Early in the summer the school moved to Heald's House, on the low-lying Dewsbury Moor—a place which soon began to affect the health of both sisters. In August, the visits of Charlotte's other friends, Mary Taylor and her sister Martha, also stopped for some weeks, and her appeals to Ellen to return grew almost desperate: '*When will you come home?*' she asks, '*Come— Come* .... Saturday after Saturday comes round and I can have no hope of hearing your knock at the door and then being told that "Miss Ellen Nussey is come". O dear, in this monotonous life of mine that was a pleasant event.'[14]

Her comments on Miss Wooler showed that Charlotte's employer was not to escape criticism. 'I am again at Dewsbury Moor engaged in the old business teach—teach—teach,' Charlotte informs the still absent Ellen, 'Miss Eliza Wooler and Mrs. Wooler are coming here next Christmas. Miss Wooler will then relinquish the school in favour of her sister Eliza—but I am happy to say the worthy dame will continue to reside in the house, with all her faults I should be sorry indeed to part with her.'[15]

In the autumn Emily again left the parsonage—this time to teach in Elizabeth Patchett's school at Law Hill near Halifax. Branwell, not to be outdone, obtained a situation as teacher in a nearby school.

For the first time all four Brontës were away from home. But not for long. Within a few months Branwell was back at Haworth,[16] and Emily soon followed him.

Of Emily's brief employment at Law Hill little is known; but her unhappiness there cannot have been entirely due to her peculiarities. Her extreme reserve with strangers was noticed; but so, too, was her generosity and considerateness towards those whom she liked. Charlotte drew a gloomy picture of the life Emily was leading. 'My sister Emily', she told Ellen on 2 October, 'has gone into a situation as teacher in a large school of near forty pupils, near Halifax. I have had one letter from her since her departure; it gives an appalling account of her duties—hard labour from six in the morning until near eleven at night, with only one half-hour of exercise between. This is slavery. I fear she will never stand it.'[17]

Charlotte was right—Emily could not stand it. Yet she remained at Law Hill longer than her sister thought possible. It is difficult to say how much of her second failure to stay away from home was due to overwork—which the loyal Charlotte may have exaggerated—and how much to Emily's misery whenever she felt confined. Freedom was the very breath of life to Emily. The girl who dealt cheerfully with the household tasks at the parsonage, who would outwalk and outstay the others, who would confront the rough tramp and master fierce animals without fear—this Emily, at Roe Head, and again at Law Hill, sank into hopeless despondency and had to be sent home before she became a complete physical and mental wreck.[18]

During the weary months away from home Emily wrote lyrics which, even more than the Gondal poems she had begun to compose, gave her the comfort of self-expression.[19] In them she was concerned chiefly to relieve her heart of its home-sickness:

A little while, a little while
The noisy crowd are barred away;
And I can sing and I can smile—
A little while I've holyday!

Where wilt thou go my harassed heart?
Full many a land invites thee now;
And places near and far apart
Hold rest for thee, my weary brow—

There is a spot mid barren hills
Where winter howls and driving rain
But if the dreary tempest chills
There is a light that warms again.

The house is old, the trees are bare
And moonless bends the misty dome
But what on earth is half so dear—
So longed for as the hearth of home?

The mute bird sitting on the stone,
The dank moss dripping from the wall,
The garden-walk with weeds o'er-grown
I love them—how I love them all!

Shall I go there? or shall I seek
Another clime, another sky,
Where tongues familiar music speak
In accents dear to memory?

Yes, as I mused, the naked room,
The flickering firelight died away
And from the midst of cheerless gloom
I passed to bright, unclouded day.

A little and a lone green lane
That opened on a common wide
A distant, dreamy, dim blue chain
Of mountains circling every side—

A heaven so clear, an earth so calm,
So sweet, so soft, so hushed an air
And, deepening still the dreamlike charm,
Wild moor-sheep feeding everywhere—

That was the scene—I knew it well
I knew the path-ways far and near
That winding o'er each billowy swell
Marked out the tracks of wandering deer.

Could I have lingered but an hour
It well had paid a week of toil
But truth has banished fancy's power
I hear my dungeon bars recoil.

Even as I stood with raptured eye
Absorbed in bliss so deep and dear
My hour of rest had fleeted by
And given me back to weary care.[20]

Branwell was home again within six months. He, it seems, returned in dudgeon, resentful of his pupils' fun at the expense of his red hair and small stature. Branwell, like Emily, panted for freedom; but having gained it, he often did not know what to do with it. He, too, was ill, chiefly because he had been drinking to forget his boredom and chagrin.[21]

Anne, however, was home soonest of all. The air of Dewsbury, so different from the sharp bracing winds of Haworth, did

not suit her. She could not have known much happiness at
school. Her spiritual struggles, her extreme shyness, and the
sight of Charlotte's own melancholy combined to depress her
unbearably. She longed for home, for the moors, for Emily.
Charlotte was jolted at last out of her self-absorption, and the
rest of the affair is best told by her. 'Anne continued wretched
ill,' she wrote to Ellen, 'neither the pain nor the difficulty of
breathing left her—and how could I feel otherwise than very
miserable? I looked upon her case in a different light to what I
could wish or expect any uninterested person to view it in.
Miss Wooler thought me a fool—and by way of proving her
opinion treated me with marked coldness—we came to a little
éclaircissement one evening—and the next day, unknown to me,
she wrote to Papa, telling him that I had reproached her bitterly,
taken her severely to task, etc., etc.—Papa sent for us the day
after he had received her letter. Meantime I had formed a firm
resolution to quit Miss Wooler and her concerns for ever—but
just before I went away she took me into her room, and, giving
way to her feelings, which in general she restrains far too
rigidly, gave me to understand that in spite of her cold repulsive
manner she had a considerable regard for me and would be
very sorry to part with me. If anybody likes me I can't help
liking them, and, remembering that she had in general been
very kind to me, I gave in and said I would come back if she
wished me—so—we're settled again for the present, but I am
not satisfied. I should have respected her far more if she had
turned me out of doors instead of crying for two days and two
nights together. I was in a regular passion, my "warm temper"
quite got the better of me. Of which I don't boast, for it was a
weakness, nor am I ashamed of it for I had reason to be angry.'[22]
Yet Charlotte remained dissatisfied with herself: 'We have entered on a New Year,' she continued. 'Will it be stained as
darkly as the last with all our sins, follies, secret vanities, and
uncontrolled passions and propensities? I trust not—but I feel
in nothing better—neither humbler nor purer . . . but however
bitterly I sometimes feel towards other people, the recollection
of your mild steady friendship consoles and softens me. I am
glad you are not such a passionate fool as myself.'[23]

Anne stayed at home, where she quickly recovered; but after
the Christmas holidays of 1837 Charlotte, her peace made with

Miss Wooler, returned to the school. During this Christmas, however, the faithful Tabby slipped and broke her leg. Miss Branwell said that she must be sent home, and a new servant engaged. The Brontë children did not agree. They determined that, as Tabby had nursed and cared for them, they would do as much for her in her old age. As a protest against their aunt's decision they decided to begin a hunger strike. They worked, but would not eat, until Miss Branwell gave way. Then the girls were kept busy, but happy, looking after the house and the invalid.[24]

Charlotte did not stay much longer at the school. She became more and more unwell, until her state was little better than Anne's. Although the sisters had not seen a great deal of each other at the school, Anne's departure broke Charlotte's one link with home and made her feel less able than ever to deal with her depression. Her relationship with Miss Wooler had been seriously strained because of their difference over Anne, and Charlotte could never feel the same again towards her. At the end of the first term of 1838 she left Heald's House for good. Ellen is told of her friend's last days at school: 'I stayed as long as I was able,' Charlotte wrote, 'and at length I neither could nor dared stay any longer. My health and spirits had utterly failed me, and the medical man I consulted enjoined me, if I valued my life, to go home. So home I went; the change has at once roused and soothed me, and I am now, I trust, fairly in the way to be myself again. A calm and even mind like yours, Ellen, cannot conceive the feelings of the shattered wretch who is now writing to you, when, after weeks of mental and bodily anguish not to be described, something like tranquillity and ease began to dawn again. I will not enlarge on the subject; to me, every recollection of the past half-year is painful.'[25]

That summer, when Emily was also at home, Mary Taylor and her sister Martha stayed at the parsonage. Their gaiety was infectious and everyone felt brighter. The Brontës were glad to be together again, and even Mr. Brontë and Miss Branwell looked benevolently on the high spirits of the young people. These few days in June 1838 must take their place as some of the happiest and liveliest ever known in the Brontës' home. 'Martha', reported Charlotte, 'has kept in a constant flow of good-humour during her stay here, and has consequently been very fascinating . . . . They are making such a noise about me I cannot write any more. Mary is playing on the piano; Martha is chattering as fast as her little tongue can run; and Branwell is standing before her, laughing at her vivacity.'[26]

But Charlotte, who was rarely without a worry, was disturbed by Mary's health: 'Her lively spirits and bright colour might delude you into thinking that all was well,' Charlotte remarked; 'But she breathes short, has a pain in her chest, and frequent flushings of fever. I cannot tell you what agony these symptoms give me. They remind me strongly of my two sisters whom no power of medicine could save.'[27] The deaths of Maria and Elizabeth were never far from her mind. She feared death for herself and for those she loved, and she always believed that consumption was the danger. This fear, only too well-founded, was never to leave Charlotte, and a great deal of her youth was sobered by it.

One evening, in the dining-room, Mary said that someone had asked her what her religion was, and she had replied that this was between God and herself. Emily, who was lying on the hearth-rug, looked up at this, and said 'That's right.' These two words were Emily's only contribution to the subject.[28]

THE END OF ANGRIA

Effect of Branwell's failure on his sisters. Anne goes to work. Charlotte becomes a governess. Her suitors. She abandons Angria. The differences between the work of Charlotte and Branwell. Emily begins to write lyrics. The troubles of Anne. Branwell meets Hartley Coleridge. His translation of Horace approved.

BRANWELL, having had no success as a writer or schoolmaster, now turned again to his portrait painting. He resumed lessons with Robinson in Leeds. Then he decided to set up for himself, and rented a studio in Fountain Street, Bradford.[1] He did in fact paint some portraits; but not enough and not well enough; he spent far too much time in the Bull's Head and at the George Hotel, where most of his set congregated.[2] This venture only lasted a few months.

In the spring of 1839 Branwell returned home abruptly, leaving a friend to complete his last work and pay overdue rent.[3] This unsuccessful fling was yet another drain on the family resources; and, as a direct consequence of it, the three girls had no sooner come together at home again than they had to think once more of looking about for posts. Charlotte and Anne both began making inquiries; Emily, Charlotte felt, would best help by looking after the housework, since it was clear that she could not bear any prolonged absence from Haworth. The idea that Anne should go was her own entirely; everyone was against it. But the youngest Brontë displayed an unexpected obstinacy, and, after considerable demur from Miss Branwell, Mr. Brontë, and Charlotte, she had her way.[4] She was, in fact, the first to obtain a post. She arranged to begin on 8 April as governess to the two elder children of Mrs. Ingham of Blake Hall, Mirfield.

A month before Anne left home, Charlotte had an unexpected chance to escape from teaching. A letter came for her from Henry Nussey—now curate at Donnington in Sussex. She said nothing to Ellen about it, and after a week, Ellen, her curiosity overcoming her, wrote to ask if Charlotte had received the letter. Yes, Charlotte replied, and the contents of the letter had rather surprised her. 'I kept them to myself, and unless you had questioned me on the subject, I would never have adverted to it. Henry says he is comfortably situated at Donnington, that his health is much improved, and that it is his intention to take pupils after Easter. He then intimates that in due course he should want a wife to look after his pupils, and frankly asks me to be that wife. Altogether the letter is written without cant or flattery, and in a common-sense style which does credit to his judgment. Now, my dear Ellen, there were in this proposal some things which might have proved a strong temptation. I thought if I were to marry Henry Nussey, his sister could live with me, and how happy I should be. But again I asked myself two questions. Do I love him as much as a woman ought to love the man she marries? Am I the person best qualified to make him happy? Alas! Ellen, my conscience answered *no* to both these questions. I felt that though I esteemed, though I had a kindly leaning towards him, because he is an amiable and well-disposed man, yet I had not, and could not have, that intense attachment which would make me willing to die for him; and, if ever I marry, it must be in that light of adoration that I will regard my husband. Ten to one I shall never have the chance again; but *n'importe*. Moreover, I was aware that Henry knew so little of me he could hardly be conscious to whom he was writing. Why, it would startle him to see me in my natural home character; he would think I was a wild, romantic enthusiast indeed. I could not sit all day long making a grave face before my husband. I would laugh, and satirise, and say whatever came into my head first. And if he were a clever man, and loved me, the whole world weighed in the balance against his smallest wish would be light as air. Could I, knowing my mind to be such as that, conscientiously say that I would take a grave, quiet young man like Henry? No, it would have been deceiving him, and deception of that sort is beneath me.'[5]

Charlotte had replied to Henry Nussey a week earlier: 'Before answering your letter you are aware that I have many reasons to feel grateful to your family, that I have peculiar reasons for affection towards one at least of your sisters, and also that I highly esteem yourself—do not therefore accuse me of wrong motives when I say that my answer to your proposal must be a *decided negative*. I have no personal repugnance to the idea of a union with you, but I feel convinced that mine is not the sort of disposition calculated to form the happiness of a man like you.'[6]

Having said as much, Charlotte was unable to resist the temptation to tell Henry Nussey exactly what kind of wife he really wanted.

'It has always been my habit', she continued gravely, 'to study the characters of those amongst whom I chance to be thrown, and I think I know yours and can imagine what description of woman would suit you for a wife. The character should not be too marked, ardent, and original, her temper should be mild, her piety undoubted, her spirits even and cheerful, and her *personal attractions* sufficient to please your eyes and gratify your just pride. As for me, you do not know me; I am not the serious, grave, cool-headed individual you suppose; you would think me romantic and eccentric; you would say I was satirical and severe. However, I scorn deceit, and I will never, for the sake of attaining the distinction of matrimony and escaping the stigma of an old maid, take a worthy man whom I am conscious I cannot render happy.'[7]

A few weeks later Anne set off to take up her first post.

'Poor child!' wrote Charlotte to Ellen, 'She left us last Monday—no one went with her—it was her own wish that she might be allowed to go alone, as she thought she could manage better and summon more courage if thrown entirely upon her own resources. We have had one letter from her since she went —she expresses herself very well satisfied, and says that Mrs. Ingham is extremely kind; the two eldest children alone are under her care, the rest are confined to the nursery—with which and its occupants she has nothing to do. Both her pupils are desperate little dunces—neither of them can read and sometimes they even profess a profound ignorance of their alphabet. The worst of it is the little monkeys are excessively indulged and she is not empowered to inflict any punishment—she is requested when they misbehave themselves to inform their Mama—which she says is utterly out of the question as in that case she might be making complaints from morning till night. So she alternately scolds, coaxes and threatens, sticks always to her first word and gets on as well as she can.[8] I hope she'll do, you would be astonished to see what a sensible, clever letter she writes. It is only the talking part that I fear—but I do seriously apprehend that Mrs. Ingham will sometimes consider that she has a natural impediment of speech.'[9]

Two months later, Charlotte left to take up her first position as private governess—to the children of John Benson Sidgwick of Stonegappe near Skipton.[10] The post was a temporary one —which, as it happened, was just as well, for it is clear that Charlotte's stay at Stonegappe would in any event have been short-lived. Charlotte and her employers did not see eye to eye. She comments on the children in a letter to Emily, 'more riotous, perverse, unmanageable cubs never grew. As for correcting them I quickly found that was entirely out of the question: they are to do as they like.'[11] And of their mother, she tells her sister: 'I said in my last letter that Mrs. Sidgwick did not know me. I now begin to see that she does not intend to know me, that she cares nothing about me except to contrive how the greatest possible quantity of labour may be squeezed out of me, and to that end she overwhelms me with oceans of needlework, yards of cambric to hem, muslin nightcaps to make, and, above all things, dolls to dress.'[12]

Charlotte's responsiveness to affection and her readiness to hero-worship any likely man she met, are shown by her first impressions of Mr. Sidgwick—who, she told Emily, was a hundred times better than his wife: 'It is very seldom that he speaks to me,' says Charlotte, 'but when he does I always feel happier and more settled for some minutes afterwards. He never asks me to wipe the children's smutty noses or tie their shoes or fetch their pinafores or set them a chair. One of the pleasantest afternoons I have spent here—indeed, the only one at all pleasant—was when Mr. Sidgwick walked out with his children, and I had orders to follow a little behind. As he strolled on through his fields with his magnificent Newfoundland dog at his side, he looked very like what a frank, wealthy, Conservative gentleman ought to be.'[13]

But in spite of Mr. Sidgwick, Charlotte was quite out of her element. The family, with Charlotte and their guests, moved to Swarcliffe near Harrogate. From here Charlotte wrote her first letter to Ellen since she left home. She asked her friend to 'imagine the miseries of a reserved wretch like me, thrown at once into the midst of a large family—proud as peacocks and wealthy as Jews—at a time when they were particularly gay, when the house was full of company—all strangers, people whose faces I had never seen before—in this state of things having the charge given me of a set of pampered, spoilt, and turbulent children, whom I was expected constantly to amuse as well as instruct. I soon found that the constant demand on my stock of animal spirits reduced them to the lowest state of exhaustion; at times I felt and I suppose seemed depressed. To my astonishment I was taken to task on the subject by Mrs. Sidgwick with a stress of manner and a harshness of language scarcely credible. Like a fool, I cried most bitterly; I could not help it—and my spirits quite failed me at first. I thought I had done my best—strained every nerve to please her—and to be treated in that way merely because I was shy and sometimes melancholy was too bad. At first I was for giving all up and going home, but after a little reflection I determined to summon what energy I had and to weather the storm. I said to myself, I have never yet quitted a place without gaining a friend. Adversity is a good school—the Poor are born to labour, and the Dependent to endure. I resolved to be patient—to command my feelings and to take what came; the ordeal, I reflected, would not last many weeks, and I trusted it would do me good. I recollected the fable of the Willow and the Oak; I bent quietly, and I trust now the storm is blowing over me.'[14]

Charlotte, however, was neither by nature nor inclination a willow. The Sidgwicks appear to have been reasonable people; but Charlotte, as a governess, was anything but reasonable; and if she resented her uneasy position, belonging neither to the family nor to the staff, her employers were likewise piqued by this silent, resentful girl, who plainly disliked the children, and held the Sidgwicks' social life in contempt. The only fact that is definitely known about this episode in Charlotte's life is that on one occasion a Bible was thrown at her.[15] However much Charlotte may have resented this, she would no doubt dislike a hot-tempered action of this kind a good deal less than coldness and petty nagging. The only attitude to herself that she could neither understand nor forgive was indifference, and it was this that made her life with the Sidgwicks so impossible. Had the Sidgwicks thrown a few more Bibles at her, Charlotte would have been more content with her lot, for she craved a strong and, if possible, a masculine hand. As it was, her good resolutions came to nothing, and, later that summer, she returned to Haworth—the only results of her stay with the Sidgwicks being a stronger prejudice than ever against the life of a governess, and the memory of a visit to Norton Conyers near Ripon, where she was told a mad woman had been imprisoned until one night the house caught fire, and she escaped.[16]

With Charlotte, Branwell, and Anne away, Emily had much work about the house, because Tabby was now able to do very little. She also had her pets, the moors and her Gondal writings. But although busy enough, and satisfied for the most part with her own company, there were times when Emily had a sense of guilt in staying at home while the others were earning money, and her self-sufficiency was undermined by a morbid conviction that she was extraordinary, set apart, unfitted for human relationships. It was at such a time that, turning like all the Brontës to the written word for self-expression, she wrote:

> I am the only being whose doom
> No tongue would ask, no eye would mourn
> I've never caused a thought of gloom
> A smile of joy since I was born.
>
> In secret pleasure, secret tears
> This changeful life has slipped away
> As friendless after eighteen years
> As lone as on my natal day.
>
> There have been times, I cannot hide,
> There have been times when this was drear
> When my sad soul forgot its pride
> And longed for one to love me here.
>
> But those were in the early glow
> Of feelings long subdued by care
> And they have died so long ago
> I hardly now believe they were.
>
> First melted off the hope of youth
> Then fancy's rainbow fast withdrew
> And then experience told me truth
> In mortal bosoms never grew.

'Twas grief enough to think mankind
All hollow, servile, insincere,
But worse to trust to my own mind
And find the same corruption there.[17]

For a time Charlotte did not try very hard to get another situation. Ellen had suggested a holiday by the sea, and Charlotte moved heaven and earth to get it. In the autumn, after arrangements and re-arrangements that would have sickened anyone less determined, and after more than one objection from Miss Branwell and Mr. Brontë, she—to Branwell's approving cry, 'a brave defeat, the doubters were fairly taken aback'[18]—finally set off with Ellen to Bridlington.[19]

This was the first time Charlotte had seen the sea, and the sight was almost too much for her. She stared at it, overcome, the tears running down her cheeks. She could not speak at first, and waved her friend away until she was able to control herself. For the rest of the day she was unusually quiet and subdued, and whenever she heard the sea, she longed to rush down to it.[20] When she was home again, after three weeks, almost her first thought was the sea: 'Have you forgot the sea by this time Ellen,' she asks; 'Is it grown dim in your mind? Or can you still see it dark blue and green and foam-white and hear it—roaring roughly when the wind is high or rushing softly when it is calm?'[21]

Emily was contemptuous of the selfish attempts to deny Charlotte her holiday by the sea. As usual her contempt found expression in verse, and, as usual, the feeling finally expressed had passed beyond the occasion which aroused it.

There was a time when my cheek burned
To give such scornful fiends the lie
Ungoverned nature madly spurned
The law that bade it not defy—
O in the ardent days of youth
I would have given my life for truth

For truth for right for liberty
I would have gladly freely died
And now I calmly bear and see
The vain man smile the fool deride
Though not because my heart is tame
Though not for fear though not for shame

My soul still chafes at every tone
Of selfish and self-blinded error
My breast still braves the world alone
Steeled as it ever was to terror—
Only I know howe'er I frown
The same world will go rolling on.[22]

Just before she left for Bridlington, Charlotte had received an unexpected compliment. At the beginning of the year Mr. Brontë, whose eyes were giving him increasing trouble, had decided to get a curate to help him.[23] The first soon obtained a living of his own,[24] but one day visited the parsonage with his curate, a lively young Irishman by the name of Bryce, fresh from Dublin University. Charlotte had an odd circumstance to tell about this visit: 'It was the first time any of us had seen him,' she explained to Ellen; 'but however, after the manner of his countrymen, he soon made himself at home. His character quickly appeared in his conversation—witty—lively ardent—clever too—but deficient in the dignity and discretion of an Englishman. At home, you know Ellen, I talk with ease and am never shy—never weighed down and depressed by that miserable *mauvaise honte* which torments and constrains me elsewhere—so I conversed with this Irishman and laughed at his jests—and though I saw faults in his character, excused them because of the amusement his originality afforded. I cooled a little indeed and drew in towards the latter part of the evening because he began to season his conversation with something of Hibernian flattery which I did not quite relish.'[25]

The two clergymen went away, and no more was thought about them. But the irrepressible Bryce, attracted as much by Charlotte's aloofness as by her early friendliness, was not finished with.

'A few days afterwards', wrote Charlotte to her friend, 'I got a letter the direction of which puzzled me, it being in a hand I was not accustomed to see. Evidently it was neither from you nor Mary Taylor, my only correspondents. Having opened and read it, it proved to be a declaration of attachment—and proposal of Matrimony—expressed in the ardent language of the sapient young Irishman! Well, thought I—I've heard of love at first sight but this beats all. I leave you to guess what my answer would be. . . .'[26]

This second offer of marriage firmly set aside—'I'm certainly doomed to be an old maid, Ellen,' remarked Charlotte play-fully, 'I can't expect another chance'[27]—and her holiday over, she turned to work again.

Also, forgetting Southey's advice, she decided to stop writing Angrian stories and begin work on a novel. 'I have now written a great many books,' runs Charlotte's apologia, 'and for a long time have dwelt on the same characters and scenes and subjects. I have shown my landscapes in every variety of shade and light which morning, noon, and evening—the rising, the meridian and the setting sun can bestow upon them. Sometimes I have filled the air with the whitened tempest of winter: snow has embossed the dark arms of the beech and oak and filled with drifts the parks of the lowlands or the mountain-pass of wilder districts. Again, the same mansion with its woods, the same moor with its glens, has been softly coloured with the tints of moonlight in summer, and in the warmest June night the trees have clustered their full-plumed heads over glades flushed with flowers. So it is with persons. My readers have been habituated to one set of features, which they have seen now in profile, now in full face, now in outline, and again in finished painting—varied but by the thought or feeling or temper or age; lit with love, flushed with passion, shaded with grief, kindled with ecstasy; in meditation and mirth, in sorrow and scorn and rap-ture; with the round outline of childhood, the beauty and ful-ness of youth, the strength of manhood, and the furrows of thoughtful decline; but we must change, for the eye is tired of the picture so oft recurring and now so familiar. Yet do not urge me too fast, reader; it is not easy to dismiss from my imagination the images which have filled it so long; they were my friends and my intimate acquaintances, and I could with little labour describe to you the faces, the voices, the actions, of those who peopled my thoughts by day, and not seldom stole strangely even into my dreams by night. When I depart from these I feel almost as if I stood on the threshold of a home and were bidding farewell to its inmates. When I strive to conjure up new images I feel as if I had got into a distant country where every face was unknown and the character of all the population an enigma which it would take much study to comprehend and much talent to expound. Still, I long to quit for a while that burning clime where we have sojourned too long—its skies flame—the glow of sunset is always upon it—the mind would cease from excitement and turn now to a cooler region where the dawn breaks grey and sober, and the coming day for a time at least is subdued by clouds.'[28]

Probably her decision to stop the work that had become so great a part of her life was influenced by the growing separation between herself and Branwell. Charlotte and he had now been writing their Angrian tales since 1829.[29] For more than ten years they had lived a great part of their lives[30] in Angria and its people as though they were realities, not just extensions of their own personalities.[31] Charlotte now broke away from the already shaky partnership. Branwell worked on intermittently with Angrian poems and tales, and Charlotte's occasional pieces are English versions of Angrian stories,[32] but the joint Angrian saga may be considered over by the end of 1839.

The amount of Branwell's writings exceeds even that of Charlotte's, but although there was a common development in their style as they grew older, the impression gained from Branwell's stories is that he never grew up. His prose, though often conventionally melodramatic, was more lively and readable than Charlotte's; he frequently produced a vivid expression, he successfully handled a complicated narrative, and he showed a surprisingly wide reading, but the content remained, from first to last, juvenile. For though Branwell was to suffer much, and to dwell sincerely enough upon his sufferings, he was incapable of prolonged or deep feeling.

Not so Charlotte. Though she was never free from faults of style, her work shows a growing maturity of thought and feeling. There is no inexplicable gap between Angria and her novels.

Although Charlotte had continued to write Angrian stories after she left Roe Head,[33] her experience there, and afterwards as a governess, undermined the hold that Angria had upon her. She wrote on, but there was a difference in her stories. At Roe Head, and as a governess, she had been forced for the first time to live with strangers, but in spite of her detestation of mixing freely with people with whom she had little or no sympathy, this contact with the outside world fostered an already strong interest in the workings of the emotions. Her Angrian stories, though possessing the same highly romantic setting, began to show people who, instead of being mere puppets, had some life and character. And it was not long before the framework itself was given up, because Charlotte's interest had passed almost entirely to the development of character.

So the interest of the later Angrian stories began slowly to move from improbable heroics into the motives for these heroics. It moved out of the romantic action into the mental activity of the Angrian figures—personalities in which, as her gift, her true interest and its possibilities unfolded, Charlotte became increasingly absorbed; until the very truth and naturalism of her characters began to demand a corresponding realism in action and background.

By this time Charlotte was not only reconciled to writing the lives of those around her; she had become positively and deeply anxious to explore this territory, superficially so hackneyed and dull, yet, in the event, rich in fascinating interest and excitement—and moreover, almost untouched by those, particularly of her own sex, who had written before her. The first experiment in this genre proved unsuccessful. Charlotte, as was to be expected, swung too far into realism, she became too imitative. The work ran to great length. Early in 1840 she sent the opening portion to Wordsworth for criticism. He dubbed it Richardsonian—an estimate with which Charlotte, however ruefully, concurred—and no more was heard of it.[34]

Tabby had never recovered fully from her accident of two years earlier. She stayed on because the four Brontës could not bear to see her, and with her their childhood, go. But now fresh misfortune befell her; and finally she left the parsonage. 'Poor Tabby', Charlotte told Ellen, 'became so lame from a large ulcer in her leg that she was at length obliged to leave us. She is residing with her sister in a little house of her own, which she bought with her savings a year or two since. She is very comfortable and wants nothing; as she is near we see her very often. In the meantime Emily and I are sufficiently busy as you may suppose—I manage the ironing and keep the rooms clean—Emily does the baking and attends to the kitchen. We are such odd animals that we prefer this mode of contrivance to having a new face among us. Besides we do not despair of Tabby's return, and she shall not be supplanted by a stranger in her absence. I excited Aunt's wrath very much by burning the clothes the first time I attempted to iron but I do better now. Human feelings are queer things—I am much happier black-leading stoves, making the beds, and sweeping the floors at home, than I should be living like a fine lady anywhere else.'[35]

This extra housework; a fresh attempt to master the technique of drawing; and, eventually, the knowledge that she must again set out as governess—'I intend to force myself to take another situation when I can get one, though I *hate* and *abhor* the very thoughts of governess-ship,' she tells Ellen[36]—all this, following the failure of her first attempt as a novelist, discouraged Charlotte from writing for some time to come. But the lesson she had learned was not to be forgotten, the power she had discovered in herself was not to remain unemployed. She took a delight in analysing the minds and hearts of everybody she met; she noted every twist and turn of character; and she had a remarkable memory—remembering every detail of local stories she had heard.

There was also another most important influence at work upon Charlotte, helping to bring out the genius latent in her, to point the true direction her mind should follow. The French novels—lent by Joshua Taylor—that she began to read at this time, though intended primarily to assist her to master the language, often struck an answering chord in her mind despite her criticism of their content. 'I have got another bale of French books from Gomersal,' she tells Ellen. 'They are like the rest, clever, wicked, sophistical and immoral—the best of it is they give one a thorough idea of France and Paris—and are the best substitute for French Conversation I have met with.'[37] This was true enough so far as it went. But it was not the whole truth, whether or not Charlotte believed it to be. Beyond her satisfaction at reading the language, beyond her disgust at the lack of moral tone in these books, there was a certain fellow-feeling between this reader and many of her authors in their main interest and in their manner of developing this interest. The acute psychological studies of Balzac, for instance, compelled the admiration of one whose genius was inclining towards the same subtle method of portraiture, however much Charlotte might deplore the use to which the Frenchman put his gift.[38]

Emily, settled fast at home after her two disastrous visits to
school, managed the house in all but name. Tabby's departure
threw much extra work upon her, as on Charlotte.[39] This
work Emily dealt with efficiently and not without a certain
pleasure, for she liked to use her hands. And although her
younger sister was there no longer to ramble with her on the
moors, to make out Gondal stories, or talk to the birds and
the wild creatures that made a rare appearance in the dell, Emily
had her consolations. She had numerous pets to care for—the
cat Tiger, the geese Victoria and Adelaide, Hero the hawk,
the occasional strays and invalids who were nursed back to
health in the warm kitchen, and in particular her own Keeper,
half mastiff, half bulldog, who needed and obtained a loving
but masterful hand.[40]

And she was free. She had the wide, bleak, desolate, yet
to her always beautiful moors. And although Anne was still
at Blake Hall and Charlotte could not fully take the younger
sister's place, Emily carried consolation, as she carried strife,
within herself. In her lyrics, she expressed her imperfectly
comprehended emotions in words which, in their deceptive
simplicity and depth of passion, have a rare power. She wrote
as she felt at the moment, careless of refinements, her critical
sense seldom permitted to interfere with what was always
primarily an outlet of emotion demanding utterance. Thus, at
this time, she would write simply enough:

> That wind, I used to hear it swelling
> With joy divinely deep;
> You might have seen my hot tears welling
> But rapture made me weep.
>
> I used to love on winter nights
> To lie and dream alone
> Of all the rare and real delights
> My lonely years had known.
>
> And oh, above the best of those
> That coming time should bear,
> Like heaven's own glorious stars they rose
> Still beaming bright and fair.[41]

Anne remained at Blake Hall, yet not happily. Her vision of
loving, dutiful pupils drinking in wisdom, of a family circle

into which she might settle inconspicuously, had long since gone. Her charges were spoiled, unloving, disrespectful.[42] She was horrified by their cruelty, saddened by their lack of honour or consideration. She shrank under the stigma of her equivocal position.[43] She pined for the Haworth moors, for the parsonage, for love and true companionship. She was driven for consolation to her Gondal game and to the writing of gentle, pious verses melancholy in tone and containing many signs of spiritual struggle.

Charlotte, stirred still by protective solicitude for her sisters, and in particular for the younger and weaker one, soon wrote gloomily to Ellen of Anne's work: 'It was one struggle of life-wearing exertion to keep the children in anything like decent order.'[44]

Branwell, during a visit to Liverpool, had made what was probably his first acquaintance with opium[45]—the taking of which had been to many, including members of his set, sanctioned by the example of Coleridge and De Quincey. This made more tolerable the rest of 1839 which he spent for the most part painting in his little studio upstairs in the parsonage, when he was not talking and drinking more than was good for him at the Black Bull and in the inns of Keighley, Halifax, and Bradford. At these places he began to run up debts which, though not large, were to prove a perpetual embarrassment to him, and even more to his family.[46] At home, when not painting, he turned again to his Angrian tales and poems. These poems, written frequently under the pseudonym of Northangerland, often reflected the influence of his elder sister in content if not in style. They showed that Charlotte had fixed in his mind an idea of the pure life and cruel martyrdom of his sister Maria.[47] But Branwell was not allowed to overlook the efforts of his sisters to replace the money he wasted, and in his better moments, which were then plentiful, he had no wish to forget what he owed to them. He had lost none of his ambition, and little confidence, but for the moment he had to be content with something less than the conquest of his chosen world; and, on the first day of 1840, he set out for Broughton-in-Furness where he was to teach the children of a Mr. Postle-thwaite.

Charlotte, whose faith in her brother had decreased as her

knowledge of his character deepened, reported his coming departure to Ellen with a certain scepticism that, as was customary with her, contained more of hope and fear than the bare words would suggest: 'Branwell, who used to enliven us, is to leave us in a few days', she wrote; 'How he will like or settle remains yet to be seen; at present he is full of hope and resolution. I, who know his variable nature, and his strong turn for active life, dare not be too sanguine.'[48] But Branwell set off happily and confidently enough. His choice of district had not been without purpose. Not only would he be earning money, but he would be near his literary giants—Wordsworth, Hartley Coleridge, De Quincey, Southey. To Coleridge and to Wordsworth for certain, and probably to all, Branwell addressed letters begging for an interview.[49]

The kindly Coleridge agreed to meet his admirer at Ambleside in June. Branwell had previously sent Coleridge his translation of two Odes from Horace. To his delight the great man's opinion of his work was favourable—the first favourable notice he had ever received—and on his return to Haworth, Branwell sent him the First Book of the Odes.[50] It is not surprising that Coleridge thought well of these Odes, for they compare favourably with other translations in English. They are, in fact, Branwell's best work, in which shape and economy are forced upon him.[51] He wrote nothing so good, apart from a few lyrics so close in manner and thought to those of Emily as almost to be indistinguishable from them. But the *Horace* was not completed at Broughton. Despite a letter foolishly braggadocio to a bosom friend at Haworth (John Brown the sexton and Master of the local Masonic Lodge and father of Martha, who was to work in the parsonage),[52] Branwell appears to have conducted himself with decorum, and to have given satisfaction to his employer. Yet a few days after meeting Coleridge he had returned to Haworth at his father's wish.[53]

A description of him at this time gives a good idea of Branwell's ability to charm, if not of his appearance. 'His complexion was fair and his features handsome; his mouth and his chin were well shaped; his nose was prominent and of the Roman type; his eyes sparkled and danced with delight, and his fine forehead made up a face of oval form which gave an irresistible charm to its possessor, and attracted the admiration of those who knew him. Added to this, his address was simple and unadorned, yet polished; but being particular with the English language in its highest form of expression, and with Yorkshire and Hibernian *patois* also, he could easily make use of the quaintest and broadest terms when occasion called for them. It was indeed amazing how suddenly he could pass from the discussion of a grave and lofty subject . . . to make his light-hearted and amusing Irish or Yorkshire sallies.'[54]

X

WILLIAM WEIGHTMAN

A new curate at the parsonage. His popularity. Reactions of the sisters. Charlotte's letters to Ellen. She reads more French novels. Effect on her writing.

MEANWHILE, excitement and even a measure of gaiety had entered the parsonage in the person of William Weightman, Mr. Brontë's new curate. This young man was distinctly handsome in a somewhat feminine style, he liked the company of women, he was gay, carefree, charming; his conversation was lively, irrepressible, beguiling. Nothing like him had been seen before at Haworth, and his effect on everyone there was immediate and remarkable.

Charlotte, after her usual preliminary acid self-defence, acted for the first time in her life in a manner not far removed from her years. Ellen, who stayed at Haworth early in the year, was captivated by the charms of the newcomer; and he, it appeared, with hers.[1] Branwell soon rated Weightman one of his best friends. Anne, when she met him, was at once swept off her feet—he was all she had dreamed of; handsome, gay, clever, and a clergyman. He noticed her, even singled her out; though, probably, with no greater seriousness than might be expected when he was faced by the prettiest of the sisters. Even Emily abated with him the repellent brusqueness she adopted towards all except her family and Ellen. Curates had been known to retreat in confusion whenever Emily—nicknamed The Major in her not too serious character as guardian of Ellen and her sisters from Weightman's attentions[2]—encountered them in the parsonage. She did not favour them with even conventional courtesy, but Weightman was made an exception. At the tea table, where he became a frequent and lively guest, Emily entered into the fun of the badinage that went on, her countenance glimmering as it always did when she enjoyed herself, smiling her rare smile, and looking at Ellen and her sisters with an expression that stayed long in the memory.[3]

It is possible that Weightman—not indeed in himself but in

82

his character as the first agreeable man Emily had ever met—
was made the hero of verses which she wrote at this time:[4]

> *If grief for grief can touch thee,*
> *If answering woe for woe,*
> *If any ruth can melt thee*
> *Come to me now!*
>
> *I cannot be more lonely,*
> *More drear I cannot be!*
> *My worn heart throbs so wildly*
> *'Twill break for thee.*
>
> *And when the world despises,*
> *When Heaven repels my prayer,*
> *Will not mine angel comfort?*
> *Mine idol hear?*
>
> *Yes by the tears I've poured thee,*
> *By all my hours of pain*
> *O I shall surely win thee*
> *Beloved, again!*[5]

Weightman took the girls to hear his lectures at the Mechanics' Institute at Keighley. The party included another cleric as
escort. Once it did not arrive back at the parsonage until midnight, to the perturbation of Miss Branwell and the secret joy
of everyone else but the sleeping Mr. Brontë.[6] Weightman
sent the girls their first and only Valentines, walking to Bradford
and back to post them in order that Miss Branwell might not
suspect letters without a postmark—a gesture which actually
drew forth an answering poem from Charlotte.[7]

Weightman bandied words fearlessly with the girls, teased
them constantly, and flirted with them whenever opportunity
permitted. He sang gallant ballads and romantic lyrics to the
accompaniment of an Anne dazed with bliss and an Emily exceptionally agreeable. His portrait in all the glory of his robes
was taken by Charlotte—a procedure which called for sittings
of inordinate length.[8] He played lively games of chess with
Mary Taylor when she visited the parsonage later in the summer, anxious to see this paragon of masculine virtues.[9] He was
soon known to all as Celia Amelia—a reference to his smooth

cheeks and curly hair.[10] In short, Weightman brought into the severe parsonage a spirit of fun and light-heartedness it did not often know—a spirit usually found in the sisters only when they were on the moors, Emily and Anne walking with arms round each other, Emily teasing the nervous Charlotte with hints of nearby cattle; or in the dining-room when Ellen was a visitor, and there would be laughter and perhaps a display by Emily of Keeper's terrifying antics and sounds when roused to mock fury.[11] These had been rare spots of colour in a grey existence. Now Weightman appeared miraculously to delight them all.

It was small wonder that Charlotte's letters to Ellen, when her friend returned home reluctantly, became for a time little more than a diary of Weightman's comings, goings, and sayings. This Weightman news was mingled with admonitions on the necessity of emotional control, and appeals to Ellen to refrain from self-delusion or the nursing of false hopes—advice by which Charlotte, without loss of face, was able to administer a timely reproof to her own imagination:

'I wish to scold you with a forty horse power for having told Martha Taylor that I had requested you "not to tell her everything," ' she reproached her friend, 'I desire to take off any embargo I may have laid on your tongue which I plainly see will not be restrained and to enjoin you to walk up to Gomersal and tell her forthwith every individual occurrence you can recollect, including Valentines, "Fair Ellen—Fair Ellen"— "Away Fond Love", "Soul Divine" and all—likewise if you please the painting of Miss Celia Amelia Weightman's portrait and that young lady's frequent and agreeable visits. By the bye I inquired into the opinion of that intelligent and interesting young person respecting you—it was a favourable one. She thought you a fine looking girl and a very good girl into the bargain. Have you received the newspaper which has been dispatched containing a notice of her lecture at Keighley?'[12] But later Charlotte is saying: 'Don't set your heart on him. I'm afraid he is very fickle . . . . I have not mentioned your name to him yet—nor do I mean to do so until I have a fair·opportunity of gathering his real mind. Perhaps I may never mention it at all, but on the contrary carefully avoid all allusion to you. It will just depend upon the further opinion I may form of his character . . . . Don't think about him—I am not afraid you will break your heart—but don't think about him.'[13]

Ellen evidently felt that attack was the best form of defence: 'I have been painting a portrait of Agnes Walton for our friend Miss Celia Amelia,' Charlotte had announced, '—you would laugh to see how his eyes sparkle with delight when he looks at it like a pretty child pleased with a new plaything.' Then Charlotte adds, 'Goodbye to you, let me have no more of your humbug about Cupid, etc., you know as well as I do it is all groundless trash.'[14]

A few weeks later, Charlotte had made up her mind about their lively acquisition: 'I am fully convinced, Ellen, that he is a thorough male-flirt, his sighs are deeper than ever and his treading on toes more assiduous. I find he has scattered his impressions far and wide—Keighley has yielded him a fruitful field of conquest . . . . I find he is perfectly conscious of his irresistibleness and is as vain as a peacock on the subject. I am not at all surprised at all this—it is perfectly natural—a handsome—clean—prepossessing—good-humoured young man—will never want troops of victims amongst young ladies. As long as you are not among the number it is all right. He has not mentioned you to me and I have not mentioned you to him—I believe we fully understand one another on the subject. I have seen little of him lately and talked precious little to him—when he was lonely and rather melancholy I had a great pleasure in cheering and amusing him—now that he has got his spirits up and found plenty of acquaintances I don't care and he does not care either.'[15]

Charlotte's life became, by her Haworth standards, quite animated at this time. She visited Ellen at Birstall and the Taylors at Gomersal; and both Ellen and Mary Taylor spent time with her. Then came some relatives from Cornwall—Mrs. Brontë's cousin, John Branwell Williams and his wife and daughter.[16] Charlotte was the image of her aunt, Charlotte Branwell, she was told. The comment was passed on to Ellen: 'Mrs. Williams sets up for being a woman of great talents, tact and accomplishment—I thought there was more noise than work. My cousin Eliza is a young lady intended by nature to be a bouncing good-looking girl. Art has trained her to be a languishing affected piece of goods. I would have been friendly with her; but I could get no talk except about the Low-Church Evangelical Clergy, the Millennium, Baptist Noel, Botany,[17] and her own Conversion.'[18] And indeed, Charlotte and the other Brontës had heard enough and to spare of this type of conversation from their aunt.

But now there was always Weightman; and Charlotte tilts at him with a gaiety rare in her, retailing his amorous escapades in some detail, interspersed with more warnings to her friend on no account to take this breaker of hearts seriously. In general Charlotte had adopted, or there had perhaps been forced upon her, a somewhat maternal attitude towards the young man: 'I know', she writes, 'Mrs. Ellen is burning with eagerness to hear something about Wm. Weightman, whom she adores in her heart, and whose image she cannot efface from her memory. I think I'll plague her by not telling her a word. To speak Heaven's truth, I have precious little to say, inasmuch as I seldom see him, except on a Sunday, when he looks as handsome, cheery, and good tempered as usual. I have indeed had the advantage of one long conversation since his return from Westmorland, when he poured out his whole, warm fickle soul in fondness and admiration of Agnes Walton . . . . No doubt there are defects in his character, but there are also good qualities. God bless him! I wonder who, with his advantages, would be without his faults. I know many of his faulty actions, many of his weak points; yet, where I am, he shall always find rather a defender than an accuser.'[19] Then Charlotte realizes that her words might be misinterpreted by the highly interested Ellen. 'You are not to suppose from all this that Mr. Weightman and I are on very amiable terms:' she protests, 'we are not at all. We are cold, distant, and reserved. We seldom speak; and when we do, it is only to exchange the most commonplace remarks. If you were to ask Mr. Weightman's opinion of my character just now, he would say that at first he thought me a cheerful, chatty kind of body, and that on further acquaintance he found me of a capricious changeful temper, never to be reckoned on. He does not know that I have regulated my manner by his, that I was cheerful and chatty so long as he was respectful, and that when he grew almost contemptuously familiar I found it necessary to adopt a degree of reserve which was not natural, and therefore was very painful to me. I find this reserve very convenient, and consequently I intend to keep it up.'[20]

Charlotte at this time had stopped writing. Her eyes suffered under any prolonged strain, she said. Yet this was not the whole truth. She was not sure what or how to write; and kind words from Coleridge[21] (to whom she had sent some manuscripts after his praise of Branwell's *Horace*) only unsettled her still further. She was hovering between the world of fantasy and the world of reality—the one discarded in deed but not yet in thought, the other at a standstill after her first unsatisfactory experiment. But a new insight, and so a new interest in the workings of the human heart, was mounting in her mind, bringing closer the moment when she was ready to begin the writing of her novels.

Joshua Taylor's French novels were playing no small part in bringing about this metamorphosis. They were helping to sharpen Charlotte's critical faculty, bringing to light her penetrating and imaginative power of observation and her ability to reveal the cause beneath the effect, the emotional impulse behind every cold, wayward, or apparently clear action. At this time Charlotte received a batch of more than forty of these novels from Gomersal. She read them earnestly, so as to master the language, yet with a certain enjoyment of the craftsmanship they displayed, despite disapproval of much of their contents.[22] Her appreciation was given grudgingly, disfigured by a racial and religious bigotry she was never to lose. Yet the fact that their psychological insight overcame her objections pointed, not only to their skill, but to the affinity that was to lead the reader herself to greatness in this kind.

XI

THREE GO TO WORK

Branwell gets work on the railway. His loneliness and degeneration. He hears local tales and repeats them at Haworth. Charlotte and Anne leave home again. The troubles of Anne. She and Emily begin the Gondal chronicles.

CHARLOTTE renewed her search for another situation, but with reluctance. Anne, after eighteen months at Blake Hall, had come home at Christmas 1840, and had not returned. Even her calm front had been broken, her ample fund of Christian resignation exhausted by the petty tyranny of her charges, and the unhelpful attitude of her employers.[1] Two months earlier, Branwell had found work for himself. While dabbling still with his painting and music, writing with fair consistency, and seeing much of his Bradford and Halifax friends, he had also been spending a good deal of his time watching the construction of the Manchester-Leeds railway, then advanced as far as the vale of Todmorden on the way to Hebden Bridge.[2] His attractive manner and his ability to interest himself in any new thing soon made him popular with the men on the line. Here he met Woolven, his London acquaintance, now in charge of the works. As a result of this meeting, Branwell, goaded partly by conscience at his idleness, partly by alarm at the debts he was incurring, obtained the post of booking clerk at Sowerby Bridge station.[3]

This step, with its tacit abandonment of ambition, was badly received by Charlotte, who despised weakness or instability of purpose. So far, she had always been hopeful of sudden regeneration, of a not-to-be-denied outburst from Branwell of brilliance and determination to succeed. Now he had voluntarily thrown in his hand. 'A distant relation of mine, one Patrick Boanerges, has set off to seek his fortune in the wild, wandering, adventurous, romantic, knight-errant-like capacity of clerk on the Leeds and Manchester Railroad,' she told Ellen sarcastically.[4] From this moment her faith in Branwell, and her intimacy with him, began to collapse.

A few months later, in March 1841, Branwell was transferred
a mile up the line to the little station of Luddenden Foot, where
he acted as booking clerk and ticket collector.[5] Luddenden Foot
was far from his home, his friends and interests. The village
consisted only of a few houses and an inn; traffic through the
station was slight; the work, what there was of it, proved
monotonous and uninteresting,[6] and Branwell soon began to
find time hanging on his hands. He wrote some good poems in
a notebook kept at this time.[7] But he could not face solitude;
without company he became frightened and morose; his thoughts
haunted him, and the memory of all that he might have done,
but had not, was a constant torment to him. His instinct to
escape unpleasantness now became a guiding principle of his
life, and clamoured for relief. Occasional visits from Francis H.
Grundy,[8] a railway engineer with whom Branwell became
friendly, broke the monotony a little, but not enough.

Branwell began to drink heavily at the Lord Nelson inn at
Luddenden. There, evening after evening, he heard tales of the
neighbouring big houses; of Ewood House,[9] home of the Lock-
woods, where Wesley had stayed. The Mrs. Lockwood of that
day had been the widow of the heavy-drinking son of Grimshaw
of the old Haworth parsonage.[10] He heard tales of Scaithcliffe
Hall, home of the Sutcliffes, where the woman who later married old Grimshaw himself was the wife of William Sutcliffe.
By the inn was the church where Grimshaw lay buried, at his
wish as near his wife as possible.[11] Of these families Branwell
learnt much as he leaned on the bar of the Lord Nelson, drinking
whisky and gin. He learnt how Grimshaw's son drank himself
to death; of old Grimshaw's journeyings and arrivals home with
strays and outcasts to be cared for; and of the crimes, the inter-
marryings, the numerous legends and tales of the hard, wild
folk who had flourished so recently in this district.

Not all these tales were new to Branwell; indeed, such stories
were staple food in his own home; Grimshaw's old parsonage[12]
was known to the Brontës by sight almost as well as their own
church; and the echoes of Grimshaw's thunderous drive of his
people to God remained a clear, inspiring, and fearful memory
to the older Haworth folk.[13] But actually to walk about Luddenden, where these sometimes great and always exciting people
had lived their stormy lives, to hear afresh and in greater detail

of them from the innkeeper and customers of the Lord Nelson
—this set Branwell's imagination racing; and to Grundy the
red-haired, bespectacled Brontë, when in his cups, would spin
such wild romances of these lonely Yorkshire folk that his
hearer was amazed. Nor was Grundy the only one to hear
Branwell's versions of these tales, half fiction, half fact; Branwell
retold the stories in the parsonage at Haworth,[14] sometimes with
Grundy again as listener.[15]

But Grundy was not always with him, at Haworth or at
Luddenden. And, left alone at Luddenden without affection or
companionship close at hand, without work or a strong hand to
direct his work, Branwell was lost. His bouts of drinking were
followed quickly by bouts of remorse no less violent than the
excesses which occasioned them.[16] He sickened time and again
of his weakness, and fell deeper into melancholy and hopelessness. His aunt's teaching of the grim Methodist morality
haunted him, denounced the uselessness, the sin of his life, and
threatened obscure, terrifying penalties.[17] His high ambitions
and his consistent failures rose up and mocked him. After a
visit to Haworth with Grundy, as after a night at the Lord
Nelson, Branwell would break into violent, tearful self-reproaches and make futile promises of amendment.[18]

As traffic on the line remained slight, as no one appeared to
oversee his duties, Branwell grew bolder, his absences from the
station became spectacular. He abandoned all pretence of
attention to work. He spent days at Haworth, at Halifax, at
Bradford, his old gay, charming, irresponsible self. A boy
was left in charge of the little station.[19] The accounts fell into
arrears.

Emily, still at home, listened, fascinated, while her brother
recounted his macabre local stories. She heard also his embellish-
ments of these stories; and they were added to the store accumu-
lating in her mind.[20] She was still without her companion, Anne,
but she had a companion in her own imagination. When night
fell and her work was done, she began more and more to dream;
and, in the darkness, she summoned visions that sometimes
soothed and sometimes excited, but always lifted her out of
loneliness and discontent. And when longings possessed her that
were too strong for silence, she expressed them in the only way
known to her.

In summer's mellow midnight
A cloudless moon shone through
Our open parlour window
And rose trees wet with dew.

I sat in silent musing
The soft wind waved my hair
It told me Heaven was glorious
And sleeping Earth was fair.

I needed not its breathing
To bring such thoughts to me
But still it whispered lowly
'How dark the woods will be!

'The thick leaves in my murmur
Are rustling like a dream,
And all their myriad voices
Instinct with spirit seem.'

I said, 'Go gentle singer,
Thy wooing voice is kind
But do not think its music
Has power to reach my mind.

'Play with the scented flower
The young tree's supple bough,
And leave my human feelings
In their own course to flow.'

The wanderer would not leave me
Its kiss grew warmer still.
'O come', it sighed so sweetly
'I'll win thee 'gainst thy will.

'Have we not been from childhood friends?
Have I not loved thee long?
As long as thou hast loved the night
Whose silence wakes my song?

'And when thy heart is laid at rest
Beneath the church-yard stone
I shall have time enough to mourn
And thou to be alone.'21

In another poem written a few months later, Emily, whose reactions to the events of the past year or two had been positive,
though unspoken, made her first clear statement of faith:

Riches I hold in light esteem
And Love I laugh to scorn
And lust of Fame was but a dream
That vanished with the morn—

And if I pray the only prayer
That moves my lips for me
Is—'Leave the heart that now I bear
And give me liberty.'

Yes, as my swift days near their goal
'Tis all that I implore—
Through life and death, a chainless soul
With courage to endure![22]

On the day this poem was written, in the beginning of March
1841, Charlotte left home to make her second attempt as private
governess. This time she was more fortunate in her employers.
She had to look after the son (six) and the daughter (eight) of
Mr. and Mrs. John White of Upperwood House, Rawdon, a
village in Airedale between Leeds and Guiseley. Her salary was
£20 a year, from which laundry bills were to be deducted.[23]
The Whites proved kindly people; and Charlotte found the
children, as she put it, 'wild and unbroken, but apparently well-
disposed'.[24] This was high praise from Charlotte, no lover of
children; and it is probable that, as a sense of humour was not
her strong point, she was as contented at Rawdon as she was
likely to be in any similar situation. But that is not saying a great
deal. Within a month of her arrival Charlotte found it necessary
to press for leave so that she might spend a recuperative week-
end with Ellen. Permission to do so, she told her friend, was
given grudgingly: 'I popped the question—and for two minutes
received no answer. Will she refuse me when I work so hard
for her? thought I. Ye-es-es, drawled Madam in a reluctant cold
tone. Thank you Madam, said I with extreme cordiality, and
was marching from the room when she recalled me with—
"You'd better go on Saturday afternoon then—when the children have holiday—and if you return in time for them to have

lessons on Monday morning I don't see that much will be lost." You *are* a genuine Turk, thought I.'[25]

Once again, she preferred the master: 'I like Mr. White extremely,' she wrote. 'Respecting Mrs. White I am for the present silent. I am trying hard to like her.'[26] And, as at Stonegappe, her pride was touched time after time by incidents which, rightly or wrongly, her very acute sense of inferiority attributed to Mrs. White's attitude. Her reaction was characteristic: 'Well can I believe that Mrs. W. has been an exciseman's daughter,' she tells Ellen, 'And I am convinced also that Mr. W.'s extraction is very low—yet Mrs. W. talks in an amusing strain of pomposity about his and her family and connexions, and affects to look down with wondrous hauteur on the whole race of "Tradesfolk" as she terms men of business. I was beginning to think Mrs. W. a good sort of body in spite of her bouncing and boasting—her bad grammar and worse orthography—but I have had experience of one little trait in her character which condemns her a long way with me. After treating a person on the most familiar terms of equality for a long time, if any little thing goes wrong she does not scruple to give way to anger in a very coarse unladylike manner—though in justice no blame could be attached where she ascribed it all. I think passion is the true test of vulgarity or refinement—Mrs. W. when put out of her way is highly offensive. She must not give me any more of the same sort or I shall ask for my wages and go.'[27]

Charlotte was also sorely tried by her difficulty in getting on terms with strangers. 'Some of my greatest difficulties', she told Ellen, 'lie in things that would appear to you comparatively trivial. I find it so hard to repel the rude familiarity of children. I find it so difficult to ask either servants or mistress for anything I want, however much I want it. It is less pain to me to endure the greatest inconvenience than to request its removal.'[28]

Even when it seems that affection for the baby of the family might make her duties less irksome, the wary Charlotte, always on the alert for an excess of emotion, in herself as in others, stops short, draws back, and offers the familiar brusque front to her little world: 'By dint of nursing the fat baby,' she says, 'it has got to know me and be fond of me. Occasionally I suspect myself of growing rather fond of it—but this suspicion clears away the moment its mamma takes it and makes a fool of it. From a bonny, rosy little morsel it sinks in my estimation into a small, petted nuisance.'[29] As for the other children, her real charges: 'The children are not such little devils incarnate as the Sidgwicks',' she tells Ellen, 'but they are over-indulged, and at times hard to manage.'[30]

To her annoyance, when Charlotte returned to Haworth for three weeks' holiday at the end of June, she just missed seeing Anne, who had been on holiday before her.[31] Anne, who had not enjoyed home life for long, had been for some months at Thorp Green, near York, where she was governess to the two daughters of the Rev. Mr. and Mrs. Robinson. The state of Anne's health still worried Charlotte. She could never forget the early deaths of Maria and Elizabeth; and Anne's occasional hectic colour, her transparent complexion, the rapidity with which she caught a chill or developed a cough filled Charlotte with uneasiness: '*I should like* to see her to judge for myself of the state of her health,' she wrote, 'I cannot trust any other person's report, no one seems minute enough in their observations.'[32]

Like Charlotte, Anne was not happy in her new position, although it promised better things than her previous situation: 'I have one aching feeling at my heart (I must allude to it though I had resolved not to),' Charlotte told Ellen. 'It is about Anne —she has so much to endure—far far more than I have. When my thoughts turn to her they always see her as a patient, perse-cuted stranger amongst people more grossly insolent, proud and tyrannical than your imagination unassisted can readily depict. I know what concealed susceptibility is in her nature—when her feelings are wounded I wish I could be with her to administer a little balm. She is more lonely—less gifted with the power of making friends even than I am.'[33]

Although something must be subtracted from the vehemence of Charlotte's championship, Anne herself wrote verses at this time that bear out some of her sister's words:

> *O! I am very weary*
> *Though tears no longer flow*
> *My eyes are tired of weeping*
> *My heart is sick of woe.*

My life is very lonely
My days pass heavily
I'm weary of repining
Wilt thou not come to me?

Oh didst thou know my longing
For thee from day to day
My hopes so often blighted
Thou wouldst not thus delay[34].

But loneliness was perhaps the least of Anne's troubles. At work in her all the time, advancing its position stealthily with every dulling disappointment, every lonely hour, every slight put upon her, was the dread of spiritual failure, of a fearful fate awaiting her soul after death. This thought also began to find expression in her poems:[35]

I have gone backward in the work
The labour has not sped
Drowsy and dark my spirit lies
Heavy and dull as lead.

How can I rouse my sinking soul
From such a lethargy?
How can I break these iron chains
And set my spirit free?

There have been times when I have mourned
In anguish o'er the past
And raised my suppliant hands on high
While tears fell thick and fast

And prayed to have my sins forgiven
With such a fervent zeal
And earnest grief—a strong desire
That now I cannot feel

And vowed to trample on my sins
And called on Heaven to aid
My spirit in her firm resolves
And hear the vows I made.

And I have felt so full of love
So strong in spirit then
As if my heart would never cool
Or wander back again.

And yet alas! how many times
My feet have gone astray
How oft have I forgot my God
How greatly fallen away!

My sins increase, my love grows cold
And hope within me dies
And Faith itself is wavering now;
Oh how shall I arise?

I cannot weep but I can pray
Then let me not despair
Lord Jesus save me lest I die
And hear a wretch's prayer.[36]

The one hope in Anne's heart was perhaps too precious even for her chief confidante, Emily, to hear. Only in a few poems could this sentimental soul murmur of a longed-for happiness with a young and handsome clergyman.[37] Weightman had been missed by Charlotte with genuine regret for the loss of a lively male opponent who awoke in her a sense, doubly delicious on account of its rarity, of her youth and her sex. Anne's regret, though not so openly expressed, was more poignant. She could only dream of Weightman, fitfully and with the ebb and flow of hopes and fears characteristic of her state. To express her feelings she turned, like the rest of her family, to her writing, and to the creatures of her imagination—to her poems, and to the Gondals.

The Brontë children had never been given to demonstrations of affection—it had been discouraged by their aunt and father—yet their emotions were unusually strong. So, gifted with an intensity of feeling incompletely understood, which they had been taught to regard cloudily as a weakness, and for which they knew no means of expression except in the words of the divine passion, some outlet became imperative.[38] This outlet had taken its expected form. While Charlotte and Branwell expended themselves in their Angrian Saga, the two younger Brontës had played their Gondal game without break since childhood. Round the inhabitants of the two islands they built a story without apparent end, and, not knowing why they did what they did, instilled into the Gondal men and women their own loves and hates, working out through them their own emotional problems, satisfying vicariously their own emotional needs.

Thus the outwardly dour Emily could languish, chained but unbroken, with her F. de Samara in a dark dungeon of the Gaaldine prison caves; she could storm and conquer in love and war with her heroic yet pitiless King Julius Brenzaida; she could give passion for passion, match guile with guile with her treacherous, beautiful, black-haired Augusta G. Almeda; she could express her mystical yearnings, sum up her simple, severe philosophy of life in the words of her A. G. Rochelle; she could sing her Gondal songs of a love that never was on earth:

Light up thy halls! 'Tis closing day;
I'm drear and lone and far away—
Cold blows on my breast, the north wind's bitter sigh
And O, my couch is bleak, beneath the rainy sky!

Light up thy halls—and think not of me;
That face is absent now, thou hast hated so to see!—
Bright be thine eyes, undimmed their dazzling shine,
For never, never more shall they encounter mine!

The desert moor is dark; there is tempest in the air:
I have breathed my only wish in one last, one burning prayer—
A prayer that would come forth although it lingered long;
That set on fire my heart, but froze upon my tongue—

And now, it shall be done before the morning rise;
I will not watch the sun ascend in yonder skies.
One task alone remains—thy pictured face to view
And then I go to prove if God, at least, be true!

Do I not see thee now? Thy black resplendent hair;
Thy glory-beaming brow, and smile how heavenly fair!
Thine eyes are turned away—those eyes I would not see;
Their dark, their deadly ray would more than madden me.

There, go, Deceiver, go! My hand is streaming wet;
My heart's blood flows to buy the blessing—To forget!
O could that lost heart give back, back again to thine
One tenth part of the pain that clouds my dark decline!

O could I see thy lids weighed down in cheerless woe;
Too full to hide their tears, too stern to overflow;
O could I know thy soul with equal grief was torn,
This fate might be endured—this anguish might be borne!

How gloomy grows the Night! 'Tis Gondal's wind that blows
I shall not tread again the deep glens where it rose—
I feel it on my face—Where, wild blast, dost thou roam?
What do we, wanderer, here, so far away from home?

I do not need thy breath to cool my death-cold brow
But go to that far land where she is shining now
Tell Her my latest wish, tell Her my dreary doom;
Say, that my pangs are past, but Hers are yet to come—

Vain words—vain, frenzied thoughts! No ear can hear me call—
Lost in the vacant air my frantic curses fall—
And could she see me now, perchance her lip would smile,
Would smile in careless pride and utter scorn the while!

But yet, for all Her hate, each parting glance would tell
A stronger passion breathed, burned in this last farewell.
Unconquered in my soul the Tyrant rules me still—
Life bows to my control, but Love I cannot kill![39]

The timid, blushing, stammering Anne could meet love with love, freely spoken, in the person of Olivia Vernon; she could sing of her beloved moors, of a modest search after fame, with the Lady Geralda; she could indulge a temperament naturally inclined to the morbid with the woes of Alexandrina Zenobia:

Methought I saw him but I knew him not
He was so changed from what he used to be;
There was no redness in his woe-worn cheeks,
No sunny smile upon his ashy lips,
His hollow, wandering eyes looked wild and fierce
And grief was printed on his marble brow;
And oh I thought he clasped his wasted hands
And raised his haggard eyes to Heaven and prayed
That he might die. I had no power to speak
I thought I was allowed to see him thus
And yet I might not speak one single word
I might not even tell him that I lived
And that it might be possible if search were made
To find out where I was and set me free.

Oh! how I longed to clasp him to my heart
Or but to hold his trembling hand in mine
And speak one word of comfort to his mind.

I struggled wildly but it was in vain
I could not rise from my dark dungeon floor
And the dear name I vainly strove to speak
Died in a voiceless whisper on my tongue.
Then I awoke and lo! it was a dream.
A dream? Alas! it was reality,
For well I know, wherever he may be,
He mourns me thus. Oh Heaven! I could bear
My deadly fate with calmness if there were
No kindred hearts to bleed and break for me.[40]

The Gondal plays had begun for both sisters as an exciting game, a rival to the Branwell-Charlotte-dominated Angrian saga; but as the obscure longings and problems of womanhood grew upon them without a corresponding growth of experience or contact with reality, the Gondal world assumed an increasingly prominent place in their lives. Both sisters wrote poems about their favourite Gondal characters. Sometimes the situations, thoughts and actions of the characters bore little or no relation to the private lives of the writers—although even the unblushing melodrama into which the Gondal stories often slipped expressed a love of violence that formed an integral part of the Brontë character. More often than not, however, a far stronger link exists between the Gondal characters and adventures and those of their creators.

Every Gondal poem, though complete in itself, advanced the saga as a whole. Emily and Anne worked, if anything, even closer together than Charlotte and Branwell on their Angrian saga; and, unlike the elder couple, their collaboration was never broken. On the eve of Anne's first journey to Thorp Green the two sisters inaugurated the Gondal Chronicles,[41] a prose record of the Gondal adventures, which called for even closer co-operation between the two than the writing of isolated and often spontaneous verses. The poems were continued—the writing of verses had long since come to be a vital creative outlet for Emily, and was scarcely less essential to Anne for meditation, inspiration, and as confessional. But the Gondal Chronicles were now occupying most of their spare time; and to Anne, reluctant to be away from home and from Emily, this community of work and thought brought some happiness.

99

XII

TO BRUSSELS

Charlotte plans to open a school. Miss Wooler's offer. News of the Taylors causes a change of plan. Charlotte persuades Miss Branwell to pay for education abroad. Reactions of the other Brontës to the new venture. Anne returns to Thorp Green. Charlotte and Emily leave for Brussels.

THE most exciting and hopeful news that the Brontë sisters had ever known was that with which Charlotte had hoped to greet Anne in the summer holiday of 1841. In fact, the news was sent by letter, as the two girls had missed one another at Haworth by a few days.[1]

Charlotte had for long been thinking hard about the future. Branwell had now to be disregarded as a money-maker, but the debts he had incurred and threatened to incur could not be forgotten. Somehow, the sisters had to make money. They longed to be together, and they wanted if possible to be at home. Charlotte had tried drawing, she had tried writing, but without success. Like Anne and Emily, she detested teaching in a school not her own, and she resented working as a governess. Moreover, Charlotte knew well enough how unfitted she was for the position: 'No one but myself', she told Ellen, 'can tell how hard a governess's work is to me—for no one but myself is aware how utterly averse my whole mind and nature are to the employment.'[2] And again: 'What dismays and haunts me sometimes is a conviction that I have no natural knack for my vocation. If teaching only were requisite it would be smooth and easy, but it is the living in other people's houses—the estrangement from one's real character—the adoption of a cold frigid apathetic exterior that is painful.'[3] Charlotte not only detested the work as work—she fretted under the discipline of people whom she could not respect. Until the time—so visionary as scarcely to seem possible—when she would gladly acknowledge the mastery of a man she could love and respect, Charlotte wanted to be her own master. To earn money was not enough;

it had to be earned in such a way as to satisfy both her pride and her ambition.

Such a chance had now come. Charlotte opened the subject during the summer holidays: 'There is a project hatching in this house', she told Ellen, who had been unable to pay a promised visit to Haworth, 'which both Emily and I anxiously wished to discuss with you . . . papa and aunt talk, by fits and starts, of our—*id est*, Emily, Anne and myself—commencing a school. I have often, you know, said how much I wished such a thing; but I never could conceive where the capital was to come from for making such a speculation. I was well aware, indeed, that aunt had money, but I always considered that she was the last person who would offer a loan for the purpose in question. A loan, however, she *has* offered, or rather intimates that she perhaps *will* offer, in case pupils can be secured, an eligible situation obtained, etc.'⁴

At first Charlotte thought of Bridlington as a likely situation for a new school.⁵ But a more practicable scheme appeared when she asked Miss Wooler for advice. Miss Wooler suggested that the Brontë girls might take over her old school at Dewsbury Moor, which her sister had just given up, and offered Charlotte the use of her furniture in return for her board.⁶ Charlotte accepted.⁷ But scarcely had she done so when her mind was turned towards a more ambitious project. Lack of money had not been the only hindrance to the success of any school the sisters might open. No less serious was the unfitness of two, if not all three, as teachers.⁸ Apart from their lack of flair for the work—a weakness which Charlotte was inclined to overlook in her eagerness to be independent—their own education scarcely fitted them to teach others. Charlotte alone possessed a reasonable grounding. None of them had been given a chance of acquiring real proficiency in the arts or languages, although by hard work they had progressed some way in both—Charlotte in particular, by her assiduous reading of Joshua Taylor's French novels.

While matters stood thus, events in the Taylor home gave Charlotte the impulse she needed to break out of her cramping environment. Joshua Taylor had died at the end of 1840, and his restless, ambitious family soon broke up. Mary Taylor, determined not to endure the humiliations of a governess's life,⁹ decided to emigrate to New Zealand.[10] Her sister Martha arranged to go to a finishing school in Brussels,[11] and in May 1841 she entered the Château de Koekelberg.[12] Mary finally decided to join her sister in Brussels for a few months before leaving for New Zealand.[13] She arrived at the school in August. These events so close to her aroused the ready ambition in Charlotte to a high pitch. In her way, she had influenced the Taylor sisters;[14] and the sight of them breaking the traces determined her to attempt a corresponding freedom for herself and her sisters.[15]

Meanwhile, Anne and Emily had arranged to write and to seal autobiographical papers. These papers were to be written on Emily's birthday, 30 July. They were to describe what the writer was doing and thinking at the time, and they were to be opened by the two sisters on the same day four years later.

In her paper of this year, Anne, once more with the Robinsons, refers hopefully to the prospect of freedom from unwelcome work, and of rejoining her family, that had been opened out by Charlotte's plans:

July the 30th, A.D. 1841

This is Emily's birthday. She has now completed her 23rd year, and is, I believe, at home. Charlotte is a governess in the family of Mr. White. Branwell is a clerk in the railroad station at Luddenden Foot, and I am a governess in the family of Mr. Robinson. I dislike the situation and wish to change it for another. I am now at Scarborough. My pupils are gone to bed and I am hastening to finish this before I follow them.

We are thinking of setting up a school of our own, but nothing definite is settled about it yet, and we do not know whether we shall be able to or not. I hope we shall. And I wonder what will be our condition and how or where we shall all be on this day four years hence; at which time, if all be well, I shall be 25 years and 6 months old, Emily will be 27 years old, Branwell 28 years and 1 month, and Charlotte 29 years and a quarter. We are now all separate and not likely to meet again for many a weary week, but we are none of us ill that I know of, and all are doing something for our own livelihood except Emily, who, however, is as busy as any of us, and in reality earns her food and raiment as much as we do.

How little know we what we are
How less what we may be!

Four years ago I was at school. Since then I have been a governess at Blake Hall, left it, come to Thorp Green, and seen the sea and York Minster. Emily has been a teacher at Miss Patchett's school, and left it. Charlotte has left Miss Wooler's, been a governess at Mrs. Sidgwick's, left her, and gone to Mrs. White's. Branwell has given up painting, been a tutor in Cumberland, left it, and become a clerk on the railroad. Tabby has left us. Martha Brown has come in her place. We have got Keeper, got a sweet little cat, and lost it, and also got a hawk. Got a wild goose which has flown away, and three tame ones, one of which has been killed. All these diversities, with many others, are things we did not expect or foresee in the July of 1837. What will the next four years bring forth? Providence only knows. But we ourselves have sustained very little alteration since that time. I have the same faults that I had then, only I have more vision and experience, and a little more self-possession than I then enjoyed. How will it be when we open this paper and the one Emily has written? I wonder whether the Gondalians will still be flourishing, and what will be their condition. I am now engaged in writing the fourth volume of Solala Vernon's life.

For some time I have looked upon 25 as a sort of era in my existence. It may prove a true presentiment, or it may be only a superstitious fancy; the latter seems more likely, but time will show.

ANNE BRONTË.[16]

Emily had her days filled with housekeeping, home study, nursing the pets at home and any wild thing that came into her hands, wandering over the moors with Keeper at her heels, and writing her Gondal Chronicles and her poems:

> Shall Earth no more inspire thee,
> Thou lonely dreamer now?
> Since passion may not fire thee
> Shall Nature cease to bow?
>
> Thy mind is ever moving
> In regions dark to thee;
> Recalls its useless roving—
> Come back and dwell with me.
>
> I know my mountain breezes
> Enchant and soothe thee still—
> I know my sunshine pleases
> Despite thy wayward will.
>
> When day with evening blending
> Sinks from the summer sky

I've seen thy spirit bending
In fond idolatry.

I've watched thee every hour—
I know my mighty sway—
I know my magic power
To drive thy griefs away.

Few hearts to mortals given
On earth so wildly pine
Yet none would ask a Heaven
More like this Earth than thine.

Then let my winds caress thee—
Thy comrade let me be—
Since nought beside can bless thee
Return and dwell with me.[17]

Emily's verses did not always express even this degree of
calm. When Anne returned to Thorp Green, and the two sisters
could no longer roam the moors arm in arm, scribble their
Gondal stories within sound of their favourite waterfall, write
their poems seated under the currant bushes in the parsonage
garden, little desks on knees, every now and then reaching up to
pick a cluster of the fruit[18]—when all this was ended, and Emily
was left to the arguments of Charlotte battling her way to independence, and to her own solitary imaginings, then the content
of her poems began to change; the stoic and pantheist began to
emerge clearly:

I see around me tombstones grey
Stretching their shadows far away.
Beneath the turf my footsteps tread
Lie low and lone the silent dead—
Beneath the turf, beneath the mould—
Forever dark, forever cold—
And my eyes cannot hold the tears
That memory hoards from vanished years
For Time and Death and Mortal pain
Give wounds that will not heal again.
Let me remember half the woe
I've seen and heard and felt below
And Heaven itself, so pure and blest
Could never give my spirit rest.
Sweet land of light! thy children fair

Know nought akin to our despair;
Nor have they felt, nor can they tell
What tenants haunt each mortal cell
What gloomy guests we hold within—
Torments and madness, tears and sin!
Well, may they live in ecstasy
Their long eternity of joy;
At least we would not bring them down—
With us to weep, with us to groan.
No—Earth would wish no other sphere
To taste her cup of sufferings drear;
She turns from Heaven a careless eye
And only mourns that we must die!
Ah mother, what shall comfort thee
In all this boundless misery?
To cheer our eager eyes awhile
We see thee smile, how fondly smile!
But who reads not through that tender glow
Thy deep, unutterable woe?
Indeed no dazzling land above
Can cheat thee of thy children's love—
We all in life's departing shine
Our last dear longings blend with thine;
And struggle still, and strive to trace
With clouded gaze, thy darling face
We would not leave our native home
For any world beyond the Tomb
No—rather on thy kindly breast
Let us be laid in lasting rest
Or waken but to share with thee
A mutual immortality.[19]

Yet even Emily was brought finally to face, with something
more than equanimity, the prospect of teaching again—tribute
indeed to Charlotte's powers of persuasion. Thus Emily's birthday paper of this summer is more optimistic than Anne's:

A PAPER to be opened
when Anne is
25 years old
or my next birthday after
if
all be well
Emily Jane Bronte. July 30th, 1841.

It is Friday evening, near 9 o'clock—wild rainy weather. I am seated in the dining-room alone, having just concluded tidying our desk boxes, writing this document Papa is in the parlour—aunt upstairs in her room. She has been reading Blackwood's Magazine to papa. Victoria and Adelaide are ensconced in the peat-house. Keeper is in the kitchen—Hero in his cage. We are all stout and hearty, as I hope is the case with Charlotte, Branwell, and Anne, of whom the first is at John White, Esq., Upperwood House, Rawdon; the second is at Luddenden Foot; and the third is, I believe, at Scarborough, inditing perhaps a paper similar to this.

A scheme is at present in agitation for setting us up in a school of our own; as yet nothing is determined, but I hope and trust it may go on and prosper and answer our highest expectations. This day four years I wonder whether we shall still be dragging on in our present condition or established to our hearts' content. Time will show.

I guess that at the time appointed for the opening of this paper we i.e. Charlotte, Anne, and I, shall be all merrily seated in our sitting-room in some pleasant and flourishing seminary, having just gathered in for the midsummer holyday. Our debts will be paid off, and we shall have cash in hand to a considerable amount. Papa, aunt, and Branwell will either have been or be coming to visit us. It will be a fine warm summer evening, very different from this bleak look-out, and Anne and I will perchance slip out into the garden for a few minutes to peruse our papers. I hope either this or something better will be the case.

The Gondalians are at present in a threatening state, but there is no open rupture as yet. All the princes and princesses of the Royalty are at the Palace of Instruction. I have a good many books on hand, but I am sorry to say that as usual I make small progress with any. However, I have just made a new regularity paper! and I mean *verb sap* to do great things. And now I must close, sending from far an exhortation, 'Courage, courage,' to exiled and harassed Anne, wishing she was here.[20]

For herself, Charlotte was all joy at the prospect her imagination unfolded. Already, tasting the exhilaration of freedom, and with the Taylor sisters in her mind's eye, she was contemplating a more spectacular emancipation. She began to make plans that a few months ago would have seemed an impossible dream. Miss Branwell had already accepted the principle of a loan. Now a further daring refinement on the original plan could be placed before her.

Charlotte's intention was now nothing less than to join a

school in Brussels in order to perfect her French before attempting to set up a school in England. But although this reason for going abroad could be put before Miss Branwell as a genuine inducement, Charlotte thought of it with an uncontrollable excitement that no plan to improve her education could alone arouse. To leave Haworth, to leave England, to cross the sea and breathe foreign air was to live for the first time. Opportunity was opening its arms to her, the world seemed laid at her feet.

True child of her father in her ambition as in her means of attaining it, Charlotte approached her aunt with the utmost dexterity. There was only this one source from which she could get the necessary help. Miss Branwell had the money; she had been saving her annuity for years. Could she be persuaded to lend it?

Two months after rejoining the Whites at Rawdon, Charlotte sent her aunt a letter, carefully composed with an eye to the recipient, in which she explained the position, cast the onus for the suggestion on others, and asked for help: 'I have heard nothing of Miss Wooler yet', she said, 'since I wrote to her intimating that I would accept her offer . . . . Meantime, a plan has been suggested and approved by Mr. and Mrs. White, and others, which I wish now to impart to you. My friends recommend me, if I desire to secure permanent success, to delay commencing the school for six months longer, and by all means contrive, by hook or by crook, to spend the intervening time in some school on the Continent. They say schools in England are so numerous, competition so great, that without some such step towards attaining superiority we shall probably have a very hard struggle and may fail in the end. They say, moreover, that the loan of £100, which you have been so kind as to offer us, will, perhaps, not be all required now, as Miss Wooler will lend us the furniture; and that, if the speculation is intended to be a good and successful one, half the sum, at least, ought to be laid out in the manner I have mentioned, thereby insuring a more speedy repayment both of interest and principal. I would not go to France or to Paris. I would go to Brussels, in Belgium. The cost of the journey there, at the dearest rate of travelling, would be £5. Living is there little more than half as dear as it is in England, and the facilities for education are equal or superior to any other place in Europe. In half a year, I could acquire a thorough familiarity with French, I could improve greatly in Italian, and even get a dash of German, i.e. providing my health continued as good as it is now. Martha Taylor is now staying in Brussels, at a first-rate establishment there. I should not think of going to the Château de Koekelberg, where she is resident, as the terms are much too high; but if I wrote to her, she, with the the assistance of Mrs. Jenkins, the wife of the British Consul,[21] would be able to secure me a cheap and decent residence and respectable protection. I should have the opportunity of seeing her frequently, she would make me acquainted with the city; and, with the assistance of her cousins, I should probably in time be introduced to connections far more improving, polished and cultivated, than any I have yet known.

'These are advantages which we would turn to vast account, when we actually commenced a school—and, if Emily could share them with me, only for a single half-year, we could take a footing in the world afterwards which we can never do now. I say Emily instead of Anne; for Anne might take her turn at some future period, if our school answered. I feel certain, while I am writing, that you will see the propriety of what I say; you always like to use your money to the best advantage; you are not fond of making shabby purchases; when you do confer a favour, it is often done in style; and depend upon it, £50, or £100, thus laid out, would be well employed. Of course, I know no other friend in the world to whom I could apply on this subject except yourself. I feel an absolute conviction that, if this advantage were allowed us, it would be the making of us for life. Papa will perhaps think it a wild and ambitious scheme; but who ever rose in the world without ambition? When he left Ireland to go to Cambridge University, he was as ambitious as I am now. I want us *all* to get on. I know we have talents, and I want them to be turned to account. I look to you, aunt, to help us. I think you will not refuse. I know, if you consent, it shall not be my fault if you ever repent your kindness.'[22]

Miss Branwell consented to advance the money. Charlotte, jubilant, unobtrusively allowed Miss Wooler's offer and her own acceptance to recede into the background, to be forgotten; she gave notice to her employers, and plunged into a delicious orgy of planning. Lille was suggested to her as a better educational centre than Brussels, but Charlotte's heart was set on

Brussels, less of a provincial town than Lille, and where she would be near the Taylor girls. She enlisted the help of the Jenkinses—Mr. Jenkins was the British chaplain in Brussels—to persuade her aunt and father that Brussels should be chosen. And sure enough, Brussels became the final choice.[23]

As excitement, hope, and anticipation mounted in Charlotte at the promise of freedom, the prospect of advancement, so her letters, whose stateliness grew in inverse proportion to the importance of the news she had to impart, took on a brisk youthfulness they had never before shown. Ecstatic visions rose before her at the thought of studying on the Continent—particularly delightful to Charlotte, so conscious of her provinciality.

Charlotte had not succeeded in replacing her intimacy with Branwell by a similar closeness to her sisters, but if she could not possess their whole confidence, at least she was now in the way of deciding their destinies. They were agreeing with her plans, and she was happy in a tingle of action which she believed would lead to the well-being of all.

Whether Emily wholly welcomed this activity on her behalf is doubtful. She was certainly dismayed to find that the Dewsbury idea had already been dropped, and that she was asked to look upon it as a pleasure and a compliment to go to school again, to live for months in a foreign country. But she recognized the sincerity of Charlotte's intentions, and with true strength of will she submitted to them.

Anne welcomed the new scheme with her usual unselfishness and good sense; she was anxious for them all to be at home together in the future, and she could see that it would eventually be to everyone's advantage if she stayed at Thorp Green to compensate a little for the Brussels expenditure.[24]

For herself, Charlotte was all excitement and triumph: 'If I could, Ellen, I would always work in silence and obscurity and let my efforts be known only by their results. Miss Wooler did most kindly propose that I should come to Dewsbury Moor and attempt to revive the school her sister had relinquished—she offered me the use of her furniture for the consideration of her board. At first I received the proposal cordially and proposed to do my utmost to bring about success—but a fire was kindled in my heart which I could not quench—I so longed to increase my attainments, to become something better than I am—a glance of what I felt I showed you in one of my former letters—only a glimpse. Mary Taylor cast oil on the flames—encouraged me, and in her own strong energetic language heartened me on —I longed to go to Brussels—but how could I get there? I wished for one at least of my Sisters to share the advantage with me, I fixed on Emily—she deserved the reward I knew—How could this point be managed? In extreme excitement I wrote a letter home which carried the point—I made an appeal to Aunt for assistance which was answered by consent. Things are not settled. Yet it is sufficient to say that we have a *chance* of going for half a year. Dewsbury Moor is relinquished, perhaps fortunately so, it is an obscure and dreary place—not adapted for a school. In my secret soul I believe there is no cause to regret it. My plans for the future are bounded to this intention: if I once get to Brussels, and if my health is spared, I will do my best to make the utmost of every advantage that shall come within my reach. When the half year is expired I will do what I can . . . .'[25]

Charlotte was home by Christmas Eve, her period as governess ended. Anne had already returned to Haworth, but she had been asked to go back to Thorp Green after the holidays[26] —the two Robinson girls, though difficult pupils, had already taken a liking to their gentle, patient teacher. Once more the family were together. The Christmas was a triumphant one for Charlotte, a time of troubled joy for Anne. Charlotte, strangely oblivious of her sister's susceptible heart, writes merrily of the antics of Weightman: 'He sits opposite to Anne at Church sighing softly and looking out of the corners of his eyes to win her attention—and Anne is so quiet, her look so downcast— they are a picture . . . .'[27]

The Brussels plan caused Branwell much heartburning. He admired Charlotte's drive, even when he could not follow her example, and even when she made him wince with her reproaches. No one with Branwell's faculty for self-criticism could hope to escape bitterness; but he was bitter because Charlotte seemed likely to succeed where he had failed, and because he knew that it was largely because of him and his extravagances that the school plan had ever been suggested. But these feelings, though sincere enough at the time, could not last, and they were soon drowned, like all his short fits of conscience, in the same way. He was still nominally in charge of Luddenden Foot station, and he appeared from time to time at home; sometimes alone and very much depressed, sometimes with Grundy, in high spirits.[28]

Emily regarded the coming departure apprehensively. Her two previous attempts to live away from the parsonage had proved disastrous. She had hoped to set up school with her sisters at Dewsbury Moor, but Charlotte's later plan was a very different affair. All Emily had to set off against a third disaster, and an absence that threatened to last even longer than six months, were Charlotte's company and her own conviction that such a step was necessary. But feel glad she could not.

All arrangements were complete. Charlotte and Emily were to join the *Pensionnat* Héger in Brussels as pupils until September.[29] This was the official plan. But in fact, Charlotte had every intention of staying at least a year out of England—she wanted experience both as pupil and teacher before opening her own school: 'Before our half-year in Brussels is completed', she tells Emily, 'you and I will have to seek employment abroad. It is not my intention to retrace my steps home till twelve months, if all continues well, and we and those at home retain good health.'[30]

Ellen paid a final visit to the parsonage in January 1842. Anne returned, heavy-hearted but acquiescent, to Thorp Green; Martha Brown, daughter of Branwell's friend, the sexton and freemason, who had succeeded Tabby, was proving so competent about the house that there had been no difficulty in allowing Anne to leave home.

In February, Mr. Brontë, Charlotte, and Emily set out for Belgium.[31]

XIII

THE PENSIONNAT HEGER

Brontës and Taylors travel to Brussels. Reactions of Charlotte and Emily to London. The Pensionnat Héger. Madame Héger. Monsieur Héger. Life at school. Failure of visits to friends. Interest of Monsieur Héger in the two girls. Special lessons. They progress. Their reactions to school life abroad. They begin to teach. Deaths of Weightman, Martha Taylor, Miss Branwell. They return home.

Mary Taylor and her brother Joe, who were also going to Brussels, joined forces with the Brontës, and all five travelled to London together. Charlotte lost no time in beginning her cultural campaign. 'In passing through London', Mary said, 'Charlotte seemed to think our business was, and ought to be, to see all the pictures and statues we could. She knew the artists, and knew where other productions of theirs were to be found. I don't remember what was seen except St. Paul's. Emily was like Charlotte in these habits of mind, but certainly never took her opinion, but always had one to offer.'[1] The party arrived at Brussels after dark. Mary and her brother went to the Château de Koekelberg; Mr. Brontë took his daughters to the *Pensionnat* Héger.

The *pensionnat* was a large, historic, somewhat gloomy old house in the Rue d'Isabelle, a short and narrow street approached down a flight of broad stone steps from the fashionable Rue Royale. At the back of the house, beyond the classrooms separated by glass corridors from one another, was a large walled garden, with paths shaded by overhanging branches of old fruit trees. In one corner of the garden was a wide arbour, almost surrounded by a trellis of vine; and over against the garden stood an academy for boys, one window of which looked down directly upon the paths and playground of the *pensionnat*.[2]

Madame Héger, the presiding genius of the *pensionnat*, was a suave, capable, industrious woman, fresh-faced and neat. When she chose, she had much charm, but she was parsimonious and entirely unscrupulous in everything that affected the interests of her school. Her desire to have it absolutely under her control had led her to set up an intricate system of spying upon the movements and conversation of pupils and staff alike; and this espionage had become such a part of the life of the school that, by the time Emily and Charlotte arrived, a slight but unmistakable haze of suspicion hovered over most of its inmates.

Her husband, Constantin Héger, was a choleric, forceful, yet kindly little man of some intellectual distinction. He was only seven years older than Charlotte; and, with his bushy black hair and moustache, his bright black eyes, abrupt gestures, his impatience, his almost childish bursts of egotism, and his uncompromising rectitude, he was both lovable and laughable. He played no active part in the management of the school. He was Professor at the Academy close by, but took classes in French at the *pensionnat*. One of his classes—of some sixty pupils—was attended by Charlotte and Emily, sitting at the end of the last row at the back of the large class-room.[3]

There were about one hundred pupils, mostly day-boarders. All but nine or ten were Bruxelloises. All were younger by several years than the twenty-six and twenty-four years old Charlotte and Emily. Most of them regarded the grown-up, reserved, and badly-dressed new arrivals with an understandable hesitancy—some even with amusement. Nor was any greater friendliness manifested by the staff, who may well have seen future rivals in these silent, hard-working English sisters.[4] But any coldness the pupils and mistresses may have shown towards the Brontë sisters was more than counterbalanced by the disdain of Charlotte and Emily. The English girls united in presenting a hard, bigoted, intolerant front to those whose religious faith they despised, whose manners they detested, and whose lack of cleverness and application Charlotte in particular castigated cruelly. A sense of strangeness, of loneliness, played some part in this attitude, which persisted throughout their entire stay at the school—but as much, at least, was due to their provincialism.

Charlotte and Emily slept in a big dormitory over the long class-room, but their beds were curtained off from those of the other girls at the end of the room. The two sisters worked together unremittingly, silently. In moments of leisure they would walk apart from the laughing, noisy throng of girls in the garden. Up and down the path farthest from the girls at play (the *allée défendue*, as it was called), bordered by fruit trees and by the garden wall, near the Academy, the two Brontë sisters would pace slowly, the taller Emily leaning upon Charlotte. They would speak to few, and few would address them, except perhaps Madame Héger, eager to know what her strange pupils were discussing. Charlotte would always answer when spoken to, and would reply to any remark addressed to both; Emily rarely spoke to anyone.[5] Both were dressed in black, ill-fitting, old-fashioned dresses. Emily, who persisted in wearing the huge, ugly, long out-of-date leg-of-mutton sleeves, and whose petticoats hung shapeless on her lanky figure,[6] presented a picture that would have been wholly comic but for her kindling, far-seeing eyes, and determined features.

At first, friends and acquaintances in the city attempted to provide the two girls with some relief from their work in strange surroundings. The attempt failed. Neither Charlotte nor Emily was to be moved from the frozen immobility into which residence in a foreign country had set them. Charlotte, indeed, occasionally overcame this paralysing reserve sufficiently to join in conversation; but in order so to do, she found it necessary to turn her back to the person she was addressing. Emily said nothing; and her silence was so defiant, so black with misery and moroseness, as to render useless the whole purpose of the gatherings.[7]

Thus the Jenkinses, and the Dixons, cousins of the Taylors, who lived in Brussels, soon lost both heart and patience with their difficult visitors; the escort, provided for the two girls between school and house, mutinied and declined further service; and the visits ended, to the mutual relief of hosts and guests alike.[8]

Then Laetitia Wheelwright, one of five English sisters who joined the school in the summer, became acquainted with Charlotte. Laetitia was as insular and intolerant as the girls from Haworth. Charlotte observed her eyeing the Belgian girls contemptuously, and her heart warmed towards this superior being —'It was so very English,' Charlotte remarked.[9] When asked by Laetitia to the hotel where the Wheelwright family lived, Charlotte brought Emily along with her. The visits proceeded along the dreary course experienced by the Jenkinses and the Dixons. There was a similar deadly silence from Emily; a similar difficulty in bringing the tongue-tied Charlotte to the point of speech; and the Wheelwrights, feeling Emily's presence too high a price to pay for the company of her sister, stopped inviting them.[10] Only at the Château de Koekelberg, alone with the Taylor girls, did Charlotte and Emily permit themselves to relax their stiff and unsociable attitude, to show anything of their Haworth selves.

Communication with strangers was always difficult for Emily. In Brussels, her unhappiness and her antipathy—immediate and uncompromising—to all she now saw and heard about her, destroyed the wish to make herself even tolerably agreeable. And on Charlotte, conscious of her sister's misery, her own painful shyness descended even more readily.[11]

It had early become clear to the Hégers that the training of Charlotte and Emily would never prosper unless their French was taken in hand. Emily's knowledge of the language, in particular, was quite inadequate. Héger therefore began to give the two sisters special lessons in French: 'They are, I suppose, to be considered a great favour,' Charlotte told Ellen, 'and I can perceive they have already excited much spite and jealousy in the school.'[12] Héger soon began to realize with what strange and rare material he had to deal. Being a man of considerable penetration, he perceived the possibilities hidden in his two silent and unprepossessing pupils. He devoted time and thought to the methods by which they could best and soonest master the French language, and so, the subjects they must learn by means of that language. He studied their characters, encouraging, even while dictating, the course their development should take.

The passing of the summer left the sisters practically as friendless as when they had arrived. Charlotte certainly made an acquaintance of Laetitia; but the only suggestion that Emily spoke to anyone in the school except the Hégers is made in Charlotte's reference to the mistresses. 'Madame Héger, the head', she wrote, 'is a lady of precisely the same cast of mind, degree of cultivation, and quality of intellect as Miss Catherine Wooler. I think the severe points are a little softened, because she has not been disappointed, and consequently soured. In a word, she is a married instead of a maiden lady. There are three teachers in the school—Mademoiselle Blanche, Mademoiselle Sophie, and Mademoiselle Marie. The first two have no particular character. One is an old maid, and the other will be one. Mademoiselle Marie is talented and original, but of repulsive and arbitrary manners, which have made the whole school, except myself and Emily, her bitter enemies.'[13]

This suggests, as might be expected, that Emily warmed to the strange, the unwanted, as she warmed to the homeless dog, the frightened or broken bird at Haworth. This instinctive alliance with the unpopular, the downtrodden, was later to exercise a profound influence on Emily and those about her. Meanwhile, she existed grimly, bitterly, waging a ceaseless fight against desolation of heart and physical collapse. The sense of imprisonment that had proved her undoing at Roe Head and again at Halifax attacked her in Brussels—attacked her with even greater virulence, surrounded as she was by foreign scenes redolent everywhere of the popery she had been taught to despise, and in a school brooded over by the espionage of Madame Héger, in which eyes were forever peering through the glass of the corridors, where footsteps seemed noiseless, and voices sank too easily to whispers. All this threatened Emily with breakdown. But she was now older; she had Charlotte; and she set herself fiercely to conquer her weakness, to wrest every ounce of educational value out of her enforced exile. She neither expected nor wanted happiness in Belgium; but she would not leave the country empty-handed.

Far different were the feelings of her sister at this time. Charlotte, for all her silence and contempt for those about her, was tasting a satisfaction, a happiness greater by far than she had dreamed the Brussels venture could ever bring. Not only was she at last acquiring knowledge vital to her progress in the world in which she longed to move—she was also discovering in Constantin Héger the masterful man she could admire intensely for his intellect and character. With her customary combination of crude mockery and bluntness of speech Charlotte hurried to disclaim—to herself as to her friend—the impression this irascible, inflexible, volatile man—so much like one of her own Angrian heroes—had made on her. 'He is professor of rhetoric,' she writes, 'a man of power as to mind, but very choleric and irritable as to temperament; a little black ugly being, with a face that varies in expression. Sometimes he borrows the lineaments of an insane tom-cat, sometimes those of a delirious hyena; occasionally, but very seldom, he discards these perilous attractions and assumes an air not above 100 degrees removed from mild and gentlemanlike.'[14]

But she submitted gladly to his dictation; nor was she ashamed to own it: 'He is very angry with me at present', she wrote, 'because I have written a translation which he chose to stigmatise as *peu correcte*. He did not tell me so, but wrote the accusation on the margin of my book, and asked in brief, stern phrase, how it happened that my compositions were always better than my translations? adding that the thing seemed to him inexplicable. The fact is, some weeks ago, in a high-flown humour, he forbade me to use either dictionary or grammar in translating the most difficult English translations into French. This makes the task rather arduous and compels me now and then to introduce an English word, which nearly plucks the eyes out of his head when he sees it. When he is very ferocious with me I cry; that sets all things straight.'[15]

She accepted her master's corrections to her devoirs meekly, hung on his words, wept when he scolded, wrote poems in which he figured prominently; and if at times her fiery temperament rose against his arbitrariness, gratitude and admiration overcame impatience, and her heart welcomed a master, even an unreasonable one. For Charlotte was not naturally self-sufficient. Her dominance at home and in friendship was self-imposed, partly by the urge of ambition, partly by the weakness or indifference of others, and partly by her strong sense of duty and warm affection for those near her. She was no law unto herself, she carried within no sense of an unconventional, all-powerful God, no awareness of an all-embracing visionary power, in contemplation of which earthly desires became contemptible, not worth fighting for. She had neither the mystical detachment of Emily nor Anne's piety. She had neither the widespread geniality nor the expansive weakness and shallowness of Branwell into which she might retreat from her emotions. Of all the Brontës, Charlotte was the most human. Of the sisters she was at heart the most feminine. Her loneliness was not left undefined in her mind. She knew well what she wanted. She was a born hero-worshipper. She looked for, longed for, a stronger will than her own, a Byronic Wellington among men whom she might serve and adore. Her hot and impetuous heart

burned for an answering human love. Her passionate desire for
an intense life called for a strong directing hand; and this, at
least, Héger was the first to provide.

Charlotte's letters made her feelings clear: 'I was twenty-six
a week or two since,' she told Ellen, 'and at this ripe time of life
I am a schoolgirl, a complete schoolgirl, and, on the whole,
very happy in that capacity. It felt very strange at first to submit
to authority instead of exercising it—to obey orders instead of
giving them; but I like that state of things. I returned to it with
the same avidity that a cow, that has long been kept on dry hay,
returns to fresh grass. Don't laugh at my simile. It is natural to
me to submit, and very unnatural to command.'[16]

To the indignant Emily, watching, this glad surrender of the
dictatorial Charlotte provided yet another reason for an obstinate refusal to bend an inch before the domineering, self-
opinionated, obstinate little professor.

Héger, after consulting his wife, decided that the sisters
would progress more quickly if they abandoned the usual grammatical grounding. He began to read them selections from great
French writers, to analyse what he had read, and then to ask
Charlotte and Emily to write devoirs on some similar subject.
He hoped thus to instil into them an appreciation of French at
its best, so that in their own use of the language they might
come instinctively to reproduce what they knew was good. He
explained the plan to his two pupils before putting it into action.
Emily protested. She saw no good to be derived from it, she
said. On the contrary, she believed that by adopting it they
would lose all originality of thought and expression. She would
have entered into an argument on the subject, but Héger, who
had already done some violence to his nature by discussing the
matter at all, would not listen further. He was not opposed by
Charlotte who, though she agreed in principle with her sister,
said that she was bound to obey her master while she was his
pupil. The plan went forward, and was succeeded by an even
more ambitious one. He read his two pupils various accounts,
by different writers, of one person or subject, asking them to
analyse the parts, reject the unnecessary or the untrue, and unite
the rest into a composite, artistic and truthful whole.[17] This
work pleased Charlotte, whose powers of analysis, always considerable, were sharpened and enriched. But Emily, though her

work rose above her sister's in power, imagination, and expression, remained unconvinced, reluctant, surly. She worked hard but without enthusiasm.[18]

'Emily works like a horse,' reported Charlotte, 'and she has had great difficulties to contend with—far greater than I have had.' But Charlotte was bound to admit in the same letter that all was not well between her sister and her teacher. 'Emily and he don't draw well together at all,' she wrote.[19] Yet, though he thought Emily egotistical and exacting compared with Charlotte, though he believed Emily exercised an unconscious tyranny over Charlotte because of Charlotte's anxiety to see her contented, it was this sullen, resentful, stubborn younger sister that Monsieur Héger admired. In her he saw a strength of character, a grasp of essentials, a depth and masculine capacity of mind that ought to lead to greatness. He found that Emily had a head for logic and a capability of argument unusual in a man and rare in a woman.[20] But he saw that the force of this gift was being impaired by an obstinacy which made Emily obtuse to all reasoning. 'She should have been a man—a great navigator,' he said; 'Her powerful reason would have deduced new spheres of discovery from the knowledge of the old; and her strong, imperious will would never have been daunted by opposition or difficulty; never have given way but with life. And yet, moreover, her faculty of imagination was such that, if she had written a history, her view of scenes and characters would have been so vivid, and so powerfully expressed, and supported by such a show of argument, that it would have dominated over the reader, whatever might have been his previous opinions or his cooler perceptions of its truth.'[21]

So far he saw, with unusual penetration. What he did not and could not see was the merry, teasing, care-free Emily of the Haworth moors; the gentle Emily with her pets, and all helpless injured creatures; the romantic Emily of the Gondal tales; the passionate Emily of the love lyrics; the mystical Emily of the poems telling of the search for that which ever beckoned yet ever eluded her.

Both sisters made great strides in their work. Charlotte rapidly became proficient in French, and obtained a useful grounding in German. She was on the whole very content with her lot, and with the advances she was making in knowledge.

'I don't deny that I sometimes wish to be in England, or that I have brief attacks of home-sickness,' she tells Ellen, 'but on the whole I have borne a very valiant heart so far—and I have been happy in Brussels because I have always been fully occupied with the employments that I like.'[22] Emily, though far from happy, was progressing with equal speed: 'Emily is making rapid progress in French, German, Music and Drawing,' Charlotte reported.[23] When the school broke up for the summer holidays, Charlotte and Emily worked on. Whatever Madame Héger's personal opinion of her two silent and hostile Yorkshire pupils, she was in no doubt whatever as to the merit of their industry or the value of their services to an astute and careful headmistress.

So it came to pass that Charlotte's original plan—to remain in Brussels or on the Continent as teacher after six months of tuition—was realized without the necessity of a search for another school. Madame Héger, prompted by her husband, whose interest in the sisters was less calculated than that of his wife, offered to keep both Charlotte and Emily at the school for a further six months. Charlotte was to be English mistress; Emily was to teach music to the younger pupils; both were to continue their own studies under Héger and the other teachers. They were to receive no salary, but were to be boarded free.

Although the summer holidays were about to begin when this offer was made and accepted, Emily was able to start teaching immediately. The five Wheelwright girls joined the school at this time; and the younger ones began pianoforte lessons at once.[24] Neither Emily nor Charlotte took a holiday; they remained busy amassing knowledge against their eventual return to a school of their own. Charlotte, who had worked and hoped for just such an event as the Hégers' offer, was contented and even gay. How much she wished to remain in Brussels was to be seen by her refusal of an opportunity which occurred at this time to earn a great deal more money in England.[25] Emily must have felt some satisfaction with her improvement in languages, music, and drawing; but she is unlikely to have shared her sister's pleasure that 'Monsieur and Madame Héger begin to recognise the valuable points of her character under her singularities'.[26] Pleasure, Charlotte certainly felt; the pleasure of the general who watches his plans working out, as she began to see the justification of her choice of Emily in the Brussels venture. But for Emily, who still disagreed uncompromisingly with Héger and despised his wife, whose longing for home and dislike of her surroundings had not altered, there remained only determination to make the school pay, in learning, for the unhappiness it was causing.

August passed, and September. The school reassembled. Emily's pupils increased in number. Charlotte began teaching English. She was not loved, she was too quiet and silent, but she made herself respected. She never lost her temper; when her pupils were irritating, impertinent, or did not attend, the only signs of annoyance she betrayed were a slight increase of colour, a momentary sparkle of the eye, and a more energetic manner; and this self-control, so different from the voluble tirades to which the girls were accustomed, had its reward in a tractable class.[27]

Then, as the sisters settled down to their work, interruption came in a form with which they were already familiar.

First, they heard that Weightman had died—Weightman, the only stranger with whom Emily had ever unbent; who had given Charlotte so many moments of lightheartedness and fun; whose tender glance and winning manner had carried away Anne's heart; whose good-comradeship had held out hope and encouragement to Branwell. He fell ill suddenly and died within a fortnight.[28]

A few days later, towards the end of October, Martha Taylor was taken ill. Her illness, similar to that of Weightman, was equally sudden and equally fatal.[29] Charlotte heard of her friend's illness one day; she hurried to the Château de Koekelberg the next morning only to find that Martha had died during the night.[30] On the last Sunday in the month Charlotte, Emily, and Mary Taylor met in the afternoon to visit the Protestant cemetery in which Martha had been buried.[31] The cemetery was three miles out of the town, and they walked there and back. 'We then', said Mary, 'spent a pleasant evening with my cousins [the Dixons, with whom Mary was then staying], and in presence of my uncle and Emily, one not speaking at all, the other once or twice.'[32]

Finally, three days later, came news that Miss Branwell was seriously ill. She was not expected to recover. Charlotte and

Emily, after consulting the Hégers, prepared to go home at once, but the next day, 3 November, they heard that their aunt had died. They decided to return to Haworth nevertheless, left Brussels three days later, and on 8 November they were back at the parsonage.[33]

XIV

HOME AND RETURN

Branwell is dismissed and returns home. His reactions to the deaths of Weightman and Miss Branwell. Charlotte and Emily home again. Their reactions to recent events. Anne gets Branwell another post. Héger urges Mr. Brontë to send his daughters back to Brussels. Charlotte's indecision. She decides to return to the Pensionnat. Emily stays at home.

BRANWELL'S stay at Luddenden Foot had come already to its inevitable end. After he had been a year at the station the company's officials suddenly arrived and examined his books. They were hopelessly in arrears, and Branwell was dismissed.[1] After a final carousal he returned to a home even more quiet than usual. All his sisters were away from home—Anne at Thorp Green, Charlotte and Emily in Brussels. Tabby lived in the village, hobbling about on her game leg, and he had for company only Martha Brown, Tabby's successor, Miss Branwell, ailing already and keeping even closer to her room, and Mr. Brontë, his eyesight now very bad, who spent most of the day in his study.[2]

To the weak and expansive Branwell, smarting from the stigma of dismissal, bitterly conscious of talent wasted and opportunities thrown away, this solitude quickly proved intolerable, and he was soon writing to Grundy, appealing for work on some other part of the railway:[3] 'After experiencing, since my return home, extreme pain and illness, with mental depression worse than either,' he wrote, 'I have at length acquired health and strength and soundness of mind, far superior, I trust, to anything shown by that miserable wreck you used to know under my name. I can now speak cheerfully and enjoy the company of another without the stimulus of six glasses of whisky; I can write, think and act with some apparent approach to resolution, and I only want a motive for exertion to be happier than I have been for years. But I feel my recovery from *almost insanity* to be retarded by having nothing to listen to except the wind moaning among old chimneys and older ash

123

trees, nothing to look at except heathery hills walked over when life had all to hope for and nothing to regret with me—no one to speak to except crabbed old Greeks and Romans who have been dust the last five thousand years. And yet this quiet life, from its contrast, makes the year passed at Luddenden Foot appear like a nightmare, for I would rather give my hand than undergo again the grovelling carelessness, the malignant yet cold debauchery, the determination to find how far mind could carry body without both being chucked into hell, which too often marked my conduct when there, lost as I was to all I really liked, and seeking relief in the indulgence of feelings which form the black spot on my character.'[4]

Grundy could do nothing for him; and it was not long before Branwell's public-house friends were once more listening to stories of his escapades at Luddenden. Branwell also wrote poetry from time to time—Angrian, religious and historical. One of the latter poems, 'The Afghan War', was printed in the *Leeds Intelligencer* of 7 May 1842.[5] This was the first time any work of the Brontës had appeared in print. Branwell was still using the pseudonym Northangerland for many of his poems, and was still seeking the advice or assistance of well-known writers. To Wordsworth, Hartley Coleridge, and De Quincey, he now added the Sheffield poet, James Montgomery, who praised his work, and advised him to turn his attention seriously to literature.[6]

But Branwell had become sceptical, not only of his talent, but of his ability to develop it. He showed a cynical delight in analysing the weakness of his character. He shared with Charlotte a power of analysis, but unlike his sister he was unable to put his knowledge to good use. Indeed, his analytical insight, with his love of dramatization and his excessive self-pity, played no small part in his eventual undoing. At the moment he told Grundy merely that Montgomery's advice and encouragement was 'All very well, but I have no great conceit of myself, and great desire for activity'—a desire which meant no more than an inability to concentrate for long upon anything.[7]

In one direction alone had Branwell's friendships held hope of improving his character—this was the friendship with Weightman. Branwell, whose affections seem to have been given almost entirely to men, admired and loved Weightman more than most of his friends; and if the gay and mercurial curate was not precisely the friend Branwell needed, there was at least some sanity and sobriety of mind beneath his charming exterior and unpredictable actions. But a few months after Branwell returned from Luddenden Foot, Weightman was taken fatally ill. Branwell spent much time with him, and was with him when he died.

By this time Miss Branwell's condition had become worse. It was plain that she had not long to live, and Branwell was obliged to watch her cruel and lingering end. Yet even in the midst of emotion genuinely felt, he could not refrain from improving upon the occasion: 'I have had a long attendance at the death-bed of the Rev. Mr. Weightman, one of my dearest friends,' he told Grundy, 'and now I am attending at the death-bed of my aunt, who has been for twenty years as my mother. I expect her to die in a few hours . . . . I had meant to have written to you . . . but one sad ceremony must, I fear, be gone through first . . . excuse this scrawl—my eyes are too dim with sorrow to see well.'[8]

Grundy, sensing a lack of sincerity or an excess of imagination in his friend, chided him; but Miss Branwell was already dead: 'As I don't want to lose a *real* friend', replied Branwell, 'I write in deprecation of the tone of your letter. Death only has made me neglectful of your kindness, and I have lately had so much experience with him, that your sister would not *now* blame me for indulging in gloomy visions either of this world or another. I am incoherent, I fear, but I have been waking two nights witnessing such agonising suffering as I would not wish my worst enemy to endure; and I have now lost the guide and director of all the happy days connected with my childhood. I have suffered such sorrow since I last saw you at Haworth, that I do not now care if I were fighting in India, since, when the mind is depressed, danger is the most effectual cure. But you don't like croaking, I know well, only I request you to understand from my two notes that I have not forgotten *you*, but *myself*.'[9]

Charlotte and Emily returned to a house of mourning. Their aunt was already buried. Anne, who had come back from Thorp Green for the funeral, was quieter and more pensive than ever. The hope that had agitated her for more than a year was dead, and resignation—that quality which seems almost inseparable from the Annes of this world—had taken its place. Branwell was shaken, morbid, irresolute about his future. Mr. Brontë had withdrawn still further behind his massive self-sufficiency.

Yet joy in the return of the two sisters could not be withheld. The sorrow for the death of Miss Branwell was more dutiful than heartfelt. Emily, who had little cause to love her aunt, was also the one to whom the recall from Brussels came as a delightful and unexpected release. Charlotte was less pleased to be home. She quickly got into touch with Ellen, showing a new determination to overcome obstacles between their meeting, and manifesting less reluctance to accept hospitality unless she could be certain of repaying in kind. Thus, when Ellen proved unable to visit the parsonage at once despite the assurance of her friend: 'Do not fear to find us melancholy or depressed. We are all much as usual'[10]—Charlotte made it her business to go over to Brookroyd for a few days. She left with Anne, who was on her way back to Thorp Green, late in November:[11] 'I'll break through ceremony, or pride, or whatever it is, and like Mahomet go to the mountain which won't or can't come to me.'[12]

A few days after a Christmas in which all the Brontës were at home together, Ellen joined them. There were once again long walks upon the moors, and long evenings of talk and music in the dining-room. Branwell was at his best at such times, his liveliness and banter adding to the general lightheartedness.[13] There was on this occasion an additional reason for Branwell's high spirits. Anne, who had by now made herself practically indispensable to the two Robinson girls, had managed another chance for her brother. He was to return with her after the Christmas holidays as tutor to the Robinson boy.[14] Branwell, though well aware, if he had chosen to examine his mind, that tutoring would soon pall on him, was in a mood of wild confidence and relief at being no longer the unemployed member of the family. He looked forward to the companionship of Anne, for whom he had affection, but no respect.[15]

Charlotte was playful, rallying Ellen upon the possible suitors at Brookroyd.[16] Emily also was in her most genial mood, joyful to be back at Haworth, pleased with Ellen's company, and with no thought of a return to Brussels to weigh down her spirits.

Emily had changed, Ellen hinted to Mary Taylor; the Brussels sojourn had rubbed off something of her roughness of manner and 'substituted several accomplishments commonly considered as ladylike'. But Mary found it hard to believe that Emily could be much altered. She wanted to know more of Ellen's opinion of this girl, not unlike herself in bluntness of manner, in steadfastness of opinion turning easily into obstinacy, in scorn of insincerity and hatred of dependence. 'I can't imagine how the newly acquired qualities can fit in, in the same head and heart that is occupied by the old ones. I can't imagine Emily turning over prints or "taking wine" with any stupid pup and preserving her temper and politeness!'[17]

The question as to whether the interrupted stay at Brussels should be resumed had been thrashed out in the family circle and with Ellen. Soon after Charlotte and Emily had decided to leave the *pensionnat,* Héger wrote to Mr. Brontë: 'A very sad event has suddenly recalled your daughters to England. Their departure, which causes us much sorrow, has my entire approbation. It is very natural that they should seek to console you for that which Heaven has so lately taken away from you, and to enable you by their presence to appreciate that which Heaven has given and still leaves you. I hope you will pardon me, Sir, if I take advantage of this circumstance to assure you of my respect. I have not the honour of knowing you personally, still I hold you in sincere veneration; for in judging of a father of a family by his children one cannot be greatly deceived; and, in view of this, the education and sentiments we have found in your daughters can only give us a very high opinion of your merit and your character. You will no doubt learn with pleasure that your daughters have made very remarkable progress in all branches of teaching, and that this progress is entirely owing to their love of work and their perseverance. With such pupils we have had but little to do; their advancement is your work more than ours. We have not had to teach them the value of time and instruction; they had learnt all that in their paternal home, and we, on our part, have had only the feeble merit of directing their efforts and providing suitable aliment for the praiseworthy activity for which your daughters are indebted to your example and teaching. May the commendation which we give to your children be some consolation to you in your present sorrow.

That is our hope in writing to you, and that will be a sweet
recompense to the Misses Charlotte and Emily for their labours.
In losing our two dear pupils we cannot hide the fact of our own
sadness and uneasiness; we are sorely pained that this sudden
separation comes to sever an affection almost paternal which we
have felt for them; and our sorrow is increased by the sight of so
much work interrupted, and so many things well begun which
only needed more time satisfactorily to complete them. In a
year each of your daughters would have been quite prepared for
any eventuality of the future; each of them while receiving instruction was at the same time acquiring the science of teaching;
Miss Emily was learning the piano, receiving lessons from the
best professor in Belgium, and she herself already had little
pupils. She was losing whatever remained of ignorance, and
also of what was worse—timidity; Miss Charlotte was beginning
to give lessons in French and to acquire that assurance, that
aplomb so necessary to a teacher; only another year and the
work would have been completed, and well completed. Then
we should have been able, if convenient to you, to offer to your
daughters, or at least to one of them, a position according with
her taste, and that pleasant independence so difficult for a young
person to find. This is not, believe me, Sir,—this is not a question
of personal interest; it is a question of affection. You will pardon
me if I speak of your children, if we interest ourselves in their
welfare, as if they were part of our family; their personal qualities, their good nature, their intense zeal, are the sole reasons
which impel us to run the risk of your displeasure. We know,
Sir, that you will weigh with better judgment, and more wisely
than we, the consequences which a complete interruption of
your daughters' studies would have on the future. You will
decide what may be done, and you will pardon our frankness
when you consider that the motive which prompted it is an
affection quite disinterested and deeply saddened by the thought
that it must resign itself to being no longer useful to your dear
children.'[18]

Charlotte was as conscious as Héger of the incompleteness of
her education at Brussels; and she was more determined than
he that what had been begun there should be brought to a satisfactory end. She had been happy at the *pensionnat*, knowing
that she was gaining knowledge and the ability to pass it on,

and that she had at last met a man of considerable intellectual stature and with a dominating personality.[19] Emily was equally determined that she would not again leave Haworth for Brussels. Her French was now good, her German tolerable, her music excellent; she believed that she could continue her studies as well at home as in Belgium; and this was her fixed intention.

There was, however, no occasion for difference of opinion. The situation clearly demanded that one of the Brontë sisters should remain in charge of the household. Tabby had emerged from her semi-retirement in the village and had insisted upon coming back to the parsonage;[20] but although her company was welcome, and by none more than by Emily, Tabby was over seventy and had to be regarded rather as companion than active help.[21] There was little question which of the sisters should remain. Anne was in demand at Thorp Green; Charlotte burned to be back at Brussels; Emily, who wished for nothing better than to stay, was more competent in the house than either of her sisters, she had been accustomed to control the household in all but name for a number of years. It was agreed without difficulty that Emily should stay behind at Haworth.

The way was therefore left clear for Charlotte to return to the *pensionnat*. Yet, for all her wish to be there, she was in two minds about the wisdom of going back. Mr. Brontë, who liked his drink, needed watchful, firm, and sympathetic attention.[22] This attention Charlotte, with some reason, felt herself best able to give. And although she was eager to bring nearer the day when she and her sisters might work and live together in a school of their own, she must even then have questioned the single-mindedness of her desire. She returned to Brussels against her conscience, she said later, prompted by what then seemed an irresistible impulse;[23] but the impulse, which was to cause her much future misery, did not pass unchallenged; and it is possible that a cordial and even affectionate letter which arrived from Madame Héger expressing the hope of seeing her former pupils back in Brussels finally decided Charlotte to leave her home once more.[24]

The lack of a companion worried her, and, when Ellen was at Haworth, she tried to persuade her friend to come to Brussels.[25] But Ellen's family would not agree,[26] and Charlotte made up her mind to go alone. How much she wanted to go back to the *pensionnat* is also shown by her refusal, within a short time of returning home, of an offer of £50 a year; this she put aside gladly for the Hégers' £16 less the cost of her German lessons.[27] So, all doubts and fears overridden for the moment, she once more packed her trunks, and, on Friday 27 January, she again left Haworth, and was back at the *pensionnat* on the Sunday evening.

XV

BRUSSELS AGAIN

Charlotte leaves for Brussels. An adventure in London. She makes good progress as teacher. Her relations with M. and Madame Héger. Her spirits fail. She goes to the confessional. Gives notice. Is persuaded to withdraw it. Gives notice again. Leaves for home.

CHARLOTTE did not arrive in Brussels without an adventure, which, like so many other of her experiences, she put to good use in later years. Her train from Leeds was late. It did not arrive at Euston until ten o'clock at night. She had intended to go to the Chapter Coffee House, where she had stayed on the previous journey to Brussels, and which was near that part of the river in which the steamers lay; but she appears to have been worried by the idea of arriving at an hour which, to Yorkshire notions, was so late and unseemly; so, taking a cab at the station, she drove straight to the wharf at London Bridge and asked a waterman to row her to the Ostend packet, which was to sail the next morning.

She later described to Mrs. Gaskell, much as she was to describe it in *Villette*, her sense of loneliness and strange excitement as she went swiftly over the dark river in the dead of that winter's night to the black hull's side, and was at first refused permission to come on deck. 'No passengers might sleep on board,' she was told with some brusqueness. She looked back to the lights and subdued noises of London—that 'mighty heart' in which she had no place—and, standing up in the rocking boat, she asked to speak to someone in authority on board the packet. He came, and her quiet, simple statement of her wish, and her reason for it, impressed the man so favourably that he allowed her to come on board, and go to a berth.[1]

The early months of this year passed happily enough for Charlotte. She was in the first flush of authority, she was filled with the pleasing sense that she was making good use of her time, and she was moving in an intellectual atmosphere very dear to her.[2] She again visited and, without the silent, sullen Emily, enjoyed herself at the Dixons', Wheelwrights', and Jenkinses', in spite of Mr. Jenkins—'that unclerical little Welsh pony', as she described him to Ellen.[3] 'I have heard from Charlotte since her arrival', Mary Taylor informed Ellen; 'she seems *content* at least, but I fear her sister's absence will have a bad effect. When people have so little amusement they cannot afford to lose *any*.'[4]

Certainly Charlotte was not able to replace Emily in any way. She made no new acquaintance, either in school or out of it: 'I ought to consider myself well off, and to be thankful for my good fortune,' she told Ellen. 'I hope I am thankful; and if I could always keep up my spirits, and never feel lonely, or long for companionship, or friendship or whatever they call it, I should do very well. As I told you before, M. and Madame Héger are the only two persons in the house for whom I really experience regard and esteem, and, of course, I cannot always be with them, nor even often.'[5] Yet she had her pleasures: 'I now regularly give English lessons to M. Héger and his brother-in-law . . . . They get on with wonderful rapidity, especially the first. He already begins to speak English very decently. If you could see and hear the efforts I make to teach them to pronounce like Englishmen, and their unavailing attempts to imitate, you would laugh to all eternity. The Carnival is just over . . . . M. Héger took me and one of the pupils into the town to see the masks. It was animating to see the immense crowds and the general gaiety, but the masks were nothing. I have been twice to the Dixons. They are very kind to me.'[6]

Her opinion of pupils and fellow-mistresses in the school was so unfavourable that she could scarcely have wished to know them any better: 'Amongst 120 persons which compose the daily population of this house', she told Branwell, 'I can discern only one or two who deserve anything like regard. This is not owing to foolish fastidiousness on my part, but to the absence of decent qualities on theirs. They have not intellect or politeness or good-nature or good-feeling. They are nothing. I don't hate them—hatred would be too warm a feeling. They have no sensations themselves and they excite none. But one wearies from day to day of caring nothing, fearing nothing, liking nothing, hating nothing, being nothing, doing nothing—yes, I teach and sometimes get red in the face with impatience at their stupidity. But don't think I ever scold or fly into a passion. If I spoke warmly, as warmly as I sometimes used to do at Roe Head, they would think me mad. Nobody ever gets into a passion here. Such a thing is not known. The phlegm that thickens their blood is too gluey to boil. They are very false in their relations with each other, but they rarely quarrel, and friendship is a folly they are unacquainted with. The black Swan, M. Héger, is the only sole veritable exception to this rule (for Madame, always cool and always reasoning, is not quite an exception).'[7]

Charlotte was especially caustic about the mistresses: 'Mdlle Blanche and Mdlle Hausse are at present on a system of war without quarter,' she explains to Emily. 'They hate each other like two cats. Mdlle Blanche frightens Mdlle Hausse by her white passions (they quarrel venomously). Mdlle Hausse complains that when Mdlle Blanche is in a fury, "elle n'a pas de lèvres". I find also that Mdlle Sophie dislikes Mdlle Blanche extremely. She says she is heartless, insincere, and vindictive, which epithets, I assure you, are richly deserved. Also I find she is the regular spy of Mme Héger, to whom she reports everything. Also she invents . . . .'[8]

But on the whole, though she was rarely free from moments of desolating loneliness, Charlotte remained for some time content with her lot in the belief that she was advancing in knowledge and in power. She was alternately soothed and excited by her contact with the intellectual exhilaration and the warm, vehement personality (so like her own, so unlike those of all the others around her) of her 'black Swan'.[9]

'There are privations and humiliations to submit to,' she told Ellen, 'there is monotony and uniformity of life—and above all there is a constant sense of solitude in the midst of numbers—the Protestant, the Foreigner, is a solitary being, whether as teacher or pupil. I do not say this by way of complaining of my own lot—for though I acknowledge that there are certain disadvantages in my present position, what position on earth is without them? and whenever I turn back to compare what I am with what I was—my place here with my place at Mrs. Sidgwick's or Mrs. White's—I am thankful.'[10] She says much the same to Branwell, who, with his acceptance of the tutorship at

Thorp Green, had been received back to some extent in her good graces: 'Except for the total want of companionship I have nothing to complain of. I have not much to do, sufficient liberty, and I am rarely interfered with. I lead an easeful, stagnant, silent life, for which, when I think of Mrs. Sidgwick, I ought to be very thankful.'[11]

As time went on, however, as the Dixons left Brussels[12] and the Wheelwrights prepared to follow suit,[13] Charlotte became too dependent upon a single source of consolation and, at times, of inspiration. She rarely spoke to anyone, certainly not to any other man, but Héger.[14] She treasured happily every little act of kindness: 'Mary Taylor', she says of her friend, now in Germany, 'has nobody to be as good to her as Monsieur Héger is to me; to lend her books, to converse with her sometimes.'[15] Again: 'From time to time he shows his kind-heartedness by loading me with books, so that I am still indebted to him for all the pleasure and amusement I have.'[16] And yet again: 'M. Héger has just been in and given me a little German Testament as a present.'[17]

Charlotte also wrote verses, not far removed from mawkish, in which a glorified Héger plays a prominent part. One poem entitled 'Master and Pupil' begins:

> *I gave, at first, attention close;*
> *Then interest warm ensued;*
> *From interest, as improvement rose,*
> *Succeeded gratitude.*
>
> *Obedience was no effort soon,*
> *And labour was no pain;*
> *If tired, a word, a glance alone*
> *Would give me strength again.*
>
> *From others of the studious band*
> *Ere long he singled me;*
> *But only by more close demand*
> *And sterner urgency.*
>
> *The task he from another took,*
> *From me he did reject;*
> *He would no slight omission brook,*
> *And suffer no defect.*

If my companions went astray,
He scarce their wanderings blamed;
If I but faltered in the way,
His anger fiercely flamed.

When sickness stayed awhile my course,
He seemed impatient still,
Because his pupil's flagging force
Could not obey his will.

One day when summoned to the bed
Where pain and I did strive
I heard him, as he bent his head,
Say, 'God, she must revive!'

I felt his hand with gentle stress,
A moment laid on mine,
And wished to mark my consciousness
By some responsive sign.

But powerless then to speak or move,
I only felt, within,
The sense of Hope, the strength of Love,
Their healing work begin.[18]

Charlotte thus raised up against herself in course of time the
thinly-veiled hostility of Madame Héger, who had not perhaps
been best pleased to see only one Brontë sister return to the
school after Christmas. Charlotte sensed this hostility and was
not backward in returning it: 'Of late days', she writes, 'M. and
Mme. Héger rarely speak to me, and I really don't pretend to
care a fig for anybody else in the establishment. You are not to
suppose by that expression that I am under the influence of
warm affection for Mme. Héger. I am convinced that she does
not like me.'[19] And later: 'Madame Héger is a politic, plausible
and interested person—I no longer trust her.'[20]

But if Madame Héger's coldness did not worry Charlotte unduly, her reactions to the changing attitude of Héger were far
different. The object of her admiration—who, like his wife,
may well have regretted the absence of his more brilliant
pupil, argumentative and sullen though she was—became more
and more cautious and aloof as Charlotte's feelings revealed

themselves; and Charlotte, whose determination to persevere in the midst of uncongeniality was dependent on the amount of attention devoted to her and her work by Héger, fell into despondency that pretended indifference did not hide. 'M. Héger is wondrously influenced by Madame, and I should not wonder if he disapproves very much of my unamiable want of sociability,' she told Emily. 'He has already given me a brief lecture on universal *bienveillance*, and, perceiving that I don't improve in consequence, I fancy he has taken to considering me as a person to be left alone—left to the error of her ways; and consequently he has in a great measure withdrawn the light of his countenance, and I get on from day to day in a Robinson-Crusoe-like condition—very lonely. That does not signify. In other respects I have nothing substantial to complain of, nor is even this a cause for complaint. Except the loss of M. Héger's goodwill (if I have lost it) I care for none of 'em.'[21]

And again: 'I rarely speak to Monsieur now.'[22]

Still, through the spring and early summer months Charlotte kept a tolerably good heart. If her homesickness was increasing, if the one person in the school for whom she cared was to be seen and heard less as time passed, yet at least she had the consolation of making progress in her work, and so, she told herself, of justifying her return to Brussels. She was in complete control of the English lessons throughout the school. She had succeeded, without the proffered aid of the Hégers, in maintaining order in a class of rebellious elder girls. And her German showed signs of improvement.[23] But her loneliness mounted as her few acquaintances prepared to leave Brussels, and as the Hégers left her to herself more and more. She had been too proud to accept their early suggestion that she should share their sitting-room: 'This . . . I cannot do. In the daytime it is a public room, where music masters and mistresses are constantly passing in and out; and in the evening I will not and ought not to intrude on M. and Madame Héger and their children.'[24] Thus she found herself almost always alone. She would walk the empty class-rooms in the evenings. In the spare hours of the day she would pace up and down the *allée défendue*, the overgrown path by the fruit trees where no pupils were allowed, and where she had walked so many hours with Emily on her arm the year before. At night, or when the class-rooms were engaged, she would lie on her bed in the large, solitary dormitory,[25] her self-chosen sitting-room and bedroom.[26] She slept badly, and her thoughts became more and more neurotic. Nevertheless, she insisted that she was better off in the *pensionnat* than she would be in England.[27] Impressions of people, places, and incidents were taking lasting shape in her mind. All that went on around her, the spoken and the unspoken life, was seized upon and dramatized in response to her insatiable interest in the emotions—an interest that combined shrewd and merciless insight with the warm intuition of her passionate nature. Her power of visionary observation was busy even then revealing the cause underlying the effect of word and deed in her everyday life, and uncovering the emotional impulse which lay beneath the outwardly commonplace, the cold, hard speech or action.

Not until the beginning of August, a few days before the school broke up for the summer holidays, did Charlotte's spirits begin to give way completely under the strain of loneliness and repressed emotion. Though she despised her pupils and fellow-teachers, their presence at least provided a welcome sensation of movement and companionship, illusory though it may have been, that was sadly missed when the school relapsed into a hot, dusty, August silence. For Charlotte, despite her sharp, and even shrewish criticism of those about her, was naturally gregarious.[28] Her heart all but failed her when she contemplated the five weeks of holiday to be lived through—the silent, desolate school in which she must eat, sleep, and occupy herself as best she could—the alien city in whose life she had no part, and which only emphasized her loneliness.[29]

But hope and ambition still lived in her. She was very homesick, she admitted to Ellen; yet before a return home could be considered, she must master her German. Then only could she come home with a satisfactory sense of fitness for the school she had planned.[30] This excuse for remaining was genuine enough, but it was not the whole truth. Charlotte was to give other reasons why she stayed on despite her unhappiness;[31] but she did not speak, then or at any other time, of what was probably the deciding factor.

In the event, the first weeks of the school holiday proved more endurable than Charlotte's imagination had pictured them.

The hot, sunny days continued, and she was able to escape the empty, depressing class-rooms of the *pensionnat* for hours at a time; she explored Brussels, pored over its art treasures, and walked at times in the country surrounding the city.[32] Yet her relief to be out of the house never satisfied her for long, for by this time she had fallen into the grip of hypochondria—or so she described it, although her depression was not without cause. Her otherwise accurate analysis of the state into which she had drifted gave her neither the strength nor the motive for its over-throw.[33] The depth of her depression is made clear by an incident in the middle of the holidays: 'Yesterday', she wrote to Emily, 'I went on a pilgrimage to the cemetery, and far beyond it on to a hill where there was nothing but fields as far as the horizon. When I came back it was evening; but I had such a repugnance to return to the house, which contained nothing that I cared for, I still kept threading the streets in the neighbour-hood of the Rue d'Isabelle and avoiding it. I found myself opposite to Ste Gudule, and the bell, whose voice you know, began to toll for evening *salut*. I went in, quite alone (which procedure you will say is not much like me), wandered about the aisles where a few old women were saying their prayers, till vespers began. I stayed till they were over. Still I could not leave the church or force myself to go home—to school I mean. An odd whim came into my head. In a solitary part of the Cathedral six or seven people still remained kneeling by the confessionals. In two confessionals I saw a priest. I felt as if I did not care what I did, provided it was not absolutely wrong, and that it served to vary my life and yield a moment's interest. I took a fancy to change myself into a Catholic and go and make a real confession to see what it was like. Knowing me as you do, you will think this odd, but when people are by themselves they have singular fancies. A penitent was occupied in confessing. They do not go into the sort of pew or cloister which the priest occupies, but kneel down on the steps and confess through a grating. Both the confessor and the penitent whisper very low, you can hardly hear their voices. After I had watched one or two penitents go and return, I approached at last and knelt down in a niche which was just vacated. I had to kneel there ten minutes waiting, for on the other side was another penitent in-visible to me. At last that went away and a little wooden door inside the grating opened, and I saw the priest leaning his ear towards me. I was obliged to begin, and yet I did not know a word of the formula with which they always commence their confessions. It was a funny position. I felt precisely as I did when alone on the Thames at midnight. I commenced with saying I was a foreigner and had been brought up a Protestant. The priest asked if I was a Protestant then. I somehow could not tell a lie, and said "Yes". He replied that in that case I could not "*jouir du bonheur de la confesse*"; but I was determined to confess, and at last he said he would allow me because it might be the first step towards returning to the true church. I actually did confess—a real confession.'[34]

Up to this point, although Charlotte's account was written with a rather forced lightness, and some apologetics which she might well have thought necessary for Emily, she had not disguised the state of mind that had driven her to such a remarkable action. But she continued in a manner more befitting the narrow creed in which she had been brought up: 'When I had done', she goes on, 'he told me his address, and said that every morning I was to go to the Rue du Parc—to his house—and he would reason with me and try to convince me of the error and enormity of being a Protestant!!! I promised faithfully to go. Of course, however, the adventure stops there, and I hope I shall never see the priest again.'[35] Whether Charlotte did or did not call at the house of the priest is not known. That she would hesitate to tell even Emily if she did so is understandable; but the action of Lucy Snowe in *Villette* cannot be taken with any certainty as a guide to the doings of her creator years earlier. Perhaps the most interesting fact is that Charlotte, by the time she re-lived this particular incident in the novel, realized that the heroine would forfeit the reader's sympathy if she were to act as Charlotte led Emily to believe she herself had acted.[36] Charlotte ended her account of the incident with a warning to Emily: 'I think you had better not tell papa of this. He will not understand that it was only a freak, and will perhaps think I am going to turn Catholic.'[37]

From this time Charlotte slipped ever deeper into melancholy and inertia. The holidays dragged on. Her only companion in the school was one of the mistresses, Mdlle Blanche, for whom Charlotte felt such an aversion that she could not bring herself even to speak to her. The days seemed to grow longer and longer, to hold in their long hours almost unendurable weariness, but she dreaded the nights even more. In the day, her thoughts were morbid and tortured by self-loathing; at night her dreams were full of misery and horror.

So far was she in the clutches of hypochondria by the time the school reassembled that neither her work nor the resounding bustle of a hundred children was able to break the spell.[38] Her nostalgia for home, which she now identified naturally if mistakenly with peace of mind, became an *idée fixe*. This longing for home was aggravated by a sense of duty neglected, which grew more insistent in the face of an unhappiness that could so easily be regarded as just punishment. She was scarcely able to regard her state of mind as anything but a sin, and all feelings became magnified out of proportion to their true importance. All she could think of was her need for home and the quiet welcome to be expected there; no questions asked; a silence which, though at times it could madden, could also heal. She recalled with wistful envy the simplicity of life at Haworth: 'I should like uncommonly to be in the dining-room at home,' she tells Emily at the beginning of October, 'or in the kitchen, or in the back kitchen. I should like even to be cutting up the hash, with the clerk and some register people at the other table, and you standing by, watching that I put enough flour, and not too much pepper, and, above all, that I save the best pieces of the leg of mutton for Tiger and Keeper, the first of which personages would be jumping about the dish and carving-knife, and the latter standing like a devouring flame on the kitchen floor. To complete the picture, Tabby blowing the fire, in order to boil the potatoes to a sort of vegetable glue! How divine are these recollections to me at this moment!'[39] Yet Charlotte had no thought of going home at that time: 'I lack a real pretext for doing so,' she tells Emily; 'it is true this place is dismal to me, but I cannot go home without a fixed prospect when I get there; and this prospect must not be a situation; that would be jumping out of the frying-pan into the fire.'[40]

She longed, too, for some kind of assurance that she was really needed at Haworth—a further incentive that would enable her, even against her will, to break the link that bound her to the *pensionnat*: 'Tell me', she writes, 'whether papa really

wants me very much to come home, and whether you do likewise. I have an idea that I should be of no use there—a sort of
aged person upon the parish.'[41] That assurance she obtained; and,
feeling desolate still, and friendless, and without hope, life at the
school suddenly seemed impossible to endure a moment longer.
She gave notice to Madame Héger.[42] 'If it had depended on her',
Charlotte explained to Ellen a few days after, ' I should certainly
have soon been at liberty, but Monsieur Héger—having heard
of what was in agitation—sent for me the day after—and pronounced with vehemence his decision that I should not leave.
I could not at that time have persevered in my intention without
exciting him to passion, so I promised to stay a while longer—
how long that will be I do not know.'[43] But Charlotte's acquies-
cence brought her no nearer happiness or peace of mind. The
next day she scribbled a note of her feelings in a school book
during a lesson:[44] 'I am very cold—there is no Fire—I wish I
were at home with papa—Branwell—Emily—Anne and Tabby
—I am tired of being among foreigners—it is a dreary life—
especially as there is only one person in this house worthy of
being liked—also another, who seems a rosy sugar plum, but
I know her to be coloured chalk.'[45]

The very repetition of the names at home helped at such
times to soften the pangs of home-sickness; pangs which the
lack of physical comfort in the school did nothing to ease. But
Charlotte held on, hoping that life at the *pensionnat* would
change if she were patient, and determined, if this were not so,
to go back to Haworth sufficiently experienced to make her
school project more likely to succeed. She was desperately afraid
of idleness, of being unwanted and a burden on her family; and
her wish to leave Brussels was by no means wholehearted. So
she defied her own homesickness and the appeals of her family
to come home, and she refused Mary Taylor's advice to join
her in Germany: 'To leave a certainty for a complete uncertainty would be to the last degree imprudent,' she declared.[46]

Another month passed. Charlotte's year was running out.
Her loneliness remained unsatisfied. Héger was kind, helpful,
interested in her work and progress, but she saw little of him.
Madame Héger rarely spoke to her: 'I know you, living in the
country, can hardly believe it possible life can be monotonous
in the centre of a brilliant capital like Brussels,' she told Ellen;

'but so it is. I feel it most in the holidays, when all the girls and teachers go out to visit, and it sometimes happens that I am left, during several hours, quite alone, with four great desolate schoolrooms at my disposition. I try to read, I try to write; but in vain. I then wander from room to room, but the silence and loneliness of all the house weighs down one's spirits like lead. You will hardly believe that Madame Héger (good and kind as I have described her) never comes near me on these occasions. She is a reasonable and calm woman, but Nelly, as to warm-heartedness she has as much of that article as Mrs. Taylor.'[47] In spite of her depression Charlotte continued to speak of herself as well satisfied with her position; and she wanted Ellen to say so to any who asked about her.[48] Little more than a month had gone by, however, before Charlotte once again abandoned her attempt to stay at the school. She could not live any longer in the midst of coldness and suspicion, and she had lost hope that her earlier happiness might return. Her year ended in January; and although there had been a time when both she and the Hégers hoped that she would stay even longer at the school, it is unlikely that any of them now wished it.

In the middle of December Charlotte told Madame Héger that she would have to go at the end of the year.[49] This time no attempt was made to change her mind, and when the year ended Charlotte left the school[50] in which she had spent many miserable hours, but which had also seen some of her happiest moments; she said good-bye to the Hégers whom she was not destined to see again; she saw the last of Brussels, in which she was never again to set foot; and in a short while she was on the seas, heading towards England, which she was never again to leave.

XVI

THE SCHOOL PLAN FAILS

Charlotte home again. Good reports of Anne and Branwell. Charlotte's depression. Development of Emily as poet. Plan to begin a school in the parsonage. It fails. Reactions of the four Brontës. Charlotte's letters to M. Héger. Branwell and Mrs. Robinson.

ON the third day of January 1844, Charlotte arrived home. Anne and Branwell had just come back from Thorp Green for Christmas, and all four Brontës were at the parsonage together for a few days. Anne brought back with her a spaniel, Flossy, that the Robinson girls had given her as a Christmas gift.[1] Anne was by this time much more than governess to the two girls; she had become their friend and confidante as well as instructor, although she deplored their worldly attitude of mind—an echo of their mother.

Branwell, by what he said, seemed to have settled down well at Thorp Green. Mr. Robinson, old and an invalid, had little to do with his son's tutor, but Mrs. Robinson, younger and attractive, had already shown him some signs of favour.[2]

Charlotte was well satisfied with what she heard of Anne and Branwell: 'They are both wondrously valued in their situations,' she told Ellen.[3] In this letter, Charlotte explained something of her feelings when leaving Héger:[4] 'I suffered much before I left Brussels,' she wrote. 'I think, however long I live, I shall not forget what the parting with M. Héger cost me; it grieved me so much to grieve him, who has been so true, kind and disinterested a friend. At parting he gave me a kind of diploma certifying my abilities as a teacher, sealed with the seal of the Athénée Royal, of which he is professor. He wanted me to take one of his little girls with me, but I refused. I was surprised also at the degree of regret expressed by my Belgian pupils, when they knew I was going to leave. I did not think it had been in their phlegmatic nature.'[5]

The peace of Haworth, for which Charlotte had longed whilst in Brussels, now began to take on another and less pleasant form: 'Haworth seems such a lonely, quiet spot buried away from the world,' she told her friend.[6] Charlotte had, indeed, exchanged one form of unhappiness for another. In satisfying her pride, and her sense of duty at Haworth, she had to bear with the absence, almost certainly final, of the stimulating influence that had drawn her back to the *pensionnat* a year before; and she was reluctant to face the thought that she had disappointed the man whom, of all people except perhaps her family, she would have wished to think well of her. Charlotte also missed the activity of the school, the sense of power she had enjoyed as mistress, and the feeling that she was doing something useful which would give her a definite place in the world. 'I do not know whether you feel as I do,' she remarked to Ellen sadly, 'but there are times now when it appears to me as if all my ideas and feelings, except a few friendships and affections, are changed from what they used to be; something in me, which used to be enthusiasm, is tamed down and broken. I have fewer illusions; what I wish for now is active exertion—a stake in life . . . it seems as if I ought to be working and braving the rough realities of the world as other people do. It is, however, my duty to restrain this feeling at present, and I will endeavour to do so.'[7]

The experience Charlotte had gained now seemed almost useless. The condition of Mr. Brontë's eyes had grown steadily worse during the past year; a cataract had formed and his sight was threatened; and, having come home to a great extent on his account, she did not feel free to leave him again even to work in England.[8] She had therefore to abandon her cherished school plan, and to refuse a good post offered her in Manchester.[9] She began to feel Haworth close in upon her ominously, its peacefulness rapidly assuming an air of stagnation. She had visions of a reluctantly cloistered spinsterhood, of a life divorced from culture, advancement, friendship—fears never long out of Charlotte's mind since she had grown up, but never so insistent as now, when she saw slipping away all hope of these essentials to happiness that had seemed within her grasp at Brussels.

A month or two after her return to England, Charlotte spent some weeks with Ellen at Brookroyd; but the friendship, though remaining steadfast and a source of comfort to Charlotte, had moved from its original emotional plane; and Charlotte's sojourn in Brussels had driven a further wedge of unshared intimacies between the two girls. There had never been any intellectual companionship between them. Now, Ellen's company was restful to Charlotte, but little more.

As a substitute for Héger, Emily afforded small comfort to her sister. The two girls walked frequently on the moors, they spent their evenings and a great part of their days together, and Charlotte at least had much to say to Emily.[10] They loved one another, Charlotte especially leaning towards Emily as Branwell lost his high place in her esteem. Yet Charlotte could not discuss the one memory of Brussels which she longed to share; she could not expect more from her sister than silent disapproval; and the knowledge that this subject lay undiscussed between them formed a barrier to complete intimacy. Even Charlotte's frequent tirades about her frustrated ambition, her sense of encirclement and futility at Haworth, could hope for no more than a patient listener in Emily. The younger girl had no wish to be elsewhere, she had lost all desire to make a name for herself in the world; and since her months in Brussels, she had moved away from the measure of agreement with Charlotte which had induced her originally to agree to the school scheme.

Ellen sent back by Charlotte some flower seeds for Emily, the gardener of the family.[11] Charlotte, returning her sister's thanks and asking, on her behalf, how the seeds should be sown, told Ellen that the parsonage cat had died. 'It is piteous to see even an animal lying lifeless,' she remarks rather sententiously, and goes on to say, 'Emily *is* sorry.'[12]

Emily's liking for animals was characteristic of the solitary, uncommunicative person with strong feelings. Animals had none of the frailties she was so ready to condemn in human beings. They were loyal, sincere, simple in thought and action —all qualities she admired. Someone who knew her said: 'She never showed regard to any human creature; all her love was reserved for animals.'[13]

The wildness and intractability of some animals also commended them to this girl of a similar nature. Yet though attracted by ferocity, which she had strength to master, Emily was also drawn by the inarticulate and helpless.

A great deal has been made, naturally enough, of Emily's dramatic encounters with animals. We hear how, with set lips, white face, and glowing eyes she punished the disobedient Keeper, striking him coldly, remorselessly, fearlessly with her bare fists at the bottom of the parsonage stairs while the rest of the family listened with beating hearts to the savage growls that turned to whines and moans.[14] We hear how, bitten by a maddened dog, she herself cauterized the wound, without a word to anyone in the house, by thrusting a red-hot poker on her arm.[15] These incidents, though they illuminate one side of Emily's character, have their complements, less stirring in the telling, but no less important as a revelation of her nature. There is Emily's determination to offer the maddened dog water to drink;[16] her gentle tending of Keeper's hurts the moment his punishment had ended;[17] her habit of reading whilst sitting before the fire on the dining-room rug with her arm round Keeper's neck;[18] her way, on the moors, of taking fledgling birds into her hands, so softly that they had no fear, and telling stories to them;[19] her frequent arrival home from the moors with one of these birds or a young rabbit, talking gently to it, confident that her words were understood:[20] these were incidents that display an Emily as real as the stern dispenser of justice, the unflinching self-doctor.

Emily accused herself of idleness while Charlotte was at Brussels, and Anne and Branwell at Thorp Green. Charlotte pooh-poohed the idea: '*You* call yourself idle! absurd, absurd!'[21] —and it is difficult to see how Emily could have found time to idle. Tabby was not able to do much in the house. A girl, Hannah, had come and gone, leaving Emily with much on her hands.[22] Mr. Brontë needed looking after more than usual because of his failing eyesight. The pets had to be exercised and cared for, the garden tended. Emily herself did the ironing and most of the cooking. She was also determined that her education, so hardly gained, should not stop abruptly because she had chosen not to return to Brussels. She was often to be seen through the open kitchen door—which looked out on to the moors—studying German by means of a book propped up before her as she kneaded the dough for the household bread.[23]

Of this time, free for the moment from self-reproach, Emily has left record:

> All day I've toiled but not with pain
> In learning's golden mine
> And now at eventide again
> The moonbeams softly shine.

There is no snow upon the ground
No frost on wind or wave
The south wind blew with gentlest sound
And broke their icy grave.

'Tis sweet to wander here at night
To watch the winter die
With heart as summer sunshine light
And warm as summer sky.

O may I never lose the peace
That lulls me gently now
Though time should change my youthful face
And years should shade my brow!

True to myself and true to all
May I be healthful still
And turn away from passion's call
And curb my own wild will.[24]

When she accused herself of idleness, however, Emily had in mind her hours of reverie: this was no new thing with her, indeed, but it fed on solitude; and, usually after dark, she would sit before the fire or lie on her bed for hours, her thoughts far away. 'I have dreamed in my life dreams that have stayed with me ever after, and changed my ideas,' Emily was to write later; 'they have gone through and through me like wine through water, and altered the colour of my mind.'[25] But for all her love of these solitary hours, she many a time felt guilty—and never more so than now, when faced by the more spectacular industry of her sisters, and even of her brother.

Yet Emily's time was not wasted as she sometimes thought. From her meditative hours, in a hollow of the moors, before the dining-room fire, watching the simmering pot in the kitchen or looking at the sky from her bedroom window, came the poems that she was writing now with ever greater assurance. This increase of lyrical power, and the subjects inspiring it were soon to be seen when she sang of her beloved stars:

Ah! why, because the dazzling sun
Restored my earth to joy
Have you departed, every one,
And left a desert sky?

All through the night your glorious eyes
Were gazing down in mine
And with a full heart's thankful sighs
I blessed that watch divine!

I was at peace, and drank your beams
As they were life to me
And revelled in my changeful dreams
Like petrel on the sea.

Thought followed thought—star followed star
Through boundless regions on
While one sweet influence near and far
Thrilled through and proved us one.

Why did the morning rise to break
So great, so pure a spell,
And scorch with fire the tranquil cheek
Where your cool radiance fell?

Blood-red he rose, and arrow-straight
His fierce beams struck my brow
The soul of Nature sprang elate,
But mine sank sad and low!

My lids closed down—yet through their veil
I saw him blazing still
And bathe in gold the misty dale
And flash upon the hill.

I turned me to the pillow then
To call back Night and see
Your worlds of solemn light again
Throb with my heart and me!

It would not do—the pillow glowed
And glowed both roof and floor
And birds sang loudly in the wood
And fresh winds shook the door.

The curtains waved, the wakened flies
Were murmuring round my room
Imprisoned there till I should rise
And give them leave to roam.

ANNE, EMILY, AND CHARLOTTE
from a painting by Branwell

EMILY'S SCHOOL AT LAW HILL

O Stars and Dreams and Gentle Night—
O Night and Stars return!
And hide me from the hostile light
That does not warm, but burn—

That drains the blood of suffering men—
Drinks tears instead of dew—
Let me sleep through his blinding reign
And only wake with you![26]

As the years passed, Emily had grown more and more pre-occupied with the struggle to discover the true vision of life. She thought at length about her purpose in the world—although, unlike most highly introspective people, she positively enjoyed the practical side of life. She worked on, thinking and dreaming; but her struggle to win complete autonomy had now become a passion; and, as time passed, she threw off, more and more, all human teaching, ideas, influences that fettered her judgement and will, and hindered absolute self-knowledge:

Often rebuked, yet always back returning
To those first feelings that were born with me
And leaving busy chase of wealth and learning
For idle dreams of things which cannot be:

Today I will not seek the shadowy region
Its unsustaining vastness waxes drear
And visions rising, legion after legion,
Bring the unreal world too strangely near.

I'll walk, but not in old heroic traces
And not in paths of high morality
And not among the half-distinguished faces
The clouded forms of long-past history.

I'll walk where my own nature would be leading—
It vexes me to choose another guide—
Where the grey flocks in ferny glens are feeding
Where the wild wind blows on the mountain side.

What have those lonely mountains worth revealing?
More glory and more grief than I can tell:
The earth that wakes one human heart to feeling
Can centre both the worlds of Heaven and Hell.[27]

This poem, with its profound and eloquent statement of Emily's philosophy, was not one of those chosen by her as worthy of a more permanent record; for in February 1844, a few weeks after Charlotte returned from Brussels, Emily had begun to transcribe what she regarded as her most satisfactory poems into two little books—one for her Gondal poems, the other for her secret, directly personal verses. Charlotte, who knew that Emily and Anne occasionally wrote poems, was not shewn these books, which were kept locked in Emily's desk.[28]

Charlotte, restless, unhappy, and passionately determined to make something of her life, though repulsed by circumstances was by no means defeated. Already she was forming a plan whereby the hopes she had aroused in her sisters, and still more in herself, might even yet be realized, and their education, acquired at so considerable an expense, might yet repay them. In June, when Branwell and Anne came home for their summer holiday, and Ellen paid a visit to the parsonage, this plan was discussed. The school, Charlotte suggested, might now be set up in the parsonage, suitably enlarged. Mr. Brontë could then be cared for, and the sisters could live together again, doing their duty to their father, and making something of themselves.[29] At no time did Charlotte suggest that she was moved by the desire to teach; it was plain that the school was merely a means to an end. The poverty of the methods by which women might then break the bonds of domesticity is shown by the fact that Charlotte faced with actual enthusiasm the prospect of teaching, which she detested. But then she had at the back of her mind an even more powerful inducement. If the school was successful, she would have the money, and the prestige, to revisit Brussels.

Branwell's part, if any, in the plan was not made clear. The three girls now possessed sufficient capital, left to them by their aunt, to set the school on its feet.[30] They would be able to pay for the proposed additions to the parsonage. All three had now gained valuable experience in the teaching of children and had mastered the subjects necessary to form a reasonable syllabus. There remained only the promise of pupils. But pupils were precisely what the Brontë sisters could not obtain. Charlotte drew up and had printed a prospectus,[31] which she sent to all parents, with children of suitable age, known to her.[32] Ellen

and other friends also distributed prospectuses. But not one
inquiry was received.[33]

The reactions of the sisters to this news varied greatly. To
Anne, this final failure of the school scheme came as a cruel
blow. She, more than any other of her family, felt the need of
home—and now more than ever before. The company of Branwell at Thorp Green, so eagerly sought by her, and for which
she had planned with such hope, was proving worse than useless. His behaviour was already causing her uneasiness and
alarm.

Branwell's intense excitement when he visited Halifax was
commented upon by his friends.[34] Charlotte also noted that her
brother was nervy and irritable during his summer holidays;[35]
but this she attributed wholly to his health: 'My poor brother
is always ill,' she wrote.[36] She was beginning to accept Branwell
as a weakling—but, for the time, with affection. Contempt and
disapproval were to come later.[37] But to Anne, living in the
same house with her brother and Mrs. Robinson, Branwell's
behaviour had another and more obvious significance—a significance necessarily lost upon Charlotte, and of which the
youngest Brontë, whose uneasiness had not yet resolved itself
into words, would not speak. Now that the school plan had
finally failed, Anne had to face, not only an indefinite separation
from her home and sisters, but also the loss of whatever peace
and contentment she had managed to build about her at Thorp
Green.

To Emily, the failure of the school plan came as an impersonal reinforcement of the struggle in her mind, and, with
Charlotte's plain unhappiness and Branwell's decline before her,
any ambition she may once have felt was finally extinguished.
She gave up all thought of material advancement, and dwelt increasingly on that which she had come to see must be master in
her house. The preservation of her integrity was her first and
chief concern:

> When weary with the long day's care
> And earthly change from pain to pain,
> And lost and ready to despair
> Thy kind voice calls me back again—
> O my true Friend, I am not lone
> While thou canst speak with such a tone!

So hopeless is the world without
The world within I doubly prize
Thy world, where guile and hate and doubt
And cold suspicion never rise—
Where thou and I and Liberty
Have undisputed sovereignty.

What matters it that all around
Danger and grief and darkness lie
If but within our bosom's bound
We hold a bright unsullied sky
Warm with ten thousand mingled rays
Of suns that know no winter days?

Reason indeed may oft complain
For Nature's sad reality,
And tell the suffering heart how vain
Its cherished dreams must always be
And Truth may rudely trample down
The flowers of Fancy newly blown.

But thou art ever there to bring
The hovering visions back and breathe
New glories o'er the blighted spring
And call a lovelier life from death
And whisper with a voice divine
Of real worlds as bright as thine.

I trust not to thy phantom bliss,
Yet still in evening's quiet hour
With never-failing thankfulness
I welcome thee benignant power
Sure solacer of human cares
And brighter hope when hope despairs.[38]

Yet her renunciation was not made without a struggle:

O, thy bright eyes must answer now,
When Reason, with a scornful brow,
Is mocking at my overthrow;
O, thy sweet tongue must plead for me
And tell why I have chosen thee!

Stern Reason is to judgement come
Arrayed in all her forms of gloom;

Wilt thou my advocate be dumb?
No, radiant angel, speak and say
Why I did cast the world away:

Why I have persevered to shun
The common paths that others run
And on a strange road journeyed on,
Heedless alike of Wealth and Power—
Of Glory's Wreath and Pleasure's Flower.

These once indeed seemed Beings divine,
And they perchance heard vows of mine
And saw my offerings on their shrine—
But careless gifts are seldom prized
And mine were worthily despised;

So with a ready heart I swore
To seek their altar stone no more,
And gave my spirit to adore
Thee, ever present, phantom thing,
My Slave, my Comrade and my King!

A slave because I rule thee still
Incline thee to my changeful will
And make thy influence good or ill—
A comrade, for by day and night
Thou art my intimate delight—

My Darling Pain that wounds and sears
And wrings a blessing out from tears
By deadening me to real cares;
And yet a king—though prudence well
Have taught thy subject to rebel—

And am I wrong to worship where
Faith cannot doubt nor Hope despair,
Since my own soul can grant my prayer?
Speak God of Visions, plead for me
And tell why I have chosen thee![39]

To Charlotte the collapse of the school scheme came as a bitter disappointment. Every effort to make something of her life had been frustrated. She seemed tied inexorably to a future of pandering to the whims of a half-blind father in an inaccessible

village far from the springs of life and action as she visualized
them. The life of literature, of art, of brilliant conversation, and
of romance after which her heart longed was reduced to books
from the library at Keighley, an eight mile walk; to her painstaking drawings; to meetings, giving little satisfaction to either
party, with the local curates, who afforded her scope only
for analysis of character and for exercise of a sharp tongue; and,
finally, to walks and talks with Emily, whom Charlotte no
more than half understood, and who could not be persuaded into
full confidence.[40]

Thus Charlotte fell into depression of mind and a corresponding weariness of body. Her life seemed purposeless. She had
little or nothing to do. Emily had long since made the ordering
of the house her prerogative, and Charlotte's inclinations were
not towards housework.[41] Soon, even worse befell. She again
strained her eyes, and had to give up drawing, reading, or writing
for hours, sometimes for days at a time.

Her depression was mainly due, however, to the silence of
Héger, to whom she had written often. His only reply, in April,
suggested a six months' interval between the letters, which threatened already to become an embarrassment.[42] Charlotte had replied at once, then again, ignoring the time limit, at the end of
July, when the school circulars were being printed: 'I am well
aware that it is not my turn to write to you,' she said, 'but as
Mrs. Wheelwright is going to Brussels and is kind enough to
take charge of a letter—it seems to me that I ought not to neglect
so favourable an opportunity of writing to you. I am very
pleased that the school-year is nearly over and that the holidays
are approaching—I am pleased on your account, Monsieur—
for I am told that you are working too hard and that your health
has suffered somewhat in consequence. For that reason I refrain
from uttering a single complaint for your long silence—I would
rather remain six months without receiving news from you
than add one grain to the weight, already too heavy, which
overwhelms you. I know well that it is now the period of compositions, that it will soon be that of examinations, and later
on of prizes—and during all that time you are condemned to
breathe the stifling atmosphere of the class-rooms—to wear
yourself out—to explain, to question, to talk all day, and then
in the evening you have all those wretched compositions to

read, to correct, almost to re-write. Ah, Monsieur! I once wrote you a letter that was less than reasonable, because sorrow was at my heart; but I shall do so no more—I shall try to be selfish no longer; and even while I look upon your letters as one of the greatest felicities known to me, I shall await the receipt of them until it pleases you and suits you to send me any. Meanwhile, I may well send you a little letter from time to time:—you have authorised me to do so. I greatly fear I shall forget French, for I am firmly convinced that I shall see you again some day—I know not how or when—but it must be, for I wish it so much, and then I should not wish to remain dumb before you—it would be too sad to see you and not be able to speak to you. To avoid such a misfortune I learn every day by heart half a page of French from a book written in familiar style: and I take pleasure in learning this lesson, Monsieur; as I pronounce the French words it seems to me as if I were chatting with you. I have just been offered a situation as first governess in a large school in Manchester, with a salary of £100 (i.e. 2,500 francs) per annum. I cannot accept it, for in accepting it I should have to leave my father, and that I cannot do. Nevertheless I have a plan—(when one lives retired the brain goes on working; there is the desire of occupation, the wish to embark on an active career.) Our parsonage is rather a large house—with a few alterations there will be room for five or six boarders. If I could find this number of children of good family, I should devote myself to their education. Emily does not care much for teaching, but she would look after the housekeeping, and, although something of a recluse, she is too good-hearted not to do all she could for the well-being of the children. Moreover, she is very generous, and as for order, economy, strictness—and diligent work—all of them things very essential in a school—I willingly take that upon myself. That, Monsieur, is my plan, which I have already explained to my father and which he approves. It only remains to find the pupils—rather a difficult thing—for we live rather far from towns, and people do not greatly care about crossing the hills which form as it were a barrier around us. But the task that is without difficulty is also without merit; there is great interest in triumphing over obstacles. I do not say I shall succeed, but I shall try to succeed—the effort alone will do me good. There is nothing I fear so much as idleness, the want of occupation, inactivity, the lethargy of the faculties: when the body is idle, the spirit suffers painfully. I should not know this lethargy if I could write. Formerly I passed whole days and weeks and months in writing, not wholly without result, for Southey and Coleridge—two of our best authors, to whom I sent certain manuscripts—were good enough to express their approval; but now my sight is too weak to write—were I to write much I should become blind. This weakness of sight is a terrible hindrance to me. Otherwise do you know what I should do, Monsieur?—I should write a book, and I should dedicate it to my literature-master—to the only master I ever had—to you, Monsieur. I have often told you in French how much I respect you—how much I am indebted to your goodness, to your advice; I should like to say it once in English. But that cannot be—it is not to be thought of. The career of letters is closed to me—only that of teaching is open. It does not offer the same attractions; never mind, I shall enter it, and if I do not go far it shall not be for want of industry. You too, Monsieur— you wished to be a barrister—destiny or providence made you a professor; you are happy in spite of it.'[43] Charlotte added a postscript: 'I have not begged you to write to me soon as I fear to importune you—but you are too kind to forget that I wish it all the same—yes, I wish it greatly. Enough: after all, do as you wish, Monsieur. If, then, I received a letter, and if I thought that you had written it *out of pity*—I should feel deeply wounded . . . . Once more goodbye, Monsieur; it hurts to say goodbye even in a letter. Oh, it is certain that I shall see you again—it must be so—for as soon as I have earned enough money to go to Brussels I shall go there—and I shall see you again if only for a moment.'[44]

Héger did not reply to this letter; and three months later, in October, when the school scheme had failed, when the thought of his former kindness and interest alone sustained Charlotte against almost complete despair, she wrote to him once more. 'I am in high glee this morning,' she told him, '—and that has rarely happened to me these last two years. It is because a gentleman of my acquaintance[45] is going to Brussels, and has offered to take charge of a letter for you—which letter he will deliver to you himself, or else his sister,[46] so that I shall be certain that you have received it. I am not going to write a long letter; in the first place, I have not the time—it must leave at once; and then, I am afraid of worrying you. I would only ask you if you heard from me at the beginning of May and again in the month of August? For six months I have been waiting a letter from Monsieur—six months' waiting is very long, you know. However, I do not complain, and I shall be richly rewarded for a little sorrow if you will now write a letter and give it to this gentleman—or to his sister—who will hand it to me without fail. I shall be satisfied with the letter however brief it be—only do not forget to tell me of your health, Monsieur, and how Madame and the children are, and the governesses and pupils. My father and sisters send you their respects. My father's infirmity increases little by little. Nevertheless he is not yet entirely blind. My sisters are well, but my poor brother is always ill. Farewell, Monsieur; I am depending on soon having your news. The idea delights me, for the remembrance of your kindness will never fade from my memory, and as long as that remembrance endures the respect with which it has inspired me will endure likewise.'[47] Charlotte adds in a postscript: 'I have just had bound all the books you gave me when I was at Brussels. I take delight in contemplating them; they make quite a little library. To begin with, there are the complete works of Bernardine de St. Pierre—the Pensées de Pascal—a book of poetry, two German books—and (worth all the rest) two discourses of Monsieur le Professeur Héger, delivered at the distribution of prizes of the Athénée Royal.'[48]

Branwell could have taken little more than a detached interest in the fortunes of the plan hatching so earnestly in the parsonage during his summer holidays. He was apparently intended to play no part in the school, but in any event he was altogether too engrossed in his own emotions. Romance of a kind had finally entered Branwell's life without waiting upon imaginative creation: 'This lady', he was to write later of Mrs. Robinson, '(though her husband detested me) showed me a degree of kindness which, when I was deeply grieved one day at her husband's conduct, ripened into declarations of more than ordinary feeling. My admiration of her mental and personal attractions, my knowledge of her unselfish sincerity, her sweet temper, and unwearied care for others, with but unrequited return where most should have been given . . . although she is seventeen years my senior, all combined to an attachment on my part, and led to reciprocations which I had little looked for. During three years I had daily "troubled pleasure soon chastised by fear"....'[49]

Whatever the exact truth (if there is such a thing) about Branwell and Mrs. Robinson, he certainly imagined himself to be passionately in love with her. She did not return his feelings, it is plain—he was simply a welcome diversion in a life of boredom—but she gave him enough encouragement for him to build his fantasies on. His letters show him to be morbid, extravagant, paranoiac, and even caddish about his relationship with her, but he could not make up something out of nothing. He was also largely at the mercy of his Brontë temperament, with its hyper-intensity of feeling, allied to a character naturally weak and still further weakened by his family's over-indulgence and too high expectations. So he flung himself into the raptures and tortures of love as he had always flung himself into every experience. He could not think seriously, or for long, of anything else.

The breach between him and his family was widened still further when Charlotte left him out of her latest plan. She thought of him as a hopeless weakling; Anne was horrified by his excesses; from Emily alone, of his three sisters, was Branwell now likely to obtain more than a passing or dutiful attention.

XVII

CALM BEFORE STORM

All the Brontës together again. Charlotte on marriage. Another letter to M. Héger. Mary Taylor off to New Zealand. She advises Charlotte to leave home. Charlotte refuses. Her dissatisfaction. Anne's troubles at Thorp Green. Emily's growing contentment. Her poems.

AT Christmas all the Brontës were again at home. Ellen asked Charlotte and Anne to spend Christmas with her. Emily was not included in the invitation.[1] In the event, none of the sisters accepted the offer, but in her letter telling Ellen that they could not come, Charlotte gave brief character sketches of her youngest sister and of Ellen, and, incidentally, of herself. Ellen had been given one of Flossy's puppies: 'The Catastrophe, which you relate so calmly about your book-muslin dress, lace bertha, etc. convulsed me with cold shudderings of horror,' exclaimed Charlotte, '—you have reason to curse the day when so fatal a present was offered you. As to that infamous little *bitch*—the perfect serenity with which you endured the disaster proves most fully to me that you would make the best wife, mother and mistress of a family in the world. You and Anne are a pair, for marvellous philosophical powers of endurance—no spoilt dinners—scorched linen, dirtied carpets—torn sofa-covers, squealing brats, cross husbands would ever discompose either of you. You ought never to marry a good-tempered man— such a union would be mingling honey with sugar.'[2]

Charlotte's thoughts were often upon a husband and lover. It was true of her, as of Anne, that the need for love came first in her life; only the nature of the love desired differed as the character of the sisters differed. All Charlotte's rough denials, all her scathing comments on men, were but so many affirmations of that which she was so busy denying. That she despised the husband-hunter, the woman who would at all costs be married, is without question; but she knew what she was missing as the years passed and the hope of a true marriage grew fainter. Underlying all her thought, all that she was to write, glowed this deep, unalterable longing for love; not the puny, self-indulgent, mercenary, ignoble relationship between man and woman she saw so often about her, but a forthright, self-forgetful union—a marriage of true minds.

Christmas passed peacefully and even gaily—the last time peace, or even a semblance of it, was to be found when all the Brontës were together. Branwell was quieter and more amenable than he had been in the summer;[3] and though Anne had no cause to feel easier about him, to Charlotte at this time he actually appeared in better health than a few months earlier.[4] The latter part of the holiday was enlivened by a visit from Mary Taylor;[5] yet the usual good effect of her brisk, hearty, and affectionate personality was overcast by the news she brought with her. For Mary had decided finally to go to New Zealand. She intended to leave England within the next few days.[6]

For Charlotte, Mary's last visit held a double sorrow. Mary it was who had taken Charlotte's recent letter to Héger at Brussels; and she had returned empty-handed. While her visitor remained at the parsonage, and in between the walks, talks, music, and occasional fun of the party, Charlotte withdrew to make yet another passionate and pathetic appeal to her master in Brussels:[7] 'Mr. Taylor has returned,' she wrote. 'I asked him if he had a letter for me. "No; nothing." "Patience," said I— "His sister will be here soon." Miss Taylor has returned. "I have nothing for you from Monsieur Héger," says she; "Neither letter nor message." Having realised the meaning of these words, I said to myself what I should say to another similarly placed: "You must be resigned, and above all do not grieve at a misfortune which you have not deserved." I strove to restrain my tears, to utter no complaint. But when one does not complain, when one seeks to dominate oneself with a tyrant's grip, the faculties start into rebellion, and one pays for external calm with an internal struggle that is almost unbearable. Day and night I find neither rest nor peace. If I sleep I am disturbed by tormenting dreams in which I see you always severe, always grave, always incensed against me. Forgive me, then, Monsieur, if I adopt the course of writing to you again. How can I endure life if I make no effort to ease its sufferings? I know that you will be irritated when you read this letter. You will say once more that I am hysterical—that I have black thoughts, etc. So be it, Monsieur; I do not seek to justify myself; I submit to every sort of reproach. All I know is that I cannot, that I will not, resign myself to lose wholly the friendship of my master. I would rather suffer the greatest physical pain than always have my heart lacerated by smarting regrets. If my master withdraws his friendship from me entirely I shall be altogether without hope; if he gives me a little—just a little—I shall be satisfied—happy; I shall have reason for living on, for working. Monsieur, the poor have not need of much to sustain them—they ask only for the crumbs that fall from the rich men's table—but if they are refused the crumbs they die of hunger. Nor do I, either, need much affection from those I love. I should not know what to do with a friendship entire and complete—I am not used to it. But you showed me a *little* of your interest when I was your pupil in Brussels, and I hold on to the maintenance of that *little* interest—I hold on to it as I would hold on to life. You will tell me perhaps—"I take not the slightest interest in you, Mademoiselle Charlotte. You are no longer an inmate of my House; I have forgotten you." Well, Monsieur, tell me so frankly. It will be a shock to me. It matters not. It would be less dreadful than uncertainty. I shall not re-read this letter. I send it as I have written it. Nevertheless, I have a hidden consciousness that some people, cold and common-sense, in reading it would say—"She is talking nonsense." I would avenge myself on such persons in no other way than by wishing them one single day of the torments which I have suffered for eight months. We should then see if they would not talk nonsense too. One suffers in silence so long as one has the strength to do so, and when that strength gives out one speaks without too carefully measuring one's words. I wish Monsieur happiness and prosperity.'[8]

Charlotte had, as usual, to wait and hope for an answer; there was nothing else she could do. Meanwhile, when her eyes allowed her, she continued to pore over whatever French newspapers and books she could lay hands upon. Desperate at Héger's indifference, she spoke of taking a position in Paris—to attempt to go again to Brussels directly was of course not to be thought of.[9] But it was a vain dream, and she knew it; she was tied to Haworth and her father. Her self-respect was shaken by thoughts of the letter she had written; yet as the days, the weeks, and months passed without reply she had to face a future so bleak as to threaten the remnants of hope and resolution within her. At Haworth, she was no one, a person without a future. Her spirits failed. She felt old and useless. 'I can hardly tell you how time gets on here,' she wrote. 'There is no event whatever to mark its progress—one day resembles another, and all have heavy, lifeless physiognomies—Sunday, baking day and Saturday are the only ones that bear the slightest distinctive mark. Meantime life wears away—I shall soon be thirty and I have done nothing yet. Sometimes I get melancholy at the prospect before and behind me—yet it is wrong and foolish to repine—and undoubtedly my duty directs me to stay at home for the present. There was a time when Haworth was a very pleasant place to me, it is not so now—I feel as if we were all buried here—I long to travel—to work—to live a life of action.'[10]

The kind of visits Charlotte was able to make occasionally did little for her. She went to Hunsworth, to be with Mary Taylor just before she left England, but the stay only heightened her dissatisfaction.[11] The occasion did not make for happiness, and some of the talks they had made matters even worse. Mary, who was pained and indignant to see Charlotte throwing away her life at Haworth, urged her to follow her own example, and to leave home. Taxed by Mary about her life at home, Charlotte 'owned she did not like it. Her health was weak. She said she would like any change at first, as she had liked Brussels at first, and she thought that there must be some possibility for some people of having a life of more variety and more communion with human kind, but she saw none for her.'[12] Mary pressed her point warmly. She told her friend that she ought not to stay at home; that to spend the next five years there, in solitude and poor health, would ruin her: 'Think of what you'll be five years hence!' Mary began; but, seeing a dark shadow come over Charlotte's face at the thought, she stopped, and told her not to cry. Charlotte did not cry, but went on walking up and down the room, and said a little later, 'But I intend to stay, Polly.'[13] Soon afterwards she left Hunsworth, not altogether sorry to be going, even though she knew she might never see her friend again. She went back to her eventless days, her unrequited longing, and her letters to Ellen—filled mostly with superficial news and diatribes against the curates who now buzzed like flies about the parsonage, avoiding encounters with Emily, but attracted to the slightly more accessible Charlotte with her sharp and lively tongue.

Anne, though busier, was not less wretched at Thorp Green than Charlotte at Haworth. The years away from home tried her clinging, affectionate nature even more than the sympathetic Charlotte realized, and she was now horrified by Branwell's behaviour and full of fears for the future—fears that Charlotte could not even dream of. The least suspicious mind could scarcely have avoided conclusions that formed themselves as the days passed at Thorp Green; the least sensitive mind could scarcely have failed to feel something of the suspense that worried Anne. Branwell was not made for concealment. His moments of delirious joy and extravagant dejection were plain for all to see; nor could the cause remain hidden for long.

The only one of the Brontës to feel some peace of mind at this time was Emily, now settled determinedly in her beloved home. Her increasing periods of calm, her moments of happiness, sometimes even of triumph, and, more rarely still, of a positive exaltation, came from her mastery of an unruly and passionate will, and from her growing sense of detachment from the life about her, even when she was in the midst of it. This remoteness, which piqued Charlotte sorely, gave Emily much satisfaction, which appears more than once in verses that show a great advance on any she had written before. But Emily does not seem to have been aware of their merit. Her mind was divided; she wanted to be a poet but she did not think of herself as a poet, and she suspected weakness in this method of expressing herself.[14] So she made light of her poems, and hid the books in which they were written; ashamed, not so much of what she wrote as of her surrender to the impulse which urged her to write. In her eyes this surrender could not be justified by talk of art. Emily would, indeed, have expressed herself pretty bluntly had anyone spoken to her in such terms.

It is precisely this fugitive, instinctive character of Emily's poems that first singles them out. Despite the occasional revision that, for all her indifferent opinion of the poems, the artist in her felt impelled to make, her verses are essentially spontaneous; and it is in this spontaneity that their charm and much of their power lie. As poet, Emily has a child's impulsive outpouring of thought and emotion, a child's directness of vision. Her poems also have the disadvantages of immaturity—in technique, which she never fully mastered, in grammatical error, in clumsy conveyance of idea, and in rhymes which are often poor and sometimes downright bad. At times, she lacks a sense of rhythm and music, and many of her lines are marred by poetic clichés, borrowed frequently from Cowper, whose influence on the Brontës was almost wholly unfortunate.

All these characteristics of the child are found in Emily as poet. Anything but childish, however, is the mastery—casual though it may seem—of word and swift unimpeded line, the depth of passion and the expression of mystic joy. Emily wrote with power because she felt strongly and saw clearly. She wrote casually because she used the medium of poetry with reluctance. She does not embellish her lines. She makes no attempt to woo the reader. Deep feeling forced utterance from her. She had something to say, and she said it, with passion, without ornament, in words of the utmost simplicity.

This simplicity often appears merely naïve, the thought crude and the expression commonplace. Emily's use of the debased poetic vocabulary of the age (of which Charlotte as poet is a lamentable example) is a handicap to full appreciation of her work. But when the literal meaning of her words is accepted, as she intended, her poems appear more and more as the sometimes great and almost always remarkable things they are. Emily's verses remained her servants. She did not cultivate verbal beauty; nevertheless it glows from her lines with sombre power.[15]

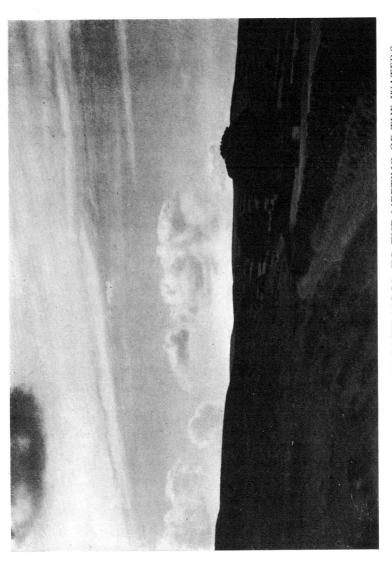

THE TRACK ACROSS HAWORTH MOOR TO THE MEETING OF THE WATERS

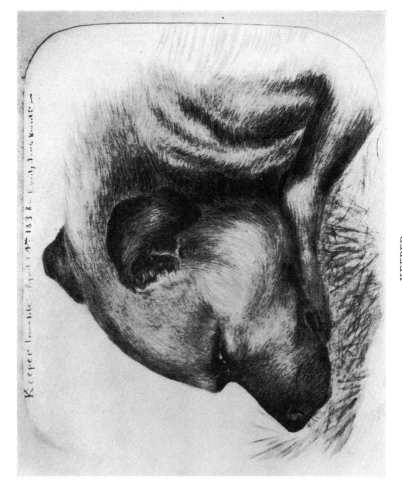

Keeper from life April 24th 1838 Emily Jane Brontë —

KEEPER.

from a water-colour sketch by Emily

XVIII

BRANWELL COMES HOME

Emily as business woman. A new curate at Haworth. A letter from M. Héger. Anne comes home. Charlotte on holiday. Branwell in disgrace. Reactions of two sisters to their brother's decline.

THIS transcendental poet was also a careful business woman, though at times a somewhat obstinate one. Emily, as the only sister at home after Miss Branwell's death, had been left to invest the money bequeathed to the Brontë sisters by their aunt. She had bought shares in the York and North Midland Railway. At this time, just before the widespread uncertainty that was to be felt in railways as a form of investment, Emily's choice had been much approved by Charlotte, who saw their legacies growing larger. 'Emily', her elder sister told Miss Wooler, 'has made herself mistress of the necessary degree of knowledge for conducting the matter, by dint of carefully reading every paragraph and every advertisement in the news papers that related to railroads, and as we have abstained from all gambling, all mere speculative buying-in and selling-out—we have got on very decently.'[1]

In May of this year, 1845, yet another curate arrived at Haworth. His advent was reported with unusual restraint by Charlotte: 'Papa has got a new curate lately, a Mr. Nicholls from Ireland. He did duty for the first time on Sunday—he appears a respectable young man, reads well, and I hope will give satisfaction.'[2]

This—from Charlotte—almost high praise of a curate is unlikely to have been due entirely to the merits of Arthur Bell Nicholls. Charlotte had at last received a letter from Héger[3]—the second in the sixteen months since she had left Brussels. Her spirits rose still higher a month later, when Anne and her brother came back to Haworth for their summer holidays, and Anne announced that she was not going to return to the Robinsons.[4] She said nothing about Branwell, who went back to Thorp Green alone after a week at home.[5] Charlotte was overjoyed;

she did not suspect the real reason for her sister's sudden decision after enduring six uncongenial years at Thorp Green without complaint: 'Anne, I am rejoiced to say has decided not to return to Mr. Robinson's', she tells Ellen contentedly. She adds significantly: '*her* presence at home certainly makes me feel more at liberty'.[6]

In high spirits, having replied to Héger, who again reminded her of the six months' interval,[7] Charlotte planned a visit to Ellen at the vicarage of Hathersage in Derbyshire, where her friend was preparing for the new vicar, her brother Henry, and his bride—for, after Charlotte's refusal, he had married elsewhere.[8] In the same letter to Ellen, Charlotte returns to normality. Mr. Nicholls, it seems, had shown his true colours since Charlotte's first mild judgement; or, more probably, his foibles had merged in Charlotte's mind with those of his fellow curates.[9]

Ellen, too, showed the interest of Victorian young ladies in the comings and goings of the younger clergy; but Charlotte brushed aside her friend's gentle comments: 'I have no desire at all to see your medical-clerical curate. I think he must be like all the other curates I have seen—and they seem to me a self-seeking, vain, empty race. At this blessed moment we have no less than three of them in Haworth Parish—and God knows there is not one to mend another.'[10] She was equal to them, however. 'The other day they all three—accompanied by Mr. Smidt[11] . . . dropped or rather rushed in unexpectedly to tea. It was Monday and I was hot and tired—still if they had behaved quietly and decently I would have served them out their tea in peace—but they began glorifying themselves and abusing dissenters in such a manner that my temper lost its balance, and I pronounced a few sentences sharply and rapidly which struck them all dumb. Papa was greatly horrified also—I don't regret it.'[12]

The 'few sentences', and the curates' discomfiture were left to her friend's imagination; but Ellen had seen others routed by Charlotte's tongue and the indignant glare of her eyes—those large, expressive eyes which many people were to find so striking in an otherwise unremarkable face. The eyes of all three Brontë girls were their only claim to beauty, except for Anne's soft hair and clear complexion.

Anne was soon walking again on the moors with Emily,

planning new Gondal chronicles, and telling her mild adventures at places she had visited. She was most anxious that Emily should see Scarborough—a particular favourite of her own—and the two girls arranged a short trip there. But their plan conflicted with Charlotte's proposed visit to Ellen, and the masterful eldest sister informed her friend: 'I have told Emily and Anne that I should not like again to put you off—and for that and for some other reasons they have decided to give up the idea of going to Scarbro' and instead, to make a little excursion next Monday and Tuesday to Ilkley or elsewhere.'[13]

The two girls gave up the idea of Scarborough, which Emily was now never to see, but they were determined to have the little excursion together. They were also determined to go, not to Ilkley, but to some place nearer than Scarborough that Anne wished Emily to see. They decided on York, whose cathedral was specially admired by Anne, and to York, therefore, both girls went forthwith. On the way they spent their time re-enacting, in the characters of various Gondal Royalists, certain sanguinary scenes of the revolution then convulsing the Gondals. From York they went to Keighley, and so home on foot. The whole excursion was completed in three days, by the second day of July.[14]

Charlotte stayed a fortnight at Hathersage, and, despite her description of herself at this time as a middle-aged person, she enjoyed herself sufficiently well to authorize her friend to beg Mr. Brontë for a further week of her company. The gossipy bedroom talks and the walks with the admiring Ellen were undeniably comforting even if the confidences between the two girls omitted the two subjects most in Charlotte's mind.[15] Ellen's request to Mr. Brontë was granted. 'If you have set your heart on Charlotte staying another week, she has our united consent,' wrote Emily in one of her brief, rare letters. 'I, for one, will take everything easy on Sunday. I am glad she is enjoying herself; let her make the most of the next seven days to return stout and hearty. Love to her and you from Anne and myself—and tell her all are well at home.'[16]

'All are well at home,' said Emily; but a few days later she and Anne had on their hands at the parsonage one who could by no stretch of imagination merit such a description. While Charlotte was away, Branwell had again come back from Thorp

Green to spend the rest of his holidays at home while the Robinson family went on to Scarborough. He had gone back to Thorp Green for a few days because he could not bear to be separated from Mrs. Robinson, but this return during his holidays had been sufficiently remarkable to confirm Mr. Robinson's suspicions. There followed hard on Branwell's heels a letter from Mr. Robinson dismissing him, and forbidding him the house.[17] This blow—inevitable though it must have seemed to any reasoning mind—fell upon the sanguine and reckless Branwell with fearful force. He sank into morbid despair, was prostrated by misery, and finally fell into a stupor. But this did not last long; Branwell could do nothing by halves: 'Eleven continuous nights of sleepless horror reduced me to almost blindness,' he tells his friend Grundy.[18] He drank continuously in an effort to escape his despair, but the remedy proved worse than the disease, and he at last had a bad bout of delirium tremens.[19]

To a household distracted by the antics of this stricken creature —now violent, now abject, now clamouring for sympathy with his loss and sufferings, in turn defiant, tearful, suicidal, threatening—Charlotte, all unsuspecting of ill, now returned. She was in particularly good spirits, reading the French newspapers that had become one of her chief pleasures, and cheered by a little adventure in the train to Keighley, where, so much did things French now mean to her, she had plucked up sufficient courage to speak to a man whom she believed to be a Frenchman: 'There was a gentleman in the railroad carriage whom I recognised by his features immediately as a foreigner and Frenchman. So sure was I of it, that I ventured to say to him in French—"Monsieur est français, n'est-ce-pas?" He gave a start of surprise, and answered immediately in his own tongue; he appeared still more astonished, and even puzzled, when after a few minutes' further conversation, I enquired if he had not passed the greater part of his life in Germany. He said the surmise was correct. I had guessed it from his speaking French with the German accent.'[20]

But for all her good spirits, Charlotte, as she afterwards told Ellen, had a presentiment of sorrow awaiting her at Haworth.[21] Anne told her for the first time why she had given up her position at Thorp Green, and why her brother had been disgraced. 'It was ten o'clock at night when I got home. I found Branwell ill; he is so very often owing to his own fault. I was not therefore shocked at first, but when Anne informed me of the immediate cause of his present illness, I was very greatly shocked. He had last Thursday received a note from Mr. Robinson sternly dismissing him, intimating that he had discovered his proceedings, which he characterised as bad beyond expression, and charging him on pain of exposure to break off instantly and for ever all communication with every member of his family. We have had sad work with Branwell since. He thought of nothing but stunning or drowning his distress of mind. No one in the house could have rest.'[22]

Charlotte regarded her brother with mounting disgust. The more he bewailed his lot and called upon the name of Mrs. Robinson, the more his eldest sister railed at him as none but she could do in that household. When Branwell recovered from his attack sufficiently to profess contrition, Charlotte packed him off for a week to North Wales to recover under the care of his faithful but not over good friend, John Brown the sexton.[23] But Charlotte had her doubts about the future: 'He promises amendment on his return,' she told Ellen, 'but so long as he remains at home I scarce dare hope for peace in the house. We must all, I fear, prepare for a season of distress and disquietude.'[24]

Charlotte was right. Branwell returned, slightly better in health, but as morbidly wretched as ever. He tortured himself and everyone round him with futile repinings, and with forebodings (actually without foundation) of Mrs. Robinson's sufferings.[25] To friends beyond reach of his voice he wrote harrowing tales of his passion, of the lack of sympathy at home, and of his desperate plight: 'I have lain during nine long weeks utterly shattered in body and broken down in mind. The probability of her becoming free to give me herself and estate never rose to drive away the prospect of her decline under her present grief. I dreaded, too, the wreck of my mind and body, which, God knows, during a short life have been severely tried.'[26]

Branwell was rarely free from his actual or potential audience; and it is no easier for the onlooker than it could have been for Branwell himself to disentangle at times the sincere emotion from the heroics and apologetics which clouded most of his words. 'Of course, you will despise the writer of all this,' he goes on to say; ' I can only answer that the writer does the same, and would not wish to live if he did not hope that work and change might yet restore him. Apologising sincerely for what seems like whining egotism . . . .'[27]

When well enough to leave the parsonage, Branwell spent most of his time begging or borrowing money—the terms were synonymous to him—from his father or village cronies so that he might again drink and forget; but, having gained fresh heart, his sense of the dramatic was roused, and led to further posturing.

So passed the summer and autumn of 1845, with Branwell veering between sober despair and drunken hope and with life in the parsonage dominated by this dreary and often alarming spectacle of weakness engulfed by a passion it had neither will nor inclination to conquer. The sight was not wholly unfamiliar to the three sisters; they were no strangers to drunkenness at home; but it now possessed a ghastly comprehensiveness which passed far beyond their worst imaginings. Branwell hid nothing, he knew nothing of reticence, and self-control had never been imposed upon him. If he did attempt to wrestle secretly with his sorrow, loneliness, and regrets, the attempts soon failed. Whether he had been hurt or had hurt himself he neither thought nor cared; sympathy he must have from some quarter —he was not particular so long as consolation was offered.[28] When his sisters would hear him, Branwell would rave of Mrs. Robinson, of her love for him, of his love for her, of her sufferings at their enforced separation, and at the hands of the iniquitous husband. When his sisters could or would not listen, when his friends did not answer his letters, when he could discover no means of obtaining more money for drink or drugs, he would subside into a sullen, shamefaced silence, broken by obscure threats of violence.[29] Occasionally he would try to pull himself together. He would repent with a violent self-condemnation that made these outbreaks scarcely less alarming than the drinking-bouts themselves; he dramatized every one of his miseries, discovering an aesthetic satisfaction in despair and repentance that made sympathy and reproof useless.[30] The Brontë sisters watched this slide of their once promising brother from self-control and normality, each in her own way reacting to this new factor in their lives. Charlotte would not speak to him when she could possibly avoid doing so, and she would not allow Ellen to see him: 'Branwell still remains at home,' she told her friend later in the year, 'and while *he* is here—*you* shall not come. I am more confirmed in that resolution the more I see of him. I wish I could say one word to you in his favour, but I cannot, therefore I will hold my tongue.'[31] Almost every letter written to Ellen at this time contains some similar refusal to allow her friend to be touched by the contamination Charlotte believed Branwell might now spread. She felt ashamed that her brother should be seen in his degradation, and she brooded bitterly upon the sacrifices made, the years cast away vainly by her sisters and herself for one whom she now saw as no better than a drunken weakling. Although she, the eldest Brontë, was no more than twenty-nine years old, Charlotte felt the weight of years and the sense of failure. Now she was able to place on her brother's shoulders no small part of the blame for this premature onset of age and fear of mediocrity.[32]

Yet all these grievances were as nothing to the humiliation with which Charlotte was obliged to recognize in Branwell's emotional problem an echo of her own. True, Branwell's behaviour at Thorp Green, which profoundly shocked Charlotte's sense of morality, had degraded his problem almost below comparison with hers; but although Charlotte could not have acted as he had done, the superficial resemblance was inescapable. Charlotte was too honest with herself not to admit this; but the very admission compelled her to react more violently against Branwell. Thus she had to face the fact that she was despising him for longings that had been in her own mind, day and night, ever since she had come back from Brussels. She could not believe herself wholly right in these feelings, although the temptation was too great for her to resist completely. But whereas she used her letters to Héger as her sole outlet, Branwell, made of weaker stuff, threw his anxiety, his grief, his misery and self-reproaches on to every shoulder that seemed at all inclined to bear them.

Here is an explanation of conduct which would otherwise seem difficult to account for. Charlotte's attitude to Branwell was not only harsh, it gives every appearance of being hypocritical, yet it is hard to believe that this woman, always so painfully direct with others, could escape some frankness with herself. Charlotte could not, with sincerity, blame Branwell for loving someone who was not free to return his feeling. Nor could she even blame him for declaring his passion, for her declarations had been little less open than his. But she could and did despise her brother for his lack of self-control. She only wrote to Héger —that was the full extent of her concession to the pressure of emotion—and she possibly succeeded in persuading herself that these letters did not reveal her feelings. Branwell, in contrast, wrote poems on his love,[33] he poured out long, melancholy, unanswerable letters to his friends, dealing in detail with his misfortunes, he whined incessantly,[34] whereas Charlotte carried on her daily life as best she could, though certain that joy had vanished from it for good. Branwell threw up work, pride, reticence; unable to face even his own thoughts, he made haste to dull and drown them—and for this he brought down upon himself the disgusted contempt of his elder sister.

Anne, on the contrary, felt no wish to vent an unsatisfied emotion on Branwell. She was no less horrified than Charlotte by her brother's excesses—she was less well fitted by nature to face them—but she possessed a philosophic resignation and a true charity. And she was not troubled by an uneasy conscience.

Anne's situation might be thought even more unfavourable than that of Charlotte or Branwell, for she had no hope of a return of her love this side eternity. Yet her mild power of endurance, together with her religious faith, enabled her to face the future calmly and even hopefully. She did not escape unhappiness, but of regrets she was innocent; and her life tended to centre more and more on dreams of what might have been, of what might yet, in some predestined future life, come to pass:

> I love the silent hour of night,
> For blissful dreams may then arise,
> Revealing to my charmed sight
> What may not bless my waking eyes.
>
> And then a voice may meet my ear
> That death has silenced long ago;
> And hope and rapture may appear
> Instead of solitude and woe.
>
> Cold in the grave for many years has lain
> The form it was my bliss to see;
> And only dreams can bring again
> The darling of my heart to me.[35]

And again, pursuing the same thought:

> *While on my lonely couch I lie,*
> *I seldom feel myself alone,*
> *For fancy fills my dreaming eye*
> *With scenes and pleasures of its own.*
>
> *That I may cherish at my breast*
> *An infant's form beloved and fair;*
> *May smile and soothe it into rest,*
> *With all a mother's fondest care.*
>
> *How sweet to feel its helpless form*
> *Depending thus on me alone;*
> *And while I hold it safe and warm,*
> *What bliss to think it is my own!*
>
> *And glances then may meet my eyes*
> *That daylight never showed to me;*
> *What raptures in my bosom rise*
> *Those earnest looks of love to see!*
>
> *To feel my hand so kindly prest,*
> *To know myself beloved at last;*
> *To think my heart has found a rest,*
> *My life of solitude is past!*[36]

With stanzas such as these Anne had found comfort in the last months at Thorp Green. Yet there were many times when her dreams faded:

> *But then to wake and find it flown,*
> *The dream of happiness destroyed;*
> *To find myself unloved, alone,*
> *What tongue can speak the dreary void!*
>
> *A heart whence warm affections flow,*
> *Creator, Thou hast given to me;*
> *And am I only thus to know*
> *How sweet the joys of love would be?*[37]

The constant humiliation and fear of exposure that Branwell's intrigue at Thorp Green brought upon her; the prevailing melancholy cast of her mind; the dread of a future life in which, not being of the elect, even her dreams must be for ever shattered: all this led to verses of misery and doubt:

> O God! if this indeed be all
> That Life can show to me;
> If on my aching brow may fall
> No freshening dew from Thee,
>
> If with no brighter light than this
> The lamp of hope may glow,
> And I may only dream of bliss,
> And wake to weary woe;
>
> If friendship's solace must decay
> When other joys are gone,
> And love must keep so far away
> While I go wandering on—
>
> Wandering and toiling without gain,
> The slave of others' will,
> With constant care and frequent pain,
> Despised, forgotten still;
>
> Grieving to look on vice and sin,
> Yet powerless to quell
> The silent current from within,
> The outward torrent's swell;
>
> While all the good I would impart,
> The feelings I would share,
> Are driven backward to my heart,
> And turned to wormwood there;
>
> If clouds must ever keep from sight
> The glories of the Sun,
> And I must suffer Winter's blight
> Ere Summer is begun,
>
> If Life must be so full of care,
> Then call me soon to Thee;
> Or give me strength enough to bear
> My load of misery.[38]

When, her warnings unheeded, her timid affection forgotten by Branwell in the heat of passion, Anne saw retribution over-

whelm her brother, she wrote the fact in the four-year biographical note which fell due on Emily's birthday of this year,
but she had for so long seen disaster coming that her comment
was mildness itself:

Thursday, July the 31st, 1845.

Yesterday was Emily's birthday, and the time when we should have
opened our 1841 paper, but by mistake we opened it today instead.
How many things have happened since it was written—some pleasant,
some far otherwise. Yet I was then at Thorp Green, and now I am only
just escaped from it. I was wishing to leave it then, and if I had known
that I had four years longer to stay, how wretched I should have been;
but during my stay I have had some very unpleasant and undreamt-of
experience of human nature. Others have seen more changes. Charlotte
has been at Mr. White's, and been twice to Brussels, where she stayed
each time nearly a year. Branwell has left Luddenden Foot, and been a
tutor at Thorp Green, and had much tribulation and ill health. He was
very ill on Thursday, but he went with John Brown to Liverpool,
where he now is, I suppose; and we hope he will be better and do better
in future. This is a dismal, cloudy, wet evening. We have had so far a
very cold, wet summer. Charlotte has lately been to Hathersage, in
Derbyshire, on a visit of three weeks to Ellen Nussey. She is now sitting
sewing in the dining-room. Emily is ironing upstairs. I am sitting in the
dining-room in the rocking-chair before the fire with my feet on the
fender. Papa is in the parlour. Tabby and Martha are, I think, in the
kitchen. Keeper and Flossy are, I do not know where. Little Dick is
hopping in his cage. When the last paper was written we were thinking
of setting up a school. The scheme has been dropt, and long after
taken up again, and dropt again, because we could not get pupils.
Charlotte is thinking about getting another situation. She wishes to
go to Paris. Will she go? She has let Flossy in, by-the-by, and he is
now lying on the sofa. Emily is engaged in writing the Emperor
Julius's Life. She has read some of it, and I want very much to hear the
rest. She is writing some poetry too. I wonder what it is about? I have
begun the third volume of *Passages in the Life of an Individual*. I wish I
had finished it. This afternoon I began to set about making my grey
figured silk frock that was dyed at Keighley. What sort of a hand shall
I make of it? E. and I have a great deal of work to do. When shall we
sensibly diminish it? I want to get a habit of early rising. Shall I succeed? We have not yet finished our *Gondal Chronicles* that we began
three years and a half ago. When will they be done? The Gondals are
at present in a sad state. The Republicans are uppermost, but the
Royalists are not quite overcome. The young sovereigns, with their

brothers and sisters, are still at the Palace of Instruction. The Unique Society, about half a year ago, were wrecked on a desert island as they were returning from Gaul. They are still there but we have not played at them much yet. The Gondals in general are not in first-rate playing condition. Will they improve? I wonder how we shall all be, and where and how situated, on the thirtieth of July 1848, when, if we are all alive, Emily will be just 30, I shall be in my 29th year, Charlotte in her 33rd, and Branwell in his 32nd; and what changes shall we have seen and known; and shall we be much changed ourselves? I hope not, for the worse at least. I for my part cannot well be flatter or older in mind than I am now. Hoping for the best, I conclude.[39]

As Branwell's excesses showed no sign of abating except during occasional bouts of repentance, there rose above Anne's horror at his glorification of what she felt was sheer wickedness a persistent fear for his soul. Beset as she was by cruel doubts as to her own salvation, there seemed to her small possibility that her brother could escape eternal damnation; and, as time went on, Branwell's shortcomings, and the effect of them upon those around her, seemed to her of little account measured by the fate awaiting him. She had many times tried to reason with him, but always in vain; he would never listen, and he brushed aside her timid, earnest warnings and her shy efforts to offer him affection as some sort of compensation for the love he expected from Mrs. Robinson.[40] But Branwell could not prevent his youngest sister from wrestling secretly with God for his soul; and this Anne did the more resolutely the nearer Branwell appeared to his inevitable end.

Of this pleading, Anne has left some record in her poems, and when Branwell fell into a passion of self-reproach, when the doctrines pressed on his childish consciousness by his aunt revived and drove him to repentance,[41] she silently expressed her thankfulness and renewed hope:

> I mourn with thee, and yet rejoice
> That thou shouldst sorrow so;
> With angel choirs I join my voice
> To bless the sinner's woe.
>
> Though friends and kindred turn away,
> And laugh thy grief to scorn;
> I hear the great Redeemer say,
> 'Blessed are ye that mourn.'

Hold on thy course, nor deem it strange
That earthly cords are riven,
Man may lament the wondrous change,
But 'there is joy in heaven!'[42]

Only later, when Branwell's course appeared irrevocable, did there rise in Anne's mind and take root in her conscience a belief that a duty lay before her. Only then did there grow in her a conviction that somehow she must make her brother an example and a warning to others.

XIX

BRANWELL AND EMILY

Emily's birthday note. Her first reaction to Branwell's decline. Her later change of view. These reactions illustrated in her poetry. Estimate of Branwell's influence upon his sisters.

EMILY, as might be expected, was the least disturbed of the three sisters by Branwell's collapse. In her birthday note she speaks about her brother in much the same terms as Anne had done; but the whole tone of the note, in contrast with her sister's, displays a steady optimism:

Haworth, Thursday, July 30th, 1845.
My birthday—showery, breezy, cool. I am twenty-seven years old today. This morning Anne and I opened the papers we wrote four years since, on my twenty-third birthday. This paper we intend, if all be well to open on my thirtieth—three years hence, in 1848. Since the 1841 paper the following events have taken place. Our school scheme has been abandoned, and instead Charlotte and I went to Brussels on the 8th of February, 1842. Branwell left his place at Luddenden Foot. C. and I returned from Brussels, November 8th, 1842, in consequence of aunt's death. Branwell went to Thorp Green as a tutor, where Anne still continued, January 1843. Charlotte returned to Brussels the same month, and after staying a year, came back again on New Year's Day 1844. Anne left her situation at Thorp Green of her own accord, June 1845. Anne and I went our first long journey by ourselves together, leaving home on the 30th of June, Monday, sleeping at York, returning to Keighley Tuesday evening, sleeping there and walking home on Wednesday morning. Though the weather was broken we enjoyed ourselves very much, except during a few hours at Bradford. And during our excursion we were, Ronald Macalgin, Henry Angora, Juliet Angusteena, Rosabella Esmaldan, Ella and Julian Egremont, Catherine Navarre, and Cordelia Fitzaphnold, escaping from the palaces of instruction to join the Royalists who are hard driven at present by the victorious Republicans. The Gondals still flourish bright as ever. I am at present writing a work on the first wars. Anne has been writing some articles on this, and a book by Henry Sophona. We intend sticking firm by the rascals as long as they delight us, which I am glad to say they do at present. I should have mentioned that last sum-

mer the school scheme was revived in full vigour. We had prospectuses printed, despatched letters to all acquaintances imparting our plans, and did our little all; but it was found no go. Now I don't desire a school at all, and none of us have any great longing for it. We have cash enough for our present wants, with a prospect of accumulation. We are all in decent health, only that papa has a complaint in his eyes, and with the exception of B., who, I hope, will be better and do better hereafter. I am quite contented for myself: not as idle as formerly, altogether as hearty, and having learned to make the most of the present and long for the future with less fidgetiness that I cannot do all I wish; seldom or never troubled with nothing to do, and merely desiring that everybody could be as comfortable as myself and as undesponding, and then we should have a very tolerable world of it. By mistake I find we have opened the paper on the 31st instead of the 30th. Yesterday was much such a day as this, but the morning was divine. Tabby, who was gone in our last paper, is come back, and has lived with us two years and a half, and is in good health. Martha, who also departed, is here too. We have got Flossy; got and lost Tiger; lost the hawk Hero, which, with the geese, was given away, and is doubtless dead, for when I came back from Brussels, I enquired on all hands and could hear nothing of him. Tiger died early last year. Keeper and Flossy are well, also the canary acquired four years since. We are now all at home, and likely to be there some time. Branwell went to Liverpool on Tuesday to stay a week. Tabby has just been teasing me to turn as formerly to 'pilloputate'. Anne and I should have picked the black currants if it had been fine and sunshiny. I must hurry off now to my turning and ironing. I have plenty of work on hand, and writing, and am altogether full of business. With best wishes for the whole house till 1848, July 30th, and as much longer as may be,—I conclude.'[1]

This cheerful note—one of the most level-headed, carefree and natural pieces of writing ever to come from a Brontë pen —shows, at such a time, the truly remarkable power of Emily's detachment from the life about her. Her formidable sanity was strengthened on this occasion by the amount of time she had spent alone with Branwell in the past few years. She was thus more familiar than Charlotte and Anne, and more hardened to the habits which foretold clearly what would happen when real trouble came his way. She thought him a poor creature often enough, but this merely aroused her pity—an emotion frequently obscured in Anne by painful hesitations of conscience, and almost entirely absent from Branwell's old playmate, Charlotte, who could do nothing by halves, and who now, hurt and disappointed by his utter collapse, could express only anger and contempt.

'Merely desiring that everybody should be as undesponding as myself. . . .' It is difficult not to think that Emily, when she wrote thus, had in mind the attitude of the family, and of Charlotte in particular, towards Branwell. Not that Emily had much use for her brother as a man, but she had even less use for the normal standards of morality, and it seems that she took up no kind of moral attitude towards him. At his worst, she would think of him as a nuisance, 'a hopeless being'.[2] In her relations with her family Emily is at her most baffling. Was it the strength of egotism or of wisdom that allowed her to pity Branwell when the others were shocked? No one can say; the poems point one way, *Wuthering Heights* the other. What seems clear is that her emotions were not seriously involved. There is no sign that Emily cared overmuch for anyone, and certainly not for Branwell. But he possessed two strong attractions for her. She admired his free and easy ways and his ready word and smile for all, with the impatient envy of the uncommunicative. And she was fascinated by the story he told so often and at such length to any who would listen. She was not shocked. Why should she be? She had dealt in horrors for years, and now before her eyes was being acted out the fate, not only of Branwell, but of one of her Gondal characters. Did not her Gondal men live hard, love desperately, die with their backs to the wall, an oath on their lips? Branwell, too, loved to the death, if his words were to be believed, and as his actions seemed likely to prove. Branwell was extravagant where Emily and Charlotte were passionate; but this essential difference Emily failed to discern. She saw in her brother's extravagant grief and in his desperate measures to allay it a certain note of grandeur. Here, it seemed to her, a King Julius rose from her Gondal pages into vital, passionate life. In just such a manner might this extension of her own personality love and hate and sorrow.

From Branwell's violent picture of Thorp Green—the jealous, harsh husband, the long-suffering, much abused wife, the knightly lover—Emily recreated without difficulty a scene which her vivid dramatic sense, tending to exaggerate and now further enhanced by long meditation upon Gondal themes of a kindred character, leaped to greet. So had she conceived it a thousand times. So had she written it in language no less fiery, no less violent than Branwell's own. The full pitifulness of the shaking, nerveless, sodden, red-headed creature, now violent, now abject, who told the tale, was obscured by the high romance of his story as he told it, and the drama of his declarations that, if he could not have his heart's desire, he counted life worthless. How should she, who spent so much of her time feeding on such romances, disentangle the truth from the lies, the lies from wishful thinking?

So Branwell won this sister's sympathy and admiration, even while he earned her contempt. His appeal to the violence in her was not made in vain. He encouraged her desire for passionate love, her appetite for melodrama. Through him, by discounting the sordid weaknesses of the tale and its teller—a process which familiarity with Branwell and his ways rendered almost second nature—Emily was able to live at second-hand a life of stormy emotion.

Emily's expression of love had been made in the pages of her Gondal manuscript book only a few months earlier. In this, perhaps her finest love lyric, she makes clear how she could enrich and ennoble the theme of love-unto-and-beyond-death that Branwell was to reiterate tirelessly:

Cold in the earth and the deep snow piled above thee!
Far, far removed cold in the dreary grave!
Have I forgot, my Only Love, to love thee,
Severed at last by Time's all-wearing wave?

Now, when alone, do my thoughts no longer hover
Over the mountains on Angora's shore,
Resting their wings where heath and fern-leaves cover
That noble heart for ever, evermore?

Cold in the earth, and fifteen wild Decembers
From those brown hills have melted into spring—
Faithful indeed is the spirit that remembers
After such years of change and suffering!

Sweet Love of youth, forgive if I forget thee
While the World's tide is bearing me along
Sterner desires and darker hopes beset me
Hopes which obscure but cannot do thee wrong—

No other sun has lightened up my heaven;
No other star has ever shone for me
All my life's bliss from thy dear life was given—
All my life's bliss is in the grave with thee.

But when the days of golden dreams had perished
And even Despair was powerless to destroy
Then did I learn how existence could be cherished
Strengthened and fed without the aid of joy

Then did I check the tears of useless passion,
Weaned my young soul from yearning after thine,
Sternly denied its burning wish to hasten
Down to that tomb already more than mine!

And even yet I dare not let it languish,
Dare not indulge in Memory's rapturous pain
Once drinking deep of that divinest anguish
How could I seek the empty world again?[3]

Emily continued for some time to interpret her brother's words in the spirit of this poem rather than in the light of his behaviour and past record. Passion for her, was, after all, an imaginative emotion with no basis in experience.

Yet this was not all, it was not even the major part of Branwell's influence upon Emily. Inevitably his experiences, and the sympathy he had won through his sister's romanticization of them, eventually provoked a violent reaction. For some years Emily had been moving slowly, with infinite difficulties, with innumerable setbacks, yet with measurable progress, towards a mastery of the elements in her nature that looked to the things of earth for final satisfaction. Her sympathy with Branwell, which seemed at first to encourage this love of life, served finally to set her with even greater firmness and certainty against it. Emily's treatment of passion, in whatever terms it found expression in her writings, is capable in the last analysis only of a spiritual interpretation. The increase of Gondal activity that Anne's return to Haworth brought about did not change the essentially spiritual character of this type of Gondal tale and poem. But Branwell's experiences, however transmuted by Emily's inexperience, could not for long hide their true ugliness.

Thus, despite her first instinctive sympathy with the highly romanticized rendering of Branwell's love affair—possibly because of it—Emily's final reaction to the sordidness of the actual details related by him, to the shade he cast upon the purity and nobility of love as she conceived it, was violent and decisive. It was expressed in her poems of the autumn after Branwell had come home, and when his continued presence had begun to belie the magic of his words. A few days before Branwell returned for the last time from Thorp Green, Emily had written her poem 'Anticipation', in which she turned back to the source of her spiritual strength:

> *How beautiful the Earth is still*
> *To thee, how full of Happiness;*
> *How little fraught with real ill*
> *Or shadowy phantoms of distress:*

> *How Spring can bring thee glory yet*
> *And Summer win thee to forget*
> *December's sullen time!*
> *Why dost thou hold the treasure fast*
> *Of youth's delight, when youth is past*
> *And thou art near thy prime?*

> *When those who were thy own compeers*
> *Equal in fortune and in years*
> *Have seen their morning melt in tears*
> *To dull unlovely day;*
> *Blest, had they died unproved and young*
> *Before their hearts were wildly wrung*
> *Poor slaves, subdued by passions strong*
> *A weak and helpless prey!*

> *'Because, I hoped while they enjoyed*
> *And by fulfilment, hope destroyed—*
> *As children hope, with trustful breast*
> *I waited Bliss and cherished Rest—*

> *'A thoughtful spirit taught me soon*
> *That we must long till life be done*
> *That every phase of earthly joy*
> *Will always fade and always cloy—*

'This I foresaw, and would not chase
The fleeting treacheries,
But with firm foot and tranquil face
Held backward from that tempting race,
Gazed o'er the sands the waves efface
To the enduring seas—

'There cast my anchor of Desire
Deep in unknown Eternity
Nor ever let my spirit tire
With looking for What is to Be.

'It is Hope's spell that glorifies
Like youth to my maturer eyes
All Nature's million mysteries—
The fearful and the fair—
Hope soothes me in the griefs I know
She lulls my pain for others' woe,
And makes me strong to undergo
What I am born to bear.

'Glad comforter, will I not brave
Unawed the darkness of the grave?
Nay, smile to hear Death's billows rave,
My guide, sustained by thee?
The more unjust seems present fate
The more my spirit springs elate
Strong in thy strength, to anticipate
Rewarding Destiny!'[4]

To this strain, at once rapt and stoical, Emily returned in
October of the same year; but now with a deeper note:

Silent is the House—all are laid asleep;
One, alone, looks out o'er the snow-wreaths deep;
Watching every cloud, dreading every breeze
That whirls the wildering drifts and bends the groaning trees—

Cheerful is the hearth, soft the matted floor
Not one shivering gust creeps through pane or door
The little lamp burns straight, its rays shoot strong and far
I trim it well to be the Wanderer's guiding star—

Frown my haughty sire, chide my angry dame;
Set your slaves to spy, threaten me with shame;
But neither sire nor dame, nor prying serf shall know
What angel nightly tracks that waste of winter snow.

In the dungeon crypts idly did I stray
Reckless of the lives wasting there away;
'Draw the ponderous bars; open, Warder stern!'
He dare not say me nay—the hinges harshly turn.

'Our guests are darkly lodged,' I whispered, gazing through
The vault whose grated eye showed heaven more grey than blue;
(This was when glad Spring laughed in awaking pride)
'Aye, darkly lodged enough!' returned my sullen guide.

Then, God forgive my youth, forgive my careless tongue!
I scoffed as the chill chains on the damp flagstones rung;
'Confined in triple walls, art thou so much to fear,
That we must bind thee down and clench thy fetters here?'

The captive raised her face, it was as soft and mild
As sculptured marble saint or slumbering, unweaned child
It was so soft and mild, it was so sweet and fair
Pain could not trace a line nor grief a shadow there!

She knew me and she sighed, 'Lord Julian, can it be,
Of all my playmates, you alone remember me?
Nay start not at my words, unless you deem it shame
To own-from conquered foe, a once familiar name—

'I cannot wonder now at aught the world will do
And insult and contempt I lightly brook from you,
Since those who vowed away their souls to win my love
Around this living grave like utter strangers move!

'Nor has one voice been raised to plead that I might die
Not buried under earth but in the open sky;
By ball or speedy knife or headsman's skilful blow—
A quick and welcome pang instead of lingering woe!

'Yet, tell them, Julian, all, I am not doomed to wear
Year after year in gloom and desolate despair;
A messenger of Hope comes every night to me
And offers, for short life, eternal liberty—

'He comes with western winds, with evening's wandering airs,
With that clear dusk of heaven that brings the thickest stars;
Winds take a pensive tone and stars a tender fire
And visions rise and change which kill me with desire—

'*Desire for nothing known in my maturer years*
When joy grew mad with awe at counting future tears;
When, if my spirit's sky was full of flashes warm,
I knew not whence they came from sun or thunderstorm;

'*But first a hush of peace, a soundless calm descends;*
The struggle of distress and fierce impatience ends;
Mute music soothes my breast—unuttered harmony
That I could never dream till earth was lost to me.

'*Then dawns the Invisible, the Unseen its truth reveals;*
My outward sense is gone, my inward essence feels—
Its wings are almost free, its home, its harbour found;
Measuring the gulf it stoops and dares the final bound!

O, dreadful is the check—intense the agony
When the ear begins to hear and the eye begins to see;
When the pulse begins to throb, the brain to think again,
The soul to feel the flesh and the flesh to feel the chain!

'*Yet I would lose no sting, would wish no torture less;*
The more that anguish racks the earlier it will bless;
And robed in fires of Hell, or bright with heavenly shine
If it but herald Death, the vision is divine.'[5]

These stanzas from a Gondal poem display the curious duality
of character in their author—on the one hand, the naïveté of
conception; on the other, the depth of vision. There is first the
Emily who devours German romances, dreams of knightly
lovers, invents the false yet fascinating King Julius, who revels
in gory battle scenes and lonely death-beds for her Gondal
characters, who can admire uncritically the extravagant boasts
of Branwell. Then, into this setting of absurd heroics and childish revelling in blood and thunder, projecting her personality
into the pasteboard heroine, Emily introduces suddenly, in
verses of great power and beauty, a mystical experience of her
own. This contradiction in Emily persisted throughout her life.
It was never resolved or explained.

Others have written at length, have spoken much, of their
wrestlings with the spirit. Emily has left only a few poems, but
in them she conveys the mystical experience as few writers
have done. This is particularly true of the poem quoted above;
the final stanzas leave the reader breathless and with the feeling

that he has undergone the experience himself. Characteristic of Emily, too, is the marked death wish expressed in these poems, and the heretical indifference to the Christian concept of heaven and hell. All her concern was for her spirit's consummation. What this consummation was, Emily several times made clear.⁶ In yet another poem written at this time, she recalled—unalloyed by Gondal heroics—a further mystical experience, one which was to end only with her death:

> *Enough of Thought, Philosopher;*
> *Too long hast thou been dreaming*
> *Unlightened, in thy chamber drear*
> *While summer's sun is beaming—*
> *Space-sweeping soul, what sad refrain*
> *Concludes thy musings once again?*
>
> 'O for the time when I shall sleep
> Without identity—
> And never care how rain may steep
> Or snow may cover me!
>
> 'No promised Heaven these wild Desires
> Could all or half fulfil—
> No threatened Hell with quenchless fires
> Subdue this quenchless will!'
>
> *So said I, and still say the same,*
> *Still to my Death will say—*
> *Three Gods within this little frame*
> *Are warring night and day.*
>
> *Heaven could not hold them all, and yet*
> *They all are held in me*
> *And must be mine till I forget*
> *My present entity.*
>
> *O for the time when in my breast*
> *Their struggles will be o'er—*
> *O for the day when I shall rest*
> *And never suffer more!*
>
> 'I saw a Spirit standing, Man,
> Where thou dost stand—an hour ago,
> And round his feet three rivers ran
> Of equal depth and equal flow—

'*A golden stream, and one like blood*
And one like sapphire, seemed to be
But where they joined their triple flood
It tumbled in a inky sea—

'*The Spirit bent his dazzling gaze*
Down on that Ocean's gloomy night
Then—kindling all with sudden blaze
The glad deep sparkled wide and bright
White as the sun, far, far more fair
Than their divided sources were!'

And even for that Spirit, Seer,
I've watched and sought my lifetime long
Sought him in Heaven, Hell, Earth and Air
An endless search—and always wrong!

Had I but seen his glorious eye
Once light the clouds that 'wilder me,
I ne'er had raised this coward cry
To cease to think and cease to be—

I ne'er had called oblivion blest
Nor stretching eager hands to Death
Implored to change for lifeless rest
This sentient soul this living breath.[7]

Later, when her capacity for suffering had been brought almost to breaking point, Emily scratched out her concluding stanza of this poem and substituted:

O let me die, that power and will
Their cruel strife may close,
And vanquished Good victorious Ill
Be lost in one repose.[8]

Branwell was the only man Emily could be said to have known intimately. Anne knew enough about other men to measure their manners and actions against those of her brother. But only Charlotte, who penetrated quickly to intimacy, and whose mind was probing incessantly for the motive behind action, was able to place Branwell with reasonable accuracy, which personal bitterness alone distorted.

To each sister, then, Branwell assumed a different aspect. To

Emily, he appeared variously as a figure not without romantic grandeur and as a weakling to be protected from himself. To Anne, he grew fast into the shape of a dreadful warning to the intemperate. To Charlotte, he became both humiliation and hindrance; and later, a psychological study of melancholy, when not contemptuous, interest; Branwell was added to that ever-increasing gallery of acute and merciless portraits of contemporaries forming in his elder sister's mind.

So Branwell at this time and for the next few years directly and indirectly affected all three sisters in their life and work. He presented each with the semblance of a human figure, a mode of living and an outlook upon life which, virtually imprisoned in the parsonage as they were, none could avoid. In due time, each in her own fashion, and according to the light in which his personality and his actions were regarded, was to set down her reactions in writings that stand to-day among their finest work. As a figure in literature, Branwell was thus destined to play no mean part; not, indeed, the part he had been encouraged to hope for and believe in; yet a form of immortality not less secure for the exchange of rôle from creator to that of pitiable, sordid, but undoubted inspiration.

XX

THE BELLS IN PRINT

Branwell prepares Charlotte for the future. Charlotte discovers and reads Emily's poems. She appeases Emily's fury. Anne produces her poems. Charlotte's plan to publish a selection from the work of all three. How she gained Emily's consent. Struggle to find a publisher. The 'Poems' are printed.

THIS was not the end of Branwell's influence on the destiny of his sisters. The most important effect of his catastrophic return home in the summer of 1845 was yet to come. It was the means of turning Charlotte, and, through Charlotte, her sisters, finally towards their true vocation.

All four Brontës wrote as a matter of course, but so far without direction. Emily and Anne wrote for pleasure, because they could best express themselves in their writings. They had no thought of publication; Emily would have scouted such an idea. Charlotte, even more than Branwell, had been rebuffed in her attempts to obtain encouragement; and, as her bad eyesight always threatened to prevent her from writing, she had tried to turn her thirst for advancement into other channels.

Now, Branwell's presence in the parsonage put an end to Charlotte's lingering hopes of establishing a school there. The need to look after him and support him also killed her cherished plan of taking a post on the continent.[1] There was now Branwell to be fed, it seemed indefinitely, at the parsonage, and, as Charlotte knew from past experience, there would be debts to settle whenever her brother bestirred himself sufficiently to visit the village or his friends further afield. Once again, the sisters had to earn some money, and, so far as Charlotte could see, their only chance was to write novels for the large and growing public who welcomed the woman novelist, then coming into her own.

As it happened, however, Branwell was the first of the four to begin writing a novel. He had come back from his short holiday little better in spirit than when he had left the parsonage: 'I returned yesterday from a week's journey to Liverpool and North Wales,' he told his friend Leyland, 'but I found during my absence that wherever I went a certain woman robed in black, and calling herself 'MISERY' walked by my side, and leant on my arm as affectionately as if she were my legal wife.'[2] Yet for all his misery and his efforts to deaden it, Branwell at this time had spasms of hard work. Six weeks after his letter to Leyland, and only two days after a complaint to Ellen by Charlotte that her brother 'makes no effort to seek a situation, and while he is at home I will invite no one to come and share our discomfort',[3] Branwell was telling his friend: 'I have, since I saw you at Halifax, devoted my hours of time snatched from downright illness, to the composition of a three volume *novel*—one volume of which is completed—and along with the two forthcoming ones, has been really the result of half a dozen by-past years of thoughts about, and experience in, this crooked path of Life.'[4] Branwell explained why he was making this effort: 'I felt that I must rouse myself to attempt something while roasting daily and nightly over a slow fire—to wile away my torment—and I knew that in the present state of the publishing and reading world a Novel is the most sale-able article, so that where ten pounds would be offered for a work the production of which would require the utmost stretch of a man's intellect, two hundred pounds would be a refused offer for three volumes whose composition would require the smoking of a cigar and the humming of a tune.'[5]

'My novel', continued Branwell, 'is the result of years of thought, and if it gives a vivid picture of human feelings for good and evil—veiled by the cloak of deceit which must en-wrap man and woman—if it records as faithfully as the pages that unveil man's heart in Hamlet or Lear, the conflicting feel-ings and clashing pursuits in our uncertain path through life, I shall be as much gratified (and as much astonished) as I should be if in betting that I could jump over the Mersey I jumped over the Irish Sea. It would not be more pleasant to light on Dublin instead of Birkenhead than to leap from the present bathos of fictitious literature on to the firmly fixed rock honoured by the foot of a Smollett or Fielding.'[6]

So, having by his behaviour forced Charlotte to choose between an effort to make money and a name with her pen, or to acquiesce in her present monotonous, unfulfilled life, Branwell further presented her with an example of the kind of work she should attempt. Whether he really finished the first volume of the proposed novel cannot be known, and is of little moment; he had written some of it and he certainly spoke of it; and even a hostile Charlotte could not entirely avoid the doings and sayings of her brother in a house where the four of them were practically on top of each other all day long. This must have helped to make Charlotte's mind ready, and finally to set her inclinations. But the spark which caught the tinder was, in a sense, accidental. All the Brontës knew that Emily wrote poems; Anne, at least, had seen and heard some of her Gondal poems; and there could, in any event, be no close-hid secret in such a household. Charlotte, who fretted against Emily's reserve, may have suspected some clue to the mystery in the verses her sister carefully printed out in little books, which she locked away in her desk. Charlotte was curious about the contents of these little books; a secret of any kind was anathema to her; and eventually, in some way that will never be known, she discovered and read one of them.

She later gave her own account of the incident: 'One day in the autumn of 1845 I accidentally lighted on a MS. volume of verse in my sister Emily's handwriting. Of course I was not surprised, knowing that she could and did write verses. I looked it over, and something more than surprise seized me—a deep conviction that these were not common effusions, nor at all like the poetry women generally write. I thought them condensed and terse, vigorous and genuine. To my ear they had also a peculiar music, wild, melancholy, and elevating. My sister was not a person of demonstrative character, nor one on the recesses of whose mind and feelings even those nearest and dearest to her could, with impunity, intrude unlicensed: it took hours to reconcile her to the discovery I had made, and days to persuade her that such poems merited ·publication.'[7]

'Of its startling excellence', she wrote of Emily's poetry, 'I am deeply convinced, and have been from the first moment the MS. fell by chance into my hands. The pieces are short, but they are very genuine; they stirred my heart like the sound of a trumpet when I read them alone and in secret. The deep excitement I felt forced from me the confession of the discovery I had made.'[8]

Charlotte then explained the reception given to her when she told Emily that she had read her poems. 'I was sternly rated at first for having taken an unwarrantable liberty.' But of this she made light; she expected it, she said, since Emily was 'of no flexible or ordinary materials'.[9]

But Charlotte not only appreciated that the verses written minutely, sometimes almost illegibly, in the notebook, were of uncommon merit; she knew also exactly what such a gift in her sister might do for all of them. 'By dint of entreaty and reason', she went on, 'I at last wrung out a reluctant consent to have the "rhymes", as they were contemptuously called, published. The author never alludes to them; or, when she does, it is with scorn. But I know no woman that ever lived ever wrote such poetry before. Condensed energy, clearness, finish—strange, strong pathos are their characteristics; utterly different from the weak diffusiveness, the laboured yet most feeble wordiness, which dilute the writings of even very popular poetesses. That is my deliberate and quite impartial opinion.'[10]

If Charlotte chose to make public even at a later date so much of the event which led up to the publication of her sister's poems, if she admitted to such opposition, something of Emily's fury and contempt can be imagined. Charlotte speaks frankly—yet she left much unsaid. However good her motive, she had pried upon Emily's privacy; and whatever Emily's opinion of her 'rhymes' as literature, as a revelation of herself they were dear, even while she despised them for bearing witness to her longing for self-expression. It was the uncovering of this personal weakness—as Emily saw it—of which she was so ashamed and which she so deeply resented. Nor did her trials end there; for it was soon made plain that, if her sister had her way, not Charlotte alone, but the stranger everywhere would see these personal poems; they were to be brandished in the face of the whole world.

Of any comprehension of Emily's real reaction, Charlotte betrays no inkling. She imputed her sister's anger and disdain to causes common to her own experience, and with characteristic persistence she braved the storm, helped by a radiant vision that the discovery had raised in her imagination. This vision was nothing less than publication of a selection from the poems of all three sisters. For such a plan to be carried out, Charlotte had first to gain Emily's consent. This was a formidable task, but

Charlotte, now afire with hope, succeeded. How she did so is best seen in her own words when describing the incident later. She soon found that an appeal to Emily's vanity was useless; her sister was not to be persuaded that her poems were worth printing. But when Emily was convinced that her sisters' poems stood little or no chance of publication if she withheld her work; when Charlotte made clear that it must be all or none; then her opposition weakened. 'Meanwhile my younger sister quietly produced some of her own compositions,' wrote Charlotte, 'intimating that since Emily's had given me pleasure I might like to look at hers. I could not but be a partial judge, yet I thought that these verses too had a sweet, sincere pathos of their own.'[11] She added: 'We had very early cherished the dream of one day becoming authors.'[12] Here was a reason that Emily found hard and, after a time, impossible to resist. She gave way.

'We agreed', continued the triumphant Charlotte, 'to arrange a small selection of our poems, and, if possible, get them printed. Averse to personal publicity, we veiled our names under those of Currer, Ellis, and Acton Bell; the ambiguous choice being dictated by a sort of conscientious scruple at assuming Christian names positively masculine, while we did not like to declare ourselves women, because—without at the time suspecting that our mode of writing and thinking was not what is called "feminine" —we had a vague impression that authoresses are liable to be looked on with prejudice; we noticed how critics sometimes used for their chastisement the weapon of personality, and for their reward a flattery which is not true praise.'[13]

But it was one thing to agree to publish poems, and quite another to get the poems published. 'The great puzzle lay in the difficulty of getting answers of any kind from the publishers to whom we applied,' explained Charlotte. 'Being greatly harassed by this obstacle, I ventured to apply to Messrs. Chambers of Edinburgh for a word of advice; *they* may have forgotten the circumstance, but *I* have not, for from them I received a brief and businesslike, but civil and sensible reply, on which we acted, and at last made way.'[14]

As a result of this advice Charlotte got in touch with Aylott and Jones of Paternoster Row, who, in January 1846, agreed to publish the little book of poems at the authors' expense. At the end of May, copies were on sale.

XXI

THE END OF M. HEGER

Tension at home during the winter. Branwell's letters. Friction between Charlotte and Emily. Anne's depression. Charlotte's last letter to M. Héger. He replies. She rejects his suggestion and breaks with him. The sisters begin to write novels. Charlotte and Ellen Nussey. Branwell's condition. Mr. Robinson's death. Branwell's hopes shattered. Reaction of the sisters to his despair.

DURING the winter of 1845–6, with Branwell a skeleton in the cupboard, the Brontës were more than ever cut off from the rest of the world.

The visit of the sculptor Leyland,[1] to whom Branwell still poured out his woes, emphasized the isolation of the family. The welcome diversion of Ellen's visits was still forbidden by Charlotte as long as Branwell stayed at home. 'He never thinks of seeking employment,' Charlotte tells Miss Wooler, 'and I begin to fear he has rendered himself incapable of filling any respectable station in life. Besides, if money were at his disposal he would only use it to his own injury—the faculty of self-government is, I fear, almost destroyed in him.'[2]

Eventually, she spent a few days with Ellen at Brookroyd, and on her return had a similar gloomy report to make: 'I went into the room where Branwell was to speak to him about an hour after I got home—it was very forced work to address him —I might have spared myself the trouble as he took no notice and made no reply—he was stupefied. My fears were not vain —Emily tells me that he got a sovereign from Papa while I have been away under the pretence of paying a pressing debt— he went immediately and changed it at a public-house—and has employed it as was to be expected. She concluded her account with saying he was a hopeless being—it is too true. In his present state it is scarcely possible to stay in the room where he is.'[3]

Branwell himself had his grievances. Not for many years had he spent such a long time at home. He missed the exhilaration of company, the intoxication of having men hang on his words, and, still more, the flattering attentions of Mrs. Robinson. To fall from this high estate to the silence of the parsonage, the long, lonely, accusing hours when the waste and weakness of his life could not be hidden from others or from himself; to have for company only those who talked rarely, who listened with reluctance, and who regarded him often with disgust, at best with pity: all this preyed on Branwell's mind, drove him to further excesses, followed by frantic repentance and futile determinings to take himself from Haworth: 'I cannot, without a smile at myself, think of my stay for three days in Halifax on a business which need not have occupied three hours,' he told Leyland of a visit in April during which he had sat to the sculptor for a medallion, 'but in truth when I fall back *on* myself I suffer so much wretchedness that I cannot withstand my temptations to get *out* of myself—and for that reason I am prosecuting enquiries about situations suitable to me whereby I could have a voyage abroad. The quietude of home, and the inability to make my family aware of the nature of most of my sufferings makes me write—

> *Home thoughts are not, with me,*
> *Bright as of yore;*
> *Joys are forgot by me,*
> *Taught to deplore!*
> *My home has taken rest*
> *In an afflicted breast*
> *Which I have often pressed,*
> *But—may no more!*[4]

Troubles never come alone—and I have some little troubles astride the shoulders of the big one. Literary exertion would seem a resource, but the depression attendant on it, and the almost hopelessness of bursting through the barriers of literary circles, and getting a hearing among publishers, make me disheartened, and indifferent; for I cannot write what would be thrown, unread, into a library fire. Otherwise I have the materials for a respectably sized volume . . . .'[5]

Branwell continued in this same letter to include morbid verses referring to the deathless love between Mrs. Robinson and himself; and he enclosed a sketch, no less morbid, of her.[6]

To Emily, the long winter brought as one of its main difficulties the possibility of friction with Charlotte. Their opposed attitudes to Branwell; the constant intercourse—unbroken even for a day—between two such strong and intense natures; the aftermath of the tension following upon Charlotte's discovery of her sister's poems; Charlotte's persistent endeavours to break down Emily's reserve; Charlotte's longing to see, or at the very least to hear from, Constantin Héger, and her knowledge that Emily both knew and disapproved of it; all this caused a struggle no less violent and prolonged in that it remained unspoken. The atmosphere, always liable to rise to sudden tension, was still further heightened by the presence in the house, day after day, of Branwell, and of Mr. Brontë, now all but blinded by cataract yet unable to have an operation.[7]

Occasionally the friction came to a head, but the real difference between them was never mentioned. One such incident concerned Emily's attitude towards the investment of the sisters' legacy from their aunt. Charlotte feared for the safety of their holdings in the railway. She tried to persuade her sisters to re-invest the money in some more settled security.[8] Anne was willing to do whatever Charlotte and Emily thought best, but Emily remained adamant; she would neither consider nor discuss an alteration of her original investment. Anne, as usual, finally sided with her, and Charlotte, fearful of offending Emily and so of placing herself further still from the complete confidence she coveted, was obliged to let the matter drop:[9] 'I cannot . . . persuade my sisters to regard the affair precisely from my point of view,' she wrote, 'and I feel as if I would rather run the risk of loss than hurt Emily's feelings by acting in direct opposition to her opinion—she acted in a most handsome and able manner for me when I was at Brussels and prevented by distance from looking after my own interests—therefore I will let her manage still and take the consequences. Disinterested and energetic she certainly is; and if she be not quite so tractable or open to conviction as I could wish, I must remember perfection is not the lot of humanity; and as long as we can regard those we love, and to whom we are closely allied, with profound and never-shaken esteem, it is a small thing that they should vex us occasionally by, what appear to us, unreasonable and headstrong notions.'[10]

Anne's outward calm began to break under the strain of months that left Branwell no nearer normality. Even the fundamental confidence between the three sisters began to show signs of disintegration under the strain of this constant close proximity to one another, to Branwell, and to their father. Anne's own plaintive lines suggest as much:

> Why should such gloomy silence reign,
> And why is all the house so drear.
> When neither danger, sickness, pain,
> Nor death, nor want, has entered here?
>
> We are as many as we were
> That other night, when all were gay
> And full of hope, and free from care;
> Yet is there something gone away.
>
> The moon without, as pure and calm,
> Is shining as that night she shone;
> But now, to us, she brings no balm,
> For something from our hearts is gone.
>
> Something whose absence leaves a void—
> A cheerless want in every heart;
> Each feels the bliss of all destroyed,
> And mourns the change—but each apart.
>
> The fire is burning in the grate
> As redly as it used to burn;
> But still the hearth is desolate,
> Till mirth, and love, with peace return.
>
> 'Twas peace that flowed from heart to heart,
> With looks and smiles that spoke of Heaven,
> And gave us language to impart
> The blissful thoughts itself had given.
>
> Domestic peace—best joy of earth!
> When shall we all thy value learn?
> White angel, to our sorrowing hearth,
> Return—oh, graciously return![11]

Charlotte had spent a wretched summer, and, the moment her time was up, she was writing again to Héger: 'The six months of silence have run their course. It is now the 18th of November; my last letter was dated (I think) the 18th of May. I may there-

fore write to you without failing in my promise. The summer
and autumn seemed very long to me; truth to tell, it has needed
painful efforts on my part to bear hitherto the self-denial which I
have imposed on myself. You, Monsieur, cannot conceive what
it means; but suppose for a moment that one of your children
was separated from you, 160 leagues away, and that you had to
remain six months without writing to him, without receiving
news of him, without hearing him spoken of, without knowing
aught of his health, then you would understand easily all the
harshness of such an obligation. I tell you frankly that I have
tried meanwhile to forget you, for the remembrance of a person whom one thinks never to see again, and whom, nevertheless, one greatly esteems, frets the mind too much; and when
one has suffered that kind of anxiety for a year or two, one is
ready to do anything to find peace once more. I have done
everything; I have sought occupations; I have denied myself
absolutely the pleasure of speaking about you—even to Emily;
but I have been able to conquer neither my regrets nor my impatience. That, indeed, is humiliating—to be unable to control
one's own thoughts, to be the slave of a regret, of a memory, the
slave of a fixed and dominant idea which lords it over the mind.
Why cannot I have just as much friendship for you, as you for
me—neither more or less? Then I should be so tranquil, so free
—I could keep silence then for six years without an effort. My
father is well but his sight is almost gone. He can neither read
nor write. Yet the doctors advise waiting a few months more
before attempting an operation. The winter will be a long night
for him. He rarely complains; I admire his patience. If Providence wills the same calamity for me, may He at least vouchsafe
me as much patience with which to bear it! It seems to me,
Monsieur, that there is nothing more galling in great physical
misfortunes than to be compelled to make all those about us
share in our sufferings. The ills of the soul one can hide, but those
which attack the body and destroy the faculties cannot be concealed. My father allows me now to read to him and write for
him; he shows me, too, more confidence than he has ever shown
before, and that is a great consolation.

'Monsieur, I have a favour to ask of you: when you reply
to this letter, speak to me a little of yourself, not of me; for I
know that if you speak of me it will be to scold me, and this

time I would see your kindly side. Speak to me therefore of your children. Never was your brow severe when Louise and Claire and Prosper were by your side. Tell me also something of the School, of the pupils, of the Governesses. Are Mesdemoiselles Blanche, Sophie, and Justine still at Brussels? Tell me where you travelled during the holidays—did you go to the Rhine? Did you not visit Cologne or Coblentz? Tell me, in short, my master, what you will, but tell me something. To write to an ex-assistant-governess (No! I refuse to remember my employment as assistant-governess—I repudiate it)—anyhow, to write to an old pupil cannot be a very interesting occupation for you, I know; but for me it is life. Your last letter was stay and prop to me—nourishment to me for half a year. Now I need another and you will give it me; not because you bear me friendship—you cannot have much—but because you are compassionate of soul and you would condemn no one to prolonged suffering to save yourself a few moments' trouble. To forbid me to write to you, to refuse to answer me, would be to tear from me my only joy on earth, to deprive me of my last privilege—a privilege I shall never consent willingly to surrender. Believe me, my master, in writing to me it is a good deed that you will do. So long as I believe you are pleased with me, so long as I have hope of receiving news from you, I can be at rest and not too sad. But when a prolonged and gloomy silence seems to threaten me with the estrangement of my master— when day by day I await a letter, and when day by day disappointment comes to fling me back into overwhelming sorrow, and the sweet delight of seeing your handwriting and reading your counsel escapes me as a vision that is vain, then fever claims me—I lose appetite and sleep—I pine away. May I write to you again next May? I would rather wait a year, but it is impossible—it is too long.'[12]

Here her self-control broke down, and she did what she had once told Héger was not to be thought of:[13] 'I must say one word to you in English—I wish I could write to you more cheerful letters, for when I read this over, I find it to be somewhat gloomy—but forgive me my dear master—do not be irritated at my sadness—according to the words of the Bible: "Out of the fulness of the heart, the mouth speaketh" and truly I find it difficult to be more cheerful so long as I think I shall never see you more. You will perceive by the defects in this letter that I am forgetting the French language—yet I read all the French books I can get, and learn a daily portion by heart—but I have never heard French spoken but once since I left Brussels—and then it sounded like music in my ears—every word was most precious to me because it reminded me of you—I love French for your sake with all my heart and soul. Farewell, my dear Master—may God protect you with special care and crown you with peculiar blessings.'[14]

So Charlotte poured out her heart in this most moving letter. Yet it seems that her desperate and poignant appeal was sent, with cruel irony, to a man whom it could only embarrass. His choice of a woman had been Mme. Héger—Charlotte's opposite in almost every way. But Charlotte could never learn that few people felt with or responded to her own intensity—mild interest, sensible affection, and self-sufficiency were all beyond her imagination. Thus she was bitterly hurt by the two people for whom she cared most passionately—Héger and Emily—both of whom, in their own way, kept her at arm's length.

When she was in Brussels she was often able to regard Héger with fair objectivity, although even then her estimate of him was far from the truth. In the *pensionnat*, Charlotte's opinion of women, never very high, sank to disgusted contempt. Mme. Héger was cunning and untrustworthy, the mistresses spiteful and small-minded, and the girls phlegmatic boors. In such a setting Héger appeared more remarkable than he was—his masculinity contrasting irresistibly with the female atmosphere she detested—and Charlotte made the profound mistake of supposing his fieriness to be the manifestation of a deep and passionate nature.

When she began writing to him she was still able to keep a reasonable balance between Héger as she knew him to be and Héger as she wanted to think of him—as her early letters to him show. But as time passed and her longing for him increased, so did her picture of him become distorted, until her heart and imagination combined to produce this desperate appeal to a man who never existed.[15] Héger's reply must have been a terrible shock. He proposed that she should in future address her letters to the Athénée.[16] His motive was a kindly one, because if Mme. Héger had had her way, the correspondence would have stopped at once.[17] But to Charlotte his suggestion was intolerable, and she never wrote to him again.

For a time she was too stunned to do more than stare aghast at this ruin, not of her hopes, for she had none, but of the vision of Héger that had sustained her through years of frustration and nothingness.

She could bear to love in vain—many women had done so—but she could not bear the thought that so much she had loved was merely the shadow of her own imagination. But Charlotte was too spirited to languish for long. Somehow, the obsession had to be exorcised. She could not talk to anyone about it, but she could write it out of herself, as she had written out lesser emotional troubles at Roe Head and so often since then. Héger was perhaps not the man she had thought him, but she had seen such a man in her imagination, she had felt deeply for him, and she had imagined a thousand times how their relationship might have developed under happier circumstances.

To this task she set herself—reversing, in crude but understandable fashion, the actual order of events and the sex of the people in the story. She called this story *The Professor*. As it developed, she began to think of publication—no impossible thought to her now that the poems were actually due to appear. She spoke to Emily and Anne. She found that Emily already had the materials for a book in her mind,[18] and that Anne had actually written the nucleus of a novel in her *Passages in the Life of an Individual*.[19]

This was quite enough for Charlotte. They would be novelists, and stake a place in the world for themselves in this way, During that winter of 1845–6 the sisters resumed their old habit of the days of Gondal and Angrian making out; they paced round the room for hours in the evening, discussing and elaborating their work.[20]

Charlotte said nothing to Ellen of Héger in her letters or during her February visit to Brookroyd; nor did she mention the forthcoming publication of the poems or the work on the three novels. With one exception—Branwell—her confidences were now reduced to minor exchanges of gossip and local news.[21] Charlotte also favoured her friend with some heavy-handed moralization in an endeavour—which met with no success—to rationalize her own emotions. Her relations with Ellen were subsiding into a passionless friendship with Charlotte taking command. 'Yours faithfully' Charlotte is signing herself in 1846 after a particularly matter-of-fact analysis of her friend's character—a far cry from the 'Darling friend' of close upon twenty years before. Yet the change indicates less a failing in Charlotte than a righting of her sense of proportion. To such a bedrock their friendship must sink if it were to continue. Charlotte, nothing if not practical where her emotions were not too strongly engaged, perceived this truth and imposed the new order on her loyal, hero-worshipping, but more sentimental friend.[22]

Of Branwell, however, Charlotte spoke freely, using Ellen as the repository of her disgust and shame at her brother's behaviour and, particularly, at his squandering of his sisters' lives and prospects. This was a rôle which neither Emily nor Anne would consent to fill. Anne was not merely shocked, she deeply pitied Branwell; already she was coming to see that his upbringing was largely responsible for his present condition; and the belief was gradually forming in her mind that it was her duty to expose this fault. Emily was alternately impressed by his protestations of undying love, and scornful of his moral collapse; yet even a weak Branwell still appealed successfully to her instinct to defend the helpless; and it seems plain that she was not at all times able to distinguish clearly between bravado and courage, empty heroics and true determination.

Branwell was therefore, in some sense, championed by his younger sisters, however much he might complain of neglect at home. Charlotte alone disdainfully avoided him; but so much did she dominate the household that Branwell might be excused for imagining at times that every hand was against him. Besides, he had never felt strongly for Emily or Anne, but he loved and respected Charlotte. He and Charlotte had worked and played together for years, and only she had the power to hurt him deeply.

It is not easy to tell where sanguinity and self-deception, truth and a particularly facile imagination meet in Branwell's accounts of his relations with Mrs. Robinson. He dramatized every thought and action. Others dramatize beneath their breath, as it were, and so comfort themselves after the prosaic fact has passed, but Branwell lived in a world of make-belief; as he thought, so he spoke. He shrank from bare facts; he would not face life; but never had he deceived himself so consistently and completely as now. That Mrs. Robinson at any time regarded the young tutor over-seriously need not be supposed. Nevertheless, she tolerated when she did not actively encourage him.[23] Branwell certainly was incapable of concealing his passion for the better part of three years, yet Mrs. Robinson made no move either to be rid of him or to keep him at arm's length while he was at Thorp Green. Branwell was not unhandsome, he could talk well and amusingly and he was in many ways lively and engaging. A woman nearly twenty years his senior might well find his attentions flattering.[24]

Mrs. Robinson cannot therefore escape responsibility for permitting such attentions, if she did no more than this. But now she had become aware that this young man's obsession might lead to serious trouble. Branwell's dismissal must have involved her in unpleasantness, yet her admirer was plainly not disposed to accept this forced parting. He wrote frantic, impassioned letters, assuming that she was suffering as greatly as himself. He also tried to send messages by way of the Robinson servants.[25]

Branwell clearly must have been given some grounds for his constant assumption that Mrs. Robinson was as distracted as he by the separation. He knew, of course, that her marriage was not a happy one. But neither that knowledge nor his own vanity would seem sufficient to explain his tireless reiteration of their mutual passion and misery. When Branwell told Grundy that: 'I received a furious letter from my employer, threatening to shoot me if I returned from my vacation,'[26] his inveterate temptation to romanticize may have transformed a plain warning to a philanderer to keep his distance into a dramatic threat more in keeping with Branwell's chosen rôle. But when he wrote that: 'When he mentioned my name—she stared at him and fainted. When she recovered she in turn dwelt upon her inextinguishable love for me—her horror at having been the first to delude me into wretchedness,'[27] the impression is that, for all their extravagance, his words are not without a basis of truth.

Then, in May 1846, Mr. Robinson died. Mrs. Robinson's policy, which, in the interests of discretion, must first have been to keep Branwell's ardour within bounds, was at once changed.

To such a woman, living in the country and tied to an elderly invalid, young Branwell had been a pleasant distraction. But to this same woman, freed of her husband, free to use her money and position, and with a promise of London society in her mind's eye, Branwell had nothing to recommend him. He, with the possibility of Mr. Robinson's death never far from his mind, had rested the most extravagant hopes on the event. These hopes it was now Mrs. Robinson's business to dispel; yet in such a manner as to prevent a scandal. How she did so was told both by the indignant Charlotte and by Branwell.[28]

Charlotte's disgust with Branwell had not lessened—she was complaining at this time that he had declined an offer to return to the railway: 'He refuses to make an effort. He will not work —and at home he is a drain on every resource—an impediment to all happiness'[29]—but this did not prevent criticism of Mrs. Robinson. The two Robinson daughters, who still wrote regularly to Anne, provided another and a more reliable source of information about Mrs. Robinson than Branwell himself. What they had to say of their mother only increased the dislike and contempt felt by Charlotte and her sisters. Mrs. Robinson proclaimed herself worldly and heartless by the way she was trying to bring up her daughters. 'We, I am sorry to say, have been somewhat more harassed than usual lately,' Charlotte told Ellen. 'The death of Mr. Robinson, which took place about three weeks or a month ago, served Branwell for a pretext to throw all about him into hubbub and confusion with his emotions. Shortly after came news from all hands that Mr. Robinson had altered his will before he died and effectually prevented all chance of a marriage between his widow and Branwell, by stipulating that she should not have a shilling if she ever ventured to reopen any communication with him. Of course, he then became intolerable. To papa he allows rest neither day nor night, and he is continually screwing money out of him, sometimes threatening that he will kill himself if it is withheld from him. He says Mrs. Robinson is now insane; that her mind is a complete wreck owing to remorse for her conduct towards Mr. Robinson (whose end it appears was hastened by distress of mind) and grief for having lost him. I do not know how much to believe of what he says, but I fear she is very ill. Branwell declares that he neither can nor will do anything for himself; good situations have been offered him more than once, for which, by a fortnight's work, he might have qualified himself, but he will do nothing except drink and make us all wretched.'[30]

Branwell was, of course, unable to share his sisters' view of Mrs. Robinson. He, like them, accepted the reason (which possessed no basis in fact) for the continued separation.[31] He reported it, no doubt with elaborations, to Leyland the day after he had been called down to the Black Bull to meet the coachman from Thorp Green. Branwell had been at work spasmodically upon a poem he had promised to send his friend: 'I should have sent you "Morley Hall" ere now,' he wrote, 'but I am unable to finish it at present from agony to which the grave would be far preferable. Mr. Robinson of Thorp Green is dead, and he has left his widow in a dreadful state of health. She sent the coachman over to me yesterday, and the account which he gave of her sufferings was enough to burst my heart. Through the will she is left quite powerless, and her eldest daughter who married imprudently is cut off without a shilling. The Executing Trustees[32] detest me, and one declares that if he sees me he will shoot me. These things I do not care about, but I do care for the life of the one who suffers even more than I do. Her Coachman said that it was a pity to see her, for she was only able to kneel in her bedroom in bitter tears and prayers. She has worn herself out in attendance on him, and his conduct during the few days before his death was exceedingly mild and repentant, but that only distressed her doubly. Her conscience has helped to agonize her, and that misery I am saved from. You, though not much older than myself, have known life. I now know it with a vengeance—for four nights I have not slept—for three days I have not tasted food—and when I think of the state of her I love best on earth, I could wish that my head was as cold and stupid as the medallion which lies in your studio. I write very egotistically but it is because my mind is crowded with one set of thoughts and I long for one sentence from a friend. What I shall *do* I know not—I am too hard to die, and too wretched to live. My wretchednesss is not about castles in the air, but about stern realities; my hardihood lies in bodily vigour; but, dear Sir, my mind sees only a dreary future which I as little wish to enter on as could a martyr to be bound to the stake.'[33] Thus Branwell gave vent to his one lasting satisfaction—a morbid and unadulterated exhibition of self-pity under the disguise of the romantic lover. He omitted nothing. Not content with the comparison of himself and the martyr, he must needs extract the last drop of pleasure from his recital by attaching a sketch of himself tied to the stake in the midst of flames. Underneath the sketch, to make assurance doubly sure, he scribbled, 'Myself'.[34]

Branwell attempted to gain some crumb of comfort for the future by messages—presumably through the Robinsons' coachman—to Mrs. Robinson and to her doctor. But, as he tells Leyland, there was no comfort to be had: 'Well, my dear Sir, I have got my finishing stroke at last—and I feel stunned into marble by the blow. I have this morning received a long, kind, and faithful letter from the medical gentleman who attended Mr. R. in his last illness and who has since had an interview with one whom I can never forget. He knows me *well*, and he pities my case most sincerely, for he declares that, though used to the rough ups and downs of this weary world, he shed tears from his heart when he saw the state of that lady and knew what I should feel. When she recovered she in turns dwelt on her inextinguishable love for me—her horror at having been the first to delude me into wretchedness, and her agony at having been the cause of the death of her husband, who, in his last hours, bitterly repented of his treatment of her. Her sensitive mind was totally wrecked. She wandered into talking of entering a nunnery; and the Doctor fairly debars me from hope in the future.'[35] Branwell then drops a tear or two on his own behalf: 'It's hard work for me dear Sir; I would bear it—but my health is so bad that the body seems as if it could not bear the mental shock. I never cared one bit about the property. I cared about herself—and always shall do. May God bless her, but I wish I had never known her! My appetite is lost; my nights are dreadful, and having nothing to do makes me dwell on past scenes—on her own self, her voice, her person, her thoughts, till I could be glad if God would take me. In the next world I could not be worse than I am in this. I am not a whiner, dear Sir, but when a young man like myself has fixed his soul on a being *worthy* of all love—and who for years, has *given* him all love, pardon him for boring a friend with a misery that has only one black end. I fully expected a change of the will, and difficulties placed in my way by powerful and wealthy men, but I *hardly* expected the hopeless ruin of the mind that I loved even more than its body.'[36]

This final end to his hopes of marrying Mrs. Robinson, however fantastic these hopes had been, was no less the end of Branwell. He had two more years to live; he was to have moments of hectic gaiety, of feverish activity, of broken repentance, of spasmodic attempts to write; yet it is true to say that he never recovered from the shock. He sank now into a stupor, largely self-induced, from which he emerged by fits and starts only to relapse again and again.

Yet neither Branwell nor his sisters ever for a moment thought that he was soon to die; and the estrangement between him and Charlotte continued to the end. Charlotte still had the power to hurt him genuinely, as he showed in his story to a friend at the Black Bull about a Sunday school pupil who was ill. The tone of this letter, and even the style of the writing, differ so markedly from Branwell's usual manner that it is difficult to believe that it was written by the man who maundered on about Mrs. Robinson. Indeed, he was not the same, for his feeling for Charlotte had no need of heroics; it was probably the most sincere attachment of his life. 'I went to see the poor little thing,' Branwell said, 'sat with her half an hour and read a psalm to her and a hymn at her request. I felt very much like praying with her too, but you see I was not good enough. How dare I pray for another, who had almost forgotten how to pray for myself? I came away with a heavy heart, for I felt sure she would die, and went straight home, where I fell into melancholy musings. I wanted somebody to cheer me. I often do; but no kind word finds its way to my ears, much less to my heart. Charlotte observed my depression, and asked what ailed me. So I told her. She looked at me with a look which I shall never forget, if I live to be a hundred years old—which I never shall. It was not like her at all. It wounded me, as if someone had struck me a blow in the mouth. It involved ever so many things in it. It was a dubious look. It ran over me, questioning and examining, as if I had been a wild beast. It said: "Did my ears deceive me, or did I hear aught?" And then came the painful baffled expression which was worse than all. It said, "I wonder if that's true?" But, as she left the room, she seemed to accuse herself of having wronged me and said, "She is my little scholar and I will go and see her." I replied not a word. I was too much cut up. When she was gone, I came over here to the Black Bull and made a night of it in sheer disgust and desperation. Why could they not give me some credit when I was trying to be good?'[37]

Charlotte said later that Branwell knew nothing of his sisters' literary ventures. But this was not the fact; and the only meaning short of a misstatement that can be attributed to Charlotte is that she personally never discussed her writings with him. But this only made more bitter the contrast between the present and the past. Branwell knew only too well that his sisters were writing and publishing; and no small part of his despair during these last years must have arisen from his exclusion from their confidence. Emily made some kind of contact with her brother on the subject, it would appear. It may well have been at this time that she gained from him some of the details used in her book. But Emily could not, even if she would, admit Branwell into the circle that wrote so industriously and with such grave, intense hope in the parsonage dining-room during the winter of 1845–6 and the following spring. And however Branwell might welcome even such a measure of intercourse, there is no doubt that it was the silence of Charlotte, his old collaborator for so many years, whom he both loved and feared beyond all others of his family, that embittered and depressed him.[38]

There was just a faint possibility that, by way of his writing, given encouragement and a reasonable faith, Branwell might even at this late hour have been brought back to some kind of happiness and usefulness. At least he would have been given harmless distraction from his morbid thoughts and habits, and might have built up once again some sort of self-respect. If Branwell could have been saved, Charlotte alone could have done it. She chose not to try. She had good reason for hardening her heart against him, but her responsibility must remain.

XXII

THE *POEMS* FAIL

The 'Poems' are published but do not sell. Charlotte's efforts to find a publisher for the novels. 'Agnes Grey' and 'Wuthering Heights' accepted: 'The Professor' rejected. Charlotte tries more publishers. She denies a report that she is to marry Nicholls. She takes her father to Manchester for an eye operation. Her depression in the lodgings. She begins 'Jane Eyre'. More trouble from Branwell. His letters of self-analysis and regrets for Mrs. Robinson. He improves slightly, and Charlotte asks Ellen to stay. Disappointment at the last moment. Her bitterness. She sends copies of the 'Poems' to famous authors. Analysis of the poems. Charlotte's responsibility for alterations to Emily's poems.

At the end of May 1846 the little book of *Poems* by Currer, Ellis, and Acton Bell was published.[1] It was a complete failure. Only two copies were sold,[2] and only three reviews appeared.[3] The reviews, however, all spoke well of the poems, and prophesied a future for Emily as poet. In any case, the three girls, with Charlotte very much the leading spirit, were already well on with their novels, and Charlotte had already approached Aylott and Jones about publishing them. She told the publishers in April that the novels were nearly finished. Her inquiry was not successful; Aylott and Jones, she was told, did not publish works of fiction.[4] Then began once more the business of sending manuscripts the rounds of the publishing houses. Anne's *Agnes Grey* (as it was finally entitled) and Emily's *Wuthering Heights* were accepted, after some hard bargaining, by T. C. Newby of Mortimer Street;[5] but Newby would not publish Charlotte's *The Professor*; nor, it seemed, would any other publisher. Charlotte, however, persisted, as she had persisted with the poems the year before; and no sooner did her manuscript return to Haworth than she readdressed it (with the rejecting publisher's name as often as not still on the wrapper, roughly scratched out) and sent it off again on its travels.[6]

At the beginning of July a rumour reached Ellen that her friend was about to be engaged to A. B. Nicholls. Charlotte promptly denied it: 'A cold far-away sort of civility are the only terms on which I have ever been with Mr. Nicholls. I could by no means think of mentioning such a rumour to him even as a joke. It would make me the laughing stock of himself and his fellow curates for half a year to come. They regard me as an old maid, and I regard them, one and all, as highly uninteresting, narrow and unattractive specimens of the coarser sex.'[7] There seems no reason to doubt Charlotte's sincerity; she was at this time less interested in men and marriage than ever before; but it is possible that a faint hope of this kind had crossed the mind of Nicholls; and it is also probable that Charlotte's apparent lack of interest in him, combined with his unpopularity in the parish (for he was outwardly stiff and unforthcoming), made him think of going back to Ireland.[8]

Mr. Brontë's cataract had become a great deal worse. He was nearly blind, but still refused to consider an operation, until, in August, Charlotte took matters into her own hands and, ignoring her father's protests, went with Emily to Manchester to find a good eye-surgeon.[9] There she made arrangements both for the operation and for lodgings in the town, if the surgeon wanted her father to stay within call.[10]

Three weeks later, Charlotte and her father settled in rooms in Boundary Street, Manchester.[11] They stayed there until the end of September, when Mr. Brontë, who had made a good recovery from the operation, was allowed to go home.[12] These five weeks in lodgings were among the worst Charlotte had ever spent in her life.[13] The greater part of the time she spent in a darkened room with her father. Mr. Brontë, who had had less and less to say to his children as the years passed, was now almost completely silent; indeed, he was for a time forbidden to talk or to be talked to. Charlotte, reluctant to leave him even on the few occasions when she could do so, was left to her own thoughts, and these were far from pleasant.[14] The continued inability to find a publisher for *The Professor* proclaimed her a failure.[15] Her old enemy, hypochondria, attacked her. She was lonely by day, haunted by night. So, tired from anxiety and watching, and unutterably depressed, she brooded on that brief part of her life which stood out above the rest. But now her longing for Héger was succeeded by a sense of shame and morbid self-reproach. Now that her father was ill and in pain, her over-sensitive conscience convicted her of failing in her duty to him. Something of this she expressed to Ellen, who asked for her help in a projected school scheme at Brookroyd: 'But if I *could* leave home Ellen—I should not be at Haworth now. I know life is passing away and I am doing nothing—earning nothing— a very bitter knowledge it is at moments—but I see no way out of the mist. More than one very favourable opportunity has now offered which I have been obliged to put aside. Probably when I am free to leave home I shall neither be able to find place nor employment—perhaps too I shall be quite past the prime of life—my faculties will be rusted—and my few acquirements in a great measure forgotten. These ideas sting me keenly some- times—but whenever I consult my conscience it affirms that I am doing right in staying at home—and bitter are its upbraid- ings when I yield to an eager desire for release. I returned to Brussels after Aunt's death against my conscience—prompted by what then seemed an irresistible impulse—I was punished for my selfish folly by a total withdrawal for more than two years of happiness and peace of mind—I could hardly expect success if I were to err again in the same way.'[16] At this time Charlotte re-lived the agonies of her second year in Brussels: ' . . . the tyranny of Hypochondria—a most dreadful doom, far worse than that of a man with healthy nerves buried in a subterranean dungeon. I endured it but a year, and assuredly I can never forget the concentrated anguish of certain insufferable moments and the heavy gloom of many long hours, besides the preter- natural horror which seemed to clothe existence and Nature, and which made life a continual waking Nightmare. Under such circumstances the morbid nerves can know neither peace nor enjoyment—whatever touches, pierces them—sensation for them is all suffering. A weary burden nervous patients conse- quently become to those about them—they know this, and it infuses a new gall, corrosive in its extreme acritude, into their bitter cup.'[17]

Yet in spite of pain and weariness and depression, her in- domitable spirit roused her to fresh effort. The conviction that she had something of greatness in her, the ever present wish to express herself, the knowledge that youth and opportunity were passing, and the proud struggle for self-respect—all worked together to spur on that small, tired, unhappy woman in her Manchester lodgings. And so, in circumstances sufficiently intimidating to the stoutest heart, Charlotte sat down in her comfortless room beside her silent father and began a new novel. *The Professor* had been returned once more to her at Manchester on the very day of Mr. Brontë's operation,[18] but Charlotte sent it off again to another publisher and, no longer content to place her hopes of fame in this one book, wrote there and then the first pages of what was to be her *Jane Eyre*[19]—pages which now stand among the best work she ever did.

Mr. Brontë made a quick and satisfactory recovery, and within a few weeks of returning home he was once more taking the services.[20] Anne was again showing signs of the delicacy which worried Charlotte: 'She had two nights last week when her cough and difficulty of breathing were painful indeed to hear and witness, and must have been most distressing to suffer. She bore it, as she does all affliction, without one complaint—only sighing now and then when nearly worn out. She has an extraordinary heroism of endurance. I admire but I certainly could not imitate her.'[21]

While Charlotte was away, Branwell had made himself even more of an embarrassment than usual; his eccentricities were no longer just a local joke. His excursions to Halifax and Bradford culminated, soon after Charlotte came home, in the arrival at the parsonage of a most unwelcome visitor: 'Nothing happens at Haworth—nothing at least of a pleasant kind,' Charlotte told Ellen. 'One little incident indeed occurred about a week ago to sting us to life—but if it gives no more pleasure for you to hear than it did for us to witness, you will scarcely thank me for adverting to it. It was merely the arrival of a Sheriff's Officer on a visit to Branwell, inviting him either to pay his debts or to take a trip to York.[22] Of course his debts had to be paid—it is not agreeable to lose money time after time in this way, but it is ten times worse to witness the shabbiness of his behaviour on such occasions.'[23] Branwell, for her, no longer deserved any consideration. She spoke of him as of some shameful burden. She had no hope of him, no faith in him, no love for him: 'But where is the use of dwelling on this subject? it will make him no better.'[24] And again, a few months later, during the first months of 1847, when she was planning for her friend to visit Haworth: 'In summer and in fine weather your visit here might be much better managed than in winter—we could go out more, be more independent of the house and of one room.'[25]

That room was where her brother spent most of his time at home—sometimes drunk, sometimes drugged, sometimes attempting to finish his promised poem, 'Morley Hall', for his friend Leyland,[26] sometimes overwhelmed by black despair and contrition, and convulsed by fear of damnation—a fear that every scoffing and blasphemous word eventually magnified an hundredfold.[27]

Early in of 1847, Branwell, smarting from a fresh rejection at Thorp Green, and finding no comfort at home unburdened himself on to the long-suffering Leyland: 'I am going to write a letter for the querulous egotism of which I must intreat your mercy, but, when I look *upon* my past, present and future, and then *into* my own self, I find much, however unpleasant, that yearns for utterance.'[28] He explains the immediate cause of his perturbation: 'This last week an honest and kindly friend has warned me that concealed hopes about one lady should be given up, let the effort to do so cost what it may. He is the Family Medical Attendant, and was commanded by Mr. Evans, M.P. for North Derbyshire to return me, unopened, a letter which I addressed to Thorp Green and which the lady was not permitted to see. She, too, surrounded by powerful persons who hate me like Hell, has sunk into religious melancholy, believes that her weight of sorrow is God's punishment, and hopelessly resigns herself to her doom. God only knows what it does cost, and will, hereafter, cost me to tear from my heart and remembrance the thousand recollections that rush upon me at the thought of four years gone by. Like ideas of sunlight to a man who has lost his sight they must be bright phantoms not to be realised again.'[29]

His tragedy, as he saw it, was increased by the importance of those whom he believed to be leagued against him and Mrs. Robinson—the usual fantasy of the paranoiac. He thought, or forced himself to think, that she remained faithful to him; and he bewailed the loss, not only of her, but (with a distinct falling away of high romance), of the material benefits she would have brought him: 'I had reason to hope that ere very long I should be the husband of a Lady whom I loved best in the world, and with whom, in more than a competence, I might live at leisure to try to make myself a name in the world of posterity, without being pestered by the small but countless botherments, which like mosquitoes sting us in the world of work-day toil. That hope, and herself, are *gone*—*She* to wither into patiently pining decline—*It* to make room for drudgery falling on one now ill fitted to bear it.'[30] How far from a decline Mrs. Robinson was, the subsequent career of that lady is sufficient evidence.[31] Branwell's analysis of himself, undertaken as usual with morbid pleasure, was a great deal more accurate—though he was unable to profit by it: 'That ill-fittedness rises from causes which I find myself able partially to overcome had I bodily strength, but with the want of that, and with the presence of daily lacerated nerves, the task is not easy. I have been in truth too much petted through life, and in my last situation I was so much master, and gave myself so much up to enjoyment, that now, when the cloud of ill-health and adversity has come upon me, it will be a disheartening job to work myself up again through a new life's battle, from the position of five years ago to that which I have been compelled to retreat with heavy loss and no gain. My army stands now where it did then, but mourning the slaughter of Youth, Health, Hope, and both mental and physical elasticity. The last two losses are indeed important to one who once built his hopes of rising in the world on the possession of them. Noble writings, works of art, music or poetry now, instead of rousing my imagination, cause a whirlwind of blighting sorrow that sweeps over my mind with unspeakable dreariness, and, if I sit down and try to write, all ideas that used to come clothed in sunlight now press round me in funeral black; for nearly every pleasurable excitement that I used to know has changed to insipidity or pain.'[32]

Branwell anticipates by a few weeks Charlotte's lament at the premature passing of youth and hope: 'I shall never be able to realize the too sanguine hopes of my friends, for at 28 I am a thoroughly *old man*—mentally and bodily—Far more so indeed than I am willing to express. God knows I do not scribble like a poetaster when I quote Byron's terribly truthful words:

> No more, no more, oh! never more on me
> The freshness of the heart shall fall like dew,
> Which, out of all the lovely things we see
> Extracts emotions beautiful and new!

I used to think if I could have for a week the free range of the

British Museum—the Library included—I could feel as though I were placed for seven days in Paradise, but now, really, dear sir, my eyes would roam over the Elgin marbles, the Egyptian saloon and the most treasured volumes like the eyes of a dead codfish.'[33]

This self-estimate was by now only too true, however dramatically Branwell chose to phrase it. Self indulgence had begun finally to deaden his finer faculties. The eager enthusiasm that had led him to pore over a map of London for hours at a time until every street was known to him,[34] the hope that had dreamed of setting eyes on the treasures of the Academy and had regarded the British Museum as the acme of delight, the fertile imagination that had built up a life within a life in the teeming conception of the Angrian kingdom—all this had dwindled with appalling speed into worse than nothingness. Not least shocking in this disintegration was the loneliness which struck at Branwell's last remnants of self-control. The more desperate the wretched man's state of mind became, the more violent grew his longing for a confidant. His father's ineffectual remonstrances and provision of money, and Emily's rough attempts at consolation proved indifferent solace for the thinly veiled horror and pity of Anne, the scathing scorn of Charlotte; they could not take the place of a man's affection and understanding. To fill such a place no one appeared. To Leyland—who with Grundy was forced willy-nilly into the role of confidant —Branwell complained bitterly of the lack of sympathy and understanding among his village acquaintances, who, doubtless, were by now tired of him: 'My rude rough acquaintances here ascribe my unhappiness solely to causes produced by my sometimes irregular life, because they have known no other pains than those resulting from excess or want of ready cash. They do not know that I would rather want a shirt than a springy step, and that my total want of happiness, were I to step into York Minster now, would be far, far worse than their want of an hundred pounds when they might happen to need it, and that if a dozen glasses or a bottle of wine drives off their cares, such cures only make me outwardly passable in company, but *never* drive off mine.'[35]

Branwell thought a great deal of the future, which his imagination presented in lurid and uniformly pessimistic terms, but no premonition of death appears to have crossed his mind. His fate was at least to be more merciful than the picture he drew of it: '*I* know only that it is time for me to be something when I am nothing; that my father cannot have long to live, and that when he dies, my evening, which is already twilight, will become night; that I shall then have a constitution still so strong that it will keep me years in torture and despair when I should every hour pray that I might die. I know that I am avoiding, while I write, one greatest cause of my utter despair—but by God, sir, it is nearly too bitter for me to allude to it!'[36]

It was as well that Branwell qualified his reluctance to discuss Mrs. Robinson, for his friends must have thought that his tragedy lay in his inability to think, talk, or write on any other subject. Thus, in this same letter, he immediately proceeds to traverse once more the same weary void of self-pity, self-delusion, dramatic accusation, and, finally, the inevitable apology: 'For four years (including one year of absence), a lady intensely loved me as I did her, and each sacrificed to that love all we had to sacrifice, and held out to each other HOPE for our guide to the future. She was all I could wish for in a woman, and vastly above me in rank, and she loved me even better than I did her. Now what is the result of these four years? UTTER WRECK. The "Great Britain" is not so thoroughly stranded as I am. I have received today, since I began my scrawl, a note from her maid, Miss Anne Marshall, and I *know* from it that she has been terrified by vows which she was forced to swear to, on her husband's deathbed, (with every addition of terror which the ghastly dying eye could inflict upon a keenly sensitive and almost *worried* woman's mind) a complete severance from him in whom lay her whole heart's feelings. When that husband was scarce cold in his grave, her relations, who controlled the whole property, overwhelmed her with their tongues, and I am *quite conscious* that she has succumbed in terror to what they have said. To no one living have I said what I now say to you, and I should not bother yourself with my incoherent account did I not believe that you would be able to understand somewhat of what I meant—though *not all*, sir—for he who is without hope, and knows that his clock is at twelve at night, cannot communicate his feelings to one who finds *his* at twelve noon.'[37]

The call of the sheriff sobered Branwell for a time. With one exception in the spring, which Charlotte reported—'Branwell has been conducting himself very badly lately, I expect from the extravagance of his behaviour and from mysterious hints he drops (for he never will speak out plainly) that we shall be hearing news of fresh debts contracted by him soon'[38]—with this one exception, he became comparatively quiet.

Charlotte, who had been steadily refusing invitations to Brookroyd because she felt unable to ask Ellen to Haworth in return, now judged that at last her friend might without too great a shock be asked to the parsonage: 'Branwell is quieter now and for a good reason: he has got to the end of a considerable sum of money of which he became possessed in the spring, and consequently is obliged to restrict himself in some degree. You must expect to find him weaker in mind, and the complete rake in appearance. I have no apprehension of his being at all uncivil to you: on the contrary, he will be as smooth as oil.'[39]

Having thus explained, prepared, warned, and reassured her friend, Charlotte fixed Whitsun as the time for the visit.[40] She had little faith in her ability to entertain a guest—even an old friend—and none at all in the attractiveness of the family and home in general: 'Prepare for much dulness and monotony,'[41] she writes pessimistically. But for all that, she makes eager plans for the meeting: 'If you can arrive at Keighley by about four o'clock in the afternoon, Emily, Anne and I will all three meet you at the station. We can take tea jovially together at the Devonshire Arms, and walk home in the cool of the evening.'[42] And again: 'I *do* trust nothing will now arise to prevent your coming . . . if it rains, I shall cry.'[43] And when Ellen asks what dress she shall wear: 'Come in black, blue, pink, white or scarlet, as you like. Come shabby or smart; neither the colour nor the condition signifies; provided only the dress contain Ellen Nussey, all will be right.'[44]

Yet all this preparation and anticipation went for nothing in the end. At the last moment Ellen was unable to come to Haworth.[45] This mild break in the monotony of life at the parsonage was denied to them all, and Charlotte had to postpone once again the hope of seeing and talking to her friend. She needed comfort. The ever-present humiliation of Branwell; the repeated failure to find a publisher for *The Professor*, or even to draw a comment from the rejecting firms; the problem of Mr. Nicholls, whose decision, recently made, to seek another living, seemed a reproach to her; and now, the disappointment over Ellen's cancelled visit: all joined in her mind with the desolating sense of time passing.[46] 'I shall be 31 next birthday,' she wrote to Ellen bitterly, 'my youth is gone like a dream, and very little use have I ever made of it. What have I done these last thirty years? Precious little.'[47]

The fate of the sisters' *Poems* lent additional despondency to her prevailing mood this spring and early summer. For this she had wrestled long, hurtful hours with Emily. For this she had imperilled the harmony that alone promised a hope of peace in the parsonage. For this she had risked the loss of an affection she was growing more and more to depend upon. The neglect of the little volume was not without cause. Charlotte's verses were pedestrian and uninspiring. Anne, in her religious poems especially, sometimes sounded a note of sincerity and depth of feeling, unmarred by sentimentality, that was not far from beauty, but, like her eldest sister, she was unable to put melody into her lines; and her mild excellences are too few in poems that, as a whole, lack unity and distinction.

So far, then, as the contributions of Charlotte and Anne are concerned, the indifference of public and reviewer alike is understandable enough. The treatment of Emily's poems is less easy to explain.

Charlotte held no high opinion of her own or of her youngest sister's poems. She saw in Emily's work, indeed, a merit outstriding the usual feminine verses of the day, yet if she is to be judged, as she must, by her amendments to these poems, it is plain that her appreciation stopped short of full understanding; for she did much to destroy Emily's careful use of punctuation and capital letters and her exact choice of words and symbols on which so much of the beauty and full sense of the poems depend. The fact is, that Charlotte, who was concerned with the heart and with morality, could never hope to understand the work of her sister, who was amoral, and concerned, in her greater poems, almost entirely with the soul. How baffled Charlotte was by some of Emily's more imaginative poems is seen in the titles she afterwards gave them, and, even more, in the utterly incongruous explanations she thought necessary to add for the benefit of the reader. It says much for Charlotte that, feeling thus out of her depth, she yet perceived the greatness of Emily's poems, and extolled and defended them.

Charlotte had little hope of a widespread sale for the poems; but her most pessimistic forecast scarcely anticipated complete failure. Her disappointment is plain in the ironic letter she sent to a number of men of letters admired by her: 'My relatives, Ellis and Acton Bell, and myself, heedless of the repeated warnings of various respectable publishers, have committed the rash act of printing a volume of poems. The consequences predicted have, of course, overtaken us: our book is found to be a drug; no man needs it or heeds it. In the space of a year our publisher has disposed but of two copies, and by what painful efforts he succeeded in getting rid of these two, himself only knows. Before transferring the edition to the trunkmakers, we have decided on distributing as presents a few copies of what we cannot sell—we beg to offer you one in acknowledgment of the pleasure and profit we have often and long derived from your works.'[48]

XXIII

JANE EYRE

*The sisters still writing their novels. 'The Tenant of Wildfell Hall'. 'The Professor'
again returned: but with a letter. Charlotte finishes 'Jane Eyre'. It is accepted and published. It becomes a literary sensation. Analysis of the book.*

CHARLOTTE at thirty-two felt old and worn and disillusioned,[1]
but, unlike Branwell, who had expressed similar feelings a
month or two earlier,[2] she was to triumph over her difficulties.
For she possessed what her brother always lacked—self-discip-
line and strength of purpose—and what he had lost for good—
the ability to work, the drive of ambition, the constant uprising
of a hope that refused to be finally crushed. Thus, whilst Branwell was lamenting the death of his dream of making a name
as writer, backed by Mrs. Robinson's money,[3] his sisters were
working hard in their spare hours when housework was done.
They walked over the moors together in the fading light,
discussing the progress of their novels, and then, at night, sat in
their room, writing, long after their father had gone to bed with
his protesting, threatening, maudlin son.[4]

If Emily wrote again after *Wuthering Heights* was finished—
and there is reason to believe that she did[5]—no trace of her
second work has been discovered. But her sisters' work during
this winter, spring, and early summer of 1846–7 has survived.
Anne, whose earlier premonitions had hardened into certainty
that it was her duty to warn as many people as possible of the
penalties of weakness and sin, worked determinedly at *The
Tenant of Wildfell Hall*. She painted from life, with her example
in the next room, drinking and drugging his life away. All
through the winter and deep into 1847 she worked with fanatical
zeal at her morality story. Unshaken by criticism and disagree-
ment with her sisters, undeterred by her misery when she considered whose fate she was portraying, she went on with her
self-appointed task—a task against which Charlotte protested
vigorously but in vain: 'She had in the course of her life been
called upon to contemplate near at hand, and for a long time,

the terrible effects of talents misused and faculties abused,' wrote Charlotte; 'hers was naturally a sensitive, reserved and dejected nature; what she saw sunk very deeply into her mind; it did her harm. She brooded over it until she believed it to be a duty to reproduce every detail (of course, with fictitious characters, incidents, and situations) as a warning to others. She hated her work, but would pursue it. When reasoned with on the subject, she regarded such reasonings as a temptation to self-indulgence. She must be honest; she must not varnish, soften, or conceal. This well-meant resolution brought on her misconstruction, and some abuse, which she bore, as it was her custom to bear whatever was unpleasant, with mild, steady patience.'[6] Yet however unsuited this work may have been to Anne's true gifts as a writer—her eye for minute observation and flair for description—and however inimical to her own interests it may have proved, the youngest Brontë wrote in *The Tenant of Wildfell Hall* a novel that can by no means be dismissed as a failure. It told a good story—a great deal more readable and exciting than the colourless *Agnes Grey*—and it contains, for its time, some remarkably plain speaking on the relations between men and women.

The Professor, which had met with an unbroken series of rejections, was sent in July by the persevering Charlotte to Smith, Elder and Company. The manuscript was returned once more; but for the first time its author received, instead of the expected rejection slip, a two-page letter from the publishers. They were not prepared to publish *The Professor*, partly because it was too short—the manuscript, they said, would fill only two of the three volumes then established as the conventional length of the novel.[7] But they were clearly interested in Charlotte's work, and expressed readiness to consider a manuscript of the right length. It was also plain that they looked for a rather more dramatic tale.[8]

Fired by this first hint of encouragement, Charlotte turned hurriedly to her unfinished novel. Like her sisters, she expressed herself naturally in the shorter novel form, and it was something of an effort to fill three volumes, but she set to work, preferring to lengthen *Jane Eyre* rather than tamper with the earlier novel already seen and criticized by the publishers. In less than a month she had finished the book and had sent it to Smith

Elder. It was soon accepted, was published on 16 October 1847,[9] and was an instant success. Within a few months a second and a third edition had been called for, and still the demand for copies persisted. *Jane Eyre* became the novel of the season; the sex and identity of the author was one of the questions of the hour among literary circles.

When the success of *Jane Eyre* was assured, Emily and Anne pressed Charlotte to tell Mr. Brontë. He was still ignorant that his children had written novels, let alone published them, and had once at least turned back the postman carrying a packet of proofs, on the ground that no one called Currer Bell lived at the parsonage. One day, Charlotte took the book into her father's study.

'Papa,' she said, 'I've been writing a book.'

'Have you, my dear?'

'Yes; and I want you to read it.'

'I'm afraid it will try my eyes too much.'

'But it is not in manuscript; it is printed.'

'My dear! you've never thought of the expense it will be! It will be almost sure to be a loss; for how can you get a book sold? No one knows you or your name.'

'But, papa, I don't think it will be a loss; no more will you, if you will just let me read you a review or two, and tell you more about it.'

Charlotte read some of the reviews to him, and then left him with the book to read. When he came into the dining-room for tea some time later, he said to Emily and Anne: 'Girls, do you know Charlotte has been writing a book, and it is much better than likely?'

Ever after that, Mr. Brontë read and marked every review of Charlotte's books, however short or unfavourable, and his pride in her authorship was tremendous.[10]

Jane Eyre deserved its success. Its story, which seems to have been based on a tale read by Charlotte a few years earlier, though melodramatic, is exciting without undue absurdity, remarkably easy to read, and difficult to lay down. The characterization is vigorous and, in general, reconcilable with the reader's experience, the book has enormous vitality, and even a characteristic of Charlotte's writing that interferes with the development of character and action—her persistent moralizing

—fell agreeably on the ears of most readers of that time. Another weakness of Charlotte as novelist—an excess of solemnity—was also acceptable to an age with a limited sense of humour.

But these essentials of a popular novel were incidental to the lasting merit of *Jane Eyre*. The book was called an autobiography but unlike *The Professor*, which was also autobiographical, Charlotte, in *Jane Eyre*, had absorbed her material sufficiently to let her art work freely; and in the person of the heroine she unfolded a tale of passion that was unique at that time in its honesty and in its curious but unmistakable impression of innocence. In her picture of the development of Jane Eyre's love, Charlotte revealed herself as a prose poet, but her powers were made clear even in the first few pages. In them, she created a real and distinctive little girl, with her sharp feelings and rapid changes of mood, who at once lays firm hold on the reader's sympathy and interest; and she also showed that she possessed a rare ability to communicate atmosphere:

'Folds of scarlet drapery shut in my view to the right hand; to the left were the clear panes of glass, protecting, but not separating me from the drear November day. At intervals, while turning over the leaves of my book, I studied the aspect of that winter afternoon. Afar it offered a pale blank of mist and cloud; near, a scene of wet lawn and storm-beat shrub, with ceaseless rain sweeping away wildly before a long and lamentable blast.'

   ·   ·   ·   ·

'Daylight began to forsake the red-room; it was past four o'clock, and the beclouded afternoon was tending to drear twilight. I heard the rain still beating continuously on the staircase window, and the wind howling in the grove behind the hall; I grew by degrees cold as a stone, and then my courage sank. My habitual mood of humiliation, self-doubt, forlorn depression, fell damp on the embers of my decaying ire. All said I was wicked, and perhaps I might be so: what thought had I been but just conceiving of starving myself to death? That certainly was a crime: and was I fit to die?' ·

   ·   ·   ·   ·

'Shaking my hair from my eyes, I lifted my head and tried to look boldly round the dark room: at this moment a light gleamed on the wall. Was it, I asked myself, a ray from the moon penetrating some aperture in the blind? No; moonlight was still, and this stirred: while I gazed, it glided up to the ceiling and quivered over my head. I can now conjecture readily that this streak of light was, in all likelihood, a gleam from a lantern, carried by someone across the lawn; but then, prepared as my mind was for horror, shaken as my nerves were by agitation, I thought the swift-darting beam was a herald of some coming vision from another world. My heart beat thick, my head grew hot; a sound filled my ears, which I deemed the rushing of wings: something seemed near me; I was oppressed, suffocated: endurance broke down; I rushed to the door and shook the lock in desperate effort. Steps came running along the outer passage; the key turned, Bessie and Abbot entered.

' "Miss Eyre, are you ill?" said Bessie.

' "What a dreadful noise! it went quite through me!" exclaimed Abbot.'[11]

The child, Jane, is the first of Charlotte's triumphs; but even more remarkable, though less noticed (perhaps because Emily, in *Wuthering Heights*, was to do it twice) is that Jane, the woman, is exactly what that child must become. Although Jane is rather unlucky in her hero, Rochester—that portmanteau of all the Byronic qualities Charlotte most admired—he acts as a fine foil to her. In one respect, he is more than this, and stands in the book in his own right; for, however unreal he may often seem, his feeling for Jane is real enough, deep, and tender with a man's tenderness; and his constant use of her name, with almost every possible nuance, sounds through the book like a refrain. Indeed, one of Charlotte's most outstanding gifts as novelist is her power of conveying love where others merely state it. The reader feels the love in Jane and Rochester and between them; and he does so, not simply because Charlotte was a writer of genius, but because she was a woman with an exceptional capacity for feeling.

The dialogues between Jane and Rochester, though most of them will not bear analysis, are almost always strangely attractive, and show, surprisingly often, a refreshing note of banter covering deep feeling.

' "Don't you think I had better take advantage of the confession, and begin and coax, and entreat—even cry and be sulky if necessary—for the sake of a mere essay of my power?"

' "I dare you to any such experiment. Encroach, presume, and the game is up."

' "Is it, sir? You soon give in. How stern you look now! Your eyebrows have become as thick as my finger, and your forehead resembles, what, in some very astonishing poetry, I once saw styled, 'a blue-piled thunder-loft'. That will be your married look, sir, I suppose?"

' "If that will be *your* married look, I, as a Christian, will soon give up the notion of consorting with a mere sprite or salamander. But what had you to ask, thing?—out with it!"

' "There, you are less than civil now; and I like rudeness a great deal better than flattery. I had rather be a *thing* than an angel." '[12]

This slightly acid tang of the interchanges—as unexpected, superficially, from Charlotte as it was rare in the love stories of the time—prevents the love scenes from cloying.

'You are not naturally austere,' says Rochester to Jane.[13] No, Charlotte was not naturally austere. She would have been fascinating had her feelings ever been allowed to express themselves freely. But the life she had led made her often appear soured, and her true personality only appeared when she began to write and to live in her writing as she wished to live. And it is this combination of an austere manner with a passionate heart that gives Charlotte (and so, Jane) her peculiar piquancy.

Even at the end of the book, from the well-worn recognition scene onwards, Charlotte avoided most of the sentimental clichés in her dialogues; and it is only necessary to think what Dickens, for instance, would have done with a blinded hero reunited to the pure young governess, to see how far Charlotte had moved from the conventions of the contemporary novel.

Thus, only a moment or two after Jane and Rochester have met, we have this kind of thing:

' "My Uncle in Madeira is dead, and he left me five thousand pounds.'

' "Ah, this is practical—this is real!" he cried: "I should never dream that. Besides, there is that peculiar voice of hers, so animating and piquant, as well as soft: it cheers my withered heart; it puts life into it —What, Janet! Are you an independent woman? A rich woman?"

' "Quite rich, sir. If you won't let me live with you, I can build a house of my own close up to your door, and you may come and sit in my parlour when you want company of an evening.' "[14]

A page or two further on, Jane is saying:

' "It is time someone undertook to rehumanise you," said I, parting his thick and long-uncut locks; "for I see you are being metamorphosed into a lion, or something of that sort. You have a 'faux air' of Nebuchadnezzar in the fields about you, that is certain: your hair reminds me of eagle's feathers; whether your nails are grown like bird's claws or not, I have not yet noticed."

' "On this arm, I have neither hand nor nails;" he said, drawing the mutilated limb from his breast, and showing it to me. "It is a mere stump—a ghastly sight! Don't you think so, Jane?"

" It is a pity to see it; and a pity to see your eyes—and the scar of fire on your forehead: and the worst of it is, one is in danger of loving you too well for all this; and making too much of you." '[15]

There is more banter, and rather more than banter.

' ". . . you talk of my being a fairy; but, I am sure, you are more like a brownie."

' "Am I hideous, Jane?"

' "Very, sir: you always were, you know."

' "Humph! The wickedness has not been taken out of you, wherever you have sojourned."

' "Yet I have been with good people; far better than you: a hundred times better; people possessed of ideas and views you never entertained in your life: quite more refined and exalted."

' "Who the deuce have you been with?"

' "If you twist in that way, you will make me pull the hair out of your head; and then I think you will cease to entertain doubts of my substantiality."

' "Who have you been with, Jane?"

' "You shall not get it out of me tonight, sir; you must wait till tomorrow; to leave my tale half-told, will, you know, be a sort of security that I shall appear at your breakfast-table to finish it. By-the-by, I must mind not to rise on your hearth with only a glass of water, then: I must bring an egg at the least, to say nothing of fried ham." '[16]

So much, then, for the conversation of these un-Victorian lovers. But this, though refreshing, was not the main difference of the book from those of its time, nor was it the cause of the fierce criticism that Charlotte had to face. Unknowingly, she had made history in the novel, as she showed the reader for the first time the heart of a woman. In *Jane Eyre* she portrayed a woman glorying in the passion that hitherto convention had tacitly assumed to be felt—and certainly expressed—by men alone. Now, without prudery, and with an innocence of mind and intention that many of her readers could neither understand nor believe, Charlotte stripped false romance from her sex, and showed that beauty could exist in the desires of a woman.

' "Do you think I can stay to become nothing to you?" [cries Jane].
"Do you think I am an automaton?—a machine without feelings?
and can bear to have my morsel of bread snatched from my lips, and
my drop of living water dashed from my cup? Do you think, because
I am poor, obscure, plain, and little, I am soulless and heartless?—You
think wrong!—I have as much soul as you,—and full as much heart!
And if God had gifted me with some beauty, and much wealth, I
should have made it as hard for you to leave me, as it is now for me to
leave you. I am not talking to you now through the medium of custom, conventionalities, nor even of mortal flesh:—it is my spirit that
addresses your spirit; just as if both had passed through the grave,
and we stood at God's feet, equal,—as we are!" '17

This magnificent challenge rings through the book and
through all the literature that has followed it. Charlotte, in
speaking for herself, had spoken for all her sex—and, criticized
and maligned though she was in many quarters as coarse and
unwomanly, the curtain she had flung aside could never be
replaced; the course of the novel had, in this vital matter, been
changed for ever.

Narrow Charlotte's world was indeed, and narrow her vision;
her style is often pompous, stilted, and cluttered with irritating
mannerisms—in particular, her lamentable tendency to personify
and apostrophize abstract qualities; but within her confined
range, and in spite of her faults of style, she writes impassioned
scenes with uncommon understanding and a real splendour of
expression.

That Charlotte's handling of love between the sexes should
be misunderstood was inevitable. Accentuating her offence in
the eyes of many was the way she expressed love. ' "We must
become one flesh," cried Rochester';18 and ' "No woman was
ever nearer to her mate than I am:" ' says Jane, ' "ever more
absolutely bone of his bone, and flesh of his flesh." '19

Never was there a more unconscious revolutionary. Those
who criticized were not to know that Charlotte was ignorant of
much that these passages in the book implied—that she wrote,
not from experience, but wholly from instinct and imagination.
Nor could readers know of the Methodist teaching, Methodist
thought, Methodist idiom in which the Brontës' lives had been
steeped; yet, so deeply was this outlook and usage a part of
Charlotte's life, that there was nothing strange to her in express-

ing Jane Eyre's love for Rochester and his for her in the language of the Passion.

Charlotte also fell foul of a smaller body of readers. She had at last avenged Maria and Elizabeth. At last, she had exposed the cruelty that sheltered under the cloak of religion, and justified itself by the poverty of the victims and the supposed good of their souls. She had forgotten nothing of the iniquitous travesty of life at Cowan Bridge; and now, in *Jane Eyre*, she introduced Maria, somewhat larger than life, and the school as thinly disguised as were all Charlotte's portraits from life. She castigated Cowan Bridge and its management with a thorough and bitter relish. The story of Helen Burns was dramatic indeed; yet, says Charlotte, 'I exaggerated nothing there. I refrained from recording much that I remember respecting her lest the narrative should sound incredible.'[20] Incredible it certainly did sound to some readers, who thought that such an attack on the school and its founder was a scandal. The school had long since been moved from Cowan Bridge; but that fact —a tacit acknowledgement of the unsuitability of the building and site—neither stirred Charlotte from her purpose nor prevented a controversy from breaking out when her Lowood was identified with Cowan Bridge.

So Charlotte at last found a publisher, and a degree of fame that she could never in her wildest dreams have imagined. In spite of the long effort to place *The Professor*, she was still the first to have a novel published. Newby had proved so dilatory— not entirely without purpose—that although *Wuthering Heights* and *Agnes Grey* were in the press before *Jane Eyre* had been sent to Smith Elder, they were not published until the following December, when Charlotte's book was on the point of going into its second edition.

'Mr. Newby,' wrote Charlotte to W. S. Williams, the Smith Elder reader, with whom she soon began a mutually appreciated correspondence, 'Mr. Newby . . . does not do business like Messrs Smith and Elder; a different spirit seems to preside at 172, Mortimer Street to that which guides the helm at 65, Cornhill. Mr. Newby shuffles, gives his word and breaks it; Messrs Smith and Elder's performance is always better than their promise. My relatives have suffered from exhausting delay and procrastination while I have to acknowledge the benefits of a management at once businesslike and gentlemanlike, energetic and considerate.'[21]

Before the publication of *Jane Eyre*, Ellen had at last spent a few days at Haworth without incident; and soon afterwards, Charlotte, her pride at ease, went to Brookroyd. She said nothing of the novels awaiting publication, for Ellen, like Mr. Brontë and everyone else, had still not been told a word of the sisters' secret. Still, in spite of the fact that Charlotte was withholding news that meant far more to her than anything she talked about, the two girls were happy enough, and Charlotte indulged in some playful scolding when presents were discovered in her box on her return to Haworth late in September; 'I have distributed the presents. Papa says I am to remember him most kindly to you. The screen will be very useful and he thanks you for it. Tabby was charmed with her cap. She said, "She never thought o' naught o' t' sort as Miss Nussey sending her aught, and she is sure she can never thank her enough for it." I was infuriated on finding a jar in my trunk. At first, I hoped it was empty, but when I found it heavy and replete, I could have hurled it all the way back to Birstall. However, the inscription A.B. softened me much. It was at once kind and villainous in you to send it. You ought first to be tenderly kissed and then afterwards as tenderly whipped. Emily is just now sitting on the floor of the bedroom where I am writing, looking at her apples. She smiled when I gave them and the collar to her as your presents, with an expression at once well pleased and slightly surprised. Anne thanks you much. All send their love.'[22]

Branwell, it appears, did not receive a gift—a melancholy reversal of the days, not so long ago, when he and Ellen made merry at Haworth and sent each other playful messages by way of Charlotte.[23]

XXIV

WUTHERING HEIGHTS

Publication of 'Agnes Grey' and 'Wuthering Heights'. Virtues and defects of Anne as novelist. Comparison between 'Jane Eyre' and 'Wuthering Heights'. Analysis of 'Wuthering Heights'.

IN December 1847 *Wuthering Heights* in two volumes and *Agnes Grey* in the third volume were at last published. The reviews were mixed. *Agnes Grey* was generally written off as pleasant but unimportant. *Wuthering Heights* was not understood by most of the reviewers, who praised its vigour or condemned its violence. Nevertheless the book sold well.[1]

In her short novel, Anne set out simply and with some charm the life of a governess. Much of the story was autobiographical. There was no trace in Anne's governess of the fiery Jane Eyre. She loved, indeed; but her mild and steadfast regard for the local curate certainly would never have exceeded the bounds of propriety. The book and its heroine display a mild but unmistakable sense of humour, which is sought in vain in *Jane Eyre*, except for some passages between Jane and Rochester, and for the humour (quite unintentional) of Charlotte's pictures of high life. Anne's descriptive powers were excellent, and her subsidiary characters have life if they usually lack interest. Her failing was that she had not the necessary imagination to translate life into art. Like Charlotte in *The Professor*, Anne made a literal transcription of emotional and factual experience.

The greatness of Emily's book was not understood in her day or for many years to come. That *Wuthering Heights* was a strange and powerful book, was clear enough; but most of the early critics were obsessed by the outward air of brutality and uncouthness that hangs over the novel, and the inhumanity of the chief male figure in the book. It was even set down by some as an earlier and inferior work by Currer Bell, hastily thrust on the market to take advantage of the success of *Jane Eyre*.[2]

Yet Emily had written a greater book than either of her sisters. She owed something to Hoffmann for her plot;[3] she owed something to her stay in Halifax for local colour;[4] she owed much to Branwell's relation of local history, to his eye for the drama of the moorland folk of earlier days, to his idiom, perhaps to his actual suggestion and written word, certainly to him as a living example of depravity;[5] she owed a great deal to her father for his early meal-time flights of imagination and tales of local legends; and to her aunt for recreating the Methodists in their heyday;[6] yet none of these explains the genius of the author. One of the first things to strike the reader is the difference between the method and attitude of *Wuthering Heights* and *Jane Eyre*. Emily's people are built up entirely by word and action; they have nothing of the introspection that plays so large a part in Charlotte's characters. As a result, the men and women in *Wuthering Heights* are seen and known as it were from a distance, but hard, bright and clear, whereas every movement of the heart and mind of *Jane Eyre* is not only known but felt. Emily's method of telling her story is objective, Charlotte's subjective, Emily wants to draw a picture, Charlotte to delve into human motives; thus the human interest is greater in *Jane Eyre* and *Villette* than in *Wuthering Heights*, even though Charlotte is often crude, dull, or unreal, and has not Emily's consistent level of expression.

Again, Emily's treatment of her characters and story is entirely amoral in contrast to the rather stifling moral tone of Charlotte at times, and of Victorian novelists in general. There are no improving or reproving asides from Emily. She was interested in cause and effect; and she gives a description, without comment, of life as she saw it.

Another difference between the work of the sisters is that Charlotte is fundamentally concerned only with love, and that only in this life, in spite of her occasional unconvincing references to reunion beyond the grave. Emily always looks out to a fuller life; death, to her, is neither an end nor a beginning but a metamorphosis, the freeing of a person's essence—a belief which she frequently expresses in her poems. *Wuthering Heights* is not in any real sense a love story, and the feeling between Catherine and Heathcliff has none of the intimate humanity of Jane's love for Rochester, or Lucy's for the Professor in *Villette*. It is scarcely possible to imagine Catherine and Heathcliff living together; easier, indeed, to imagine them disembodied, in the form of rough winds. Catherine's death is therefore artistically inevitable—it breaks the only barrier to the fulfilment of her affinity with Heathcliff.

Yet again, Charlotte is felt to be playing a part in her book. She takes sides. She is Jane, and she suffers, loves, hates, and agonizes, not only with Jane, but for her. This sense of personal passion gives the book its power and life, but leads also to its inequalities, so that from time to time one has the sense of reading an indignant tract. In *Wuthering Heights*, on the contrary, there is to be found none of the emotional writing that makes *Jane Eyre* at once a profound study of the human heart and a string of melodramatic scenes.

Emily was primarily an intellectual writer. Unlike Charlotte, she shows no sign in her book that she had ever felt sexual passion. And although she deals in scenes of naked passion, fierceness, and brutality, and although the supernatural is implicit throughout the book, it is all described so calmly and in so matter-of-fact a manner that the story is given a reality and a credibility that it would never have, told by another hand and in another way. For all its strangeness, it is a well-balanced, unhysterical novel; as much so, in its way, as the novels—apparently furthest removed from Emily—of Jane Austen.

X Here she differed, not only from Charlotte, but from the whole world of Victorian novelists. Anne's poor shade of *Wuthering Heights*—*The Tenant of Wildfell Hall*—has its brutalities also, but, like the rest of the Victorians, Anne's brutal scenes are too often improbable. In *Wuthering Heights* we have a phenomenon of its age, a unique combination of mysticism and naturalism. It is both a fine story of living people and an exposition of Emily's philosophy, using these people as symbols.

Emily achieved all this in several ways: by her almost faultless use of words, by her sense of proportion, her skilful construction, and her thorough knowledge of people and background. Surely and with great power she drew into vigorous life the Haworth moors when Wesley was riding and preaching fierily over the land, when Jabez Bunting was thundering from his pulpit, when Grimshaw stormed about the parish fighting for the souls of his people. Nor was she content to summon the spirit of that time and those people; she drew upon the actual events in their lives—as dramatic as their preaching—to form her plot;[7] and, in the man Joseph, she exorcized once and for all the spell cast by Miss Branwell in her teaching of predestination.[8]

Even the apparently loose construction of *Wuthering Heights* proves on closer examination to be close knit and skilfully planned.[9] Every detail has its place in the progression of the plot. Every word of the apparently rambling story, with its telling tossed from mouth to mouth, has its purpose, and contributes its part to the building up of plot, atmosphere, and verisimilitude.

The choice of Lockwood—a shallow, town-bred nonentity—to open the book is masterly. His inept comments turn the reader's sympathy to the people at Wuthering Heights, and help to give them credibility in spite of their uncouthness and brutality. Through Lockwood, too, the reader's curiosity is awakened, and the desire to unravel the curious relationships of the people at Wuthering Heights becomes almost overwhelming. This skilful use of Lockwood is continued with Nelly Dean, who—kindly but limited and matter-of-fact—balances the violence around her, gives it reality, and at times, by her comments, even induces a favourable reaction to it.

What moved Emily to write *Wuthering Heights*? The occasion was plain enough. The sisters had each agreed to write a novel. They would gather in the parsonage dining-room of an evening, Emily often on the rug before the fire, desk on knees, and the tawny, heavy-breathing Keeper leaning as close to her as possible, Anne with her long-haired Flossy or a cat to be stroked, her desk before her, or all three sisters pacing thoughtfully round and round the table. As they gathered thus, evening after evening, they certainly discussed the progress and to some extent the problems of their books. But the books of all three had been in mind, and partly written, before this discussion began. And Emily did not take kindly to advice.[10] Her motive in writing the book—if the unconscious movement of a writer's mind can be so called—is made clear in *Wuthering Heights*. But the actual warp and woof of the story, the nature of the plot—what influenced or dictated this?

It is difficult not to believe that Branwell was at the back of his sister's mind when she began her novel. It is difficult not to see in the relations of Heathcliff and Catherine an imaginative echo of what Emily conceived the relations of her brother and

Mrs. Robinson to have been. How could it be otherwise? Branwell was the only man with whom the sisters had been on terms of intimacy. In him they had reposed great hopes. For him they had made great sacrifices. They had been taught to give him first place in the family. Round him they had built a halo of masculine virtues; a halo enhanced by the unlikeness of Branwell to themselves, by his engaging manners, easy flow of conversation, and entire absence of self-consciousness, his unblushing self-confidence in his own abilities and brilliant future.

Charlotte, shrewdest, most experienced, warmest-hearted, and most ambitious of the three sisters, had reacted most violently to the Branwell finally stripped of his pretensions. She regarded with a passion of indignation the years, the money, the affection thrown away upon a wastrel. The result in her work was the Crimsworth of *The Professor*[11]—a study, outside the main course of the book, of what she had described as a moral madness.[12]

With Anne, horrified and pitiful at the sight of her brother's collapse, the eventual result in her work was the *Tenant of Wildfell Hall*. In that book Branwell did indeed take first place, but as a warning to the world.

Only to Emily, without Charlotte's ambition or knowledge of the world, and without Anne's fearful certainty of Branwell's damnation, did her brother appear as something of an inspiration. Of all three sisters she had seen most of him. She had seen the Branwell of Luddenden Foot, ablaze with lurid stories of local feud and passion. She had seen Branwell possessed with sudden energy and hope, writing for dear life, until the mood left him or a more congenial occasion tempted him forth. She had seen him in a delirium of passion for Mrs. Robinson. She had seen him break up, his life wrecked and all hope gone because of this passion. Her imagination could picture without effort his life as one lost for love.

So, in Emily's book too, Branwell takes a prominent place. But this time, not as a warning. Whether he can be seen in Heathcliff[13] or Hindley or Linton Heathcliff is something that will never be known. Possibly he, or a part of him, is in all, possibly in none. But one thing seems certain—that Branwell and his tales from Luddenden Foot acted as a releasing medium for *Wuthering Heights* in Emily.

Charlotte, while recognizing the power and originality of the book, as she had at once perceived the greatness in Emily's poetry, frankly deplored this exercise of her sister's imagination. She of course failed to understand the book—its mystic philosophy, its amorality, were quite foreign to her—and she fastened, naturally, upon Heathcliff. After admitting that even the first Catherine was not 'destitute of a certain strange beauty in her fierceness, or of honesty in the midst of perverted passion and passionate perversity',[14] Charlotte passes on to a defence, in itself a criticism, of Heathcliff:

'Heathcliff, indeed, stands unredeemed; never once swerving in his arrow-straight course to perdition, from the time when "the little black-haired, swarthy thing, as dark as if it came from the devil", was first unrolled out of the bundle and set on its feet in the farm-house kitchen, to the hour when Nelly Dean found the grim, stalwart corpse laid on its back in the panel-enclosed bed, with wide-gazing eyes that seemed "to sneer at her attempt to close them, and parted lips and sharp white teeth that sneered too". Heathcliff betrays one solitary human feeling, and that is *not* his love for Catherine; which is a sentiment fierce and inhuman: a passion such as might boil and glow in the bad essence of some evil genius; a fire that might form the tormented centre—the ever-suffering soul of a magnate of the infernal world; and by its quenchless and ceaseless ravage effect the execution of the decree which dooms him to carry Hell with him wherever he wanders. No; the single link that connects Heathcliff with humanity is his rudely confessed regard for Hareton Earnshaw—the young man whom he has ruined; and then his half-implied esteem for Nelly Dean. These solitary traits omitted, we should say he was child neither of Lascar nor gipsy, but a man's shape animated by demon life—a Ghoul—an Afreet.'[15]

This is all perfectly true, and quite beside the point. So is Charlotte's exoneration of her sister for bringing Heathcliff to life: 'Whether it is right or advisable to create beings like Heathcliff, I do not know: I scarcely think it is. But this I know; the writer who possesses the creative gift owns something of which he is not always master—something that at times strangely wills and works for itself. He may lay down rules and devise principles, and to rules and principles it will perhaps for years live in subjection; and then, haply without any warning of revolt, there comes a time when it will no longer consent to "narrow the vallies, or be bound with a band in the furrow"— when it "laughs at the multitude of the city, and regards not the crying of the driver"—when refusing absolutely to make ropes out of sea-sand any longer, it sets to work on statue-hewing, and you have a Pluto, or a Jove, a Tisiphone or a Psyche, a Mermaid or a Madonna, as Fate or Inspiration direct. Be the work grim or glorious, dread or divine, you have little choice left but quiescent adoption. As for you—the nominal artist— your share in it has been to work passively under dictates you neither delivered nor could question—that would not be uttered at your prayer, nor suppressed nor changed at your caprice. If the result be attractive, the World will praise you, who little deserve praise; if it be repulsive, the same World will blame you, who almost as little deserve blame.'[16]

So wrote Charlotte, stirred as often before into loyal defence of those she loved. Years earlier her indignation would have been confined to her own small circle. Now she had authority. She had words. They are good words, well spoken. Yet they scarcely mask the disapproval of the writer. Emily's anger, had she known that Charlotte was to discuss her work publicly, may be imagined—and so can her sardonic smile if she had read her sister's defence of the book.

Charlotte loved Emily deeply. She loved her the more as Branwell fell in favour. She loved her the more as she bruised herself against the barrier that stood between them. She understood her very well up to a point. But full understanding and fellow-feeling were impossible, if only because Emily would have none of it. Thus Charlotte writes of Emily, of her unobtrusiveness, of how a secluded life explained her retiring manner and habits: 'In Emily's nature the extremes of vigour and simplicity seemed to meet. Under an unsophisticated culture, inartificial tastes, and an unpretending outside, lay a secret power and fire that might have informed the brain and kindled the veins of a hero; but she had no worldly wisdom; her powers were unadapted to the practical business of life; she would fail to defend her most manifest rights, to consult her most legitimate advantage. An interpreter ought always to have stood between her and the world. Her will was not very flexible, and it generally opposed her interest. Her temper was magnanimous, but warm and sudden; her spirit altogether unbending.'[17] Linking Anne with Emily, Charlotte says: 'They had no thought of filling their pitchers at the well-spring of other minds; they always wrote from the impulse of nature, the dictates of intuition and from such stores of observation as their limited experience had enabled them to amass. I may sum up all by saying, that for strangers they were nothing, for superficial observers less than nothing; but for those who had known them all their lives in the intimacy of close relationship, they were genuinely good and truly great.'[18]

This portrait of her sister is beautiful, but it is only a list of Emily's characteristics. To the essence of the woman who could write *Wuthering Heights* Charlotte remained as one blind. How could she be otherwise? She and Emily were as different in their essential nature as any two people could be.

Branwell would probably have appreciated *Wuthering Heights* more than Charlotte or Anne, though possibly for the wrong reasons. He would have read himself into Heathcliff with pleasure. But it is not clear whether he considered himself injured by Emily's use of material he had supplied, or whether this sense of injury was manufactured later by too zealous friends. Certainly he claimed much of *Wuthering Heights* as his own; but, anxious to the last to be thought a great artist, he was not above claiming, and even reading out as his, something he had not written. His friends believed him, in some instances actually stating that they recognized parts of the novel as being word for word what Branwell had read or repeated to them before the publication of the book.[19] That he contributed something directly and a great deal indirectly to his sister's work is at least possible, and it cannot be said with certainty that Branwell did not make a preliminary draft of what, later, in Emily's hands, became the *Wuthering Heights* we know—the remarkable likeness of some of his finer poems to Emily's forbids too hasty an assumption of this kind.[20] But all the prose of his that has survived is so poor, and so unlike the published novel, that it seems incredible that he could have written any of *Wuthering Heights* as we have it to-day.[21] He was also physically and mentally ill when the book was written.

The judgements of Charlotte and the reviewers were unduly influenced by Heathcliff and the moral problem such a character presented. This tendency in criticism of *Wuthering Heights* has persisted, although the moral aspect of Heathcliff is now less considered than his unreality. Taken in isolation, he is difficult to accept; but Emily did not present him so; on the contrary, she was careful to place him always in relation to characters whose reality is beyond doubt. In any case, much criticism of the book, from Charlotte onwards, though understandable, misses the mark. It assumes that Heathcliff is the focal point of the story, but this is true only in a technical sense. He certainly gives the book unity, but its vitality and human interest are provided by the two Catherines. The elder Catherine is one of the most exciting women ever created by a novelist—the perfect example of the passionate woman without tender feelings. She fulfils three functions in the book. She lends reality to the melo-dramatically conceived Heathcliff; she is one of the main symbols illustrating Emily's mystic philosophy; and her tempestuous personality gives the story much of its vivacity. The reader may detest or admire Catherine, but he cannot avoid being fascinated by her, just as everyone in the book is fascinated, including, above all, Heathcliff himself. Heathcliff is obsessed by Catherine, more than Catherine by Heathcliff.

It is a triumph for Emily's art that when this fascinating creature dies the reader is quickly captivated anew by the younger Catherine. She, too, is a masterly portrait, both as child and young woman. She is plainly the daughter of the elder Catherine, yet not to be mistaken for her; and she carries on successfully her mother's functions of giving life to the book and reality to Heathcliff. Neither woman is remotely like Emily herself, nor anyone she had ever met—they are true creations of the imagination.

The popular impression of *Wuthering Heights* as wholly rough and violent can only survive a superficial first reading. In fact, the more lasting quality of the book is its lyricism; and it contains many pastoral and domestic scenes. The episode where young Catherine rides over to Wuthering Heights is typical of childhood, and rich in wise observation.

'Catherine came to me, one morning, at eight o'clock, and said she was that day an Arabian merchant, going to cross the Desert with his caravan; and I must give her plenty of provision for herself and beasts: a horse, and three camels, personated by a large hound and a couple of pointers. I got together good store of dainties, and slung them in a basket on one side of the saddle; and she sprang up as gay as a fairy, sheltered by her wide-brimmed hat and gauze veil from the July sun, and trotted off with a merry laugh, mocking my cautious counsel to avoid galloping, and come back early. The naughty thing never made her appearance at tea. One traveller, the hound, being an old dog and fond of its ease, returned; but neither Cathy, nor the pony, nor the two pointers were visible in any direction; and I despatched emissaries down this path, and that path, and at last went wandering in search of her myself. There was a labourer working at a fence round a plantation, on the borders of the grounds. I enquired of him if he had seen our young lady.

' "I saw her at morn," he replied; "she would have me to cut her a hazel switch, and then she leapt her galloway over the hedge yonder, where it is lowest, and galloped out of sight."

'You may guess how I felt at hearing this news. It struck me directly she must have started for Penistone Craggs. "What will become of her?" I ejaculated, pushing through a gap which the man was repairing, and making straight to the high-road. I walked as if for a wager, mile after mile, till a turn brought me in view of the Heights; but no Catherine could I detect, far or near. The Craggs lie about a mile and a half beyond Mr. Heathcliff's place, and that is four from the Grange, so I began to fear night would fall ere I could reach them. "And what if she should have slipped in clambering among them," I reflected, "and been killed, or broken some of her bones?" My suspense was truly painful; and, at first, it gave me delightful relief to observe, in hurrying by the farm-house, Charlie, the fiercest of the pointers, lying under a window, with swelled head and bleeding ear. I opened the wicket and ran to the door, knocking vehemently for admittance. A woman whom I knew, and who formerly lived at Gimmerton, answered: she had been servant there since the death of Mr. Earnshaw.

' "Ah," said she, "you are come a seeking your little mistress! don't be frightened. She's here safe: but I'm glad it isn't the master."

' "He is not at home then, is he?" I panted, quite breathless with quick walking and alarm.

' "No, no," she replied: "both he and Joseph are off, and I think they won't return this hour or more. Step in and rest you a bit."

'I entered, and beheld my stray lamb seated on the hearth, rocking herself in a little chair that had been her mother's when a child. Her hat was hung against the wall, and she seemed perfectly at home, laughing and chattering, in the best spirits imaginable, to Hareton— now a great, strong lad of eighteen—who stared at her with considerable curiosity and astonishment: comprehending precious little of the fluent succession of remarks and questions which her tongue never ceased pouring forth.

' "Very well, Miss!" I exclaimed, concealing my joy under an angry countenance. "This is your last ride, till papa comes back. I'll not trust you over the threshold again, you naughty, naughty girl!"

' "Aha, Ellen!" she cried, gaily, jumping up, and running to my side. 'I shall have a pretty story to tell tonight: and so you've found me out. Have you ever been here in your life before?"

' "Put that hat on, and home at once," said I. "I'm dreadfully grieved at you, Miss Cathy: you've done extremely wrong! It's no use pouting and crying: that won't repay the trouble I've had, scouring the country after you. To think how Mr. Linton charged me to keep you in; and you stealing off so! it shows you are a cunning little fox, and nobody will put faith in you any more."

' "What have I done?" sobbed she, instantly checked. "Papa charged me nothing: he'll not scold me, Ellen—he's never cross, like you!"

' "Come, come!" I repeated. "I'll tie the riband. Now, let us have no petulance. Oh, for shame. You thirteen years old, and such a baby!"

'This exclamation was caused by her pushing the hat from her head, and retreating to the chimney out of my reach.

' "Nay," said the servant, "don't be hard on the bonny lass, Mrs. Dean. We made her stop: she'd fain have ridden forwards, afeard you should be uneasy. But Hareton offered to go with her, and I thought he should: it's a wild road over the hills."

'Hareton, during the discussion, stood with his hands in his pockets, too awkward to speak; though he looked as if he did not relish my intrusion.

' "How long am I to wait?" I continued, disregarding the woman's interference. "It will be dark in ten minutes. Where is the pony, Miss Cathy? And where is Phoenix? I shall leave you unless you be quick; so please yourself."

' "The pony is in the yard," she replied, "and Phoenix is shut in there. He's bitten—and so is Charlie. I was going to tell you all about it; but you are in a bad temper, and don't deserve to hear."

'I picked up her hat, and approached to reinstate it; but perceiving that the people of the house took her part, she commenced capering round the room; and on my giving chase, ran like a mouse over and under and behind the furniture, rendering it ridiculous for me to pursue. Hareton and the woman laughed, and she joined them, and waxed more impertinent still; till I cried, in great irritation—

' "Well, Miss Cathy, if you were aware whose house this is, you'd be glad enough to get out."

' "It's *your* father's, isn't it?" said she, turning to Hareton.

' "Nay," he replied, looking down, and blushing bashfully.

'He could not stand a steady gaze from her eyes, though they were just his own.

' "Whose, then—your master's?" she asked.

'He coloured deeper, with a different feeling, muttered an oath, and turned away.

' "Who is his master?" continued the tiresome girl, appealing to me. "He talked about 'our house,' and 'our folk.' I thought he had been the owner's son. And he never said, Miss: he should have done, should-n't he, if he's a servant?"

'Hareton grew black as a thunder-cloud, at this childish speech. I silently shook my questioner, and at last succeeded in equipping her for departure.

' "Now, get my horse," she said, addressing her unknown kins-man as she would one of the stableboys at the Grange. "And you may come with me. I want to see where the goblin-hunter rises in the marsh, and to hear about the *fairishes,* as you call them: but make haste! What's the matter? Get my horse, I say."

' "I'll see thee damned before I be *thy* servant!" growled the lad.

' "You'll see me *what?*" asked Catherine in surprise.

' "Damned—thou saucy witch!" he replied.

' "There, Miss Cathy! you see you have got into pretty company," I interposed. "Nice words to be used to a young lady! Pray don't begin to dispute with him. Come, let us seek for Minny ourselves, and begone."

' "But Ellen," cried she, staring, fixed in astonishment. "How dare he speak so to me? Mustn't he be made to do as I ask him? You wicked creature, I shall tell papa what you said.—Now then!"

'Hareton did not appear to feel this threat; so the tears sprung into her eyes with indignation. "You bring the pony," she exclaimed, turning to the woman, "and let my dog free this moment!"

' "Softly, Miss," answered the addressed: "you'll lose nothing by being civil. Though Mr. Hareton, there, be not the master's son, he's your cousin; and I was never hired to serve you."

' "*He* my cousin!" cried Cathy, with a scornful laugh.

' "Yes, indeed," responded her reprover.

' "Oh, Ellen! don't let them say such things," she pursued in great trouble. "Papa is gone to fetch my cousin from London: my cousin is a gentleman's son. That my——" she stopped, and wept outright; upset at the bare notion of relationship with such a clown.

' "Hush, hush!" I whispered, "people can have many cousins and of all sorts, Miss Cathy, without being any the worse for it; only they needn't keep their company, if they be disagreeable and bad."

' "He's not—he's not my cousin, Ellen!" she went on, gathering fresh grief from reflection, and flinging herself into my arms for refuge from the idea.

'I was much vexed at her and the servant for their mutual revelations; having no doubt of Linton's approaching arrival, communicated by the former, being reported to Mr. Heathcliff; and feeling as confident that Catherine's first thought on her father's return would be to seek an explanation of the latter's assertion concerning her rude-bred kindred. Hareton, recovering from his disgust at being taken for a servant, seemed moved by her distress; and, having fetched the pony round to the door, he took, to propitiate her, a fine crooked-legged terrier whelp from the kennel, and putting it into her hand bid her wisht! for he meant naught. Pausing in her lamentations, she surveyed him with a glance of awe and horror, then burst forth anew.'[22]

Again, there is the charming scene of Catherine and her letters to Linton Heathcliff—a fine example of Emily's character-drawing:

'. . . in the evening, when she had retired to her room, and I went to help her to undress, I found her crying, on her knees by the bed-side.

' "Oh, fie, silly child!" I exclaimed. "If you had any real griefs, you'd be ashamed to waste a tear on this little contrariety. You never had one shadow of substantial sorrow, Miss Catherine. Suppose, for a minute, that master and I were dead, and you were by yourself in the world: how would you feel then? Compare the present occasion with such an affliction as that, and be thankful for the friends you have, instead of coveting more."

' "I'm not crying for myself, Ellen," she answered, "it's for him. He expected to see me again tomorrow, and there, he'll be so disappointed: and he'll wait for me, and I shan't come!"

' "Nonsense!" said I, "do you imagine he has thought as much of you as you have of him? Hasn't he Hareton for a companion? Not one in a hundred would weep at losing a relation they had just seen twice, for two afternoons. Linton will conjecture how it is, and trouble himself no further about you."

' "But may I not write a note to tell him why I cannot come?" she asked, rising to her feet. "And just send those books I promised to lend him? His books are not as nice as mine, and he wanted to have them extremely, when I told him how interesting they were. May I not, Ellen?"

' "No, indeed! no, indeed!" replied I with decision. "Then he would write to you, and there'd never be an end of it. No, Miss Catherine, the acquaintance must be dropped entirely: so papa expects, and I shall see that it is done."

' "But how can one little note——" she recommenced, putting on an imploring countenance.

' " Silence!" I interrupted. "We'll not begin with your little notes. Get into bed."

'She threw at me a very naughty look, so naughty that I would not kiss her good-night at first: I covered her up, and shut her door, in great displeasure; but, repenting half-way, I returned softly, and lo! there was Miss standing at the table with a bit of blank paper before her and a pencil in her hand, which she guiltily slipped out of sight, on my re-entrance.

' "You'll get nobody to take that, Catherine," I said, "if you write it; and at present I shall put out your candle."

'I set the extinguisher on the flame, receiving as I did so a slap on my hand, and a petulant "cross thing!". I then quitted her again, and she drew the bolt in one of her worst, most peevish humours. The letter was finished and forwarded to its destination by a milk-fetcher who came from the village; but that I didn't learn till some time after-wards. Weeks passed on, and Cathy recovered her temper; though she grew wondrous fond of stealing off to corners by herself; and often, if I came near her suddenly while reading, she would start and bend over the book, evidently desirous to hide it; and I detected edges of loose paper sticking out beyond the leaves. She also got a trick of coming down early in the morning, and lingering about the kitchen, as if she were expecting the arrival of something; and she had a small drawer in a cabinet in the library, which she would trifle over for hours, and whose key she took special care to remove when she left it.

'One day, as she inspected this drawer, I observed that the play-things and trinkets, which recently formed its contents, were trans-muted into bits of folded paper. My curiosity and suspicions were roused; I determined to take a peep at her mysterious treasures; so, at night, as soon as she and my master were safe up stairs, I searched and readily found among my house keys one that would fit the lock. Having opened, I emptied the whole contents into my apron, and took them with me to examine at leisure in my own chamber. Though I could not but suspect, I was still surprised to discover that they were a mass of correspondence—daily, almost, it must have been—from Linton Heathcliff: answers to documents forwarded by her. The earlier dated were embarrassed and short; gradually, however, they expanded into copious love letters, foolish as the age of the writer rendered natural, yet with touches, here and there, which I thought were bor-rowed from a more experienced source. Some of them struck me as singularly odd compounds of ardour and flatness; commencing in strong feeling, and concluding in the affected, wordy way that a schoolboy might use to a fancied, incorporeal sweetheart. Whether they satisfied Cathy, I don't know; but they appeared very worthless trash to me. After turning over as many as I thought proper, I tied them in a handkerchief and set them aside, re-locking the vacant drawer.

'Following her habit, my young lady descended early, and visited the kitchen: I watched her go to the door, on the arrival of a certain little boy; and, while the dairy maid filled his can, she tucked something into his jacket pocket, and plucked something out. I went round by the garden, and laid wait for the messenger; who fought valorously to defend his trust, and we spilt the milk between us; but I succeeding in abstracting the epistle; and, threatening serious consequences if he did not look sharp home, I remained under the wall and perused Miss Cathy's affectionate composition. It was more simple and more eloquent than her cousin's: very pretty and very silly. I shook my head, and went meditating into the house. The day being wet, she could not divert herself with rambling about the park; so, at the conclusion of her morning studies, she resorted to the solace of the drawer. Her father sat reading at the table; and I, on purpose, had sought a bit of work in some unripped fringes of the window curtain, keeping my eye steadily fixed on her proceedings. Never did any bird flying back to a plundered nest, which it had left brim-ful of chirping young ones express more complete despair in its anguished cries and flutterings, than she by her single "Oh!" and the change that transfigured her late happy countenance. Mr. Linton looked up.

' "What is the matter, love? Have you hurt yourself?" he said.

'His tone and look assured her *he* had not been the discoverer of the hoard.

' "No, papa——" she gasped. "Ellen! Ellen! come up-stairs—I'm sick!"

'I obeyed her summons, and accompanied her out.

' "Oh, Ellen! you have got them," she commenced immediately, dropping on her knees, when we were enclosed alone. "O, give them to me, and I'll never never do so again! Don't tell papa. You have not told papa, Ellen, say you have not! I've been exceedingly naughty, but I won't do it any more!"

'With a grave severity in my manner, I bid her stand up.

' "So," I exclaimed, "Miss Catherine, you are tolerably far on, it seems: you may well be ashamed of them! A fine bundle of trash you study in your leisure hours, to be sure: why it's good enough to be printed! And what do you suppose the master will think, when I display it before him? I haven't shown it yet, but you needn't imagine I shall keep your ridiculous secrets. For shame! and you must have led the way in writing such absurdities: he would not have thought of beginning, I'm certain."

'"I didn't! I didn't!" sobbed Cathy, fit to break her heart. "I didn't once think of loving him till——"

' "*Loving!*" cried I, as scornfully as I could utter the word. "*Loving!* Did anybody ever hear the like! I might just as well talk of loving the miller who comes once a year to buy our corn. Pretty loving, indeed! and both times together you have seen Linton hardly four hours in your life! Now here is the babyish trash. I'm going with it to the library; and we'll see what your father says to such *loving*."

'She sprang at her precious epistles, but I held them above my head; and then she poured out further frantic entreaties that I would burn them—do anything rather than show them. And being really fully as inclined to laugh as scold—for I esteemed it all girlish vanity—I at length relented in a measure, and asked—

'"If I consent to burn them, will you promise faithfully, neither to send nor receive a letter again, nor a book (for I perceive you have sent him books), nor locks of hair, nor rings, nor playthings?"

'"We don't send playthings!" cried Catherine, her pride overcoming her shame.

'"Nor anything at all, then, my lady!" I said. "Unless you will, here I go."

'"I promise, Ellen!" she cried, catching my dress. "Oh, put them in the fire, do, do!"

'But when I proceeded to open a place with the poker, the sacrifice was too painful to be borne. She earnestly supplicated that I would spare her one or two.

'"One or two, Ellen, to keep for Linton's sake!"

"I unknotted the handkerchief, and commenced dropping them in from an angle, and the flame curled up the chimney.

'"I will have one, you cruel wretch!" she screamed, darting her hand into the fire, and drawing forth some half consumed fragments, at the expense of her fingers.

'"Very well—and I will have some to exhibit to papa!" I answered, shaking back the rest into the bundle, and turning anew to the door.

'She emptied her blackened pieces into the flames, and motioned me to finish the immolation. It was done; I stirred up the ashes, and interred them under a shovel full of coals; and she mutely, and with a sense of intense injury, retired to her private apartment. I descended to tell my master that the young lady's qualm of sickness was almost gone, but I judged it best for her to lie down a while. She wouldn't.

246

dine; but she reappeared at tea, pale, and red about the eyes, and marvellously subdued in outward aspect.

'Next morning, I answered the letter by a slip of paper, inscribed, "Master Heathcliff is requested to send no more notes to Miss Linton, as she will not receive them." And, thenceforth, the little boy came with vacant pockets.'[23]

Quotations such as these, which could be taken from many parts of the book, illustrate the next and final point about *Wuthering Heights*—that none of Emily's great merits as a novelist so far set out would be of much account if they were not conveyed in that splendid vehicle, her prose.

Emily is one of the great English prose-writers. Her prose in *Wuthering Heights* has the mark of true genius; again and again her words sound as though she had that moment invented them. And she uses these words like the poet she is, with an economy, a rhythm, and a beauty that perfectly convey the sense and feeling.

Her writing always has distinction, but there are many times when it goes far beyond this. For instance, the last paragraph of the book, often quoted and yet impossible to resist.

'I lingered round them, under that benign sky: watched the moths fluttering among the heath and hare-bells; listened to the soft wind breathing through the grass; and wondered how any one could ever imagine unquiet slumbers for the sleepers in that quiet earth.'[24]

But there are many lesser-known passages, sometimes of dialogue, sometimes of description, where Emily's prose is similarly inspired.

'. . . and this—I should know it among a thousand—it's a lapwing's. Bonny bird; wheeling over our heads in the middle of the moor. It wanted to get to its nest, for the clouds had touched the swells, and it felt rain coming.'[25]

And:

' "The snow is quite gone down here, darling," replied her husband; "and I only see two white spots on the whole range of moors: the sky is blue, and the larks are singing, and the becks and brooks are all brim full." '[26]

'The becks and brooks are all brim full'—phrases like this sing out of almost every page, sometimes alone, sometimes in a flood of word-music, as in this, perhaps the loveliest passage she wrote:

'One time, however, we were near quarrelling. He said the pleasantest manner of spending a hot July day was lying from morning till evening on a bank of heath in the middle of the moors, with the bees humming dreamily about among the bloom, and the larks singing high up over head, and the blue sky and bright sun shining steadily and cloudlessly. That was his most perfect idea of heaven's happiness: mine was rocking in a rustling green tree, with a west wind blowing, and bright white clouds flitting rapidly above; and not only larks, but throstles, and blackbirds, and linnets, and cuckoos pouring out music on every side, and the moors seen at a distance, broken into cool dusky dells; but close by great swells of long grass undulating in waves to the breeze; and woods and sounding water, and the whole world awake and wild with joy.'[27]

XXV

THE BELLS BECOME BRONTËS

Charlotte's reaction to her success. Her new correspondents. She writes regularly to Williams. Her views on Jane Austen. Her dedication to Thackeray. Defence of 'Jane Eyre'. Illness of the sisters and failing health of Branwell. Charlotte begins a new book. Anne finishes 'The Tenant of Wildfell Hall'. It is published. Confusion about the identity of the sisters. Charlotte and Anne go to London to make themselves known to the publisher. Charlotte's description of the visit. Anne pained by reviews of her book. Emily annoyed by the revelation of her identity. Charlotte tells Ellen to deny reports that she has published a novel.

CHARLOTTE bore her success well. In her letters to Smith Elder her thanks appear excessive, and her language, sometimes flowery, sometimes stately, is not in character; but this was a small departure from the genuine Charlotte for so big and so sudden a change in her fortunes. She had not lost the sense of unworthiness and of incredulity that hangs about the newly fortunate, and she was truly grateful for the interest shown in her work when no other publisher would look at it. She was pleased, too, by her correspondence with Williams, however self-conscious her letters appear. For the first time since leaving Brussels—in many respects, for the first time in her life—she was able to write fully and frankly on literature and the arts in general, to hear news about writers hitherto only distant names to her, to make earnest comparisons between this and that journal, this and that reviewer, and even, later, to unburden herself on more personal subjects. All this was now poured out gladly to the fatherly, kind-hearted, if rather uninspired Williams, and at last Charlotte began to feel herself a part—even if a somewhat remote part—of the great world of culture she had dreamed about and craved after for so many years.

Soon, she was also writing, infrequently, to well known writers of the day who admired her book. Chief among these were G. H. Lewes, Thackeray, and R. H. Horne. Lewes, whose praise of *Jane Eyre* was mixed with a good deal of criticism, warned Charlotte to beware of melodrama, and not to stray far from her own experience. 'When I first began to write,' replied Charlotte, 'so impressed was I with the truth of the principles you advocate, that I determined to take Nature and Truth as my sole guides, and to follow in their very footprints; I restrained imagination, eschewed romance, repressed excitement; over-bright colouring too, I avoided, and sought to produce something which should be soft, grave and true. My work (a tale in one volume) being completed, I offered it to a publisher. He said it was original, faithful to nature, but he did not feel warranted in accepting it; such a work would not sell. I tried six publishers in succession; they all told me it was deficient in "startling incident" and "thrilling excitement", that it would never suit the circulating libraries . . . .'[1]

'Is not the real experience of each individual very limited?' Charlotte asked Lewes. 'And, if a writer dwells upon that solely or principally, is he not in danger of repeating himself, and also of becoming an egotist?' She pleaded for the use of the imagination, that 'strong, restless faculty, which claims to be heard and exercised: are we to be quite deaf to her cry, and insensate to her struggles? When she shows us bright pictures, are we never to look at them, and try to reproduce them? And when she is eloquent, and speaks rapidly and urgently in our ear, are we not to write to her dictation?'[2]

Lewes followed up his letter with a review of *Jane Eyre* in which he advised the author, in her next novel, to follow Jane Austen as an example of writing within her own experience. This stirred Charlotte to many words. Flattered, but in no way awed, she embarked with gusto upon further discussion: 'If I ever *do* write another book, I think I will have nothing of what you call "melodrama"; I *think* so, but I am not sure. I *think* too, I will endeavour to follow the counsel which shines out of Miss Austen's "mild eyes", "to finish more and be more subdued"; but neither am I sure of that. When authors write best, or, at least, when they write most fluently, an influence seems to waken in them, which becomes their master—which will have its own way—putting out of view all behests but its own, dictating certain words, and insisting on their being used, whether vehement or measured in their nature; new-moulding characters, giving unthought-of turns to incidents, rejecting carefully elaborated old ideas, and suddenly creating and adopting new ones. Is it not so? And should we try to counteract this influence? Can we indeed counteract it?'[3]

She hastened to make acquaintance with Jane Austen. She obtained the book to which Lewes referred with so much admiration, *Pride and Prejudice*. As she read, her indignation grew with her astonishment: 'What did I find? An accurate daguerreo-typed portrait of a common face; a carefully fenced, highly cultivated garden with neat borders and delicate flowers; but no glance of a bright, vivid physiognomy, no open country, no fresh air, no blue hill, no bonny beck. I should hardly like to live with her ladies and gentlemen, in their elegant but confined houses. . . . I can understand admiration of George Sand . . . she is sagacious and profound; Miss Austen is only shrewd and observant.'[4] Unluckily Charlotte did not read the one book of Jane Austen which might have persuaded her to take a more sympathetic and understanding view of her great predecessor. To her, Jane Austen's treatment of the emotions was insipid, she lacked romantic fire, had no passion, no poetry, no heady flight of imagination. Such a writer was anathema to her. She could not understand such deliberate restriction of subject and mood. Because Jane Austen contented herself with a limited world, Charlotte assumed her to be without imagination and passion. Had she read *Persuasion* she might have thought differently. The possibility that greatness could assume many forms did not apparently occur to her. Lewes, in his reply, did nothing to mend matters. On the contrary, he made the mistake of attempting to retreat from the position he had taken up, while insisting still upon the reverence due to Jane Austen. 'What a strange lecture comes next in your letter!' exclaimed the incensed Charlotte. 'You say I must familiarise my mind with the fact that "Miss Austen is not a poetess, has no 'sentiment' (you scornfully enclose the word in inverted commas), "no eloquence, none of the ravishing enthusiasm of poetry"; and then you add, I *must* "learn to acknowledge her as *one of the greatest artists, of the greatest painters of human character*, and one of the writers with the nicest sense of means to an end that ever lived." '[5]

'The last point only will I ever acknowledge,' declared Charlotte vehemently.[6] Lewes, by taking up this indefensible position, had touched his correspondent where she was most sensitive. Jane Austen, he said, lacked poetry, lacked sentiment, yet must be reverenced as one of the greatest artists. The implication to Charlotte was plain, if mistaken; Lewes had said in effect that neither poetry nor sentiment was essential to greatness. Yet these qualities were precisely those in which *Jane Eyre* excelled.

She fought his dictum: 'Can there be a great artist without poetry? What I call—what I will bend to, as a great artist, then —cannot be destitute of the divine gift. But by *poetry*, I am sure, you understand something different to what I do, as you do by "sentiment". It is *poetry*, as I comprehend the word, which elevates the masculine George Sand, and makes out of something coarse something godlike. It is "sentiment" in my sense of the term—sentiment jealously hidden, but genuine, which extracts the venom from that formidable Thackeray, and converts what might be corrosive poison into purifying elixir. If Thackeray did not cherish in his large heart deep feeling for his kind, he would delight to exterminate; as it is, I believe, he wishes only to reform. Miss Austen being, as you say, without "sentiment", without *poetry*, maybe *is* sensible, real (more *real* than *true*), but she cannot be great.'[7]

To Thackeray, whose work Charlotte venerated, the second edition of *Jane Eyre* was dedicated. Thackeray, an admirer of the book, expressed his appreciation of the honour. But Charlotte soon discovered that, unwittingly, she had caused her hero embarrassment rather than pleasure. She found, to her dismay, that truth and fiction had followed similar paths; the plot of *Jane Eyre*, in some of its more striking particulars, followed the circumstances of Thackeray's own domestic life with uncomfortable precision. His wife was not in her right mind; he, like Rochester, had been obliged to keep her in seclusion for some years. The Dedication, appearing in January 1848, gave a joyous fillip to the literary circles still busy speculating about the authorship of *Jane Eyre*. It now became clear that Currer Bell must be the governess of Thackeray's children, and *Jane Eyre* the fictive treatment of an actual romance. Charlotte, when told briefly, and without complaint, by Thackeray in his letter of thanks, could only protest her innocence and deep regrets, and bewail to Williams the unhappy coincidence.[8]

But despite embarrassments and disagreements, these contacts with cultured and well known people gave Charlotte immense satisfaction, and she spent much of her time writing and reading the now frequent letters. She began to apply her rigid moral standards to literature in a manner that must have astonished her correspondents, especially when they recalled some of the reviews of *Jane Eyre*. So, with Branwell in mind, she writes of Rochester: 'You say that no man who had intellect enough to paint a picture, or write a comic opera, could act as he did; you say that men of genius and talent may have egregious faults, but they cannot descend to brutality or meanness. Would that the case were so! . . . Would that intellect could preserve from low vice! . . . Lewes is nobly right when he says that intellect is not the highest faculty of man, though it may be the most brilliant; when he declares that the *moral* nature of his kind is more sacred than the *intellectual* nature. . . . There is something divine in the thought that genius preserves from degradation, were it but true; but Savage tells us it was not true for him, Sheridan confirms the avowal, and Byron seals it with terrible proof. You probably never knew a Cecil Chamberlayne. If you had known such a one you would feel that Lewes has rather subdued the picture. Without moral firmness, without a clear sense of right and wrong, without the honourable principle that makes a man rather proud than ashamed of honest labour, there are no guarantees from even deepest baseness.'[9]

And of the maniac, she replies to criticism, again with an eye on Branwell: 'I agree that the character is shocking, but I know that it is but too natural. There is a phase of insanity which may be called moral madness in which all that is good or even human seems to disappear from the mind and a fiend nature replaces. The sole aim and desire of the being thus possessed is to exasperate, to molest, to destroy, and preternatural ingenuity and energy are often exercised to that dreadful end.'[10]

A consideration of Mirabeau also made her think of Branwell: 'I find a little difficulty in telling you what I think of the "Life of Mirabeau",' she wrote to Williams. 'I have often felt called upon to approve the ability and tact of the writer . . . but I have also been moved frequently to disapprobation . . . it is his manner of treating Mirabeau's errors that offends. Could you with confidence put this work into the hands of your son, secure that its perusal would not harm him—that it would not leave on his mind some vague impression that there is a grandeur in vice committed on a colossal scale? Whereas, the fact is, that in vice there is no grandeur; that it is, on whatever side you view it, and in whatever accumulation, only a foul, sordid and degrading thing. The fact is, that this Mirabeau was a mixture of divinity and dirt; that there was no divinity whatever in his errors—they were all sullying dirt; that they ruined him, brought down his genius to the kennel, deadened his nature and generous fine sentiments, made all his greatness as nothing; that they cut him off in his prime, obviated all his aims, and struck him dead in the hour when France most needed him. Mirabeau's Life and Fate teach, to my perception, the most depressing lesson I have read for years. One would fain have hoped that so many noble qualities *must* have made a noble character, and achieved noble ends. No—the Mighty Genius lived a miserable and degraded life, and died a dog's death, for want of self-control—for want of morality—for lack of religion. One's heart is wrung for Mirabeau after reading his life, and it is not of his greatness we think, when we close the volume, so much as of his hopeless recklessness, and of the sufferings, degradation and untimely end in which it issued.'[11]

All three sisters had influenza in this bitter winter of 1847–8. Charlotte and Emily recovered well, but Anne, as usual, had difficulty in getting strong again, and her cough lingered long after she was up and about—to the concern of Charlotte, always afraid that Anne would go the way of Maria and Elizabeth.[12] But Branwell, not Anne, was to be the next victim of consumption in the house. Early in the New Year he had shown obvious signs that the disease was far advanced in him; he had fainting fits at the Talbot and Old Cock inns at Halifax, followed by fits at home; and he had an appalling cough.[13] Charlotte obviously had no idea how ill he was; her natural kindliness had been overlaid by years of disgust and irritation, and she could no longer regard her brother normally: 'We have not been very comfortable here at home lately,' she told Ellen, 'far from it indeed—Branwell has contrived by some means to get more money from the old quarter—and has led us a sad life with his absurd and often intolerable conduct—Papa is harassed day and night—we have little peace—he is always sick, has two or three times fallen down in fits—what will be the ultimate end God knows.'[14]

By this time, Branwell could no longer concentrate on his writing, but he still spoke of what he had done and hoped to do, and asked Leyland to return his poem 'Caroline' and a manuscript volume, which may possibly be 'Morley Hall' or part of it—the epic on the ancestral seat of the Leyland family which Branwell had promised to write for the sculptor.[15] He also still amused himself by grotesque drawings of himself in dissipation and despair. In his letter to Leyland, for instance, there are sketches of Branwell with his cronies at the Talbot, and of himself alone with a rope round his neck, just about to be 'turned off'.[16]

Williams urged Charlotte to send him another novel as soon as possible; and although she protested that she could not write in haste or to order, she was soon at work again.[17] At first she tried to revise *The Professor* and make the more subjective treatment of her Brussels experiences that was later to appear as *Villette*[18]—but this was soon put aside; she found the pressure of recent emotion still too strong and too close for the necessary detachment. So she began a new book. It opened with a bitter attack on the curates of Haworth, rather larger than life; for their chatter still angered Charlotte. But the book—a tale of the Chartist riots, the stories of which, heard at Roe Head, Charlotte had never forgotten—was designed primarily to do honour to Ellen and Emily, the two heroines.

While she wrote slowly, *Jane Eyre* continued to sell well. In April a third edition was published, and this too was soon sold out. To this edition Charlotte appended a disclaimer of the authorship of *Wuthering Heights* and *Agnes Grey*—for there had been frequent suggestions in the press that these novels were in fact the work of the one author. This author, however, was not always said to be Currer Bell.[19] *Jane Eyre* was sometimes attributed to the author of *Wuthering Heights*; and Newby, who was more businesslike than honourable, encouraged this belief in his advertisements of *Wuthering Heights* and *Agnes Grey*, regardless of the annoyance of Emily and Anne.[20]

Later in this Spring of 1848, Anne finished *The Tenant of Wildfell Hall*. The task had been as hard as anything Anne could have set herself. Anyone less fitted to portray the steady slide of a man to perdition through a career of dissoluteness and vice, it would be difficult to imagine, and it is a triumph for Anne that the book is so interesting to read.[21] It is an ably written and in parts absorbing story, and contains some sound analysis of character. If Huntingdon is less villainous and a great deal more attractive than Anne would have had him appear, the fact is that she was simply not capable of portraying real heartlessness and abandon. Nevertheless *The Tenant of Wildfell Hall* does no discredit to the company in which it found itself. By virtue of it, and not solely as a sister of Emily and Charlotte, Anne deserves remembrance.

In June, the book was published in England and was offered to an American publisher. Newby told this publisher that *The Tenant of Wildfell Hall* was, as far as he knew, the work of the author responsible for the three previous books written by the Bells. Williams heard of this, and at once told Charlotte. He explained that Smith Elder had promised the American publisher the second work by the author of *Jane Eyre*, and that Newby, hearing of the promise, had stepped in and had tried to substitute Anne's second book for Charlotte's as yet uncompleted *Shirley*. Charlotte did not hesitate: 'On the very day I received Smith and Elder's letter,' she told Mary Taylor in one of the letters that passed regularly between Haworth and New Zealand, 'Anne and I packed up a small box, sent it down to Keighley, set out ourselves after tea, walked through a snowstorm to the station, got to Leeds, and whirled up by the night train to London with the view of proving our separate identity to Smith and Elder, and confronting Newby with his *lie*. We arrived at the Chapter Coffee House (our old place, Polly, we did not well know where else to go) about eight o'clock in the morning. We washed ourselves, had some breakfast, sat a few minutes, and then set off in queer inward excitement to 65 Cornhill. Neither Mr. Smith nor Mr. Williams knew we were coming—they had never seen us—they did not know whether we were men or women, but had always written to us as men.'[22]

It was on Saturday, 9 July, that the two sisters, Anne on her first visit to London, Charlotte almost as complete a stranger, walked up from Paternoster Row to Cornhill.[23] Neither pleasure nor fame could tempt them from their Yorkshire home; but a hint to Charlotte of an injustice being done to Smith Elder, a suggestion to Anne that her name was being used to deprive her sister and publisher of their legitimate rights, was enough to send both sisters post-haste to London, without thought of escort or comfort. So great was their indignation, so eager were they to right the wrong that had been done, that they never considered writing to the publisher; an immediate personal visit, they felt, would alone meet the case.

They felt rather nervous as they neared the offices of Smith Elder, but were too excited to feel tired after their all-night journey: 'We found 65 to be a large bookseller's shop, in a street almost as bustling as the Strand. We went in, walked up to the counter. There were a great many young men and lads here and there; I said to the first I could accost: "May I see Mr. Smith?" He hesitated, looked a little surprised. We sat down and waited a while, looking at some books on the counter, publications of theirs well known to us, of many of which they had sent us copies as presents. At last we were shown up to Mr. Smith. "Is it Mr. Smith?" I said, looking up through my spectacles at a tall young man. "It is." I then put his own letter into his hand directed to Currer Bell. He looked at it and then at me again. "Where did you get this?" he said. I gave my real name: Miss Brontë. We were in a small room—ceiled with a great skylight—and explanations were rapidly gone into; Mr. Newby being anathematised, I fear, with undue vehemence. Mr. Smith hurried out and returned with one whom he introduced as Mr. Williams, a pale, mild, stooping man of fifty, very much like a faded Tom Dixon. Then followed talk—talk—talk, Mr. Williams being silent, Mr. Smith loquacious.'[24]

As the Brontës still wanted to remain anonymous, it was arranged that they should be introduced as the Misses Brown to any friends of their publisher; for George Smith intended to make their visit to London a pleasant one; he would have fêted them, had they been willing, but they were not.

'Mr. Smith said we must come and stay at his house, but we were not prepared for a long stay and declined this also; as we took our leave he told us he should bring his sisters to call on us that evening. We returned to our inn, and I paid for the excitement of the interview by a thundering headache and harassing sickness. Towards evening, as I got no better and expected the Smiths to call, I took a strong dose of sal-volatile.

It roused me a little; still, I was in grievous bodily case when they were announced. They came in, two elegant young ladies, in full dress, prepared for the Opera—Mr. Smith himself in evening costume, white gloves, etc. We had by no means understood that it was settled we were to go to the Opera, and were not ready. Moreover, we had no fine, elegant dresses with us, or in the world. However, on brief rumination I thought it would be wise to make no objections—I put my headache in my pocket, we attired ourselves in the plain, home-made country garments we possessed, and went with them to their carriage, where we found Mr. Williams. They must have thought us queer, quizzical-looking beings, especially me with my spectacles. I smiled inwardly at the contrast, which must have been apparent, between me and Mr. Smith as I walked with him up the crimson-carpeted staircase of the Opera House and stood amongst a brilliant throng at the box door, which was not yet open. Fine ladies and gentlemen glanced at us with a slight, graceful superciliousness quite warranted by the circumstances. Still, I felt pleasantly excited in spite of headache and sickness and conscious clownishness; and I saw Anne was calm and gentle, which she always is.'[25]

Charlotte was by no means overawed by the occasion, and, as usual, her critical sense was working busily. She analysed freely and remembered what she saw and heard. Most of that night was to find another and a longer life in Charlotte's novels. 'The performance was Rossini's opera of the "Barber of Seville",' she continued, 'very brilliant, though I fancy there are things I should like better. We got to the Exhibition of the Royal Academy and the National Gallery, dined again at Mr. Smith's, then went home with Mr. Williams to tea and saw his comparatively humble but neat residence and his fine family of eight children. A daughter of Leigh Hunt's was there. She sang some little Italian airs which she had picked up among the peasantry in Tuscany, in a manner that charmed me. On Tuesday morning we left London laden with books which Mr. Smith had given us, and got safely home. A more jaded wretch than I looked when I returned it would be difficult to conceive. I was thin when I went, but was meagre indeed when I returned; my face looked grey and very old, with strange, deep lines ploughed in it; my eyes stared unnaturally. I was weak and yet restless. In a while, however, the bad effects of excitement went off and I regained my normal condition. We saw Mr. Newby.'[26]

The meeting with Newby resulted in a second edition of the *Tenant of Wildfell Hall* with a preface by Anne, dated 22 July. 'I would have it to be distinctly understood', she wrote, 'that Acton Bell is neither Currer nor Ellis Bell, and therefore let not his faults be attributed to them.'[27]

Some of the reviews of her second book pained Anne, because they misrepresented her intentions. 'You will have seen some of the notices of *Wildfell Hall*,' Charlotte wrote to Williams, 'I wish my sister felt the unfavourable ones less keenly. She does not *say* much, for she is of a remarkably taciturn, still, thoughtful nature, reserved even with her nearest of kin, but I cannot avoid seeing that her spirits are depressed sometimes. The fact is, neither she nor any of us expected that view to be taken of the book which has been taken by some critics. That it had faults of execution, faults of art, was obvious, but faults of intention or feeling could be suspected by none who knew the writer. For my own part, I consider the subject unfortunately chosen—it was one the author was not qualified to handle at once vigorously and truthfully. The simple and natural—quiet description and simple pathos are, I think, Acton Bell's forte. I liked *Agnes Grey* better than the present work.'[28]

So Anne, who in her quieter way was as unapproachable as Emily, suffered silently as she saw her motives misconstrued, her taste questioned, and her moral warning either unhealthily enjoyed or mistakenly condemned. To a temperament naturally despondent, this fate of her great effort to right a wrong depressed her. So intense was Charlotte's anxiety, and so acute her impotence to penetrate her sisters' reserve, that she was driven to express her worry and helplessness to comparative strangers. Anne, indeed, was sufficiently kind to give confidence where she saw that the withholding of it was causing pain, but even she had a limit beyond which she could not bring herself to go—if not to Emily, then certainly not to Charlotte. Emily was even less forthcoming.

Meanwhile Charlotte continued happily enough to discuss solemnly with Williams the respective merits of Rochester, Huntingdon, and Heathcliff: 'You say Mr. Huntingdon reminds you of Mr. Rochester. Does he? Yet there is no likeness between the two; the foundation of each character is entirely different. Huntingdon is a specimen of the naturally selfish, sensual, superficial man, whose one merit of a joyous temperament only avails him while he is young and healthy, whose best days are his earliest, who never profits by experience, who is sure to grow worse the older he grows. Mr. Rochester has a thoughtful nature and a very feeling heart; he is neither selfish nor self-indulgent; he is ill-educated, misguided; errs, when he does err, through rashness and inexperience: he lives for a time as too many other men live, but being radically better than most men, he does not like that degraded life, and is never happy in it. He is taught the severe lessons of experience and has sense to learn wisdom from them. Years improve him; the effervescence of youth foamed away, what is really good in him still remains. His nature is like wine of a good vintage, time cannot sour, but only mellows him. Such at least was the character I meant to portray. Heathcliff, again, of *Wuthering Heights* is quite another creation. He exemplifies the effects which a life of continued injustice and hard usage may produce on a naturally perverse, vindictive, and inexorable disposition. Carefully trained and kindly treated, the black gipsy-cub might possibly have been reared into a human being, but tyranny and ignorance made of him a mere demon. The worst of it is, some of his spirit seems breathed through the whole narrative in which he figures: it haunts every moor and glen, and beckons in every fir-tree of the Heights.'[29]

A further result of the London visit was that the neglected *Poems* of the three sisters was given another chance of publication. Smith Elder took over the copyright as well as the remaining sheets of the *Poems* from Aylott and Jones, and issued it under their own imprint.

But the visit brought trouble with Emily. She had agreed to the publication of her poems and her novel on the understanding that her pen name was always used. But in the excitement of meeting her publishers, Charlotte did more than demonstrate that there were in fact a Currer and an Acton Bell. She explained the full story of the three sisters and their real names. When, on returning home, Charlotte confessed her slip, Emily expressed deep resentment at this breach of faith—she had a horror of being publicly known and discussed. So Charlotte wrote hastily

THE GARDEN OF THE *PENSIONNAT* HÉGER

BRANWELL
from a medallion by Leyland

to Williams: 'Permit me to caution you not to speak of my sisters when you write to me. I mean, do not use the word in the plural. Ellis Bell will not endure to be alluded to under any other appellation than the nom de plume. I committed a grand error in betraying his identity to you and Mr. Smith. It was inadvertent—the words "we are three sisters" escaped me before I was aware. I regretted the avowal the moment I had made it; I regret it bitterly now, for I find it is against every feeling and intention of Ellis Bell.'[30]

Charlotte, though far from averse to the publication of her writings, was scarcely less anxious than Emily to preserve her anonymity: 'It is very kind and right in you to answer "Currer Bell" to all enquiries respecting the authorship of *Jane Eyre*,' she wrote to Williams. 'That is the only name I wish to have mentioned in connexion with my writings. "Currer Bell" only I am and will be to the public. If accident or design should deprive me of that name, I should deem it a misfortune—a very great one. Mental tranquillity would then be gone; it would be a task to write, a task which I doubt whether I could continue. If I were known, I should ever be conscious in writing that my book must be read by ordinary acquaintances, and that idea would fetter me intolerably.'[31]

No small part of Charlotte's objection to her authorship becoming known to those about her was due to the use which she made of friends and acquaintances in her books. Few authors have drawn their characters so freely from life; and most of Charlotte's circle can be traced without difficulty. Eventually, a character recognized himself in *Shirley*,[32] but until this happened Charlotte's precautions were thorough. She did not tell her father for some time, and she did not mention her writing to Ellen Nussey, yet, inconsistently, she actually corrected the proofs of *Jane Eyre* when visiting Brookroyd.[33] And, as if this were not enough, she more than once gave the proofs to her friend to post, with the publisher's name clearly marked.[34] Ellen, hurt by this lack of confidence, finally asked Charlotte if there were any truth in the rumour that she had published a book. Acquaintances, she said, were telling her news that she should have heard first from Charlotte herself. Charlotte's reply was disingenuous and in her worst vein of vulgar and heavy-handed humour that Ellen so often brought out: 'I have given

no one a right either to affirm, or hint, in the most distant manner, that I am "publishing"—(humbug!). Whoever has said
it—if any one has, which I doubt—is no friend of mine. Though
twenty books were ascribed to me, I should own none. I scout
the idea utterly. Whoever, after I have distinctly rejected the
charge, urges it upon me, will do an unkind and an ill-bred
thing. The most profound obscurity is infinitely preferable
to vulgar notoriety: and that notoriety I neither seek nor will
have. If, then, any Birstallian or Gomersallian should presume
to bore you on the subject,—to ask you what "novel" Miss
Brontë has been "publishing"—you can just say, with the distinct firmness of which you are perfect mistress when you
choose, that you are authorised by Miss Brontë to say, that she
repels and disowns every accusation of the kind. You may add,
if you please, that if any one has her confidence, you believe you
have, and she has made no drivelling confessions to you on the
subject.'[35]

XXVI

THE DEATH OF BRANWELL

Bright prospects for the three girls. Branwell's health fails rapidly. His last letters. News of Mrs. Robinson. Grundy pays a final visit. The death of Branwell. Charlotte falls ill. Her estimate of her brother.

AT this time, in the summer of 1848, the Brontë girls seemed within sight of a good life and a secured future. Their books had been published and had sold well. All had been able in this way to express themselves freely and to feel that their gifts had not been wasted; and to Charlotte, who cared most, had come the greatest success. All had a reasonable hope of independence and the prospect of a slightly less spartan existence. True, their acquaintance remained small and their life restricted, but, to two of them at least, this was no evil. Anne loved her home and the quiet life there; and she was resigned to the lack of husband and children. Emily wanted neither, content to be as she was and where she was. And even Charlotte's craving for love had been overlaid, for the time, by her success as a writer, and by the friends and correspondents her fame had brought her. All three were feeling their powers as writers, they were still young, and they had great hopes of their future work—Charlotte was halfway through *Shirley*, Anne and Emily writing or thinking of writing books that will now never be known. Branwell remained, but familiarity inured them to much of his behaviour; it also hid from them the change taking place in him. He was now not merely ill; he was dying; but no one, not even Branwell himself, in spite of his constant protestations that he was a physical wreck, seemed to realize the truth. He continued to drink himself into a stupor at Halifax; to run himself and others into debt; to plead with Leyland and Grundy for a chance to redeem himself as a worker and make something of his life; to avow his deathless passion for Mrs. Robinson; and, occasionally, to collapse into a wild fit of repentance for his misspent life. Charlotte still spoke of her brother with disgust—mingled now with resignation—but showed no awareness of the seriousness of his condition.

A few months after his fits at Halifax and at home, Branwell was again found in the Old Cock at Halifax, begging Leyland: 'For mercie's sake come and see me, for I have sought for you till I dare not risk my knee and my eyesight any more this evening. I shall have a bad evening and night if I do not see you!'[1] A week or two more, and he was at home, imploring Leyland to help him: 'Mr. Nicholson has sent to my Father a demand for the settlement of my bill owed to him immediately under penalty of a Court Summons. I have written to inform him that I shall soon be able to pay him the balance left in full —for that I will write to Dr. Crosby, and request an advance through his hands which I am sure to obtain, when I will remit my amount owed, at once, to the Old Cock. I have also given John Brown this morning Ten shillings which John will certainly place in Mr. N's hands on Wednesday next. If he refuses my offer and presses me with law, I am RUINED. I have had five months of such utter sleeplessness, violent cough and frightful agony of mind that jail would destroy me for ever. I earnestly beg you to see Nicholson and tell him that my receipt of money on asking, through Dr. Crosby, is morally certain. If you conveniently can, see Mrs. Sugden of the Talbot, and tell her that on receipt of the money I expect so shortly I will transmit her the whole or part of the account I owe her. Excuse this scrawl. Long have I resolved to write to you a letter of five or six pages, but intolerable mental wretchedness and corporeal weakness have utterly prevented me.'[2] Another day and, unable to leave home, and without money, he had a note slipped down to John Brown: 'I shall feel very much obliged to you if you can contrive to get me five pence worth of Gin in a proper measure. Should it be speedily got I could perhaps take it from you or Billy at the lane top, or, what would be quite as well, sent out for, to you. I anxiously ask the favour because I know the good it will do me. *Punctually* at Half-past Nine in the morning you will be paid the 5d out of a shilling given me then.'[3]

Yet another friend, Grundy, came over to Haworth: 'As he never came to see me, I shortly made up my mind to visit him at Haworth, and was shocked at the wrecked and wretched appearance he presented. Yet he still craved for an appointment of any kind, in order that he might try the excitement of change; of course uselessly . . . .'[4]

264

'Of course uselessly . . . .' Branwell's friends knew him better than he knew himself. What they could do for him they did. They may not have been wise friends, they were certainly not the best friends for a man like him; but they were loyal even to the point of folly.

Mrs. Robinson's daughters had been over to see Anne at Haworth. They wrote frequently, sometimes every day.[5] Their mother, it appeared, was only waiting for the death of Sir Edward Scott's wife in order to marry him; 'whose infatuated slave, it would appear, she is', reported the disgusted Charlotte. 'A worse woman, I believe, hardly exists; the more I hear of her the more deeply she revolts me.'[6] Her mounting detestation of Mrs. Robinson did not, however, produce any reaction in favour of her brother. She had no pity for him, but she was becoming used to him. 'Branwell is the same in conduct as ever; his constitution seems shattered. Papa, and sometimes all of us, have sad nights with him, he sleeps most of the day, and consequently will lie awake at night. But has not every house its trial?'[7]

The news of Mrs. Robinson's impending marriage left Branwell without hope. He failed rapidly through the summer, but he kept to his feet; and though he talked often enough of death, neither he, nor his family, nor the doctor who had now begun to attend him, was prepared for his sudden end. Grundy came again to see his friend—for the last time, though neither he nor Branwell knew it: 'From the little inn I sent for him to the great, square, cold-looking Rectory. I had ordered a dinner for two, and the room looked cosy and warm, the bright glass and silver pleasantly reflecting the sparkling fire-light, deeply toned by the red curtains. Whilst I waited his appearance, his father was shown in. Much of the Rector's old stiffness of manner had gone. He spoke of Branwell with more affection than I had ever heretofore heard him express, but he also spoke almost hopelessly. He said that when my message came, Branwell was in bed, and had been almost too weak for the last few days to leave it; nevertheless, he had insisted upon coming, and would be there immediately. We parted, and I never saw him again. Presently the door opened cautiously, and a head appeared. It was a mass of red, unkempt, uncut hair, wildly floating round a great, gaunt forehead; the cheeks yellow and hollow, the mouth fallen, the thin white lips not trembling but shaking, the sunken eyes, once small, now glaring with the light of madness,—all told the sad tale but too surely. I hastened to my friend, greeted him in my gayest manner, as I knew he best liked, drew him quickly into the room, and forced upon him a stiff glass of hot brandy. Under its influence, and that of the bright, cheerful surroundings, he looked frightened—frightened of himself. He glanced at me for a moment, and muttered something of leaving a warm bed to come out into the cold night. Another glass of brandy, and returning warmth gradually brought him back to something like the Brontë of old. He even ate some dinner, a thing which he said he had not done for long; so our last interview was pleasant, though grave. I never knew his intellect clearer. He described himself as waiting anxiously for death—indeed, longing for it, and happy, in these his sane moments, to think it was so near. He once again declared that death would be due to the story I knew, and to nothing else.'[8]

On Friday, 22 September, Branwell was in the village as usual. The following day he took to his bed. On Sunday morning he died.[9] Tradition has it that he insisted upon dying on his feet.[10] He seems, certainly, to have met his end with courage and dignity. Indeed, he showed during the last few days of his life a new spirit: 'His demeanour, his language, his sentiments', wrote Charlotte, 'were all singularly altered and softened.'[11] And she added: 'This change could not be owing to the fear of death, for till within half an hour of his decease he seemed unconscious of danger.'[12] Particularly noticeable was the change in his attitude towards the family: 'all bitterness seemed gone'.[13]

Charlotte fell ill on the very day of her brother's death. She had been ailing; and the awe and trouble of Branwell's sudden end proved too much for her. She could not accompany the little cortège that passed a day or two later through the gate that led from garden to churchyard. For days afterwards she suffered torments. Her disgust and contempt fell away, and she could think only of Branwell as he used to be and as he might have been. Her remorse and her grief were terrible; and she dreaded the nights, fearing her dreams even more than her waking thoughts.[14] Her letters of this time did not mention her true feelings (they were too dreadful to be written about) but actually show a sense of relief rather than sorrow. Thus she told Williams a few days after the death of Branwell: 'It is not permitted us to grieve for him who is gone as others grieve for those they lose. The removal of our only brother must necessarily be regarded by us rather in the light of a mercy than a chastisement. Branwell was his father's and his sisters' pride and hope in his boyhood, but since manhood the case has been otherwise. It has been our lot to see him take a wrong bent; to hope, expect, wait his return to the right path; to know the sickness of hope deferred, the dismay of prayer baffled; to experience despair at last—and now to behold the sudden early obscure close of what might have been a noble career. I do not weep from a sense of bereavement —there is no prop withdrawn, no consolation torn away, no dear companion lost—but for the wreck of talent, the ruin of promise, the untimely dreary extinction of what might have been a burning and a shining light. My brother was a year my junior. I had aspirations and ambitions for him once, long ago —they have perished mournfully. Nothing remains of him but a memory of errors and sufferings. There is such a bitterness of pity for his life and death, such a yearning for the emptiness of his whole existence as I cannot describe.'[15]

As the days passed Charlotte slipped deeper into the sententiousness that so often attended her less sincere moments: 'When I looked on the noble face and forehead of my dead brother (Nature had favoured him with a fairer outside, as well as a finer constitution than his sisters) and asked myself what had made him go ever wrong, tend ever downwards, when he had so many gifts to induce to, and aid in an upward course, I seemed to receive an oppressive revelation of the feebleness of humanity; of the inadequacy of even genius to lead to true greatness if unaided by religion and principle.'[16]

The consolations offered by an extension of this manner of thought were plain enough. Was it not easy, was it not positively consoling to see, by fixing one's gaze firmly on the Branwell of the past few years, not the premature and unnecessary eclipse of talent and of hope, but the merciful act of an all-wise providence? Charlotte accepted such consolation. 'Many', she writes, 'under the circumstances, would think our loss rather a relief than otherwise. In truth, we must acknowledge, in all humility and gratitude, that God has greatly tempered judgment with mercy.'[17]

THE DEATH OF EMILY

*Emily catches a chill. It turns to inflammation of the lungs. Charlotte's alarm. Her
efforts to help rebuffed. Emily's attitude. She refuses to see a doctor and will not discuss
her illness. Charlotte writes to a specialist. She loses hope. The death of Emily.*

BRANWELL was dead, but his influence on the lives of the three
remaining Brontës was not ended. Emily caught a chill at her
brother's funeral, and never left the parsonage again alive. At
first Charlotte, with eyes all for the weakly Anne, took no
alarm: 'Emily and Anne are pretty well, though Anne is always
delicate, and Emily has a cough and cold at present'[1]—so Ellen
was informed early in October. Three weeks later, Charlotte
was showing some uneasiness: 'Emily's cold and cough are
very obstinate. I fear she has pain in the chest, and I sometimes
catch a shortness in her breathing, when she has moved at all
quickly. She looks very, very thin and pale. Her reserved
nature occasions me great uneasiness of mind. It is useless to
question her; you get no answers. It is still more useless to
recommend remedies; they are never adopted. Nor can I shut
my eyes to the fact of Anne's great delicacy of constitution. The
late sad event has, I feel, made me more apprehensive than
common. I cannot help feeling much depressed sometimes.'[2]

Four days after writing this letter, Charlotte had forced herself
to realize and put into words the fact that Emily was suffering
from more than a cough or cold: 'I am better, but others are ill
now,' she tells Williams. 'Papa is not well, my sister Emily has
something like a slow inflammation of the lungs, and even our
old servant, who has lived with us nearly a quarter of a century,
is suffering under serious indisposition. I would fain hope that
Emily is a little better this evening, but it is difficult to ascertain
this. She is a real stoic in illness: she neither seeks nor will accept
sympathy. To put any questions, to offer any aid, is to annoy;
she will not yield a step before pain and sickness till forced; not
one of her ordinary avocations will she voluntarily renounce.
You must look on and see her do what she is unfit to do, and not

dare to say a word—a painful necessity for those to whom her health and existence are as precious as the life in their veins. When she is ill there seems to be no sunshine in the world for me. The tie of sister is near and dear indeed, and I think a certain harshness in her powerful and peculiar character only makes me cling to her more.'[3] Then Charlotte realizes what she has been saying: 'But this is all family egotism (so to speak) —excuse it, and, above all, never allude to it, or to the name Emily, when you write to me. I do not always show your letters, but I never withhold them when they are inquired after.'[4] Another five days, and Emily had become too ill to write. But she could still enjoy reading, and she smiled with pleasure when Charlotte told her that Smith Elder were to send more books for them to read.[5]

Towards the end of November, Williams wrote recommending homoeopathic treatment: 'I put your most friendly letter into Emily's hands as soon as I had myself perused it,' wrote Charlotte, 'taking care, however, not to say a word in favour of homeopathy—that would not have answered. It is best usually to leave her to form her own judgment, and *especially* not to advocate the side you wish her to favour; if you do, she is sure to lean in the opposite direction, and ten to one will argue herself into non-compliance. Hitherto she has refused medicine, rejected medical advice; no reasoning, no entreaty, has availed to induce her to see a physician.'[6] Williams's recommendation met with no greater success: 'Mr. Williams' intention was kind and good,' said Emily, 'but he was under a delusion: Homeopathy is only another form of quackery.'[7] But Charlotte hoped on: 'She may reconsider this opinion and come to a different conclusion: her second thoughts are often the best.'[8]

Charlotte, who had just received an unfavourable review from the *North American Review*,[9] describes her sisters as they hear the reviewer's comments: 'Today, as Emily appeared a little easier, I thought the "Review" would amuse her, so I read it aloud to her and Anne. As I sat between them at our quiet but now somewhat melancholy fireside, I studied the two ferocious authors. Ellis, the "man of uncommon talents, but dogged, brutal, and morose," sat leaning back in his easy-chair drawing his impeded breath as he best could, and looking, alas! piteously pale and wasted; it is not his wont to laugh, but he smiled half-amused and half in scorn as he listened. Acton was sewing, no emotion ever stirs him to loquacity, so he only smiled too, dropping at the same time a single word of calm amazement to hear his character so darkly portrayed.'[10]

The next day, in a letter to Ellen, Charlotte allowed herself for a moment to face the possible end of her sister's illness. For the first time, she abandoned her instinctive pretence of linking Emily's illness with the passing ailment of Anne or her father: 'I told you Emily was ill, in my last letter. She has not rallied yet. She is *very* ill. I believe, if you were to see her, your impression would be that there is no hope. A more hollow, wasted, pallid aspect I have not beheld. The deep, tight cough continues; the breathing after the least exertion is a rapid pant; and these symptoms are accompanied by pains in the chest and side. Her pulse, the only time she allowed it to be felt, was found to beat 115 per minute. In this state she resolutely refuses to see a doctor, she will not give an explanation of her feelings, she will scarcely allow her illness to be alluded to. Our position is, and has been for some weeks, exquisitely painful. God only knows how all this is to terminate. More than once, I have been forced boldly to regard the terrible event of her loss as possible and even probable. But nature shrinks from such thoughts. I think Emily seems the nearest thing to my heart in this world.'[11] Charlotte could no longer conceal her grief and despair: 'Never in all her life had she lingered over any task that lay before her,' she wrote of her sister, 'and she did not linger now. She sank rapidly. She made haste to leave us. Yet, while physically she perished, she grew stronger than we had yet known her. Day by day, when I saw with what a front she met suffering, I looked on her with an anguish of wonder and love. I have seen nothing like it; but, indeed, I have never seen her parallel in anything. Stronger than a man, simpler than a child, her nature stood alone. The awful point was, that, while full of ruth for others, on herself she had no pity; the spirit was inexorable to the flesh; from the trembling hand, the unnerved limbs, the faded eyes, the same service was exacted as they had rendered in health. To stand by and witness this, and not dare to remonstrate, was a pain no words can render.'[12]

Yet to stand by and see her sister, unaided and uncomplaining, fight the gathering power of death was a fate Charlotte could not avert; all her love, her pleas, her prayers were without effect; she grieved and agonized to no end; she beat herself again and again—always in anguish and always in vain—against a stubborn and indomitable purpose. Emily resented any thought, any suggestion of her sex as necessarily the weaker. Compassion, or the making of allowances on this score, humiliated her. She would neither seek nor accept aid for a weakness that, according to her spartan, self-imposed discipline, must be shown no mercy. She would not acknowledge the body's dependence upon any power other than the mind that possessed it. She neither wanted nor admitted relief or cure by any other agency than nature. Her growing weakness humiliated her, and she fought it with stubborn fury, turning away help with sullen pride the more her body cried for it. At no time would Emily have tolerated interference in her private life with any pretence of patience. Now, she repelled every suggestion that she should see a doctor,[13] she refused to reveal or even to discuss her symptoms,[14] she was offended when any reference to her state was made.[15]

Nor was that all. Emily had just seen Branwell redeem himself by the manner of his end; she had seen him die for a romantic passion with a bravado that appealed to her ready sense of the violent and the heroic; she had seen him keep to his feet until the day before his death; she had seen him meet death defiantly on his feet. So Emily rebuffed Charlotte's advances brusquely, would give her sister's anxious love no satisfaction. Charlotte's sympathetic attentions would have annoyed her at any time: how much more so now, just after she had seen Charlotte ignore the dying Branwell until the last days of his life.

Charlotte, almost distracted by this forced inaction, could find no comfort anywhere. Mr. Brontë said, mournfully, that once he had hoped, as Charlotte now hoped, when his eldest children had been stricken by the same disease, but that he could hope no more.[16] Anne, who had never recovered completely from her illness of the preceding winter, was showing signs of the strain on a constitution naturally weak, of watching, first the long drawn out tragedy of Branwell, then—far more poignant—Emily's fierce and silent fight for life. She could not comfort Charlotte; she was too pessimistic and fatalistic. She also respected Emily's fanatical determination to deal with her illness alone, and so she interfered as little as she could. Every evening in silence, Anne and Charlotte watched their weak and emaciated but defiant sister drag herself up the stairs one by one; night after night they lay in their beds, listening, appalled, to her deep, hollow cough; every morning, they waited for it to begin again; and every day, when they saw Emily again, they had to face, as expressionless as they could force themselves to be, the cheeks a little more hectic, the eyes a little more hollow, and the struggle for breath a shade more desperate and unavailing.[17]

Anne, though uncomplaining, suffered little less than Charlotte as day by day she came ever nearer to losing the sister who had been her playmate, inspiration, and strength from childhood. Yet she was comforted by the years of understanding between them; and her innate piety helped her to feel resigned. Charlotte's grief was not softened by such thoughts. The consolations that had served her in the hours after the death of Branwell did not avail her here. She talked from time to time of submission to God's Will, but she could not submit. Death to her, for all her occasional pious platitudes, was final; and she could not bear the thought of an end to Emily before she had even known her. So she raged and agonized, but there was no help for it; Emily pursued her way out of life, aloof, untouchable, unmoved.

This frustrating sense of exclusion from a hidden Emily was no new thing. But only after Charlotte had parted company with Branwell, had placed Ellen in her true, limited sphere of friendship, and had disciplined her longing for Héger, did she gain the power through suffering to imagine something of what she was missing.[18]

Charlotte's dramatic sense and her weakness for rhetoric were to cause her more than once to write of Emily and Anne in words that would have been better left unsaid—but Emily also inspired some of her noblest passages of prose.[19] How much of Charlotte's present misery was due to helplessness in the face of her sister's stoicism, how much to the knowledge that with all her love she was unable to touch the essential Emily, and that soon the mystery would elude her for ever— this cannot be known. For the second time she suffered deeply because she could not get near the person she loved, and for the second time she suffered uselessly, because she could never have been more intimate than she was, either with Héger or with Emily.

Even if Charlotte had realized this, she had neither the coldness nor the hardness to accept it. For her, to love was to possess and be possessed, to share complete intimacy and trust; but this she was never to get from anyone, and least of all from Emily, now further from Charlotte than ever before because of the primitive instinct, so strong in her, to die alone.

Emily advanced to meet her end calmly and even with disdain. She asked no pity and she gave none. She suffered greatly but her sufferings were of the body only. She had never feared death. For her, as many of her poems show, it was a release. To her, life was the prison. All her adult life she had been in revolt, sometimes vocal, often sullen and silent, against the imprisonment of the aspiring soul. The body—that faulty, fallible mechanism, heir to many ills, muffling the mystic vision; the intellect—at its best a feeble, uncertain flicker, obscuring more of the truth than it illuminated; these, in Emily's eyes, were hindrances to the full, free life of the imagination; chains that arrested all efforts to span the gulf between her two worlds. Hence the meditation upon death that sounds through so much of her work. The grave was familiar enough to the Brontës, both as the physical background to their lives and as an integral part of their common vocabulary and thought. So, in Emily's poems, what might have been no more than a morbid concentration upon the dissolution of the body became the expression of a joy glimpsed only in moments of revelation, and a lament for the bonds that held her from fulfilment.

Now, though her body fought for life doggedly, with an animal's instinctive recoil from disease, Emily harboured this traitor who opened the gates of her citadel and let the enemy in. For years she had been longing for the moment of emancipation, dreaming of it, writing about it; and, despite the wrench of the flesh, she would not if she could at this late hour draw back. In her way, she loved Charlotte, and she loved Anne, but she was a solitary creature, detached, remote, and, by ordinary standards, unfeeling. Those who watched her die, the thwarted, passionately loving Charlotte especially, suffered in mind even more cruelly than Emily suffered bodily. They paid the penalty that falls always upon those who love the Emily Brontës of this world.

Towards the end of November, Ellen asked if she could help at the parsonage, but Emily so bitterly resented the suggestion, both as an implication that her state of health needed attention, and as an unwarranted intrusion upon Ellen's kindness, that Charlotte was obliged to refuse.[20] But it was not in Charlotte's nature entirely or for long to lose hope. 'I hope still,' Charlotte told her friend, 'for I *must* hope— she is dear to me as life—if I let the faintness of despair reach my heart I shall become worthless. The attack was, I believe, in the first place, inflammation of the lungs; it ought to have been promptly met in time, but she would take no care, use no means; she is too intractable. I *do* wish I knew her state and feelings more clearly.'[21]

Williams sent Charlotte the book on homoeopathy,[22] and Charlotte finally persuaded Emily to read it, but could only extract the admission that homoeopathy 'could not do much harm'.[23] Charlotte, however, did not share the view of Williams; she yearned for medical opinion and advice: 'It is easy my dear sir, to say that there is nothing in medicine, and that physicians are useless, but we naturally wish to procure aid for those we love when we see them suffer; most painful is it to sit still, look on and do nothing. Would that my sister added to her many great qualities the humble one of tractability! I have again and again incurred her displeasure by urging the necessity of seeking advice, and I fear I must yet incur it again and again.'[24]

But Charlotte's importunity met with no reward. Emily declared that 'no poisoning doctor' should come near her.[25] Her weakness increased, her cough grew more violent, her body more wasted; but still she carried out all her usual tasks about the house.[26] In spite of nights of pain and discomfort, she still rose at seven in the morning and stayed up until ten in the evening. She would allow no one but herself to attend to the animals, she would not let any one put so much as a hand to her elbow to guide her uncertain steps.[27] The very suggestion that she needed help was sufficient to rouse anger that her sisters dared not provoke.[28] At last, this inaction became more than Charlotte could bear: 'I have endured such tortures of uncertainty that at length I could endure it no longer .... I have written, unknown to her, to an eminent physician in London, giving as minute a statement of her case and symptoms as I could draw up, and requesting an opinion.'[29] This last desperate attempt to avert Emily's death was a failure. The doctor's reply was too obscure to be helpful. He sent medicine but Emily would not take it.[30]

Every day she grew weaker. On the morning of 19 December she had not sufficient strength to finish dressing, but she came downstairs alone, still refusing help.[31] Charlotte lost hope when she saw her. 'Moments as dark as these I have never known,' she wrote to Ellen that morning.[32] Even then, Emily showed so stoical a front that Charlotte had no idea how soon the end was to come.[33] Emily attempted to work as usual, but when Charlotte returned from a hurried walk on the moor with a scrap of heather to cheer her, Emily could not see what she held in her hand.[34]

At midday, Emily whispered that she would see a doctor,[35] but it was too late. She lay on the couch while her sisters, helpless and in silent dread, watched her last struggle. 'It was very terrible,' said Charlotte. 'She was torn conscious, panting, reluctant though resolute out of a happy life.'[36] But Emily's long fight ended at last. About two o'clock in the afternoon she turned her eyes from the sun and died.[37]

Emily had written her epitaph nearly three years before her death:

> No coward soul is mine
> No trembler in the world's storm-troubled sphere
> I see Heaven's glories shine
> And Faith shines equal arming me from fear.
>
> O God within my breast
> Almighty ever-present Deity
> Life, that in me hast rest
> As I Undying Life, have power in thee.
>
> Vain are the thousand creeds
> That move men's hearts, unutterably vain,
> Worthless as withered weeds
> Or idlest froth amid the boundless main.
>
> To waken doubt in one
> Holding so fast by thy infinity
> So surely anchored on
> The steadfast rock of Immortality.

With wide-embracing love
Thy spirit animates eternal years
Pervades and broods above,
Changes, sustains, dissolves, creates and rears.

Though Earth and moon were gone
And suns and universes ceased to be
And thou wert left alone
Every Existence would exist in thee

There is not room for Death
Nor atom that his might could render void
Since thou art Being and Breath
And what thou art may never be destroyed.[83]

Cold in the earth and the deep snow piled above thee!
Far, far removed cold in the dreary grave!
Have I forgot, my Only love, to love thee,
Severed at last by Time's all severing wave?

Now, when alone, do my thoughts no longer hover
Over the mountains on Angora's shore,
Resting their wings where heath and fern leaves cover
Thy noble heart forever, ever more?

Cold in the earth, and fifteen wild Decembers
From those brown hills have melted into spring —
Faithful indeed is the spirit that remembers
After such years of change and suffering!

Sweet Love of youth, forgive if I forget thee
While the World's tide is bearing me along
Sterner desires and darker Hopes beset me
Hopes which obscure but cannot do thee wrong —

No other Sun has lightened up my heaven;
No other Star has ever shone for me
All my life's bliss from thy dear life was given —
All my life's bliss is in the grave with thee

But when the days of golden dreams had perished
And even Despair was powerless to destroy
Then did I learn how existence could be cherished
Strengthened and fed without the aid of joy

Then did I check the tears of useless passion,
Weaned my young soul from yearning after mine,
Sternly denied its burning wish to hasten
Down to that tomb already more than mine!

And even yet, I dare not let it languish,
Dare not indulge in Memory's rapturous pain
Once drinking deep of that divinest anguish
How could I seek the empty world again?

EMILY'S POEM 'COLD IN THE EARTH'
reproduced (exact size) from two pages of her manuscript book of Gondal poems

ANNE
from a water-colour sketch by Charlotte

XXVIII

THE DEATH OF ANNE

Signs of consumption in Anne just before Emily's death. She falls ill. The doctor says there is no hope. Her patience in illness and willingness to try Charlotte's many remedies. Her one wish to go to Scarborough long frustrated. She goes at last, but too late. Description by Ellen of Anne's last days.

THUS, within three months, two of the Brontës were dead. Both deaths were unexpected, sudden, dramatic, entirely characteristic, and it is difficult to believe that either Emily or Branwell would have wished to die in any other way. To those remaining, however, the manner in which their numbers had been halved came as an appalling shock; and Charlotte, at least, must have felt that she had suffered enough with the loss of Emily. Yet death had not finished with the Brontës; it struck again; but this time its work was made easy.

Anne had never entirely recovered from the effect of her illness of the previous winter. Her constitution, never strong, had been weakened by years of unhappiness, an unhappiness that began when, alone at Thorp Green, she had heard of the death of Weightman. This frustration of her longing to be married and to have children—expressed again and again in her poems[1]—had to be borne through years of loneliness, away from the place which made up her only other happiness. Nor was this all; for in her many solitary hours the fear of damnation fastened upon her, and she had neither the hope, nor the activity, nor the company, nor the strength of will needed to throw it off. Three years of isolation at Thorp Green had been Anne's lot. Then, as if she had not endured enough, she had to spend more than two years at the same place in worse than solitude; with a brother whose behaviour filled her with shame. There followed the years of Branwell's degradation at home, his death, and, final overwhelming blow, Emily's terrible illness and death.

A week before Emily died, Charlotte wrote apprehensively about Anne's frequent pains in the side. This was during a visit of the Robinson girls: 'They seemed overjoyed to see Anne; when I went into the room, they were clinging round her like two children—she, meantime, looking perfectly quiet and passive.'[2] This is a characteristic picture. Anne's surface placidity extended beyond moments of pleasure; she was equally restrained in trouble and in pain. She had never allowed personal sorrows to bear upon anyone, least of all those she loved, and she did not allow them to do so now, when faced with her hardest and loneliest struggle. She did everything possible to make ready to pass from the world, if go she must, with the least discomfort and sorrow to those about her.

For Anne's fate was quickly determined. Emily had been dead barely three weeks when her sister, victim once again of influenza, was given by the doctor what amounted to a death sentence. Ellen Nussey, on a visit, describes the occasion: 'I found the family wonderfully calm and sustained, but anxious respecting Anne. Mr. Brontë enquired for the best doctor in Leeds. Mr. Teale was recommended; and came to Haworth. Anne was looking sweetly pretty and flushed, and in capital spirits for an invalid. While consultations were going on in Mr. Brontë's study, Anne was very lively in conversation, walking round the room supported by me. Mr. Brontë joined us after Mr. Teale's departure, and, seating himself on the couch, he drew Anne towards him and said, "My *dear* little Anne." That was all—but it was understood. Charlotte afterwards told me that Mr. Teale said—The disease of consumption had progressed too far for cure; and he thought so seriously of the case, he took the trouble to acquaint my friends and urge them to call me home from my visit.'[3]

Charlotte, afraid of the truth, would not at once admit it: 'Anne and I sit alone and in seclusion as you fancy us, but we do not study; Anne cannot study now, she can scarcely read; she occupies Emily's chair—she does not get well. A week ago we sent for a Medical Man of skill and experience from Leeds to see her; he examined her with the stethoscope; his report I forbear to dwell on for the present; even skilful physicians have often been mistaken in their conjectures . . . . When we lost Emily I thought we had drained the very dregs of our cup of trial, but now when I hear Anne cough as Emily coughed, I tremble lest there should be exquisite bitterness yet to taste.'[4]

George Smith offered to send a famous doctor of his acquaintance[5] to see Anne; but Mr. Brontë refused, partly through pride, and partly because he felt fatalistic about the disease that had carried off so many of his children.[6] Charlotte, however, unknown to her father, applied to this doctor for advice,[7] but his answer was not reassuring.[8]

Charlotte seemed to suffer more for her dead sister than for the dying one; not necessarily because she loved Anne less, but because the advance of death was made by Anne's resignation and lack of struggle to seem less terrible, less evident, than in Emily: 'The feeling of Emily's loss does not diminish as time wears on—it often makes itself most acutely recognized. It brings, too, an inexpressible sorrow with it, and then the future is dark . . . . I must confess that in the time which has elapsed since Emily's death there have been moments of solitary, deep, inert affliction far harder to bear than those which immediately followed our loss.'[9]

Her work on *Shirley*, which she forced herself to continue whenever possible, seemed futile and meaningless: 'Worse than useless did it seem to attempt to write what there no longer lived an "Ellis Bell" to read; the whole book, with every hope founded on it, faded to vanity and vexation of spirit.'[10]

Emily's illness and her death-day had fixed themselves in Charlotte's memory with horror that left little room for any other violent emotion.[11] Again and again she spoke of those dreadful last moments:[12] 'We saw Emily torn from the midst of us when our hearts clung to her with intense attachment and when—loving each other as we did—it seemed as if—might we but have been spared to each other—we could have found complete happiness in our mutual society and affection.'[13] And again: 'I cannot forget Emily's death-day; it becomes a more fixed, a darker, a more frequently recurring idea in my mind than ever; it was very terrible . . . . But it *will not do* to dwell on these things.'[14]

But this preoccupation with the end and the loss of Emily was made possible only by the self-effacement of Anne, as marked in illness as in health: 'There is some feeble consolation in thinking we are doing the very best that can be done,' Charlotte wrote. 'The agony of forced, total neglect, is not now felt, as during Emily's illness. Never may we be doomed to feel such agony again. It was terrible.'[15] Everything that relieved the mind of Charlotte—though it could not help Anne—the younger sister suffered meekly and without complaint.[16] Blisters, cod-liver oil ('it smells and tastes like train oil',[17] said Charlotte), carbonate of iron, vegetable balsam, hydropathy— all the painful and futile curatives of the day—Anne endured with patience, with stoicism, and in silence, until persistent sickness and inability to eat showed the anxious Charlotte that yet another supposed remedy had failed, another avenue of escape from death was cut off.[18]

It seemed, however, that Anne's patience bore its own reward; for the progress of the disease was both less painful and less marked than it had been with Emily: 'Her illness has none of the fearful, rapid symptoms which appalled in Emily's case,' wrote Charlotte. 'Her mind seems generally serene and her sufferings hitherto are nothing like Emily's.'[19] So Charlotte, if weighed down by the fear that Anne's end was inevitable, had the edge taken off her grief by the willingness with which the patient bent to her command. Charlotte could lull her forebodings in a turmoil of preparation; she could be incessantly up and doing, not watching in agonized powerlessness.[20] So quietly were her sister's sufferings borne, so unobtrusive was Anne's steady decline, that Charlotte was able to finish the second volume of *Shirley* and send the manuscript to her publishers for their comments.[21]

Anne made only one request. She begged that she might be taken as early as possible to the sea; and that the place might be Scarborough. There she believed she might find health, if health were to be granted her.[22] Even in this matter she thought of others. She was ready to pay for the journey and lodgings,[23] and, though longing for Charlotte's company, she asked Ellen to go with her, so that Charlotte could stay with her father and be freed from anxiety on her account.[24] Yet this one wish of Anne, simple though it appeared, met many obstacles—so many, indeed, that it seemed doubtful whether the dying girl would ever be allowed to reach Scarborough before the advance of her disease rendered a journey impossible. Charlotte passed on her sister's suggestion to Ellen; but she informed her friend privately that both she and Mr. Brontë objected to it because of the trouble to Ellen if Anne were suddenly to be taken worse away from home.[25] Ellen, who, like so many who knew Anne, loved her—the two would have been better fitted as friends than Ellen and Charlotte, if friendships were formed by reason—would not decline the proposal outright. She told Anne with truth how gladly she would accompany her; but hinted at the reluctance of friends to let her go.[26]

Anne, feeling with the passing of every day that time was being lost, and ever more sure that the sea offered the one hope of recovery, displayed a pertinacity she rarely exerted on her own behalf; yet even then, with a larger purpose behind the wish: 'I thank you greatly for your kind letter, and your ready compliance with my proposal as far as the *will* can go at least,' she replied. 'I see, however, that your friends are unwilling that you should undertake the responsibility of accompanying me under present circumstances. But I do not think there would be any great responsibility in the matter. I know, and everybody knows, that you would be as kind and helpful as any one could possibly be, and I hope I should not be very troublesome. It would be as a companion, not as a nurse, that I should wish for your company; otherwise I should not venture to ask it. As for your kind and often repeated invitations to Brookroyd, pray give my sincere thanks to your mother and sisters, but tell them I could not think of inflicting my presence upon them as I now am. It is very kind of them to make so light of the trouble, but there must be more or less, and certainly no pleasure, from the society of a silent invalid stranger. I hope, however, that Charlotte will by some means make it possible to accompany me after all. She is certainly very delicate, and greatly needs a change of air and scene to renovate her constitution. And then your going with me before the end of May is apparently out of the question unless you are disappointed in your visitors; but I should be reluctant to wait till then if the weather would at all permit an earlier departure. You say May is a trying month, and so say others. The early part is often cold enough, I acknowledge, but according to my experience, we are almost certain of some fine warm days in the latter half, when the laburnums and lilacs are in bloom; whereas June is often cold, and July generally wet. But I have a more serious reason than this for my impatience of delay. The doctors say that change of air or removal to a better climate would hardly ever fail of success in consumptive cases, if the remedy be taken *in time*; but the reason why there are so many disappointments is that it is generally deferred till it is too late. Now I would not commit this error, and, to say the truth, though I suffer much less from pain and fever than I did when you were with us, I am decidedly weaker, and very much thinner. My cough still troubles me a good deal, especially in the night, and, what seems worse than all, I am subject to great shortness of breath on going upstairs or any slight exertion. Under these circumstances, I think there is no time to be lost. I have no horror of death; if I thought it inevitable, I think I could quietly resign myself to the prospect, in the hope that you, dear Miss Nussey, would give as much of your company as you possibly could to Charlotte, and be a sister to her in my stead. But I wish it would please God to spare me, not only for papa's and Charlotte's sakes, but because I long to do some good in the world before I leave it. I have many schemes in my head for future practice, humble and limited indeed, but still I should not like them all to come to nothing, and myself to have lived to so little purpose. But God's will be done.'[27]

This letter was written in the first days of April 1849. Almost two months were to pass before Anne obtained her way, and it was then too late. If there had ever been hope of her recovery, it no longer existed when at last she was allowed to leave the parsonage. First of all, the doctor insisted upon waiting for the warmer weather before the journey was attempted. Then, when the warmer weather came, late in April, Charlotte was afraid of allowing her sister to travel on account of Anne's now pitiable weakness, her exhaustion after taking a few steps.[28] Not until the last weeks of May did she succeed in persuading Charlotte, Mr. Brontë and the doctor to let her go without further delay. Throughout these last weeks Charlotte was tortured by misgivings. She could not bear to speak of the journey, so grievously did she doubt whether it would be wise to go, or even possible.[29] Anne's eagerness, her hope, her joy at the thought of Scarborough, were so many knives at the heart of her sister; as were her silent sorrow and surprise at the lack of response from Charlotte. 'There must be *some* improvement before I can feel justified in taking her away from home,' Charlotte told Ellen at the beginning of May. 'Yet to delay is painful;

for, as is *always* the case, I believe, under the circumstances, she seems herself but half conscious of the necessity for such delay. She wonders, I believe, why I don't talk more about the journey; it grieves me to think she may even be hurt by my seeming tardiness. She is very much emaciated, far more so than when you were with us; her arms are no thicker than a little child's. The least exertion brings a shortness of breath. She goes out a little every day, but we creep rather than walk.'[30]

So the days dragged on. Anne had lost what was most dear to her—'the sight of my sister Anne's very still but deep sorrow wakens in me such fear for her that I dare not falter,'[31] Charlotte had written after Emily's death—but a strong religious sense of duty forbade any wish for an end to her life.[32] There was much to be done in the world. And so she looked forward to Scarborough, to returning health, and to a life of service and fulfilment if not of active happiness.[33]

Anne's entreaties finally took effect. Rooms were taken at Scarborough,[34] and to her joy, both Ellen and Charlotte said they would come with her. The two sisters agreed to meet Ellen at Leeds on Wednesday, 23 May.[35] Although Charlotte was persuaded at last to hope for some miracle from the sea air, she could not set aside cruel misgivings as she looked at Anne: 'She is more emaciated than Emily was at the very last,' she writes, 'her breath scarcely serves her to mount the stairs however slowly. She sleeps very little at night—and often passes most of the forenoon in a semi-lethargic state.'[36]

On the day appointed for the first stage of the journey, Ellen waited in vain for the sisters at Leeds. Anne was too ill to move.[37] The next day, she had recovered slightly, but she could no longer walk by herself—she had to be carried into the chaise and into the trains. But she insisted upon making the journey;[38] in her, too, the indefatigable Brontë spirit burned brightly. Ellen hurried over to the parsonage in time to start the journey again;[39] and it is she who completes the account of Anne's last days.

'She left her home May 24, 1849—died May 28. Her life was calm, quiet, spiritual; *such* was her end. Through the trials and fatigues of the journey she evinced the pious courage and fortitude of a martyr. Dependence and helplessness were ever with her a far sorer trial than hard, racking pain.

'The first stage of our journey was to York; and here the dear invalid was so revived, so cheerful, and so happy, we drew consolation, and trusted that at least temporary improvement was to be derived from the change which *she* had so longed for, and her friends had so dreaded for her.

'By her request we went to the Minster, and to her it was an overpowering pleasure; not for its own imposing and impressive grandeur only, but because it brought to her susceptible nature a vital and overwhelming sense of omnipotence. She said, while gazing at the structure, "If finite power can do this, what is the . . . ?" and here emotion stayed her speech, and she was hastened to a less exciting scene.

'Her weakness of body was great, but her gratitude for every mercy was greater. After such an exertion as walking to her bedroom she would clasp her hands and raise her eyes in silent thanks, and she did this not to the exclusion of wonted prayer, for that too was performed on bended knee, ere she accepted the rest of her couch.

'On the 25th we arrived at Scarborough; our dear invalid having, during the journey, directed our attention to every prospect worthy of notice.

'On the 26th we drove on the sands for an hour; and lest the poor donkey should be urged by its driver to a greater speed than her tender heart thought right, she took the reins and drove herself. When joined by her friend she was charging the boy-master of the donkey to treat the poor animal well. She was ever fond of dumb things, and would give up her own comfort for them.

'On Sunday, the 27th, she wished to go to church, and her eye brightened with the thought of once more worshipping her God among her fellow creatures. We thought it prudent to dissuade her from the attempt, though it was evident her heart was longing to join in the public act of devotion and praise.

'She walked a little in the afternoon, and meeting with a sheltered and comfortable seat near the beach, she begged we would leave her and enjoy the various scenes near at hand, which were new to us but familiar to her. She loved the place, and wished us to share her preference.

'The evening closed in with the most glorious sunset I ever witnessed. The castle on the cliff stood in proud glory, gilded by the rays of the declining sun. The distant ships glittered like burnished gold; the little boats near the beach heaved on the ebbing tide, inviting occupants. The view was grand beyond description. Anne was drawn in her easy chair to the window, to enjoy the scene with us. Her face became illuminated almost as much as the glorious scene she gazed upon. Little was said, for it was plain that her thoughts were driven by the

imposing view before her to penetrate forwards to the regions of un-
fading glory. She again thought of public worship, and wished us to
leave her, and join those who were assembled at the house of God.
We declined, gently urging the duty and pleasure of staying with her,
who was now so dear and so feeble. On returning to her place by the
fire she conversed with her sister upon the propriety of returning to
their home. She did not wish it for her own sake, she said; she was
fearing others might suffer more if her decease occurred where she
was. She probably thought the task of accompanying her lifeless
remains on a long journey was more than her sister could bear—more
than the bereaved father could bear, were she borne home another and
a third tenant of the family vault in the short space of nine months.

'The night passed without any apparent accession of illness. She rose
at seven o'clock, and performed most of her toilet herself, by her
expressed wish. Her sister always yielded such points, believing it
was the truest kindness not to press inability when it was not acknowledged. Nothing occurred to excite alarm till about 11 a.m. She then
spoke of feeling a change. "She believed she had not long to live.
Could she reach home alive, if we prepared immediately for departure?"
A physician was sent for. Her address to him was made with perfect
composure. She begged him to say "how long he thought she might
live—not to fear speaking the truth, for she was not afraid to die."
The doctor reluctantly admitted that the angel of death was already
arrived, and that life was ebbing fast. She thanked him for his truthfulness, and he departed to come again very soon. She still occupied her
easy chair, looking so serene, so reliant; there was no pining for grief
as yet, though all knew the separation was at hand. She clasped her
hands, and reverently invoked a blessing from on high: first upon her
sister, then upon her friend, to whom she said, "Be a sister in my
stead. Give Charlotte as much of your company as you can." She
then thanked each for her kindness and attention.

'Ere long the restlessness of approaching death appeared, and she
was borne to the sofa. On being asked if she were easier she looked
gratefully at her questioner, and said "It is not *you* who can give me
ease, but soon all will be well through the merits of our Redeemer."
Shortly after this, seeing that her sister could hardly restrain her grief,
she said, "Take courage, Charlotte, take courage." Her faith never
failed, and her eye never dimmed till about two o'clock, when she
calmly, and without a sigh, passed from the temporal to the eternal.
So still and so hallowed were her last hours and moments. There was
no thought of assistance or of dread. The doctor came and went two
or three times. The hostess knew that death was near, yet so little
was the house disturbed by the presence of the dying, and the sorrow

of those so nearly bereaved, that dinner was announced as ready, through the half-opened door, as the living sister was closing the eyes of the dead one. She could now no more stay the welled-up grief of her sister with her emphatic and dying "Take courage", and it burst forth in brief but agonizing strength. Charlotte's affection, however, had another channel, and there it turned in thought, in care, and in tenderness. There was bereavement, but there was not solitude; sympathy was at hand, and it was accepted.'[40]

So died Anne Brontë, as she had lived—self-effacing, reserved, her thought all for others. But there was one change. At last, towards the end, the calm front she showed to her world ceased to be a façade hiding her dread that salvation was not for her. Alone of all the Brontës, Anne died finally without a struggle and without regret. To the end she was the comforter, not the comforted.[41]

Of this quiet, patient, melancholy figure, little record has remained. 'Anne's character was milder and more subdued,' said Charlotte, comparing her two sisters; 'she wanted the power, the fire, the originality of her sister, but was well endowed with quiet virtues of her own. Long-suffering, self-denying, reflective, and intelligent, a constitutional reserve and taciturnity placed and kept her in the shade, and covered her mind, and especially her feelings, with a sort of nun-like veil, which was rarely lifted.'[42]

Charlotte described correctly. The picture that emerges from her youngest sister's words, from her novels and her poems, is not a colourful one. Yet though she naturally disliked putting herself forward, Anne was in any case most unfavourably placed for expression of her own individuality. Flanked to right and left by genius, she has too often been judged a nonentity. If her sisters' fame has cast a little of its brilliance on her, it has equally overshadowed her own dimmer light. She was beloved by all. From her, in spite of shyness, could be expected always the welcoming smile and word that might be denied by her sisters. She was truly charitable, and even on such a man as George Smith, seeing her for a few hours, she left an impression of her own mild radiance: 'She is a gentle, quiet, rather subdued person, by no means pretty, yet of a pleasing appearance. Her manner was curiously expressive of a wish for protection and encouragement, a kind of constant appeal which invited sympathy.'[43]

Anne endured much and said little. Her thoughts and her wishes were simple and, like her troubles, were kept to herself. Like all the Annes of this world, she passed through life, as she wished, unnoticed. Yet without her the world would have appeared to her sisters and brother an even less satisfactory place; and the life of genius would have proved even harder than genius itself makes it.

Like Emily, Anne wrote her own epitaph. This, her last complete poem, was written after the doctor's verdict had been passed on to her by her father:

A dreadful darkness closes in
On my bewildered mind;
O let me suffer and not sin,
Be tortured yet resigned.

Through all this world of blinding mist
Still let me look to Thee
And give me courage to resist
The Tempter till he flee.

Weary I am, O give me strength
And leave me not to faint;
Say Thou wilt comfort me at length
And pity my complaint.

I've begged to serve Thee heart and soul,
To sacrifice to Thee
No niggard portion, but the whole
Of my identity.

I hoped amid the brave and strong
My portioned task might lie,
To toil amid the labouring throng
With purpose pure and high.

But thou hast fixed another part,
And Thou hast fixed it well;
I said so with my bleeding heart
When first the anguish fell.

For Thou hast taken my delight
And hope of life away
And bid me watch the painful night
And wait the weary day.

The hope and the delight were Thine,
I bless Thee for their loan;
I gave Thee while I deemed them mine
Too little thanks I own.

Shall I with joy Thy blessings share
And not endure their loss,
Or hope the martyr's Crown to wear
And cast away the Cross?

These weary hours will not be lost,
These days of passive misery,
These nights of darkness, anguish-tost,
If I can fix my heart on Thee.

Weak and weary though I lie
Crushed with sorrow, worn with pain,
I may lift to Heaven mine eye
And strive and labour not in vain.

That inward strife against the sins
That ever wait on suffering;
To watch and strike where first begins
Each deed that would corruption bring;

That secret labour to sustain
With humble patience every blow;
To gather fortitude from pain
And hope and holiness from woe.

Thus let me serve Thee from my heart
Whatever be my written fate
Whether thus early to depart
Or yet a while to wait.

If Thou shouldst bring me back to life
More humbled I should be
More wise, more strengthened for the strife,
More apt to lean on Thee.

Should death be standing at the gate,
Thus should I keep my vow,
But hard whate'er my future fate,
So let me serve Thee now.[44]

EPILOGUE

CHARLOTTE

Charlotte stays near Scarborough. Continues 'Shirley'. She describes the return home. Her loneliness. She finishes 'Shirley'. It is published and well received. Analysis of the book. She wins a new admirer—James Taylor. She goes to London. Description of her meeting with Thackeray and other literary celebrities. The authorship of her novels revealed in London and Yorkshire. She pays another visit to London. Meets G. H. Lewes. Her happiness in the Smith home. Smith's description of her. Mutual liking. Visit to Edinburgh with him. Taylor still trying to win her favour. She visits the Lakes. Meets and likes Mrs. Gaskell. Prepares a new edition of 'Wuthering Heights' and 'Agnes Grey'. Correspondence with Dobell. Her loneliness and unhappiness at home. Reads much but cannot make progress with 'Villette'. Visits Harriet Martineau. Correspondence with Smith. Her views on marriage with Smith or Taylor. She discourages Taylor. Visits London again—sees Rachel, the Poet Laureate, Thackeray, the Crystal Palace. Goes to Manchester to see Mrs. Gaskell. Depression at home during the winter. Failure to continue 'Villette'. Visits Ellen and misses Smith at the parsonage. Further depression and illness at home. Goes to the sea for a month. Refuses to visit London until the book is finished. Sends off completed manuscript. It is favourably received by the publishers. Renewed interest in Taylor. Proposal and rejection of Nicholls. 'Villette' published. Analysis of the book. Final visit to London. She breaks with Harriet Martineau. Another visit to Mrs. Gaskell. Diatribe against Thackeray's lectures. Nicholls leaves Haworth but he and Charlotte correspond. She decides to accept him. Her father won over. They are married. Dismay of her friends. Her own doubts. She finds some happiness. Illness and death.

WITH the death of Anne the record proper of the four Brontës comes to an end. Charlotte had still six years to live. She was to publish two more novels, to meet the famous, to gain an honoured admission to the world she had admired and envied for so long. She was to make new friendships; to receive two more proposals of marriage, and, finally, to be married. Yet it is true to say that with Branwell, Emily, and Anne there died much that was most characteristic, most admirable, and most lovable in their eldest sister. From the time of Emily's terrible death struggle, Charlotte never entirely lost the sense of desolation and futility. Her fame was almost useless, for she had none with whom to share and enjoy it.[1] Between her few friends and herself there was little intimacy and less understanding; to none could she give, for from none did she receive, the love she craved. Her marriage, when it came, came soberly and without illusion.

After Anne's death, Charlotte stayed with Mr. Brontë in the parsonage, now bare in every sense, and there she was to die. Her father could not be left alone: so Charlotte said; but that was not the only reason why she remained at Haworth. The little she saw of the world she had coveted for so long convinced her that she was unfitted to take part in it. This longed-for expansion of her life had come too late. She was thirty-three, over-serious and excessively self-conscious; above all, the tragic history of her family, which she could never forget, gave her a peculiar sense of isolation, and prevented her from mixing freely with other people. She was to have moments of excitement, of hope, even of happiness, but by far the greater part of the few years left to her was one long struggle against despair. For this, she, like all the Brontës, knew only one remedy. After the death of Emily, she set herself to continue the second volume of *Shirley*. She wrote, doggedly, unhappily, whenever occasion offered, during Anne's illness. She took the manuscript to Scarborough, hoping to make use of it if her sister should recover and convalesce there. When that hope failed, she still wrote on, first at Filey, then at the farm at Easton, where she stayed with Ellen at her father's suggestion after Anne's burial at Scarborough.[2]

But the solitary return home could not be put aside for long: 'I got home a little before eight o'clock,' Charlotte told Ellen in the third week of June. 'All was clean and bright waiting for me—Papa and the servants were well—and all received me with an affection which should have consoled. The dogs seemed in strange ecstasy. I am certain they regarded me as the harbinger of others—the dumb creatures thought that, as I was returned, those who had been so long absent were not far behind. I left Papa soon and went into the dining-room. I shut the door. I tried to be glad that I was come home. I have always been glad before—except once—even then I was cheered, but this time joy was not to be the sensation. I felt that the house was all silent—the rooms were all empty. I remembered where the three were laid—in what narrow dark dwellings—never were they to reappear on earth. So the sense of desolation and bitterness took possession of me—the agony that *was to be undergone*—that *was not* to be avoided came on . . . .

The great trial is when evening closes and night approaches. At that hour we used to assemble in the dining-room—we used to talk. Now I sit by myself—necessarily I am silent. I cannot help thinking of their last days—remembering their sufferings, and what they said and did, and how they looked . . . .'[3]

Charlotte again referred to her sisters' dogs when she wrote to Williams soon afterwards: '. . . Emily's large house-dog which lay at the side of her dying-bed, and followed her funeral to the vault, lying in the pew crouched at our feet while the burial service was being read—and Anne's little spaniel. The ecstasy of these poor animals when I came in was something singular. At former returns from brief absence they always welcomed me warmly, but not in that strange, heart-touching way. I am certain they thought that, as I was returned, my sisters were not far behind—but here my sisters will come no more. Keeper may visit Emily's little bedroom as he still does day by day—and Flossy may look wistfully round for Anne—they will never see them again, nor shall I—at least the human part of me. I must not write so sadly—but how can I help thinking and feeling sadly? In the daytime, effort and occupation aid me—but when evening darkens something within my heart revolts against the burden of my solitude, the sense of loss and want grows almost too much for me. I am not good or amiable in such moments, I am rebellious, and it is only the thought of my dear Father in the next room, or of the kind servants in the kitchen, or some caress of the poor dogs which restores me to softer sentiments and more rational views. As to the night, could I do without bed I would never seek it. Waking I think, sleeping I dream of them, and I cannot recall them as they were in health —still they appear to me in sickness and suffering. Still, my nights were worse after the first shock of Branwell's death. They were terrible then—and the impressions experienced on waking were at that time such as we do not put into language. Worse seemed at hand than was yet endured—in truth worse awaited us. All this bitterness must be tasted—perhaps the palate will grow used to the draught in time and find its flavour less acrid. This pain must be undergone. Its poignancy, I trust, will be blunted one day.'[4]

So she tried to set aside desolating loneliness, to fight the memories that rushed into her mind, to forget the silence of the parsonage, the dreariness of the future, to overcome her occasional rebellion against stagnation and obscurity; and a stern concentration on *Shirley* was the instrument she used: 'Labour must be the cure,' she told Williams, 'not sympathy. Labour is the only radical cure for rooted sorrow.'[5] But the cure was not made without pain: 'Sometimes when I wake in the morning and know that solitude, remembrance and longing are to be almost my sole companions all day through, that at night I shall go to bed with them, that they will long keep me sleepless, that next morning I shall wake to them again—I have a heavy heart of it. But crushed I am not—yet: nor robbed of elasticity, nor of hope, nor quite of endeavour. Still I have some strength to fight the battle of life. I am aware and can acknowledge I have many comforts, many mercies—still I can *get on*. But I do hope and pray that never may you or any one I love be placed as I am. To sit in a lonely room—the clock ticking loud through a still house—and to have open before the mind's eye the record of the last year with its shocks, sufferings, losses, is a trial.'[6]

Williams suggested a companion, but Charlotte would have none of it: 'To take a church and stony churchyard for her prospect, the dead silence of a village parsonage—in which the tick of the clock is heard all day long—for her atmosphere, and a grave, silent spinster for her companion? I should not like to see youth thus immured.'[7]

'My work is my best companion,' she again assured both him and herself. 'For society, long seclusion has in a great measure unfitted me. I doubt whether I should enjoy it if I might have it. Sometimes I think I should, and I thirst for it, but at other times I doubt my capability of pleasing or deriving pleasure. The prisoner in solitary confinement—the toad in the block of marble—all in time shape themselves to their lot.'[8]

Her work and her own dour courage carried Charlotte through the first months of loneliness. When, at the end of August, the book was finished at last, she said as much to Williams: 'Whatever now becomes of the work, the occupation of writing it has been a boon to me. It took me out of dark and desolate reality into an unreal but happier region.'[9]

The publishers questioned the wisdom of allowing the first chapter of *Shirley*—the merciless satire on the local curates—to remain unaltered. But Charlotte stood firm. She would not alter what she had written.[10] This bitter opening to the book met with further criticism when *Shirley* was published late in 1849, though on the whole the reception of the book was favourable. It sold well. But there was no tendency among critics or literary circles to make it the sensation that *Jane Eyre* had been.

Reviewers and public alike were right. *Shirley* lacks unity, and betrays the conditions under which so much of it was written. Its two heroines and two heroes confuse the sympathies of the reader, and the narrative flow is fatally interrupted by the introduction, halfway through the book, of Shirley herself. The treatment of the women's emotions is more akin to the conventions laid down by the Victorian novelists, and in that respect the book is inferior to *Jane Eyre*. The men are even less convincing than those in the earlier book. And Shirley—the Emily that might have been—though charming and superficially unconventional, shows obvious signs of Charlotte's valiant but too conscious attempt to do honour to her sister. Charlotte said that Shirley was Emily as she would have been had her life been set in happier circumstances—but this was wishful thinking. Charlotte here, as always, credited Emily with feelings like her own; and so in *Shirley* she draws a girl much like herself emotionally, with some of Emily's more obvious characteristics superimposed. This pathetic effort to immortalize an Emily that never existed was among the last of Charlotte's misreadings of her sister. But these misreadings were inevitable—for Charlotte, feminine to her finger-tips, could never understand Emily's impersonal and unfeminine view of life, and the way she reserved all her deepest feelings for the spiritual and imaginative world.

The first part of *Shirley*, however, contains work almost as good as anything Charlotte was to write. Her treatment of the growth of Caroline's love for Robert Moore is beautifully done. The whole course of the girl's feeling, as well as the character of Caroline, are truly conceived and finely executed. Here Charlotte showed, what was not plain in *Jane Eyre*, her ability to create convincing emotion in an ordinary person, gentle, sweet, and blameless—a romanticized synthesis of Ellen Nussey and Anne. The background is conscientiously sketched in, too much so, and shows the limitation of Charlotte's imagination. She often fails when she attempts to describe something that she has neither seen nor experienced. What she could do when drawing on her actual knowledge of people is shown in her treatment of the Yorke family—in which Mr. Taylor, Mary Taylor, and Martha Taylor are brought to racy, undeniable life.

Earlier in the year Charlotte had acquired another correspondent from Smith Elder—a James Taylor, who, with her permission, had been told of her identity. Taylor had joined with Williams in criticism—without avail—both of the opening chapters of *Shirley* and of the unreality of her heroes. Now, he called at Haworth to collect the manuscript of the final volume.[11] He spent the day at the parsonage and was very much taken with Charlotte, but she was not so certain about him: 'Mr. Taylor—the little man—has again showed his parts; of him I have not yet come to a clear decision; abilities he has, for he rules the firm, he keeps 40 young men under strict control of his iron will. His young superior likes him, which, to speak truth, is more than I do at present; in fact, I suspect he is of the Helstone order of men—rigid, despotic, and self-willed. He tries to be very kind, and even to express sympathy sometimes, but he does not manage it. He has a determined, dreadful nose in the middle of his face, which, when poked into my countenance, cuts into my soul like iron. Still, he is horribly intelligent, quick, searching, sagacious, and with a memory of relentless tenacity. To turn to Williams after him, or to Smith himself, is to turn from granite to easy down or warm fur.'[12]

After his visit to Haworth, Taylor began writing to Charlotte. She replied; but the correspondence which followed was, on Charlotte's part, one of cautious dignity.

In November she paid a visit to London—urged by her publishers and by her own restlessness. There was some talk of the Wheelwrights—her Brussels acquaintances—putting her up in their London house; but George Smith protested so strongly in favour of his right to the honour that Charlotte finally spent most of her time as his mother's guest.[13]

In this house occurred the most momentous event of her visit—the first meeting with Thackeray.[14] But neither this nor her further meeting with him a few days later afforded Charlotte much satisfaction. She found herself tongue-tied before her 'Titan',[15] and she by no means appreciated Thackeray's sense of humour.[16]

Before introducing the two authors, Smith had impressed upon Thackeray Charlotte's earnest desire to preserve her incognita. But Thackeray could not resist the opportunity, when smoking his after-dinner cigar, to make a pointed allusion to the scent of Rochester's cigar—quoting a well known and much criticized passage from *Jane Eyre*. When Charlotte saw, by the smiles of other guests, that the allusion was understood, she was furious, and she showed it.[17] Thackeray, however, remained unperturbed and impenitent. A few days later, entertaining Charlotte at his own house, he repeated his offence. On the way down to dinner he addressed her as Currer Bell. She tossed her head and said 'she believed there were books being published by a person named Currer Bell . . . but the person he was talking to was Miss Brontë—and she saw no connection between the two.'[18]

Charlotte was, in fact, as incapable of entering into the spirit of such a joke as she was of passing off an allusion with tact; but Thackeray was unimaginative not to see that her life had been too serious, repressed, and circumscribed (and recently, much too sad) to permit her to dabble in pleasantries. She had no help from him, nor, it seems, from many of the other celebrities she met; and in consequence, she made heavy weather of the conversation that floated back and forth in the Smith and Thackeray drawing-rooms. Her directness was a disadvantage in such company; and even her careful eloquence of letter and novel forsook her in an atmosphere where the brilliant saying counted so much more than the thing said. She despised the literary chit-chat, and usually felt as out of place as she looked. And the nervous excitement caused by this unaccustomed whirl of events made her still less able to deal with the social round; in addition to her usual indigestion, she suffered from sickness and violent headaches.

'I can still see the scene quite plainly,' wrote Thackeray's daughter, 'the hot summer evening, the open windows, the carriage driving to the door as we all sat silent and expectant; my father, who rarely waited, waiting with us; our governess and my sister and I all in a row, and prepared for the great event. We saw the carriage stop, and out of it sprang the active, well-knit figure of Mr. George Smith, who was bringing Miss Brontë to see our father. My father, who had been walking up and down the room, goes out into the hall to meet his guests, and then, after a moment's delay, the door opens wide, and the two gentlemen come in, leading a tiny, delicate, serious, little lady, pale, with fair straight hair, and steady eyes. She may be a little over thirty; she is dressed in a little *bargee* dress, with a pattern of faint green moss. She enters in mittens, in silence, in seriousness; our hearts are beating with wild excitement. This, then, is the authoress, the unknown power whose books have set all London talking, reading, speculating; some people even say our father wrote the books—the wonderful books. To say that we little girls had been given *Jane Eyre* to read scarcely represents the facts of the case; to say that we had taken it without leave, read bits here and read bits there, been carried away by an undreamed-of and hitherto unimagined whirlwind into things, times, places, all utterly absorbing, and at the same time absolutely unintelligible to us, would more accurately describe our state of mind on that summer's evening as we looked at Jane Eyre—the great Jane Eyre—the tiny little lady. The moment is so breathless that dinner comes as a relief to the solemnity of the occasion, and we all smile as my father stoops to offer his arm; for, though genius she may be, Miss Brontë can barely reach his elbow. My own personal impressions are that she is somewhat grave and stern, especially to forward little girls who wish to chatter. Mr. George Smith has since told me how she afterwards remarked upon my father's wonderful forbearance and gentleness with our uncalled-for incursions into the conversation. She sat gazing at him with kindling eyes of interest, lighting up with a sort of illumination every now and then as she answered him. I can see her bending forward over the table, not eating, but listening to what he said as he carved the dish before him. I think it must have been on this very occasion that my father invited some of his friends in the evening to meet Miss Brontë—for everybody was interested and anxious to see her. Mrs. Brookfield, Mrs. Carlyle, Mr. Carlyle himself was present, so I am told, railing at the appearance of cockneys upon Scotch mountain sides; there were also too many Americans for his taste, "but the Americans were as gods compared to the cockneys," says the philosopher. Besides the Carlyles there were Mrs. Elliott and Miss Perry, Mrs. Proctor and her daughter, most of my father's habitual friends and companions . . . . It was a gloomy and a silent evening. Every one waited for the brilliant conversation which never began at all. Miss Brontë retired to the sofa in the study and murmured a low word now and then to our kind governess, Miss Truelock. The room looked very dark, the lamp began to smoke a little, the conversation grew dimmer and more dim, the ladies sat around still expectant, my father was too much perturbed by the gloom and the silence to be able to cope with it at all. Mrs. Brookfield, who was in the doorway by the study, near the corner in which Miss Brontë was sitting, leant forward with a little common-place, since brilliance was not to be the order of the evening. "Do you like London, Miss Brontë?" she said; another silence, a pause, then Miss Brontë answers, "Yes and No", very gravely.'[19]

Another visit paid by Charlotte at this time passed off more successfully. A month earlier she had sent a copy of *Shirley* to Harriet Martineau: 'For her character—as revealed in her works —I have a lively admiration—a deep esteem,' she told Williams. Now, hearing that Harriet Martineau was in London, Charlotte asked if she might call.[20]

'I thought her the smallest creature I had ever seen (except at a fair),' wrote Harriet Martineau, 'and her eyes blazed, as it seemed to me. She glanced quickly round; and my trumpet pointing me out, she held out her hand frankly and pleasantly. I introduced her, of course, to the family; and then came a moment which I had not anticipated. When she was seated by me upon the sofa, she cast up at me such a look—so loving, so appealing—that, in connection with her deep mourning dress, and the knowledge that she was the sole survivor of her family, I could with the utmost difficulty return her smile, or keep my composure. I should have been heartily glad to cry. We soon got on very well; and she appeared more at her ease that evening than I ever saw her afterwards, except when we were alone . . . . She was glad of the opportunity to consult me about certain strictures of the reviewers which she did not understand, and had every desire to profit by. I did not approve the spirit of these strictures, but I thought them not entirely groundless. She besought me then, and repeatedly afterwards, to tell her, at whatever cost of pain to herself, if I saw her afford any justification of them.'[21]

Mrs. Gaskell, who had written a complimentary note to

Charlotte after reading *Shirley*, but who had not met her, also recorded what she had heard of this meeting: '. . . as the clock struck, in walked a very little, bright-haired sprite, looking not above 15, very unsophisticated, neat and tidy; she sat down and had tea with them, her name being still unknown; she said to H.M. "What did you really think of *Jane Eyre*?" H.M. "I thought it a first-rate book," whereupon the little sprite went red all over with pleasure. After tea, . . . withdrew and left Sprite to a 2 hours tête-a-tête with H.M. to whom she revealed her name and the history of her life . . . particulars which H.M. is not at liberty to divulge any more than her name, which she keeps a profound secret; but Thackeray does *not*.'²²

Charlotte's connexion with Currer Bell was now to become an open secret, however. In London, Thackeray spread the news. In Yorkshire, the people and places of *Shirley*—so much more obviously the product of a local author than *Jane Eyre*—directed the attention of the curious to the mysterious and bulky correspondence exchanged between London and the parsonage.²³ So that when Ellen, now in the secret, came to spend the Christmas of 1849 with her friend at Haworth, she told her that many people were asking about the book and its author, and some were angry at Charlotte's unsparing use of them as characters. Charlotte was not disturbed: 'All you tell me about the notoriety of *Shirley* in Dewsbury &c. is almost as good as an emetic to me—I should really "go off at side" if I thought too much about it.'²⁴

Indeed, Charlotte felt positively disappointed at the mild reception given to the book by the curates. Nicholls, who played a minor part in *Shirley*, gave the author a foretaste of the hollow victory to come: 'Mr. Nicholls, having finished *Jane Eyre*, is now crying out for the "other book"—he is to have it next week—much good may it do him.'²⁵ Eight days later, Charlotte was reporting in some perplexity: 'Mr. Nicholls has finished reading *Shirley*, he is delighted with it. John Brown's wife seriously thought he had gone wrong in the head as she heard him giving vent to roars of laughter as he sat alone, clapping his hands and stamping on the floor. He would read all the scenes about the curates aloud to papa, he triumphed in his own character.'²⁶ This was surprising enough, but the true victims remained: 'Some of the clergy will not like *Shirley*: I confess the work has one prevailing fault—that of too tenderly and partially veiling the errors of "the Curates". Had Currer Bell written all he has seen and knows concerning these worthies, a singular work would have been the result.'[27] And again: 'What Mr. Grant will say is another thing.'[28]

But, alas, Mr. Grant showed a good humour that proved most disconcerting: 'I quite expected to have had one good scene at least with him,' said Charlotte, 'but as yet nothing of the sort has occurred.'[29] So she was obliged to content herself with a more general statement. 'Certain of the Clergy have thought proper to be bitter against the work—some of them good men in their way—but men in whom the animal obviously predominates over the intellectual—I smile inwardly when I hear of their disapprobation.'[30]

But this was a rare excitement in a painfully unvaried existence. Her yearly journey to London, an occasional exchange of visits with Ellen, the growing friendship with Mrs. Gaskell and Harriet Martineau—these were the high-lights of the years to come.

At present, her chief interest, apart from the books still sent to her by Smith and Williams, was long-drawn-out discussions of the matrimonial chances, fortunes, and misfortunes of Ellen's friends. For the rest, there was day after dull day of loneliness, grief, and ill-health.[31] It is pathetic to see how Charlotte reproaches herself for coming to depend more and more on the letters from her publishers. She despised herself for this weakness, but it persisted; this one link with the world of culture and fame had made itself a necessity.[32] For although she could write letters, she could make no headway with another book, despite constant encouragement from London—the words, the thoughts would not come.

.   .   .   .   .   .

One of Charlotte's most pleasant friendships of these years was with Mrs. Gaskell, whom she met through a fellow York-shireman. This man—Sir James Kay-Shuttleworth—considered it his duty to foster local genius. His attempts to lionize Charlotte were unwelcome; and if Mr. Brontë had not displayed a childish eagerness for his daughter to be made much of by the titled and the famous, Shuttleworth would probably have been

given short shrift. As it was, Charlotte submitted to his patronage with an ill grace. But Shuttleworth was a persistent man; he
and his wife invaded the parsonage early in 1850, and would not
leave until Charlotte had said when she would return the visit.[33]

Her visit to Gawthorpe Hall passed off somewhat better than
she had feared.[34] But Shuttleworth, it appeared, was saving
his protégée for London. He begged Charlotte not to allow
anyone else to introduce her into the 'Oceanic life' of the
capital.[35] Charlotte was dismayed. Although she looked forward
eagerly to her yearly London visit—the most she would permit
herself—she detested the late nights, the parties, the dinners, the
host of new faces, the constant threat of being lionized. The
very thought of this upset her even before she set foot in the
London train. Yet this was precisely what Shuttleworth as
host seemed anxious to loose on her.[36]

At the last moment, illness—for a wonder, not hers—forced
Charlotte to postpone her departure until the Shuttleworths had
left town.[37] Then, at the end of May, she arrived at the Smith
house once more for what was to be her most pleasant visit.
The fortnight she had allowed herself slipped quickly into a stay
of twice that time. She sat to Richmond for a portrait in
crayons. Thackeray called on her; and she, by that time more
used to London life, and so more herself, felt 'moved to speak
of his shortcomings'—an interview that Smith, the only other
person present, described inadequately as 'a queer scene'.[38]

Charlotte now met G. H. Lewes for the first time.[39] There had
been a painful break in their correspondence. Lewes's review of
Shirley, in which he emphasized the sex of the author as part
explanation of the failings of the book,[40] hit Charlotte in her
tenderest spot. 'I can be on my guard against my enemies, but
God deliver me from my friends!' she exclaimed with Angrian
hauteur the moment she had read the review.[41] There had been
explanations[42] and a reconciliation of sorts,[43] but the friendship,
such as it was, could not be revived—Charlotte found it hard at
any time to forgive criticism, even when she sought it.[44] Yet
when she met Lewes, she could not dislike him: 'I could not feel
otherwise to him than half sadly, half tenderly —a queer word
the last—but I use it because the aspect of Lewes's face almost
moves me to tears, it is so wonderfully like Emily- her eyes, her
features, the very nose, the somewhat prominent mouth, the

forehead, even at moments, the expression.'[45] Lewes, a poor judge of character, was unable to get the measure of his small, unimpressive visitor: 'A little, plain, provincial, sickly-looking old maid,' was his view of her.[46]

At the Smiths' home Charlotte was happier than she had been since the death of her sisters. She was treated kindly and without fuss, like a member of the family, and this made her more natural—so much so that George Smith had to revise his first opinion of her. After his first meeting with Charlotte he had written: 'She was very small, and had a quaint old-fashioned look. Her face seemed too large for her body. She had fine eyes, but her face was marred by the shape of the mouth and by the complexion. There was but little feminine charm about her; and of this fact she herself was uneasily and perpetually conscious. It may seem strange that the possession of genius did not lift her above the weakness of an excessive anxiety about her personal appearance. But I believe that she would have given all her genius and her fame to have been beautiful. Perhaps few women ever existed more anxious to be pretty than she, or more angrily conscious of the circumstance that she was *not* pretty.'[47] This was true enough as far as it went; Charlotte desired beauty and charm, at times with intense longing; but she would not have given up one iota of her moral and emotional integrity in exchange for good looks—especially when she saw them, as so often, linked with stupidity, vanity and self-indulgence. But whatever Smith thought of Charlotte when they first met, he began, during the present London visit, to see a great deal more in her; even her 'little feminine charm' and the difference in their ages (she was a good half-dozen years older) did not prevent his increasing interest. And although his mother was not altogether pleased with the way things were going, the 'sensible' Charlotte began to show signs of having her head slightly turned.[48]

A visit to Ellen, paid immediately after Charlotte left London towards the end of June, was broken for a brief stay in Edinburgh at the invitation of Smith, who had gone there to fetch home his young brother.[49] This excursion was to have been extended to a short tour of the Highlands, but Charlotte could not finally make the journey. They were both greatly disappointed, but the two days in Edinburgh and the visit to Abbotsford and Melrose gave Charlotte some of her most pleasant memories.[50] She often spoke of this Scottish visit,[51] and from that time her letters to Smith became not only more frequent but occasionally positively playful. Struggling against faint thoughts of how this agreeable comradeship might develop, Charlotte tried hard to think of her publisher as a younger brother.

In addition to the parcels of books sent by Smith Elder, Charlotte now received from Smith a portrait of Wellington, still her hero. To Mr. Brontë, Smith sent at the same time Richmond's completed portrait of Charlotte, giving great pleasure. Both portraits were hung up 'in the best light and most favourable position'.[52]

Meanwhile, Charlotte's most serious suitor, Taylor, was keeping his cause in mind by regular dispatch of the *Athenaeum* to Haworth.[53] But Charlotte, aware of his intentions, was cautious: 'I cannot consider myself placed under any personal obligation by accepting this newspaper,' she informs the highly interested Ellen, 'for it belongs to the establishment of Smith & Elder.'[54] Taylor, however, did himself no harm by the thought, if he did himself little good; for Charlotte continued: 'This little Taylor is deficient neither in spirit nor sense.'[55]

This year, 1850, was particularly eventful for Charlotte. The persevering Shuttleworth had still to be satisfied; fully recovered from his illness, he now clamoured for Charlotte's company at a house he had taken at Windermere, and with much reluctance she went to the Lakes in August for a week.[56] A great many of her gloomy forebodings were to be realized during the week —'He [Shuttleworth] very kindly showed me the scenery—*as it can be seen from a carriage*—and I discerned that the "Lake Country" is a glorious region—but I only half enjoyed it—because I was only half at my ease,' she told Miss Wooler later.[57] 'Decidedly, I find it does not agree with me to prosecute the search of the picturesque in a carriage.'[58] And her final judgement of her host was: 'I scarcely desire a continuation of the interest he professes in me—were he to forget me, I could not feel regret.'[59]

For one meeting at Windermere, however, Charlotte had cause for gratitude. The day after she arrived, Mrs. Gaskell came to stay: and the correspondence that began between them from this time strengthened into a friendship which, whatever its limitations, provided Charlotte with much needed kindness, and future generations with a popular biography. Mrs. Gaskell told a friend about Charlotte as she first saw her: 'She is (as she calls herself) *undeveloped*, thin and more than half a head shorter than I, soft brown hair, not so dark as mine; eyes (very good and expressive, looking straight and open at you) of the same colour, a reddish face; large mouth and many teeth gone; altogether plain, the forehead square, broad and *rather* overhanging. She has a very sweet voice, rather hesitates in choosing her expressions, but when chosen they seem without an effort, *admirable* and *just*, befitting the occasion. There is nothing overstrained but perfectly simple.'[60] This, with Smith's description, comes a great deal nearer the truth about Charlotte's appearance than the other London versions and Richmond's flattering portrait; and, considered together with the later photographs of Mr. Brontë, and with Charlotte's remarks on the similarity of the features of Emily and Lewes, there seems little doubt that Branwell, whatever his technical shortcomings as a portrait painter, had one essential virtue—he could catch a likeness.

The two women spent the greater part of their time at Windermere together; and Mrs. Gaskell heard much of the history of Charlotte and her family.[61] She became interested in the story, and in the one who told it; she felt both pity and respect for Charlotte—feelings which grew as she saw more of her. Together they visited Fox How, where Matthew Arnold, then young, lived with his widowed mother: 'She suffered the whole day from an acute headache brought on by apprehension of the evening,' Mrs. Gaskell reported of Charlotte.[62] As for Charlotte, she, too, wrote favourably of her new friend; but, doubtful of her powers of arousing affection, she remained guarded. This kind but slightly gushing woman both attracted and repelled her. 'I was truly glad of her companionship. She is a woman of the most genuine talent—of cheerful, pleasing and cordial manners and—I believe—of a kind and good heart.'[63]

.   .   .   .   .   .

Jane Eyre continued to sell well. A cheaper, one-volume edition—the fifth—had been put out earlier in the year.[64] In the September *Palladium* appeared an article by Sydney Dobell on the works of the Bells. It was in the main highly appreciative, particularly of *Wuthering Heights*.[65] But Dobell maintained the view—still widely held even then—that the works had been written by one person. The unwelcome suggestion that, on the strength of the popularity of *Jane Eyre*, the author had published earlier and inferior works, had more than once infuriated Charlotte—not least because of the implication that her sisters' novels would not have been accepted on their own merits.

Dobell, indeed, made no such suggestion—his enthusiasm for *Wuthering Heights* placed the book in many respects above *Jane Eyre*—and Charlotte was intensely grateful for this late and solitary tribute to Emily's book. But she was troubled once more by the general injustice to the memory of her sisters. When, after negotiation with the elusive Newby, Williams suggested that Charlotte might like to edit a new edition of her sisters' novels, to be published by Smith Elder, she seized the opportunity to make clear once for all, the separate identities of Currer, Ellis, and Acton Bell.[66] All that autumn she laboured at the texts of *Agnes Grey* and *Wuthering Heights*—at her wish *The Tenant of Wildfell Hall* was not to be reprinted.[67]

Charlotte also went once more through her sisters' papers to try to find more verses worthy, in her view, of inclusion in the volume. As she turned over the written sheets in the two small desks that would never again be used by their owners, she suffered a repetition of her mental agony when she returned alone from Scarborough to the parsonage more than a year before.[68] But she struggled through the days and weeks and months, fortified by the desire that was now little less than a passion, to set up a printed monument worthy of her dead sisters.

The eventual form of this monument was not exactly what they—or at least, Emily—would have desired. Anne's work was not interfered with—if the suppression of *Wildfell Hall* is left out of consideration—but Charlotte laid a heavy hand on Emily's novel and poems. Once before—when the sisters' poems were first published—Charlotte had apparently 'improved' Emily's contributions when the proofs were corrected. An element of doubt exists in this instance, however. But now there was no doubt at all who was making corrections. Charlotte altered *Wuthering Heights*, modifying the dialect[69] and softening the forthrightness of many passionate scenes; and, worse still, she altered the poems with an astonishing lack of sensibility, making them at times almost a mockery of Emily's intentions. Charlotte added a Preface which was in effect an apology for *Wuthering Heights*—or for those parts of it which had met with the fiercest criticism. She also wrote a Biographical Notice of Ellis and Acton Bell—a beautiful and moving piece of prose—in which she made clear how the novels had come to be written, and described her sisters as they appeared to her.[70] In this Notice, Charlotte referred to Dobell's review and to his belief, despite her denials, that the three Bells were one person. When the book appeared in December, she had a copy sent to Dobell with a complimentary note.[71]

Dobell, young, enthusiastic, and, where he admired, given to extravagance, sought Charlotte's acquaintance with no uncertain fervour: 'Surely we are marked out for friendship?' he exclaimed. 'Entering so nearly at once the adjoining provinces of literature, both young, both unknown, both (and both in a first work) singularly fortunate . . . are there not sufficient resemblances in the general features of our affairs to believe it probable that the affinity is deeper?'[72] He asked Charlotte to visit him at his Cheltenham home, describing its soft beauty. He ended with an apology: 'If I have already spoken to you too freely of other things, my dear Miss Brontë—if what I have written seems hardly in keeping with a first letter—recollect that I have long been a brother to you in my thoughts. . . .'[73]

With her usual frankness, though showing some signs of accommodating herself to Dobell's style, Charlotte told this enthusiast the true position of affairs: 'Your letter is very kind —your offered friendship is very welcome; but first—you must understand me. You say, I am young. No. I daresay people still call me "young" by courtesy, but really young I am not, and young I no longer consider myself. . . . I am a journeyer at noontide, desirous of some rest already, and with the dim still time of afternoon in prospect. You think chiefly what is to be done and won in life; I—what is to be suffered. . . .'[74]

Charlotte, who was not quite thirty-five years of age at this time, concluded: 'If ever we meet, you must regard me as a grave sort of elder sister.'[75]

Dobell was not disconcerted: 'That you are not "young" I cannot believe,' he replied, 'even on your own testimony. The heart of Jane Eyre will never grow old.'[76] He admitted his own lack of years: 'You are right in thinking that my "havings in years" are but small (I claim but twenty-seven)' he wrote. But for all that: 'I have little faith in arithmetic . . . . Try me by my own standard, and, some day or other, I will make you look up to me as a very grey old man; showing you how very often I have been by my grave; aye, have felt myself lowered into its shadow.'[77] He sent her some melancholy verses: '. . . for present proof that I am not altogether ignorant of sorrow.'[78] Following Charlotte's acknowledgement and appreciation of the verses came fresh invitations—to Cheltenham and to Switzerland.[79] Charlotte refused the invitations,[80] but the correspondence continued—and so did the mutual regard for each other's work.

The refreshing, if somewhat flowery, flattery of the Dobell letters was welcomed by Charlotte, even when she pooh-poohed them, as a change from her austere existence. But they also had a less pleasant effect, for they emphasized the almost intolerable monotony of life at the parsonage. Mr. Brontë had never been a companion to his children; now, the selfishness of the aging hypochondriac made him an almost complete recluse. Tabby was old, and called for comfort and attention rather than giving it. The few people who made their way to the lonely house were either curious sightseers who had heard of the parson's novelist daughter; dull, facetious or flirtatious curates; or toadying relatives. Only the silent, admiring Nicholls offered any prospect of relief; and he was not only painfully shy, so that he had great difficulty in addressing a coherent remark to Charlotte, but was of the despised tribe of curates.[81] For the rest, there were persistent headaches and indigestion, silence, loneliness; a never satisfied longing for intellectual companionship; dreams, growing steadily more improbable, of love given and returned; and, worst of all, memories of Emily and Anne and Branwell insistently filling her mind. Wherever she looked, wherever she walked, Charlotte saw something to remind her of them—the sofa on which Emily died, the stone stairs up which she had laboured, refusing help, the kitchen fire round which all had sat merrily years before, the little desks of

Anne and Emily, the dining-room table on which she and
Branwell, happy and industrious children, wrote their Angrian
stories—the list had no end.[82]

Now, having forced herself to read through her sisters' papers
once again, Charlotte felt lonelier than ever. The moors—
that one bleak link with health and normality—were worse than
useless.[83] Emily and Anne haunted them, and she came to shrink
so much from the pang of recollection at every familiar spot that,
eventually, she could not bring herself to go outside the house.[84]
Her health grew worse, and her misery greater. Anyone would
have found such a life almost intolerable, but she continued to
reproach herself again and again for finding it so: 'I feel to my
deep sorrow—to my humiliation—that it is not in my power
to bear the canker of constant solitude. I had calculated that
when shut out from every enjoyment, from every stimulus
but what could be derived from intellectual exertion, my mind
would rouse itself perforce. It is not so; even intellect, even
imagination, will not dispense with the ray of domestic cheerfulness, with the gentle spur of family discussion. Late in the
evening and all through the night I fall into a condition of
mind which turns entirely to the Past, to memory, and memory
is both sad and relentless.'[85]

'I am both angry and surprised', she told Ellen, 'for not growing accustomed or at least resigned to the solitude and isolation
of my lot. But my late occupation left a result for some days and,
indeed, is still very painful. The reading over of papers, the re-
newal of remembrances brought back the pang of bereavement
and occasioned a depression of spirits well nigh intolerable. For
one or two nights I scarcely knew how to get on till morning,
and when morning came I was still haunted with a sense of
sickening distress . . . . I thought to find occupation and interest
in writing when alone at home, but hitherto my efforts have
been very vain, the deficiency of every stimulus is so complete.'

Charlotte even dreaded—while she desired—the occasional
visit to London; the aftermath proved too bitter: 'You will
recommend me, I daresay, to go from home, but that does no
good, even could I again leave Papa with an easy mind. I cannot
describe what a time I had of it after my return from London,
Scotland etc., there was a reaction that sunk me to the earth—
the deadly silence, solitude, desolation were awful, the craving

for companionship, the hopelessness of relief, were what I should dread to feel again.'[86]

In fact, her life in the parsonage did eventually become too much for her. But for the time her loneliness and wretchedness made her so morbid that she lost all sense of proportion, and began to blame herself for enjoying even the few pleasures she had—such as the letters and books her publishers sent her—few and harmless enough in all conscience. She persisted in regarding her enjoyment as undeserved, and felt that she must make her own pleasure, if she were to have it at all.[87]

The books contained in themselves an additional source of reproach. As she read, Charlotte compared the author's ease of style and large output with her own difficulty in writing. She had revised her first novel, *The Professor*, but to no purpose, for it had been again rejected—for the seventh time.[88] She had now begun to write her fourth novel, *Villette*, but it dragged woefully. For days on end she could not write a line that satisfied her. She refused a suggestion from Smith Elder that she should take advantage of the popular serial form of publication. She could not write to order, she said.[89] But the suggestion disturbed her; for while she preserved her integrity by refusing, she blamed herself for not writing more quickly.

Just before Christmas, Charlotte escaped from her home for a few days. Harriet Martineau had asked her to stay at her house at Ambleside; and there, overlooking the wintry beauty of Windermere, and cared for by her rough but hearty hostess, Charlotte surrendered to the spell of that masterful woman, watching with amazement and envy her early morning activity; enjoying, even when she could not agree with, the masculine forcefulness and clarity of the Martineau conversation every evening; admiring the planned day, carried out with military precision; and even allowing herself, without protest, to listen —in a state, surely, of partial mesmerism—to expositions of decidedly unorthodox religious beliefs.[90]

Such a visit as this, however, was an event almost without parallel in Charlotte's life. Her greatest consolation and source of pleasure was still the correspondence with George Smith. She wrote to this youthful head of her publishers in a manner much unlike her usual rather heavy-handed style. Sometimes the affectionate frankness of an elder sister was the dominating note of her letters; sometimes a humorous tenderness crept in; and even, what reads suspiciously like coyness. Like Dobell, Smith proposed a visit to the Continent during the coming summer; he wished Charlotte to join him in a trip up the Rhine. This, too, Charlotte declined, but in words that, for her, were positively honeyed.[91] But Smith was eligible where Dobell was not. Smith was a man to Charlotte; Dobell no more than a complimentary letter-writer.

Whether Charlotte took seriously these attentions—which could have been mainly a matter of good business—one cannot feel sure. She kept her own counsel. But she did make one comment to Ellen: 'That hint about the Rhine disturbs me; I am not made of stone, and what is mere excitement to him is fever to me. However, it is a matter for the future, and long to look forward to. As I see it now, the journey is out of the question, for many reasons. I rather wonder he should think of it—I cannot conceive either his mother or his sisters relishing it, and all London would gabble like a countless host of geese.'[92]

Ellen, of course, scented marriage in the air; and a number of charges and denials passed between Brookroyd and Haworth.[93] If such an idea ever entered Smith's head, he soon thought better of it; and Charlotte, though certainly flattered by his attentions, and woman enough to linger over what might have been, was too sensible not to see clearly what their relationship must be: 'I think those "fixed intentions" you fancy are imaginary,' she told Ellen. 'I think the "undercurrent" amounts simply to this—a kind of natural liking and sense of something congenial. Were there no vast barrier of age, fortune, etc., there is perhaps enough personal regard to make things possible which are now impossible. If men and women married because they like each other's temper, look, conversation, nature and so on—and if besides, years were more nearly equal, the chance you allude to might be admitted as a chance. But other reasons regulate matrimony—reasons of convenience, of connection, of money. Meanwhile, I am content to have him as a friend—and pray God to continue to me the commonsense to look on one so young, so rising and so hopeful in no other light.'[94]

This letter is a good example of how Charlotte used Ellen to check her own optimism, much as Jane Eyre used her self-portrait. But Smith's attentions remained a great pleasure to one so cut off from the general run of men. They kept down much of the interest that Dobell's letters might otherwise have created in Charlotte, and they all but settled the fate of the persevering Taylor. Charlotte, indeed, writing again to Ellen, was sensible enough to see that Taylor would make a more suitable husband. 'You are to say no more about "Jupiter" and "Venus",' she commanded; 'what do you mean by such heathen trash? The fact is, no fallacy can be wilder, and I won't have it hinted at even in jest, because my commonsense laughs it to scorn. The idea of the "little man" shocks me less—it would be a more likely match, if "matches" were at all in question, which *they are not*. He still sends me his little newspaper—and the other day there came a letter of a bulk, volume, pith, judgment and knowledge, worthy to have been the product of a giant. You may laugh as much and as wickedly as you please, but the fact is there is a quiet constancy about this, my diminutive and red-haired friend, which adds a foot to his stature, turns his sandy locks dark, and altogether dignifies him a good deal in my estimation. However, I am not bothered by much vehement ardour—there is the nicest distance and respect preserved now, which makes matters very comfortable.'[95]

Yet, appreciate Taylor as she might at a distance and on reflection, Charlotte could not overcome a certain physical revulsion in his presence. Thus when he, a little later, called at the parsonage on his way back from Scotland, told her that he was soon going to India, and, it seems, asked her to marry him, Charlotte gave him no encouragement.

'The resemblance to Branwell struck me forcibly,' she reported, 'it is marked. He is not ugly, but very peculiar; the lines in his face show an inflexibility, and I must add, a hardness of character which do not attract. As he stood near me, as he looked at me in his keen way, it was all I could do to stand my ground tranquilly and steadily, and not to recoil as before.'[96] So the two parted, never to meet again; Taylor, wanting to marry Charlotte; she, curiously drawn towards him in his absence, but unable to consider marriage without a shudder when she was face to face with him.[97]

·   ·   ·   ·   ·   ·

At the end of May 1851 Charlotte spent a month in London.

She stayed again with the Smiths,[98] but this time she adventured, for her, far afield. She breakfasted with Rogers, the Poet Laureate. She heard Thackeray lecture, before his fashionable audience, on the English Humorists.[99] She went to the theatre and watched, with fascinated horror, the famous French tragédienne Rachel in *Camille* and *Les Horaces*—an experience she was later to recreate with great power, in *Villette*.[100] She heard the famous preachers of the day, D'Aubigny, Melvill, and Maurice.[101] She made short work of a confirmation service held by Cardinal Wiseman—'impiously theatrical'. She visited several times, once at least accompanied by a distinguished scientist, the Great Exhibition, then all the rage.[102] Altogether, she had little time to herself. She was undoubtedly gratified by the attention she received as a famous author—she would have been more than human if she had not been. She was stimulated, too, by the people she met and by what she saw and heard—Thackeray's lecturing and Rachel's acting were unforgettable—yet she was unable to find happiness or even peace of mind. The London life distracted her, certainly; but it also wore her out, so unaccustomed was she to excitement of any kind. So it was with relief that she left for Manchester in June, to pay her first visit to Mrs. Gaskell.[103] She enjoyed the comparative quiet of Mrs. Gaskell's home, although even here her dislike of meeting strangers, and her frozen behaviour when she did, put a great strain on herself and her friends.

Home again, Charlotte resumed her cheerless existence. Mr. Nicholls left for his holiday in Ireland, 'inviting himself on the eve thereof to come and take a farewell cup of tea; good, mild, uncontentious.'[104] Mr. Brontë, Martha, Tabby, in turn fell ill. Autumn browned the purple hills in a night. Storms of rain beat upon the house, and the equinoctial gales blew about it. No one called, and Charlotte began to fall back into melancholia as winter drew on. Tormenting images returned. She slept badly.[105] But she struggled on: 'It is useless to tell you how I live—I endure life—but whether I enjoy it or not is another question. However, I get on. The weather, I think, has not been good lately, or else the beneficial effects of change of air and scene are evaporating. In spite of regular exercise the old headaches and wakeful nights are coming upon me again, but I *do* get on . . . .'[106]

It is easy to read the despair behind the conventional phraseology: 'Some painful mental worry I have gone through this autumn, but there is no use dwelling on all that . . . life is a struggle.'[107] So Charlotte dismissed the horror—for it was becoming no less—of the Haworth winters. But it was one thing to tell Ellen what must be done, and quite another thing to do it.

Yet she refused all invitations. Ellen, Harriet Martineau, Mrs. Gaskell, Mrs. Forster—they all pressed her to visit them, but all were refused.[108] The constant sickness at Haworth—the old people needed nursing from week to week—accounted partly for these refusals, but was not the main reason. Later, when the household had returned to normal, Charlotte still held out: 'Sometimes the strain falls on the mental, sometimes on the physical part of me; I am ill with neuralgic headache, or I am ground to the dust with deep dejection of spirits.'[109] But she continued: 'As to running away from home every time I have a battle of this sort to fight, it would not do: besides, the "weird" would follow. As to shaking it off, that cannot be.'[110] One can only wonder at Charlotte's determination to stand alone, and at her victory in the extraordinary contest—one small, lonely, bereaved woman against ill health, isolation, haunting thoughts, piercing memories, bad dreams. Miserable at home, she could find no peace away from it. If she accepted these invitations, she would despise herself afterwards, and she knew by experience that time away from home only unfitted her still more for the struggle. 'It may be a dreary thought . . . but I must absolutely get accustomed to a life of solitude; there is no other plan.'[111]

Charlotte had long since set aside the winter for work. During the long, dark evenings she planned to write without interruption. She struggled to do so, oppressed by a growing sense of guilt at her failure to finish *Villette*. Her attitude towards Smith Elder far transcended an author's natural loyalty to his publisher even in those days of personal transactions. Her entertainment by the Smiths; her friendly and, at times, absorbingly interesting correspondence with Smith and Williams; their boxes of books sent regularly to Haworth for her pleasure; the admiration of Taylor and the attentions of Smith: all had contributed to magnify Charlotte's original gratitude for Smith

Elder's kindly reception of *The Professor* after its rough handling elsewhere, and for their subsequent acceptance of *Jane Eyre*— a gratitude which the furore of that book and the success of *Shirley* had done nothing to diminish. She remained far more concerned that her publishers should not suffer loss through her than that she herself should profit. She had felt anxious for Smith Elder, not only when her novels first appeared, but when each succeeding edition was mooted, in case the publishers should lose money. Now she felt that to enjoy friendship with them and to produce no new novel in return was unfair, and even unfriendly. She did not wait for reproaches that *Villette* was not finished, she blamed herself bitterly, and in so doing the relentless woman added yet another load to her sick conscience, and made the writing of her novel even more difficult. For she would not allow her slow progress to force her into hackwork. She was determined that this book, like its predecessors, should be as good as she could make it. She wrote only when moved to write; and having written, and felt that it was good, she could not be persuaded to alter a word.[112] 'If my health is spared', she told George Smith, 'I shall get on with it as fast as is consistent with its being done, if not well, yet as well as I can do it, *not one whit faster*. When the mood leaves me (it has left me now, without even leaving as much as a word of a message when it will return) I put by the MS and wait till it comes back again; and God knows I sometimes have to wait long—*very* long it seems to me.'[113]

Unlike Harriet Martineau, who 'knows nothing about my Quakerlike waiting on the spirit; that is not her plan nor her nature,'[114] Charlotte believed that 'one should only write out of the fulness of one's heart spontaneously'. And this she literally did.[115]

.   .   .   .   .   .

The comparison came about at this time because Harriet Martineau had asked Charlotte to forward to Smith Elder a novel she wished to publish anonymously. Charlotte agreed and the novel, *Oliver Weld*, was eventually sent to Smith.[116]

By November, Charlotte had at last settled down to her writing. She refused a visit to London for this reason. She also made clear to Smith Elder that *Villette* was not to be published before the following autumn even if ready earlier. She was determined to allow precedence to Thackeray's *Esmond* which Smith Elder were to publish—and which they had sent to her in manuscript—and to the Martineau book.[117] Her consideration for this last proved unnecessary. The novel was finally rejected by Smith on the ground that its treatment of religion might offend a large public. This refusal caused some embarrassment to Charlotte. 'I scarcely feel inclined to venture on trying to influence Miss M. any more,' she told Smith. 'There is a peculiar property in her which must sooner or later be recognized as a great inconvenience by such of her acquaintance as admire her intellectual powers and her many excellent personal qualities without being able to agree in her views; she is prone to mistake liking for agreement, and with the sanguine eagerness of her character thinks to sweep you along with her in her whirlwind course. This will not do.'[118]

The next day, however, Charlotte announced that she had ventured after all to try to influence her friend. Showing no mean sanguinity herself, she tried to explain to Harriet Martineau where she had failed, and she even indicated the course that formidable woman should pursue: 'What Mr. Smith wanted and expected was another "Deerbrook". He did not want for politics or theology. "Deerbrook" made you beloved wherever it was read. "Oliver Weld" will not have this effect. It is powerful, it is vivid; it must strike, but it will rarely please. You think perhaps it will do good? Not so much good as "Deerbrook" did. Better the highest part of what is in your own self than all the political and religious controversy in the world. Rest a little while; consider the matter over, and see whether you have not another "Deerbrook" in your heart to give England.'[119]

Charlotte remained adamant about publication dates, however, in spite of the rejection of the Martineau book, but her prohibition was unnecessary. Within a few weeks of settling to work, the death of Emily's dog, Keeper,[120] and all the memories it revived, brought Charlotte low.[121] She suffered from an appalling list of ailments—frequent sickness, headache, almost incessant toothache, fever, depression, and pains in the chest—all of which merged into a violent and prolonged attack of influenza.[122]

After a hard struggle with this illness, and an equally stiff tussle with a doctor who seemed almost wholly on the side of the enemy, Charlotte began to recover[123]—but not before she had passed through another bout of fearful depression: 'It cannot be denied that the solitude of my position was fearfully aggravated by its other evils,' she wrote. 'Some long, stormy days and nights there were when I felt such a craving for support and companionship as I cannot express. Sleepless, I lay awake night after night; weak and unable to occupy myself, I sat in my chair day after day, the saddest memories my only company.'[124]

She went to Brookroyd, in an effort to shake off the after effects of her influenza; and so, to her chagrin, missed the first and only visit of George Smith to the parsonage: 'I *do* wish now I had delayed my departure from home a few days longer, that I might have shared with my father the true pleasure of receiving you at Haworth Parsonage. And a pleasure your visit would have been, as I have sometimes dimly imagined but never ventured to realize.'[125]

There followed an invitation, the like of which Charlotte had never before been able to bring herself to give: 'I shall be returning in about a week, but if you must make your excursion before that time, and if you came northwards and would call at Brookroyd, I am desired to tell you that you would have the warmest Yorkshire welcome. My friends would like to see you. You would find me there, but not exactly ill now; I have only a sort of low intermittent fever which still hangs about me....'[126] But apparently Smith was not able to go.

Even when she returned home, Charlotte had neither strength nor heart for work: 'Expect no good of Currer Bell this summer,' she told Smith.[127] 'For nearly four months now I have not put pen to paper,' she said in reply to another invitation. 'My work has been lying untouched and my faculties have been rusting for want of exercise; further relaxation is out of the question, *and I will not permit myself to think of it.* My publisher groans over my long delays; I am sometimes provoked to check the expression of his impatience with short and crusty answers.'[128] Two months later, at the end of May, the work still lay idle. Charlotte gave up the fight, and went off by herself to the coast, at Filey, where she spent a month.[129]

She returned rested, and determined to put an end to *Villette*, but her purpose was handicapped almost at once by a breakdown in her father's health. Mr. Brontë had a seizure which threatened the loss of his sight, and he relapsed into the fretfulness and depression which was to become ever more characteristic of his old age.[130] Charlotte went on with her writing as well as she was able. The summer visit to London was abandoned: 'I determined in my own mind that I would not again come to London except under conditions that are yet unfulfilled,' she told Mrs. Smith, who had asked her to stay again with them. 'A treat must be *earned* before it can be *enjoyed*, and the treat which a visit to you affords me is yet unearned, and must remain so for a time—how long I do not know.'[131]

Even Ellen was not permitted to come to the parsonage until *Villette* had been finished.[132] But this resolve weakened under the pressure of loneliness and poor health, and, early in October, when the second volume of the novel was nearing its end, Charlotte gave way:[133] 'Ellen has only been my companion one little week,' she informed Miss Wooler, who was wondering why Charlotte had abandoned her declared intention not to receive or visit friends until her work was done. 'I would not have her any longer,' Charlotte continued, 'for I am disgusted with myself and my delays—and consider it was a weak yielding to temptation in me to send for her at all. But in truth my spirits were getting low—prostrate sometimes—and she has done me inexpressible good.'[134] Ellen had done her good; this week stimulated Charlotte sufficiently to enable her to get on with her work; and by the end of the month she had sent the first two volumes of *Villette* to her publishers.[135] Three weeks later she had completed and sent off the third.[136]

Already Charlotte had received favourable comments from Smith Elder on the first and second volumes;[137] now, at Brookroyd for a rest, she awaited her publisher's verdict on the third with great impatience.[138] She was very strung up and sensitive, and the book meant so much to her that, not hearing from George Smith by return of post, she prepared to leave instantly for London, afraid her work had so disappointed the publishers that they could not bring themselves to write and say so.[139] Fortunately she was persuaded to wait one more day, and the next morning Smith's letter arrived. He and Williams criticized some parts of the third volume, but their general judgement, as of the previous volumes, was favourable.[140]

The end of *Villette* was a sad time for Charlotte. Although she had trouble in writing the book, she had been living in Brussels while she wrote—a Brussels in which she and her ideal Héger were together and in love. Now that was at an end—there was no more to be said, and there no longer seemed any hope of escaping, by her imagination, the joyless and loveless life facing her. At this point she began getting letters from Taylor again. He wrote soon after he arrived in India, and then again, a long letter[141]—and in desperation Charlotte began to wonder whether she ought not to have encouraged him rather than lead a life of utter frustration. She could not make up her mind—or perhaps she did not yet know it. She criticized Taylor's letters when sending them to Ellen,[142] and her eventual reply to his second letter was phrased with the utmost propriety, not to say frigidity.[143] Yet when Taylor, tiring at last, stopped writing, Charlotte began to speculate on his doings and his reasons for silence. 'I hear nothing,' she told Ellen, 'and you must quite understand that if I feel any uneasiness, it is not the uneasiness of confirmed and fixed regard, but that anxiety which is inseparable from a state of absolute uncertainty about a somewhat momentous matter. I do not know, I am not sure myself that any other termination would be better than lasting estrangement and unbroken silence, yet a good deal of pain has been and must be gone through in that case.'[144]

Indifference always made Charlotte respect people more, and increased her interest in them. This had been so with Emily and Héger, and now she had a similar reaction, though less strong, to Taylor's attitude. For a time she could not keep from the subject. Only three days later she was again writing: 'Many Mails have come in from India since I was at Brookroyd—and always when the day came round (I know it now) expectation would be on the alert, but disappointment knocked her down. I have not heard a syllable, and cannot think of making enquiries at Cornhill. Well, long suspense in any matter usually proves somewhat cankering, but God orders all things for us, and to his will we must submit.'[145]

Four months passed. 'You ask about India,' Charlotte wrote

to Ellen. 'Let us dismiss the subject in a few words and not recur to it. All is silent as the grave. Cornhill is silent too.'[146]

.   .   .   .   .   .

Just before Christmas 1852, another, if not a new, admirer declared himself. For a long time Charlotte had known that Arthur Bell Nicholls, Mr. Brontë's curate, was very much attracted to her. Ellen had noticed Nicholls' interest in Charlotte, and had more than once rallied her about it, but Charlotte would never discuss the matter seriously. In the parsonage, she successfully kept the shy and respectful man at a distance, and for this very reason he seemed negligible to her, differing from the other curates only because he was obviously a good man. His goodness was, in fact, his only claim on Charlotte's attention, for he appeared in every other way totally unsuited to her— unintellectual, bigoted, puritanical, and with no presence. But eventually his feelings became too strong to be repressed, and suddenly, this winter evening, he proposed.

'Papa', Charlotte wrote, 'has minutely noticed all Mr. Nicholls' low spirits, all his threats of expatriation, all his symptoms of impaired health, noticed them with little sympathy and much indirect sarcasm. On Monday evening Mr. Nicholls was here to tea. I vaguely felt without clearly seeing, as without seeing I have felt for some time, the meaning of his constant looks, and strange, feverish restraint. After tea I withdrew to the dining-room as usual. As usual, Mr. Nicholls sat with papa till between eight and nine o'clock. I then heard him open the parlour door as if going. I expected the clash of the front door. He stopped in the passage: he tapped: like lightning it flashed on me what was coming. He entered—he stood before me. What his words were you can guess; his manner—you can hardly realize—never can I forget it. Shaking from head to foot, looking deadly pale, speaking low, vehemently yet with difficulty—he made me for the first time feel what it costs a man to declare affection where he doubts response. The spectacle of one ordinarily so statue-like, thus trembling, stirred, and overcome, gave me a kind of strange shock. He spoke of sufferings he had borne for months, of sufferings he could endure no longer, and craved leave for some hope. I could only entreat him to leave me then and promise a reply on the morrow. I asked him if he had spoken to papa. He said, he dared not. I think I half led, half put him out of the room. When he was gone I immediately went to papa, and told him what had taken place. Agitation and anger disproportionate to the occasion ensued; if I had loved Mr. Nicholls and had heard such epithets applied to him as were used, it would have transported me past my patience; as it was, my blood boiled with a sense of injustice, but papa worked himself into a state not to be trifled with, the veins on his temples started up like whipcord, and his eyes became suddenly bloodshot. I made haste to promise that Mr. Nicholls should on the morrow have a distinct refusal.'[147]

Charlotte duly refused Nicholls, but, annoyed by her father's unreason, and surprised and moved by Nicholls' depth of feeling, she refused him gently.[148]

Ellen followed every move with eager interest. How was Mr. Brontë treating Nicholls?[149]

'I only wish you were here to see papa in his present mood,' replied Charlotte; 'you would know something of him. He just treats him with a hardness not to be bent, and a contempt not to be propitiated. The two have had no interview as yet: all has been done by letter. Papa wrote, I must say, a most cruel note to Mr. Nicholls on Wednesday.'[150] But Mr. Brontë was digging a pit for himself. Charlotte, having discovered what was in the note, decided that she must make some amends to Nicholls: 'In his state of mind and health (for the poor man is horrifying his landlady by entirely rejecting his meals) I felt that the blow must be parried, and I thought it right to accompany the pitiless despatch by a line to the effect that, while Mr. Nicholls must never expect me to reciprocate the feeling he had expressed, yet at the same time I wished to disclaim participation in sentiments calculated to give him pain; and I exhorted him to maintain his courage and spirits.'[151]

Thus Charlotte on the progress of Nicholls' suit, her language growing in stateliness as she sought to convince her friend—and herself—of her unconcern.[152] She by no means agreed with her father's chief objection to Nicholls: 'I am afraid that papa thinks a little too much about his want of money; he says that the match would be a degradation, that I should be throwing myself away, that he expects me, if I marry at all, to do very differently; in short, his manner of viewing the subject is, on the whole, far from being one in which I can sympathize. My own objections arise from a sense of incongruity and uncongeniality in feelings, tastes, principles.'[153]

Nicholls resigned his curacy at Haworth but made no move to leave.[154] He had made himself unpopular in the parsonage by daring to lift his eyes to Charlotte; but this unpopularity, like Mr. Brontë's violent injustice of speech, did Nicholls no harm with her: 'I am sorry for one other person whom nobody pities but me,' she commented to her faithful listener at Brookroyd. 'Martha is bitter against him. John Brown says *he should like to shoot him.* They don't understand the nature of his feelings —but I see now what they are. Mr. Nicholls is one of those who attach themselves to very few, whose sensations are close and deep, like an underground stream, running strong but in a narrow channel. He continues restless and ill, he carefully performs the occasional duty, but does not come near the church, procuring a substitute every Sunday.'[155]

Nicholls then wrote to Mr. Brontë asking permission to withdraw his resignation. Mr. Brontë would agree only if Nicholls gave his written promise never again to broach 'the obnoxious subject' either to him or to Charlotte. Nicholls would not give this promise, nor did he make any motion of leaving; he simply stayed on, dropping dark hints about his future.[156] 'I feel persuaded the termination will be—his departure for Australia. Dear Nell, without loving him I don't like to think of him suffering in solitude, and wish him anywhere so that he were happier. He and Papa have never met or spoken yet.'[157]

In the midst of this unhappy deadlock, with her sympathies, but no more than her sympathies, aroused, Charlotte set off to London on her long-deferred visit. This was now timed to coincide with the publication of *Villette*;[158] and Charlotte, who stayed once more with the Smiths, spent much of her time reading proofs of the book.[159]

Villette was published on 28 January 1853. It met with a good reception and it deserved one.[160] Although it has many of the faults of style and construction of her earlier novels, *Villette* not only ranks with the great love stories of the world, but is unique among them. In it, Charlotte proclaims her belief that love between man and woman is the finest thing in life. No new idea, this—the oldest in literature—but Charlotte went further, and it is in this further declaration that her greatness lies. She affirmed that love—romantic, sexual love—was not the prerogative of the young and attractive, but was absolutely universal. Something of this sort she had attempted in *Jane Eyre*, where, against all conventions, she made her heroine plain and physically insignificant. But she more than balanced the supposed lack of romance in Jane herself with the novelettish Rochester.

Now, in *Villette*, she wrote that rarest of all things, a romance of real life, in which neither hero nor heroine is at all heroic, and neither possesses, by fictional standards, a single romantic quality. And it is Charlotte's triumph that we see Lucy and M. Paul at once as they are—an unattractive schoolmistress and an irritable, middle-aged professor—and as they appeared to each other through their love, transformed and desirable. And, such is her art, and such the truth of the book, that *Villette*, though quieter and superficially more ordinary than *Jane Eyre*, is even more exciting.

In *Villette*, Charlotte magnificently justified her faith in the universality of love, she at last wrote out Heger and her whole experience in Brussels, and she told an absorbing story that is essentially true to life. The often criticized first half of the book is in fact artistically right, and the effectiveness of the second half depends upon it. Lucy, beguiled by romantic circumstances and a prepossessing appearance, is led naturally to imagine that she is in love with Dr. John, while all the time her real affinity is in front of her eyes, regarded by her with amusement and some impatience—an experience common to many men and women.

If Charlotte fails to convince the reader completely of the truth of Lucy's experience it is because of her drawing of Dr. John. She makes him too uninteresting, an unsuccessful blend of George Smith and William Weightman. She had been attracted by both these men, but not deeply interested in them, which may account for her failure to bring this type of man to life. To the reader, Dr. John seems merely a dull catalogue of virtues and good features, and a dim shadow compared with the vital personality of M. Paul. To some extent, of course, Charlotte desired this contrast, but she overdid it; and so, unfortunately, reflects on the intelligence of Lucy, who, the reader feels, is herself stupid to be interested in him. Nevertheless, the comparative dullness of the Lucy-Dr. John relationship helps to heighten the interest of the love story.

No one who has read *Villette* can forget the feeling of excited anticipation when Lucy leaves Dr. John to his colourless marriage, and turns to her irascible, lovable little professor. The movement of the book quickens from this moment, as the love between Lucy and Paul develops through scene after charming scene—the incident of the broken spectacles, Paul's evening reading in the study, the pastoral idyll of his birthday breakfast—their meetings and conversations are all so good that it would be invidious to quote any of them. The story sweeps on with increasing impetus and excitement until the breathless moment when Madame Beck makes her last attempt to separate them, and Lucy cries 'My heart will break!' and Monsieur Paul thunders 'Laissez-moi!' Charlotte conveys with great speed and economy—in the last third of the book— the growing depth and tenderness of their love. It is true, it is moving and it is beautiful.

The physical passion between Lucy and Paul is implicit all through their love story, and is all the more striking for its restraint. Lucy's desire for Paul is subtly communicated when she watches him caressing his spaniel. When Paul grips Lucy's hand in the garden, as they are confronted by Père Silas and Madame Beck, a more powerful sense of attraction and depth of attachment is conveyed than by pages of passionate protestations. Nothing, in fact, is more surprising than the economy with which Charlotte handles such moments, in contrast to her wordiness at other, less important, times. There is scarcely a passage between the lovers that could not be read to a child, yet some critics took offence, the undercurrent of passion is so unmistakable.

Surprising, too, is the manner in which Charlotte blends humour with this passion. She not only admits humour into such a serious theme, but actually carries off the rare blend with consummate success.

Apart from the love story, Charlotte's outstanding achievement in *Villette* is Madame Beck, and the pages introducing her are among the best in the book. For once, Charlotte's artistry completely overcame her prejudiced view of people antipathetic to her. Her blacks and whites dropped away, and she added to the clear-sightedness of dislike an unusual detachment, presenting a woman who, although the evil genius of the story, has a charm which fascinates and an authority which commands respect. 'I say again, Madame was a very great and a very capable woman.' And the reader believes it.

Charlotte had already shown, in *Jane Eyre*, her gift for creating atmosphere. In *Villette*, this gift is employed on a far wider scale. Her description of Lucy's fantasies in the deserted school is desolating in its exact reproduction of nerves strung to the pitch of hysteria:

... 'for nine dark and wet days, of which the Hours rushed on all turbulent, deaf, dishevelled—bewildered with sounding hurricane—I lay in a strange fever of the nerves and blood. Sleep went quite away. I used to rise in the night, look round for her, beseech her earnestly to return. A rattle of the window, a cry of the blast only replied—Sleep never came!

.   .   .   .   .   .

'One evening—and I was not delirious: I was in my sane mind, I got up—I dressed myself, weak and shaking. The solitude and the stillness of the long dormitory could not be borne any longer; the ghastly white beds were turning into spectres—the coronal of each became a death's head, huge and sun-bleached—dead dreams of an elder world and mightier race lay frozen in their wide gaping eyeholes.'[161]

Hard things have been said about Charlotte's writing, and certainly she can be long-winded and prosy to an exasperating degree. But her faults arise from an excess of imagination and feeling, not a lack of them. At her worst it is solid food, however indigestible. At her best, it is very good indeed. She can be as simple and fresh as Emily:

'The morning broke calm as summer, with singing of birds in the garden, and a light dew-mist that promised heat.'[162]

She can paint the weather with vitality and grandeur:

'Strong and horizontal thundered the current of the wind from north west to south-east; it brought rain like spray, and sometimes, a sharp, hail like shot; it was cold and pierced me to the vitals. I bent my head to meet it, but it beat me back. My heart did not fail at all in this conflict; I only wished that I had wings and could ascend the gale, spread and repose my pinions on its strength, career in its course, sweep where it swept.'[163]

Her vocabulary is large, her choice of adjectives sensitive, and she powerfully conveys the movement of wind and snow, and the sensations of heat and cold:

'The keen, still cold of the morning was succeeded, later in the day, by a sharp breathing from Russian wastes: the cold zone sighed over the temperate zone, and froze it fast. A heavy firmament, dull, and thick with snow, sailed up from the north, and settled over expectant Europe. Towards afternoon began the descent. I feared no carriage would come, the white tempest raged so dense and wild.'

'. . . the drift darkened the lower panes of the casement, and, on looking out, one saw the sky and air vexed and dim, the wind and snow in angry conflict. There was no fall now, but what had already descended was torn up from the earth, whirled round by brief shrieking gusts, and cast into a hundred fantastic forms.'[164]

But when all is said, *Villette* must stand or fall by its love story. There will always be readers, like Harriet Martineau, to whom the book's fine writing and characterization cannot compensate for the—to them—morbid obsession with one emotion. But for those who share or sympathize with Charlotte's philosophy of life, *Villette* will always be a book apart, remarkable and unforgettable.

. . . . . .

Charlotte's visit to London—her last—was also her quietest. She was no longer the literary wonder of the day.[165] On previous visits she had seen that part of London, and those things in it, which others had urged upon her. Now, left a great deal to herself, she went where her own sombre inclination led her —the prisons of Newgate and Pentonville, the Bank, the Royal Exchange, the Foundling Hospital, and Bethlehem Hospital.[166]

Charlotte saw little of her host, George Smith. He was overworked, but even when free he had not so much time as formerly to spare for her—he was engaged to be married.[167] At much the same time Charlotte at last heard something of Taylor in India: 'There are complaints of his temper and nerves being rendered dreadfully excitable by the hot climate,' she told Ellen: 'It seems he is bad to live with. . . .'[168]

When she reached home early in February[169] she found the tension between Nicholls and her father as acute as ever. The situation was beginning to get on Nicholls' nerves, and, when the Bishop paid a visit to the parsonage, he seems to have made everyone thoroughly uncomfortable: 'I thought he made no effort to struggle with his dejection,' commented Charlotte, 'but gave way to it in a manner to draw notice; the Bishop was obviously puzzled by it. Mr. Nicholls also showed temper once or twice in speaking to Papa: Martha was beginning to tell me of certain "flaysome" looks also, but I desired not to hear of them. The fact is, I shall be most thankful when he is well away; I pity him, but I don't like that dark gloom of his. He dogged me up the lane after the evening service in no pleasant manner, he stopped also in the passage after the Bishop and the other clergy were gone into the room, and it was because I drew away and went upstairs that he gave that look which filled Martha's soul with horror. She, it seems, meantime, was making it her business to watch him from the kitchen door. If Mr. Nicholls be a good man at bottom, it is a sad thing that nature has not given him the faculty to put goodness into a more attractive form. Into the bargain of all the rest he managed to get up a most pertinacious and needless dispute with the Inspector, in listening to which all my old unfavourable impressions revived so strongly, I fear my countenance could not but show them.'[170]

Charlotte, however, was already adopting a possessive attitude towards Nicholls. This is not surprising. Nicholls made his feelings plain at a crucial time in Charlotte's life. Everything seemed to be falling away from her. *Villette* was written and published, and it is doubtful whether she had material for another book, or felt any compulsion to write one. Smith was on the verge of marriage. Taylor wrote no more. Even Williams seemed to have little to say to her. Finally, there came a break with Harriet Martineau.

Relations between the two friends had been somewhat strained since the refusal of *Oliver Weld* by Charlotte's publishers, and the rather patronizing letter from Charlotte. Now they were severed completely. A short while before, Miss Wooler had appealed to Charlotte to give up Harriet Martineau because of her free-thinking. Charlotte refused: 'I do not feel that it would be right to give Miss Martineau up entirely. There is in her nature much that is very noble; hundreds have forsaken her—more, I fear, in the apprehension that their fair names may

suffer if seen in connection with hers than from any pure con-
victions such as you suggest—of harm consequent on her fatal
tenets. With these fair-weather friends I cannot bear to rank.
And for her sin, is it not one of those which God and not man
must judge? To speak the truth, my dear Miss Wooler, I believe
if you were in my place, and knew Miss Martineau as I do, if
you had shared with me the proofs of her rough but genuine
kindliness, and had seen how she secretly suffers from abandonment, you would be the last to give her up; you would separate
the sinner from the sin, and feel as if the right lay rather in
quietly adhering to her in her strait—while that adherence is
unfashionable and unpopular—than in turning on her your
back when the world sets the example.'[171]

The day after this letter was written *Villette* was published,
and Charlotte asked Harriet Martineau for her opinion of it.
She begged for candour, for honest judgement, for the whole
truth.[172] The older woman tried to avoid carrying out her
promise, but Charlotte insisted.[173] Harriet Martineau, therefore,
unwillingly replied: 'I have but one thing to say; but it is not a
small one. I do not like the love, either the kind or the degree of
it; and its prevalence in the book, and effect on the action of it,
help to explain the passages in the reviews which you consulted
me about, and seem to afford *some* foundation for the criticisms
they offered.'[174]

Charlotte was deeply hurt. She could forgive any amount of
free-thinking, if she thought the free-thinker was sound at
heart, but to dislike the love in *Villette* was to dislike Charlotte
and everything she most believed in. 'I know what love is as I
understand it; and if man or woman should be ashamed of feeling such love, then there is nothing right, noble, faithful, truthful, unselfish in this earth, as I comprehend rectitude, nobleness,
fidelity, truth and disinterestedness.'[175]

Harriet Martineau, so different in temperament, could not
know how deeply her criticism would wound. She tried to
appease Charlotte, but Charlotte would have none of it.[176] The
love between Lucy and Paul expressed Charlotte's faith in life,
her religion—and anyone who did not share that faith was a
heretic, beyond the pale.

Only Mrs. Gaskell now remained as an active link with the
world that Charlotte had desired so fervently to enter; and to

Manchester she went for a week in April. But Mrs. Gaskell, though good for Charlotte in some ways, and very kind to her, had only a limited understanding of her difficult guest. 'Miss Brontë had expected to find us alone,' she wrote, 'and although our friend was gentle and sensible after Miss Brontë's own heart, yet her presence was enough to create a nervous tremor. I was aware that both of our guests were unusually silent; and I saw a little shiver run from time to time over Miss Brontë's frame . . . and the next day Miss Brontë told me how the unexpected sight of a strange face had affected her. It was now two or three years since I had witnessed a similar effect on her, in anticipation of a quiet evening at Fox How; and since then she had seen many and various people in London; but the physical sensations produced by shyness were still the same; and on the following day she laboured under severe headache. I had several opportunities of perceiving how this nervousness was ingrained in her constitution, and how acutely she suffered in striving to overcome it. One evening we had, among other guests, two sisters who sang Scottish ballads, exquisitely. Miss Brontë had been sitting quiet and constrained till they began "The Bonnie House of Airlie", but the effect of that and "Carlisle Yetts", which followed, was as irresistible as the playing of the Pipe of Hamelin. The beautiful clear light came into her eyes; her lips quivered with emotion; she forgot herself, rose, and crossed the room to the piano where she asked eagerly for song after song. The sisters begged her to come and see them the next morning, when they would sing as long as ever she liked; and she promised gladly and thankfully. But on reaching the house her courage failed. We walked some time up and down the street; she upbraiding herself all the while for her folly, and trying to dwell on the sweet echoes in her memory rather than on the thought of a third sister who would have to be faced if we went in. But it was of no use; and dreading lest this struggle with herself might bring on one of her trying headaches, I entered at last and made the best apology I could for her non-appearance. Much of this nervous dread of encountering strangers I ascribed to the idea of her personal ugliness, which had been strongly impressed upon her imagination early in life, and which she exaggerated to herself in a remarkable manner. "I notice", said she, "that after a stranger has once looked at my face he is careful not to let his eyes wander to that part of the room again!" A more untrue idea never entered into anyone's head. Two gentlemen who saw her during this visit, without knowing at the time who she was, were singularly attracted by her appearance; and this feeling of attraction towards a pleasant countenance, sweet voice, and gentle timid manner was so strong in one as to conquer a dislike he had previously entertained to her works.

'There was another circumstance that came to my knowledge, at this period', continues Mrs. Gaskell, 'which told secrets about the finely strung frame. One night I was on the point of relating some dismal ghost story, just before bedtime. She shrank from hearing it, and confessed that she was superstitious, and prone at all times to the involuntary recurrence of any thoughts of ominous gloom which might have been suggested to her. She said that on first coming to us she had found a letter on her dressing table from a friend in Yorkshire, containing a story which had impressed her vividly ever since—that it mingled with her dreams at night and made her sleep restless and unrefreshing.

'One day we asked two gentlemen to meet her at dinner,' concluded Mrs. Gaskell, 'expecting that she and they would have a mutual pleasure in making each other's acquaintance. To our disappointment she drew back with timid reserve from all their advances, replying to their questions and remarks in the briefest manner possible, till at last they gave up their efforts to draw her into conversation in despair, and talked to each other and my husband on subjects of recent local interest. Among these Thackeray's Lectures (which had lately been delivered in Manchester) were spoken of, and that on Fielding especially dwelt upon. One gentleman objected to it strongly as calculated to do moral harm, and regretted that a man having so great an influence over the tone of thought of the day as Thackeray should not more carefully weigh his words. The other took the opposite view. He said that Thackeray described men from the inside, as it were; through his strong powers of dramatic sympathy he identified himself with certain characters, felt their temptations, entered into their pleasures, etc. This roused Miss Brontë, who threw herself warmly into the discussion. . . .'[177]

Charlotte had already expressed herself on this subject two years earlier, when she had heard Thackeray lecture in London.

She thought of Branwell as she listened: 'It was a painful hour,' she said. 'That Thackeray was wrong in his way of treating Fielding's character and vices my conscience told me. . . . Had Thackeray owned a son, grown or growing up, and a son brilliant but reckless—would he have spoken in that light way of courses that lead to disgrace and the grave? He speaks of it all as if he had never been called on to witness the actual consequences of such failings; as if he had never stood by and seen the final result of it all. I believe, if only once the prospect of a promising life blasted at the outset by wild ways had passed close under his eyes, he never *could* have spoken with such levity of what led to its piteous destruction. Had I a brother yet living, I should tremble to let him read Thackeray's lecture on Fielding.'[178]

.   .   .   .   .   .

This week in Manchester convinced Charlotte, if she needed convincing, that she must make the best of Haworth. Even the quiet excitement of Mrs. Gaskell's home depressed rather than stimulated her, and showed her that she was too late to fit herself for any kind of life outside the one she knew. For years she had looked out impatiently from Haworth to a world in which she would find opportunity, understanding, and a fuller life. Now she realized that, though there was little chance of happiness at home, there was nothing at all anywhere else.

She came back to face a summer of almost unrelieved misery. She was again ill, and had to put off Mrs. Gaskell's return visit[179] —the one bright spot in her immediate future. But although the cause of her illness was nominally influenza, she fell ill again this summer only because her powers of resistance were giving way after years of unhappy brooding. Loneliness and frustration were responsible for her state now, as before, but a new worry was added—the feud between Nicholls and her father. Nicholls had gone to a new curacy, a few miles away, but Mr. Brontë still spent a great deal of his time violently abusing him. He also had prolonged fits of depression, and Charlotte's sense of duty was tried to the uttermost.[180] Mr. Brontë's objections to Nicholls were twofold. He thought that if Charlotte must marry she should only marry someone with money and a position; and he did not want to be left alone.[181] And although Charlotte criticized her father's attitude, she felt that she ought to stay with him. The new curate was neither so hard-working nor so considerate as Nicholls, and this was fresh ground for grievance to Mr. Brontë.[182] His continued injustice increased Charlotte's wish to make some kind of redress to Nicholls,[183] and when he wrote to her she replied.[184] The correspondence continued, and Nicholls soon began to visit Haworth and to meet Charlotte at the house of his friend Grant. Mr. Brontë knew nothing of this.[185]

When Mrs. Gaskell did come to Haworth, in September, she found Charlotte excited but worried by the meetings and correspondence with Nicholls, and, in her own tactful words, 'I could not but deeply admire the patient docility which she displayed in her conduct towards her father.'[186] Charlotte did not feel able to tell her father until her own mind was clearer;[187] when she did, after some months of uncertainty, she found his resistance had weakened, largely because he had by that time discovered how excellent a curate he had lost in Nicholls.[188] 'It was very hard and rough work at the time,' Charlotte reported in January 1854, 'but the issue after a few days was that I obtained leave to continue the communication.'[189] The two men met; Nicholls was received at the parsonage, 'but not pleasantly'. Mr. Brontë remained 'very, very hostile—bitterly unjust'.[190] Charlotte, however, saw much of Nicholls for the next few days. 'All I learnt inclines me to esteem and if not love—at least affection.'[191]

Charlotte told Nicholls of the great obstacles that lay before him. He persevered, and in April he had his way. 'Papa's consent is gained—his respect, I believe, is won,' Charlotte told Ellen, 'for Mr. Nicholls has in all things proved himself disinterested and forbearing. He has shown, too, that while his feelings are exquisitely keen, he can freely forgive. Certainly I must respect him, nor can I withhold from him more than cool respect. In fact, dear Ellen, I am engaged.'[192] She still refused to anticipate happiness.[193] 'I am still very calm, very inexpectant. What I taste of happiness is of the soberest order. I trust to love my husband—I am grateful for his tender love to me. I believe him to be an affectionate, a conscientious, a high-principled man, and if, with all this, I should yield to regrets, that fine talents, congenial tastes and thoughts are not added, it seems to me I should be most presumptuous and thankless.'[194]

If Charlotte had doubts, her friends had even more. Ellen was dismayed. She did not think Nicholls was suitable for Charlotte, and she suspected that he would discourage her friendships. Mrs. Gaskell felt vaguely uneasy, even though marriage was the thing she had always most wished for her. She was also afraid that this marriage might put a stop to Charlotte's writing.[195]

'It has cost me a good deal to come to this,' Charlotte told Catherine Winkworth on a visit—her last—to the Gaskells in May. 'You will have to care for his things, instead of his caring for yours?' she was asked. 'Yes, I can see that beforehand,' Charlotte replied. And to the further question: 'But when you have been together so long already you know what his things are, very well. He is very devoted to his duties, is he not?— and you can and would like to help him in those?' Charlotte agreed: 'I have always been used to those, and it is one great pleasure to me that he is so much beloved by all the people in the parish; there is quite a rejoicing over his return. But those are not everything, and I cannot conceal from myself that he is *not* intellectual; there are many places into which he could not follow me intellectually.'[196] Again, to the same friend: 'He is a Puseyite and very stiff; I fear it will stand in the way of my intercourse with some of my friends; but I shall always be the same in my heart towards them. I shall never let him make me a bigot.'[197]

These misgivings crowded Charlotte's mind during the next few weeks, but she told herself that Nicholls was a good man, that he loved her and depended on her. Moreover, he had agreed to come back to Haworth as curate, and to live in the parsonage, leaving Mr. Brontë his own rooms.[198]

Nicholls wanted to be married early in the summer. After some hesitation, Charlotte agreed.[199] They were married at Haworth on 29 June 1854. Of Charlotte's friends, only Ellen and Miss Wooler were present. Miss Wooler gave Charlotte away, Mr. Brontë at the last moment saying that he did not feel well enough to go to the church.[200] Charlotte and her husband left the same day for their honeymoon, in Ireland.[201] They came back to the parsonage on the first day of August.

In every way, as Charlotte said, the marriage was a good, sound arrangement—more than this, she would not have claimed.[202] Yet she was happier than she had expected. It was not marriage as Charlotte knew marriage could be, but it gave her an interest in life when all other interests seemed dead. She had no illusions about her husband,[203] but she had not anticipated how pleasant it would be to be cared for—the more autocratically, the better. And to look after a man who was grateful for every kindness—this, too, was a new pleasure. Best of all, perhaps, she had little time to think.[204] 'I have not a minute,' she told Ellen.[205] The Sunday and day schools, entertaining fellow clergy, visiting parishioners—all this, together with feeding and caring for two men, now took up most of her day.[206]

Ellen saw her only once. Her other friends saw her no more.[207] Even her letters were cut short by Nicholls standing over her as she wrote, eager to walk on the moors;[208] and after he had read some of her letters to Ellen, he asked that they should all be burned.[209] Ellen, indignant with him for interfering, refused to do so unless he gave his word not to read any future letters. He, too, refused, so the letters survived.[210]

It is not possible to say what the outcome of this marriage would have been, had Charlotte lived long enough to face its full implications. For the short time left to her, the change in the conditions of her life had a good effect on her health and spirits: 'I have had only one headache,' she told Ellen, after she had been married for some months.[211] Soon she found she was going to have a child, and this, too, pleased her at first.[212] But the improvement was only a superficial one. Her constitution had been completely worn out during the last few years.

In the autumn, during one of the walks of which her husband was so fond, Charlotte was caught on the moors during a rainstorm. She took a chill.[213] She appeared to have thrown it off, but, after a reluctant visit to the Shuttleworths early in the New Year, she fell ill.[214] She had a high fever, she could neither eat nor sleep, and she was constantly sick.[215]

Nicholls was beside himself with anxiety.[216] 'I find my husband the tenderest nurse, the kindest support—the best earthly comfort ever woman had,' Charlotte told Ellen in one of her last letters.[217] But he could not save her. She had no fight left. She grew weaker,[218] and on the last day of March 1855 she died.[219]

BIBLIOGRAPHY AND NOTES

BIBLIOGRAPHY

MANUSCRIPTS

Poems by Charlotte Brontë. Shorter Collection.
Letters of Charlotte Brontë. Brotherton Collection: Leeds University.
Letters of Charlotte Brontë. Haworth Parsonage Museum.
Poems by Branwell Brontë. Haworth Parsonage Museum.
Poems by Branwell Brontë. Brotherton Collection: Leeds University.
Letters of Branwell Brontë. Haworth Parsonage Museum.
The Angrian Works of Charlotte and Branwell Brontë. Bonnell Collection: Haworth Parsonage Museum; Law Collection; Berg Collection: New York Public Library; Lowell Collection: Widener Collection: Harvard University Library; Ashley Library Bequest: British Museum; J. Pierpont Morgan Library; A. Edward Newton Library; Henry E. Huntington Library; Brotherton Collection: Leeds University.
Gondal Poems by Emily Brontë. Smith Bequest: British Museum.
Poems by Emily Brontë. Ashley Library Bequest: British Museum.
Poems by Emily Brontë. Bonnell Collection: Haworth Parsonage Museum.
Poems by Emily Brontë. Berg Collection: New York Public Library.
Poems by Emily Brontë. University of Texas.
Diary fragment by Emily Brontë. Bonnell Collection: Haworth Parsonage Museum.
Birthday Notes by Emily and Anne Brontë. Law Collection.
Poems by Emily and Anne Brontë. Law Collection.
Poems by Anne Brontë. Haworth Parsonage Museum.
Works and Letters of the Rev. Patrick Brontë. Haworth Parsonage Museum.
Letters of Mrs. Gaskell, the Rev. A. B. Nicholls, and Miss Ellen Nussey. Haworth Parsonage Museum.

PUBLISHED WORKS

CHARLOTTE, BRANWELL, EMILY, AND ANNE

Brontë Poems. Selections from the Poetry of Charlotte, Emily, Anne, and Branwell Brontë. Edited by Arthur C. Benson, 1915.

CHARLOTTE, BRANWELL, AND EMILY

The Orphans, and other Poems, by Charlotte, Emily, and Branwell Brontë. Edited by Thomas J. Wise, 1917.

CHARLOTTE, EMILY, AND ANNE

Poems, by Currer, Ellis, and Acton Bell. 1846.
Poems, by Charlotte, Emily, and Anne Brontë. 1893.
Poems, by Charlotte, Emily, and Anne Brontë. 1902.

BIBLIOGRAPHY

CHARLOTTE

Jane Eyre. An Autobiography, edited by Currer Bell. 3 vols. 1847.

Shirley. A Tale, by Currer Bell. 3 vols. 1849.

Villette, by Currer Bell. 3 vols. 1853.

The Professor. A Tale, by Currer Bell. 2 vols. 1857.

The Last Sketch—Emma. A fragment of a story by the late Charlotte Brontë. 'Cornhill Magazine', April 1860.

The Adventures of Ernest Alembert. A Fairy Tale, by Charlotte Brontë. Edited by Thomas J. Wise, 1896.

Early Romances of Charlotte Brontë: (1) *A Leaf from an Unopened Volume, or the Manuscript of an Unfortunate Author.* 'Poet-lore', Vol. IX, Spring 1897. (2) *The Green Dwarf.* 'Poet-lore', Vol. IX, Autumn 1897.

Jane Eyre, to which is added *The Moores*, an unpublished fragment by Charlotte Brontë. With an introduction by W. Robertson Nicoll, 1902.

The Tales of the Islanders, by Charlotte Brontë, 31 June 1829–30 July 1830. 'Nash's Magazine', December 1911.

The Four Wishes. A Fairy Tale, by Charlotte Brontë. Edited by Clement Shorter, 1918.

The Twelve Adventurers and Other Stories, by Charlotte Brontë. Edited by Clement Shorter, 1925.

The Spell. An Extravaganza, by Charlotte Brontë. Edited by G. E. Maclean, 1931.

Legends of Angria. Compiled from the early writings of Charlotte Brontë, by Fannie E. Ratchford, 1933.

Poems, by Charlotte Brontë (Currer Bell). 1882.

Richard Coeur De Lion and Blondel. A Poem by Charlotte Brontë. Edited by Thomas J. Wise. With an Introduction by Clement Shorter, 1912.

Saul and Other Poems, by Charlotte Brontë. Edited by Thomas J. Wise, 1913.

The Violet. A Poem written by Charlotte Brontë at the age of fourteen. Edited by Clement Shorter, 1916.

The Red Cross Knight and Other Poems, by Charlotte Brontë. Edited by Thomas J. Wise, 1917.

The Swiss Emigrant's Return and Other Poems, by Charlotte Brontë. Edited by Thomas J. Wise, 1917.

Latest Gleanings. A series of Unpublished Poems by Charlotte Brontë. Edited by Clement Shorter, 1918.

Darius Codomannus. A Poem by Charlotte Brontë written at the age of eighteen years. Edited by Thomas J. Wise, 1920.

The Complete Poems of Charlotte Brontë. Edited by Clement Shorter, 1923.

Unpublished Letters of Charlotte Brontë, 'Hours at Home', Vol. 2, June–September 1870 (H.H.).

Thackeray and Charlotte Brontë. Being some hitherto Unpublished Letters to her publishers by Charlotte Brontë. Edited by Clement Shorter, 1919.

Four Letters from Charlotte Brontë to M. Constantin Héger, edited by Marion H. Spielman, 'The Times', 29 and 30 June 1913. (TIMES.)

The Story of the Brontës: Their Home, Haunts, Friends, and Works—Part Second—Charlotte's Letters, edited and privately printed by J. Horsfall Turner, 1885–9. (TURNER.)

CHARLOTTE AND BRANWELL

The Poems of Charlotte and Branwell Brontë. Edited by Thomas J. Wise and John Alexander Symington, 1934. (PCB.)

The Miscellaneous and Unpublished Writings of Charlotte Brontë and Patrick Branwell Brontë. Edited by Thomas J. Wise and John Alexander Symington, 2 vols. 1936, 1938. (MISC.)

BRANWELL

The Odes of Horace. First Book. Translated by Branwell Brontë. Edited by John Drinkwater, 1923. (DRINKWATER.)

EMILY AND ANNE

Wuthering Heights. A Novel, by Ellis Bell, in 3 vols., with *Agnes Grey,* by Acton Bell, 1847.

Wuthering Heights and *Agnes Grey,* by Ellis and Acton Bell. A new edition, revised, with a Biographical Notice of the Authors, a Selection from their Literary Remains, and a Preface, by Currer Bell. 3 vols. 1850.

The Poems of Emily Jane Brontë and Anne Brontë. Edited by Thomas J. Wise and John Alexander Symington, 1934. (PEA.)

EMILY

Relics of Emily Brontë, by Clement Shorter. 'The Woman at Home', August 1897.

The Complete Works of Emily Brontë. Edited by Clement Shorter. With Introductory Essay by W. Robertson Nicoll. Vol. I, *Poetry,* 1910. Vol. II, *Prose, Wuthering Heights,* 1911. (CWEB.)

The Complete Poems of Emily Jane Brontë. Edited by Clement Shorter. Arranged and collected, with Bibliography and Notes, by C. W. Hatfield, 1923.

Emily Brontë's Poems. Some Textual Corrections and Unpublished Verses, by Davidson Cook. 'The Nineteenth Century and After', August 1926.

Gondal Poems, by Emily Jane Brontë. Edited by Helen Brown and Joan Mott, 1938. (GONDAL.)

The Complete Poems of Emily Jane Brontë. Edited by C. W. Hatfield, 1941. (HATFIELD.)

Emily Brontë: Poems. Selected, with an Introduction by Philip Henderson, 1947.

ANNE

The Tenant of Wildfell Hall, by Acton Bell, 3 vols. 1848.

Self-Communion. A Poem by Anne Brontë. Edited by Thomas J. Wise, 1900.

Dreams, and Other Poems, by Anne Brontë. Edited by Thomas J. Wise, 1917.

The Complete Poems of Anne Brontë. Edited by Clement Shorter. With a Bibliographical Introduction by C. W. Hatfield, 1920.

BIBLIOGRAPHICAL

BONNELL A. *A Catalogue of the Books, Letters, Manuscripts, and other Brontë relics in the Bonnell Collection.* Prepared by Henry H. Bonnell, 1922.

COOK A. *Brontë Manuscripts in the Law Collection* by Davidson Cook, 'The Bookman', November 1925.

DRY. *Brontë Sources*, by Florence S. Dry, 1937.

MUSEUM. The Brontë Society Catalogue of the Museum Library. The Brontë Society Catalogue of the Bonnell Collection: Brontë Parsonage Museum.

WISE A. *A Bibliography of the Writings in Prose and Verse of the Members of the Brontë Family*, by Thomas J. Wise, 1917.

WISE B. *A Brontë Library.* A catalogue of printed books, manuscripts and autograph letters by the members of the Brontë family. Collected by Thomas J. Wise, 1929.

WOOD A. *A Bibliography of the Works of the Brontë Family*, by Butler Wood, BST. Part I.

WOOD B. *A Supplement to the Bibliography of the Brontë Family*, by Butler Wood, BST. Part VI.

BIBLIOGRAPHY

BST. Brontë Society Transactions.

C.B. *Letters on Charlotte Brontë*, by Mrs. Gaskell. Edited by Clement Shorter, n.d.

C.P.S. *The Structure of 'Wuthering Heights'*, by C.P.S[anger], 1926.

GASKELL A. *The Life of Charlotte Brontë*, by E. C. Gaskell, 1857.

GASKELL B. *The Life of Charlotte Brontë*, by Mrs. Gaskell, with Introduction and Notes by Clement K. Shorter, 1900.

GRUNDY A. *Pictures of the Past: Memories of Men I have met and Places I have seen*, by Francis H. Grundy, 1879.

HARRISON A. *Methodist Good Companions*, by G. Elsie Harrison, 1935.

HARRISON B. *Haworth Parsonage*, by G. Elsie Harrison, 1937.

HARRISON, C. *The Clue to the Brontës*, by G. Elsie Harrison, 1948.

LEYLAND A. *The Brontë Family, with special reference to Patrick Branwell Brontë*, by Francis A. Leyland, 1886.

LEYLAND B. *Patrick Branwell Brontë:* A Complete Transcript of the Leyland Manuscripts, showing the Unpublished Portions, 1925.

NUSSEY. *Reminiscences of Charlotte Brontë*, by A Schoolfellow, 'Scribner's Monthly', Vol. II, May 1871.

RATCHFORD A. *The Brontës Web of Childhood*, by Fannie Elizabeth Ratchford, 1941.

ROBINSON. *Emily Brontë*, by A. Mary F. Robinson, 1883.

S.H. *The Brontës: Their Lives, Friendships and Correspondence.* The Shakespeare Head Brontë, edited by Thomas James Wise and John Alexander Symington, 1932.

SHORTER. *The Brontës: Life and Letters*, by Clement Shorter, 1908.

WILLIS A. *The Authorship of 'Wuthering Heights'*, by Irene Cooper Willis, 1926.

WISE C. *The Ashley Library.* A Catalogue of Printed Books, Manuscripts and Autograph Letters collected by T. J.Wise, 1922.

SUPPLEMENTARY BIBLIOGRAPHY

The under-mentioned works, dealing wholly or in part with the Brontës, are of interest, and reference to many of them is made in the Notes following.

ACB. *The Life of Edward White Benson: sometime Archbishop of Canterbury*, by A. C. Benson, 1899.

ABERCROMBIE. *The Brontës Today*, by Lascelles Abercrombie, BST. Part XXXIV, 1924.

ARMINIAN. 'The Arminian Magazine', 1778, 1785, 1795.

ARNOLD. *Letters of Matthew Arnold*, 1848-88, collected and arranged by George W. E. Russell, 1895.

ATHENAEUM A. A review of *Wuthering Heights* and *Agnes Grey* in 'The Athenaeum', 25 December 1847.

ATHENAEUM B. A review of *Jane Eyre* in 'The Athenaeum', 23 October 1847.

ATHENAEUM C. A review of Mrs. Gaskell's *Life of Charlotte Brontë*: 4 April 1857.

ATHENAEUM D. Letter of Apology from Mrs. Gaskell in 'The Athenaeum', 6 June 1857.

ATHENAEUM E. A review of *The Tenant of Wildfell Hall* in 'The Athenaeum', 8 July 1848.

ATHENAEUM F. A review of *The Professor* in 'The Athenaeum', 13 June 1857.

ATHENAEUM G. A review of *Poems* by Currer, Ellis and Acton Bell in 'The Athenaeum', 4 July 1846.

ATLAS. A review of *Wuthering Heights* in 'The Atlas', 1848. Bonnell Collection: Haworth Parsonage Museum.

BAKER. *History of the English Novel*, by E. A. Baker, Vol. VIII, 11-80, 1937.

BALD. *Women Novelists of the Nineteenth Century*, by Marjory A. Bald, 1923.

BATHO. *The Brontës*, by E. C. Batho and Bonamy Dobrée in *The Victorians and After*, 1938.

BAYNE. *Two Great Englishwomen, Mrs. Browning and Charlotte Brontë*, by Peter Bayne, 1881.

BENSON, E. F. *Charlotte Brontë*, by E. F. Benson, 1932.

BENSON, A. C. Introduction to *Brontë Poems*, 1915.

BENTLEY. *The Brontës*, by Phyllis E. Bentley, 1947.

BIRRELL. *Life of Charlotte Brontë*, by Augustine Birrell, 1887.

BLOOMFIELD. *Wuthering Heights*, by Louis Bloomfield, 'Time and Tide', 20 March 1948.

BONNELL B. *Charlotte Brontë, George Eliot, Jane Austen: Studies in their Works*, by Henry H. Bonnell, 1902.

BRADBY. *The Brontës and other Essays*, by G. F. Bradby, 1932.

BRIDGES. *The Poems of Emily Brontë*, by Robert Bridges, No. 9 in *Collected Essays*, 1932.

BRITANNIA. A review of *Wuthering Heights* in 'Britannia', 1848. Bonnell Collection: Haworth Parsonage Museum.

BRONTEANA. The Rev. Patrick Brontë, A.B., His Collected Works and Life. Edited by J. Horsfall Turner, 1898.

BROOKFIELD. *Mrs. Brookfield and Her Circle*, by C. & F. Brookfield, 1905.

BUNTING. *The Life of Jabez Bunting*, with notices of Contemporary Persons and Events, by Thomas Percival Bunting, Vol. I, 1859.

CALDWELL. *Alice Brontë*, by George Caldwell, 'Christian Herald', March 1882.

CAUTLEY. *Old Haworth Folk who knew the Brontës*, by C. Holmes Cautley, 'The Cornhill Magazine', July 1910.

CAZAMIAN. *Charlotte and Emily Brontë*, by Louis Cazamian in *A History of English Literature, Modern Times*, 1927.

CECIL. *Early Victorian Novelists*, by Lord David Cecil, 1934.

CENTENARY. Mrs. Gaskell Centenary Number, 'The Bookman', September 1910.

CENTURY. *Mr. Brontë*, by T. Wemyss Reid, 'The Nineteenth Century', 1896.

CHADWICK A. *In the Footsteps of the Brontës*, by Mrs. Ellis H. Chadwick, 1914.

CHADWICK B. *Emily Brontë as a Lawyer*, by Mrs. Ellis H. Chadwick, 'The Bookman', November 1926.

CHAMBERS A. *A Winter Day in Haworth*, 'Chambers's Journal', 1868.

CHAMBERS B. Branwell, Emily, and Anne Brontë in *Chambers's Cyclopaedia of English Literature*, Vol. I, 1901.

CHILDE. *The Literary Background of the Brontës*, by Wilfred Roland Childe, BST. Part LIV, 1944.

CKS A. *Charlotte Brontë and Her Sisters*, by Clement K. Shorter, 1895.

CKS B. *Charlotte Brontë and Her Circle*, by Clement K. Shorter, 1896.

CKS C. *The Brontës and Their Circle*, by Clement K. Shorter, 1914.

CKS D. *Who Wrote 'Wuthering Heights'?* by Clement K. Shorter, 'Woman at Home', August 1897.

CLARKE. *Haworth Parsonage*, by Isabel Clarke, 1927.

COLIN. *Charlotte Brontë and Monsieur Héger:* by B. M. Colin, 'The Sketch', 5 June 1896.

COOK B. *Miniature Magazines of Charlotte Brontë*. With unpublished Poems from an original MS. in Ashley Library. By Davidson Cook, 'The Bookman', December 1926.

CORNISH. *These Were the Brontës*, by Dorothy Helen Cornish, 1940.

CORY. *Letters and Journals of William Johnson Cory*, 1897.

COTTAGE. 'The Cottage Magazine or Plain Christian's Library', Vol. XI, 1822.

COWAN BRIDGE. *The Brontës at Cowan Bridge*, by Angus M. Mackay, 'The Bookman', October 1894.

CROSS, J. W. *Life of George Eliot*, by J. W. Cross, 3 vols. 1885.

CROSS, W. L. *Charlotte Brontë*, by Wilbur L. Cross in *The Development of the English Novel*, 1899.

DEARDEN. A Letter from William Dearden relative to the Rev. Patrick Brontë, 'The Examiner', July 1857; an article in the *Halifax Guardian*, June 1867.

DELAFIELD. *The Brontës: Their Lives recorded by their Contemporaries*, compiled with an introduction by E. M. Delafield, 1935.

DEMBLEBY. *The Key to the Brontë Works*, by John Malham Dembleby, 1911.

DIARY. *Diary of A. C. Benson*, 1926.

DIMNET. *The Brontë Sisters*, by Ernest Dimnet, new edition with appendix, 1927.

DOBELL A. *Currer Bell*, by Sydney Dobell, 'The Palladium', September 1851. BST. Part XXVIII, 1918.

DOBELL B. *Life and Letters of Sydney Dobell*, edited by E.J. (Emily Jolly), 1878.

DODDS A. *Gondaliand*, by Madeleine Hope Dodds, 'Modern Language Review', January 1923.

DODDS B. *A Second Visit to Gondaliand*, by Madeleine Hope Dodds, 'Modern Language Review', January 1926.

DOWDEN. *Correspondence of Robert Southey with Caroline Bowles*, edited by Edward Dowden, 1881.

EB. *L'Amour Filial*, 5 August 1842; *Portrait le Roi Harold avant la Bataille de Hastings*, June 1842. Essays by Emily Brontë, Brontë Parsonage Museum. Translated by Dorothy H. Cornish in *The Brontës' Study of French*, B.S.T. Part LVII, 1947.

ELTON A. *The Brontës*, by Oliver Elton in *A Survey of English Literature, 1830 to 1880*, Vol. II, 1920.

ELTON B. *Emily Brontë*, by Oliver Elton in *The English Muse*, 1933.

ENCYCLOPAEDIA. Charlotte, Branwell, Emily, and Anne Brontë in *Encyclopaedia Britannica*, eleventh edition, 1910–11, and fourteenth edition, 1929.

EXAMINER A. A review of *Jane Eyre* in 'The Examiner', 1847.

EXAMINER B. A review of *Wuthering Heights* in 'The Examiner', 1848. Bonnell Collection: Haworth Parsonage Museum.

FLOWER. Letter from Ellen Nussey to Mrs. Flower, 29 June 1883, about *Emily Brontë* by A. Mary F. Robinson. Haworth Parsonage Museum.

FOTHERINGHAM. *The Work of Emily Brontë and the Brontë Problem*, by James Fotheringham, B.S.T. Part XI, 1900.

GARLAND. *Jane Eyre's School*, by F. A. Garland. 'Belgravia', Vol. V, 1868.

GARRS. An Interview with Nancy Garrs in 'Heckmondwike Herald and Courier, 22 September 1882. Haworth Parsonage Museum.

GEOGRAPHY. *The Brontë Country*, by William Sharp in *Literary Geography and Travel Sketches*, 1912.

GEORGE SMITH A. *The Brontës*, by George Smith, 'The Cornhill Magazine', May 1873.

GEORGE SMITH B. *Charlotte Brontë*, by George M. Smith, 'The Cornhill Magazine', December 1900.

GEORGE SMITH C. *In the Early Forties*, by George Smith, 'The Critic', January 1901.

GEORGE SMITH D. *Reminiscences of George Murray Smith*, 1923.

GLEAVE. *Emily Brontë: An Appreciation*, by J. J. Gleave, 1904.

GOLDRING. *Charlotte Brontë, the Woman. A Study*, by Maude Goldring, 1916.

GOSSE. *The Challenge of the Brontës*, by Edmund Gosse, BST Part XIII, 1903.

GREEN, J. J. *The Brontë-Wheelwright Friendship*, by Joseph J. Green, 'The Friends Quarterly Examiner', January 1916.

GREEN, JULIEN. *Charlotte Brontë*, by Julien Green in *Suite Anglaise*, 1927.

GRIERSON, E. *Where Charlotte Brontë went to School*, by Elizabeth Grierson, 'The Sunday Magazine', June 1905.

GRIERSON, H. *Emily Brontë*, by H. J. C. Grierson and J. C. Smith in *A Critical History of English Poetry*, 1944.

GRIMSHAW, B. *A Comparison Between Emily Brontë and Charlotte Brontë*, by Beatrice Grimshaw, 'John O'London's Weekly', 4 October 1924.

GRIMSHAW, W. *Some Account of the Life and Ministry of the Rev. William Grimshaw: Vicar of Haworth in Yorkshire*, 'The Arminian Magazine', 1795.

BIBLIOGRAPHY

GROOM. *The Brontës*, by Bernard Groom in *A Literary History of England*, 1929.

GRUNDY B. *Mr. Grundy and Branwell Brontë* (review), and letter from Mr. Grundy. 'The Athenaeum', 3 and 21 May 1879. Haworth Parsonage Museum.

GUARDIAN. *Who Wrote Wuthering Heights?* by William Dearden, 'Halifax Guardian', 15 June 1867.

HALDANE, R. B. *Emily Brontë's Place in Literature*, by R. B. Haldane. BST Part XI, 1901.

HALDANE, E. S. *Mrs. Gaskell and Her Friends*, by Elizabeth S. Haldane, 1930.

HALE. *Anne Brontë: Her Life and Writings*, by Will T. Hale. Indiana University Studies, Vol. 16, No. 83, 1929.

HALIFAX. Halifax Antiquarian Society Transactions, 1908.

HANSON A. *The Local Colour of Wuthering Heights*, by T. W. Hanson, BST Part XXXIII, 1923.

HANSON B. *Emily Brontë's Footprints*, by T. W. Hanson, 'Municipal Libraries Readers' Guide', February 1910.

HARDY. *William Grimshaw, incumbent of Haworth, 1742-63*, by R. Spence Hardy, 1860.

HARRISON. *Charlotte Brontë's Place in Literature*, by Frederic Harrison, 1895.

HAWORTH. *Haworth Past and Present, A History of Haworth, Stanbury and Oxenhope*, by J. Horsfall Turner, 1879.

HEGER. *Miss Brontë and Monsieur Héger*, 'British Weekly', 31 July 1913.

HINKLEY. *The Brontës: Charlotte and Emily*, by Laura L. Hinkley, 1945.

HOFFMAN N. *Rolandsitten; or the Deed of Entail*. Translated from *Das Majorat* by R. P. Gillies in German Tales, Vol. I, 1826.

HOLLOWAY. *An Hour with Charlotte Brontë*, by Laura C. Holloway, 1884.

HOLROYD. *Currer Bell and Her Sisters*, by Abraham Holroyd, 1887.

HUMPHRY WARD A. *'Wuthering Heights'*, by Mrs. Humphry Ward. BST Part XV, 1905.

HUMPHRY WARD B. Introductions to Brontë Works, Haworth Edition.

HYDE. *The Story of Early Gaelic Literature*, by Douglas Hyde, 1898.

INSH. *Haworth Pilgrimage*, by George P. Insh, 1944.

JACK. *The Brontës*, by A. A. Jack in *Cambridge History of English Literature*, Vol. XIII, 1916.

JERROLD. A review of *Wuthering Heights* in 'Douglas Jerrold's Weekly Newspaper' 1848. Bonnell Collection: Haworth Parsonage Museum.

JUVENILIA. Early Fragments by the Brontës first published. BST Parts XXIX, XXX, XXXVI, XXXVII, XLI, XLII, XLIII, XLIV.

KAVANAGH. *The Symbolism of 'Wuthering Heights'*, by Colman Kavanagh, 1920.

KINSLEY. *Pattern for Genius*, by Edith Ellsworth Kinsley, 1937.

KNEVETT. *Charlotte Brontë's School in Brussels*, by Edgar de Knevett, BST Part XXXIV, 1924.

LAMONT. *An Analysis of 'Wuthering Heights'*, by H. F. Lamont. Rutgers University (unpublished).

LANGBRIDGE. *Charlotte Brontë, A Psychological Study*, by Rosamond Langbridge, 1929.

LAYCOCK. *Methodist Heroes of the Great Haworth Round, 1734-1784*, by John William Laycock, 1909.

LAW A. *Emily Jane Brontë and the Authorship of 'Wuthering Heights'*, by Alice Law, 1925.

LAW B. *Patrick Branwell Brontë*, by Alice Law, 1923.

LEE A. *Charlotte Brontë in London*, by Sydney Lee, BST Part XIX, 1909.

LEE B. *Charlotte Brontë and the East Riding*, by P. F. Lee, BST Part IV, 1896.

LEWES A. *Jane Eyre*, a review by George Henry Lewes, 'Westminster Review', Vol. 48, 1847.

LEWES B. *Jane Eyre*, a review by George Henry Lewes, 'Fraser's Magazine', 1847.

LEWES C. *Shirley*, a review by George Henry Lewes, 'Westminster Review', Vol. 52, 1849.

LEWES D. *Charlotte Brontë*, a review by George Henry Lewes, 'Westminster Review', Vol. 53, 1850.

LEWES E. *Jane Eyre and Shirley*, a review by George Henry Lewes, 'Edinburgh Review', January 1850.

LEWIS. *'The Tenant of Wildfell Hall'*, by Naomi Lewis, 'The New Statesman and Nation', 17 August 1946.

LEY. *A Vida Trágica das Irmãs Brontë*, by C. D. Ley, 1943.

LOCKHART. *The Life and Letters of John Gibson Lockhart*, by Andrew Lang, 1897.

LONGBOTTOM. *'Wuthering Heights' and Patrick Brontë*, by John Longbottom, 'Yorkshire Notes and Queries', February 1905.

LUCAS. *An Introduction to the Psychology of 'Wuthering Heights'*, by Peter D. Lucas, 1943.

LUSK. *Brontë Genius at its Source*, by J. B. Lusk, BST Part VII, 1897.

MASEFIELD. *Women Novelists, from Fanny Burney to George Eliot*, by Muriel Masefield, 1934.

MACDONALD A. *The Brontës at Brussels*, by Frederika Macdonald, 'Woman at Home', July 1894.

MACDONALD B. *Monsieur Héger*, by Frederika Macdonald, 'The Bookman', June 1896.

MACDONALD C. *The Secret of Charlotte Brontë*, followed by some Reminiscences of the real Monsieur and Madame Héger, by Frederika Macdonald, 1914.

MACFARLANE. *Divide the Desolation*, by Kathryn Jean Macfarlane, 1936.

MACLEAN. *Unpublished Essays in Novel Writing by Charlotte Brontë*, by George Edwin Maclean, BST Part XXVI, 1916.

MAETERLINCK. *Wisdom and Destiny*, by Maurice Maeterlinck, 1905.

MACKAY A. *The Brontës: Fact and Fiction*, by Angus M. Mackay, 1897.

MACKAY B. *A Crop of Brontë Myths*, by Angus M. Mackay, 'Westminster Review', October 1895.

MACKAY C. *On the Interpretation of Emily Brontë*, by Angus M. Mackay, 'Westminster Review', August 1898.

MACKAY D. *The Brontës*, by Angus M. Mackay, 'The Bookman', October, 1904.

MAIS. *Why We Should Read 'Wuthering Heights'*, S. P. B. Mais, 1921.

MARGESSON. *The Brontës and Their Stars*, by Maud Margesson, 1928.

MARTINEAU A. *The Autobiography of Harriet Martineau*, 1877.

MARTINEAU B. *Harriet Martineau*, by Theodora Bosanquet, 1927.

MASSON. *The Brontës*, by Flora Masson, 1912.

MATTHEWS, T. *The Brontës*, by Thomas S. Matthews, 1934.

MATTHEWS, W. *Charlotte Brontë: A Tribute to her Genius*, by W. Matthews, 1897.

MEEKER. *Haworth, Home of the Brontës*, by Claude Meeker, 'Cincinnati Times and Star', 14 February 1895.

MERCURY. *Currer Bell*, 'Belfast Mercury', April 1855.

METHODIST A. 'Methodist Magazine', 1799, 1812, 1939.

METHODIST B. *A History of Methodism in Ireland*, by C. H. Crookshank, 1886.

METHODIST C. *An Address to the Methodists in Birstall Circuit*, by an old Methodist, 1797.

MILLMORE. *A Brief Life of the Brontës*, by Royston Millmore, 1947.

MOEWES. *Currer Bell*, by Frank Moewes, 'Courtag sheilage', No. 30, 'zur Bossischen Zeitung', No. 374, Berlin, 26 July 1914.

MOORE. *The Life and Eager Death of Emily Brontë*, by Virginia Moore, 1936.

MOORE SMITH. *The Brontës at Thornton*, by C. C. Moore Smith, 'The Bookman', October 1904.

MORGAN. *Emily Brontë*, by Charles Morgan in *The Great Victorians*, 1932.

MYLES. *The Life and Writings of the late Rev. William Grimshaw*, by William Myles, 1813.

N.A. Review of *Jane Eyre, Wuthering Heights*, and *The Tenant of Wildfell Hall*, 'North American Review', October 1848.

NEWTON, A.E. 'The Brontë Country', by A. Edward Newton in *Derby Day and Other Adventures*, 1934.

NEWTON, J. *Memoirs of the Life of the late Rev. William Grimshaw*, by John Newton, 1799.

NICHOLLS A. *The Late Mr. Arthur Bell Nicholls*, by Clement K. Shorter, 'The Sphere', December 1906.

NICHOLLS B. *The Late Rev. A. B. Nicholls*, by H. E. Wroot, BST Part XVI, 1906.

NICOLL A. *Charlotte Brontë*, by W. Robertson Nicoll, *Chambers's Cyclopaedia of English Literature*, Vol. I, 1901.

NICOLL B. *Emily Brontë*, by W. Robertson Nicoll, 'British Weekly', October 1908.

NOWELL. Letter from Mr. Brontë about William Nowell, 'Leeds Mercury', 15 December 1810.

O'BYRNE. *The Gallic Source of the Brontë Genius*, by Cathal O'Byrne, 1933.

OCAMPO. *Emily Brontë, Terra Incognita*, by V. Ocampo, 1938.

OFFOR. *The Brontës: Their Relation to the History and Politics of their Time*, by Richard Offor, 1943.

OLIPHANT A. *Annals of a Publishing House, William Blackwood and his Sons, Their Magazine and Friends*, by Mrs. Oliphant, 1897.

OLIPHANT B. *The Sisters Brontë*, by Margaret O. Oliphant, 1897.

PIGOT. Pigot's Yorkshire Directory, 1828.

PRITCHETT. *Wuthering Heights*, by V. S. Pritchett in 'The New Statesman and Nation', 22 June 1946.

QUARTERLY. Review of *Jane Eyre*, 'Quarterly Review', No. clxvii, December 1848.

QUINCEY. *De Quincey Memorials*, by Alexander H. Japp, 1891.

RAMSDEN. *The Brontë Homeland*, by J. Ramsden, 1897.

BIBLIOGRAPHY

RATCHFORD B. *The Brontës' Web of Dream*, by Fannie Elizabeth Ratchford, 'Yale Review', 1931.

RATCHFORD C. *War in Gondal: Emily Brontë's last Poem*, by Fannie E. Ratchford, 'The Trollopian', December 1947.

RAYMOND. *In the Steps of the Brontës*, by Ernest Raymond, 1948.

REID A. *Charlotte Brontë*, by T.Wemyss Reid, 1877.

REID B. *The Memoirs of Sir Wemyss Reid*, edited by S. J. Reid, 1905.

REVUE A. Review of *Jane Eyre* in the 'Revue des Deux Mondes', Vol. XXIV, 1848.

REVUE B. Review of *Shirley* in the 'Revue des Deux Mondes', Vol. XXV, 1849.

RITCHIE A. *Letters of Anne Thackeray Ritchie*, edited by Hester Ritchie, 1924.

RITCHIE B. *Some Memoirs*, by Lady Ritchie, 1904.

ROMIEU. *The Brontë Sisters*, by Emilie and Georges Romieu, 1931.

ROWE. *The Maternal Relatives of the Brontës*, by J. Hambley Rowe, 1923.

SAINTSBURY. *The Position of the Brontës as Origins in the History of the English Novel*, by George Saintsbury, BST. Part IV, 1899.

SCRUTON A. *The Birthplace of Charlotte Brontë*, by William Scruton, 1884.

SCRUTON B. *Thornton and the Brontës*, by William Scruton, 1898.

SEARLE. *Branwell Brontë*, by George Searle Phillips, 'The Mirror', December 1872.

SENIOR. *Patrick Brontë*, by James Senior, 1921.

SHAEN. *Memorials of Two Sisters, Susanna and Catherine Winkworth*. Edited by their Niece, Margaret J. Shaen, 1908.

SHARPE. *A Few Words about 'Jane Eyre'*, by W. Sharpe, 1855.

SHEPHEARD. *A Vindication of the Clergy Daughters' School and the Rev. W. Carus Wilson from the Remarks in 'The Life of Charlotte Brontë'*, by the Rev. H. Shepheard, 1857.

SHERRARD. *The Brontë Portraits:* Letters from Mrs. Ellis H. Chadwick and the Rev. James Sherrard, 'Morning Post', March 1914.

SIMPSON. *Emily Brontë*, by Charles Simpson, 1929.

SINCLAIR A. *The Three Brontës*, by May Sinclair, 1914.

SINCLAIR B. Introductions by May Sinclair to Second Edition of *The Three Brontës* and to Brontë Works in 'Everyman's Library'.

SMITH. *Emily Brontë—A Reconstruction*, by J. C. Smith, 'Essays and Studies', Vol. IV, 1914.

SONNINO. *Tre Anime Luminose fra le Nebbie Nordiche: Le Sorelle Brontë*, by Georgina Sonnino, 1903.

SOUTHEY. *The Life and Correspondence of Robert Southey*, edited by his Son, the Rev. Charles Cuthbert Southey, second edition, 1849–50.

SOUTHWART. *Brontë Moors and Villages from Thornton to Haworth*, by Elizabeth Southwart, 1923.

SPENS. *Charlotte Brontë*, by Janet Spens, 'Essays and Studies', Vol. XIV, 1924.

SPHERE. *Letters of Patrick Brontë to Mrs. and Miss Burder*, 'The Sphere', August 1913.

SPIELMANN. *The Inner History of the Brontë-Héger Letters*, by Marion H. Spielmann, 'The Fortnightly Review', April 1919.

STEPHEN. 'Charlotte Brontë', by Leslie Stephen in *Hours in a Library*, Vol. III, 1879.

STOLLARD. *The Brontës and their Visits to Leeds*, by M. L. Stollard, 'Yorkshire Evening Post', 7 May 1919.

STORES-SMITH. *Charlotte Brontë*, by J. Stores-Smith, 'The Free Lance', March 1868.

STUART A. *The Brontë Country: Its Topography, Antiquities and History*, by J. A. Erskine Stuart, 1888.

STUART B. *The Literary Shrines of Yorkshire*, by J. A. Erskine Stuart, 1892.

STUART C. *The Brontë Originals*, by J. A. Erskine Stuart, 'Huddersfield Examiner', January and February 1927.

STUART D. *The Brontë Nomenclature*, by J. A. Erskine Stuart, BST Part III, 1894.

SUGDEN. *A Short History of the Brontës*, by K. A. R. Sugden, 1929.

SWINBURNE A. *A Note on Charlotte Brontë*, by Algernon Swinburne, 1877.

SWINBURNE B. *Miscellanies*, by Algernon Swinburne, 1886.

SWINBURNE C. Review of *Emily Brontë* by A. Mary F. Robinson, 'The Athenaeum', 16 June 1883.

SYMONS A. *Emily Brontë*, by Arthur Symons in *Figures of Several Centuries*, 1916.

SYMONS B. *Emily Brontë*, by Arthur Symons in *Dramatis Personae*, 1923.

TAHON. *La Rue Isabelle et le Jardin des Arbalétriers*, by Victor Tahon, 1912.

TAYLOR. *Miss Miles: or a Tale of Yorkshire Life Sixty Years Ago*, by Mary Taylor, 1890.

TENNYSON. *Alfred, Lord Tennyson, A Memoir*, by Hallam, Lord Tennyson, 1895.

TRAZ. *La Famille Brontë*, by R. de Traz, 1939.

VAUGHAN. *Charlotte and Emily Brontë: a Comparison and a Contrast*, by C. E. Vaughan, BST. Part XXII, 1912.

VICTORIAN. *The Brontës*, by Hugh Walker in *The Literature of the Victorian Era*, 1910.

WADE. *Charlotte Brontë As I Knew Her*. A chat with the Rev. J. C. Bradley (the curate 'David Sweeting' of *Shirley*), by George A. Wade, 'Great Thoughts', 17 October 1908.

WALTERS. *The Spell of Yorkshire*, by J. Cuming Walters, 1931.

WARD. *The Brontës*, by A. W. Ward, *Dictionary of National Biography*, Vol. VI.

WESLEY A. *The Journal of John Wesley*, edited by Nehemiah Curnock, 1909–16.

WESLEY B. *The Letters of John Wesley*, edited by John Telford, 1931.

WESLEY C. *The Life of the Rev. J. Wesley*, by Henry Moore, 1824.

WESLEY D. *Memorials of the Wesley Family*, by G. J. Stevenson, 1887.

WESLEY E. *The Lives of Early Methodist Preachers*, edited by Thomas Jackson, 1871.

WESLEY F. *Early Methodist People*, by Leslie F. Church, 1948.

WESLEY G. *The Life of Mrs. Mary Fletcher*, by Henry Moore, 1818.

WEST. *Charlotte Brontë*, by Rebecca West in *The Great Victorians*, 1932.

WHATELEY. *English Life, Social and Domestic, in the Nineteenth Century*, by Mrs. Whateley, 1847.

WHITE. *The Miracle of Haworth*, by W. Bertram White, 1937.

WILLIAMS. *Emily Brontë*, by A. M. Williams, 'Temple Bar Magazine', July 1893.

WILLIS B. *The Brontës*, by Irene Cooper Willis, 1933.

WILSON. *All Alone: The Life and Private History of Emily Jane Brontë*, by Romer Wilson, 1928.

WILLY. *Emily Brontë: Poet and Mystic*, by Margaret Willy, 'English', Autumn 1946.

WOODHOUSE. *Woodhouse Grove School: Memorials and Reminiscences*, by J. T. Slugg, 1885.

WOOLF. *Jane Eyre and Wuthering Heights*, by Virginia Woolf in *The Common Reader:* First Series, 1925.

WORDSWORTH. *Memoirs of William Wordsworth*, by Christopher Wordsworth, 1851.

W.P.P. *Jottings on Currer, Ellis and Acton Bell*, by W.P.P., 1856.

WRIGHT, J. C. *The Story of the Brontës*, by J. C. Wright, 1925.

WRIGHT A. *The Brontës in Ireland: or Facts Stranger than Fiction*, by William Wright, 1893.

WRIGHT B. *Mrs. Heslip and the Brontës in Ireland*, by William Wright, 'The Sketch', 10 March 1897.

WRIGHT C. *More Light on the Brontës in Ireland*, by William Wright, BST Part IV, 1897.

WROOT A. *Sources of Charlotte Brontë's Novels*, by Herbert E. Wroot, 1935.

WROOT B. *Centenary Memorial of Charlotte Brontë:* by Herbert E. Wroot, 1916.

WROOT C. *Shirley at Home*, by Herbert E. Wroot, 'Ludgate Magazine', May 1896.

WROOT D. *The Persons and Places of the Brontë Novels*, by Herbert E. Wroot, BST Part XLV, 1906.

YATES A. *The Father of the Brontës: His Life and Works at Dewsbury and Hartshead*, by W. W. Yates, 1897.

YATES B. *The Brontës at Dewsbury*, by W. W. Yates, BST Part III, 1894.

YATES C. *Who Wrote 'Wuthering Heights'? More about Branwell Brontë*, by W. W. Yates, 'Dewsbury Reporter', 24 March 1894.

YORKSHIREMAN. *The Taylors of Gomersal; Nancy Wainwright, Charlotte Brontë's Nurse; Martha Brown*, 'The Yorkshireman', 1879.

YOUNG. *Early Victorian England*, edited by G. M. Young, 1935.

NOTES

CHAPTER I

Note Page

1   1   *S.H.I.* 6, Note 2; *Rowe; Harrison C*, 37–42.

2   See quotation from Charles A. Federer in the 'Yorkshire Daily Observer', 30 July 1907; *S.H.I.* 6, Note 3.

3   Fennell was godson of John Fletcher, friend of John Wesley; *Woodhouse.*

4   See *S.H.I.*, Chapters 1 and 2; *Yates A.*

5   See notice of the marriage in the 'Gentleman's Magazine', 1813. Part I, Vol. LXXXIII, p. 179.

6   *Yates A.* See *Wesley A* IV, VII.

7   *Wright A* and *B*; the answer to *Wright* in *Mackay A*, 85–187; *Brontëana*; introduction to *Turner*; *BST* Part III; *Hyde* 49; *S.H.I.* 3–4, Notes 2 and 3; *Harrison C*, 1–9.

8   *Birrell* 17–23.

9   *Cottage Poems*, 1811; *The Rural Minstrel*, 1813; and *The Cottage in the Wood: or the Art of becoming Rich and Happy*, 1815. See *Brontëana*.

10   See *Gaskell B* 41, 441; *CKS B*.

11   2   *S.H.I.* 8–27. There is some doubt about the exact birth date of Maria. Only her christening—23 April 1814—is certain. See *Mackay D; Moore Smith.*

12   Later godparent, with his wife, to Charlotte. It has been suggested that Charlotte's fees at Roe Head were paid by Mrs. Atkinson; *Chadwick A* 91.

13   *Scruton A* and *B*.

14   *Moore Smith*; *S.H.I.* 36–45, 85–7.

15   See reprint of Baptismal Registers, *S.H.I.* 35.

16   *Gaskell B* 11–35; *Leyland A* I. 20–5; *S.H.I.* 58.

17   *Gaskell B* 34.

18   With the children's nurse, Nancy Garrs; *Garrs.*

19   Population about 5,000; *Pigot.*

20   4   *Nussey.*

21   See *The Structure of Haworth Parsonage*, by Mrs. C. Mabel Edgerley; *BST* Part XLVI, 1936.

CHAPTER II

1   5   Afterwards Sowden's Farm.

2   Both he and Whitefield preached at Haworth several times between 1757 and 1790; *Wesley A*, Vol. VII.

3   1742–63; *Laycock.*

Note	Page	
4	5	*Hardy; Newton; Myles; Grimshaw; Arminian*, 1795.
5		The Haworth church used by the Brontës was built by Grimshaw in 1755. All except the tower was rebuilt in 1880.
6	6	*Bunting; Harrison B*, 20–1.
7		*Harrison B*, 17–18; *Harrison C*, 1–27; *Wesley E*, III; *Wesley A*, III–VII; *Wesley B*, III; *Methodist B*.
8		*Gaskell B* 11–35; *Cottage* 244; *S.H.I.* 37–8, 58; *Haworth; Moore Smith*.
9		*Cottage* 244; *S.H.I.* 59.
10		Ibid.
11		Ibid.
12		*Gaskell B* 50.
13	7	Letter of 25 August 1850 from Mrs. Gaskell to Catherine Winkworth; *S.H.III.* 143; *Gaskell B* 50; *Haldane, E. S.*
14		*Moore Smith; S.H.I.* 38.
15		Letter of 21 April 1823 from Patrick Brontë to Mrs. Burder, 'Sphere', 23 August 1913; *CKS C.* 34–5; *S.H.I.* 60–2.
16	8	Letter of 28 July 1823 from Patrick Brontë to Miss Burder, 'Sphere', 23 August 1913; *CKS C.* 35–8; *S.H.I.* 62–4.
17	9	Letter of 8 August 1823 from Mary D. Burder to Patrick Brontë, 'Sphere', 30 August 1913; *CKS C.* 38–40; *S.H.I.* 64–6.
18		'Sphere', 30 August 1913; *CKS C.* 40–3; *S.H.I.* 66–8.
19		*Gaskell B* 50.
20	10	Ibid.; *Shorter* I; *Wesley D, E, F, G; Methodist B*.
21		*Gaskell B* 58–9.
22		*Cottage* 244; *S.H.I.* 59.
23	11	*Gaskell A* I. 34–60; *Gaskell B* 36–59; *Examiner; Reid A* 19–23; *CKS C.* 16–17, 27–55; *Mackay A* 16–19; *S.H.I.* 46–52.
24		*Nussey; S.H.I.* 111–12.
25		Extracts from the School Register were printed in the 'Journal of Education', January 1900; *S.H.I.* 69, Note.
26	12	1792–1859; see School prospectus in *Robinson* 28–30; *Mackay D; S.H.II.* 150.
27		*Gaskell B* 64, Note; *Harrison C*, 62–70.
28	13	*Gaskell A* I. 62–80; *Gaskell B* 62–79; *Shepheard;* the correspondence between A. B. Nicholls and Carus Wilson in the 'Daily News', 'Leeds Mercury', and 'Halifax Guardian' in 1857; *Shorter* II, appendix; *S.H.I.* 70–3, IV. 297–314; *Cowan Bridge; Chadwick A* 78.
29		In much of their poetry, both Branwell and Emily were to show themselves preoccupied with the solitary child and—in Branwell particularly—its death.
30		*Gaskell B* 81.
31	14	*Harrison B*.
32	15	See *Tabitha Aykroyd*, by Mrs. C. Mabel Edgerley; *BST* Part LI, 1941.

NOTES

CHAPTER III

Note *Page*

1 17 It is possible, as suggested in *Ratchford A* 11, that the section on Africa in Anne's Goldsmith's *Grammar of General Geography,* 1832, Brontë Museum, may have stimulated the children's interest in this part of the world. And this interest was doubtless increased a few years later, when MacGregor Laird led the first expedition up the Niger.

2 Gaskell B 87; *The History of the Year,* 12 March 1829, by Charlotte; Introduction to the *History of the Young Men,* 15 December 1830, by Branwell; also Chapter 2 of the *History; Misc.* I, 2, 63, 66.

3 Parry and Ross were Arctic explorers whose exploits were at this time much in the public eye.

4 And inspired, of course, by their readings of *The Arabian Nights.*

5 Chapters 3 and 4 of the *History of the Young Men,* by Branwell; also *A Romantic Tale,* by Charlotte; *Misc.* I, 6, 75-6, 78-9; see also *The Twelve Adventurers,* by Charlotte.

6 18 *Misc.* I, 2; 'Cosmopolitan Magazine' October 1911.

7 Gaskell B 86-7; *The History of the Year,* by Charlotte; *Misc.* I, 1-2; *Cautley.*

8 On 7 May 1831.

9 The *History of the Young Men; Misc.* I, 63-95.

10 'The Origin of the O'Deays is as Follows', Bonnell Collection.

11 'Nash's Magazine', December 1911; *Misc.* II, 467.

12 19 Gaskell B 84-5; *Misc.* II, 467.

13 20 Gaskell B 88-9; *Misc.* II, 468.

14 Chapter 6 of the *History of the Young Men;* Charlotte's *Character and Description of the Duke of Wellington; Misc.* I, 37-8, 90-5.

15 Amy Lowell Collection, Harvard University Library.

16 Gaskell B 102.

17 21 Amy Lowell Collection, Harvard University Library; *Ratchford A* 19.

18 A great deal has been written, from Mrs. Gaskell onwards, about the Brontë Juvenilia. Much of it has now been printed; and the remainder of what is known to exist has been described in detail in *Ratchford A* and *B.* Angrian extracts were printed by Mrs. Gaskell and succeeding biographers. Some were then published separately—see Bibliography. In *Misc.* and *PCB* a considerable amount of Angrian writings has now been printed. A list of Brontë manuscript books was printed in *CKS B* 68-73; *Wise A and B; Wood A and B; Ratchford* A. For the strong Methodist influence on the juvenile writings, see *Harrison C,* 12-17.

19 22 See list of Gondal countries in Goldsmith's *Grammar of General Geography;* Sinclair, 199, 201, 209; *Ratchford A and B; Hinkley.*

20 Most writers on the Brontës have, of recent years, attempted a

reconstruction of the Gondal Story—May Sinclair, Madeleine Hope Dodd's *Gondaliand*, *Ratchford A* and *B* and now Laura Hinkley—but all contain serious points of difference, and suggest that more must be known before the story can be adequately told.

The only available references to the Gondal saga are to be found in the poems of Emily and Anne, and in their birthday notes. None of the prose narratives has come to light, and much of the saga is therefore conjectural. Of the attempts to knit the story together, with Emily's poems providing the main source, the outline printed as an appendix to *Hinkley* is perhaps the most comprehensive; and to this, the present brief sketch (to help the reader to make his own deductions) is most indebted.

The action takes place in two islands: Gondal, in the North Pacific, an island with physical characteristics strongly resembling those of Yorkshire; and Gaaldine, a tropical island in the South Pacific. The main characters are: Julius Brenzaida, Alfred Sidonia, Alexander of Elbë, Rosina, and Augusta Geraldine Almeda.

Julius is King or Prince of Angora, in the northern part of Gondal. He loves Princess Rosina of Alcona in southern Gondal, but in company with other Gondal Kings, he invades, conquers, and partitions Gaaldine, and there marries Geraldine Sidonia of Zedora, assuming the Crown of Almedore.

A child, Augusta Geraldine Almeda, is born when Julius has returned to Gondal. Geraldine attempts to follow him with the child, but is drowned during the voyage. The child escapes, reaches Gondal, and is acknowledged by Julius as his heir.

Julius marries his first love, Rosina, and so unites all Gondal under his sway except for the state of Exina, whose lord, Gerald, has always been his chief rival, both in Gondal and in Gaaldine.

Some nobles of Exina, instigated by Gerald, assassinate Julius. One, Arthur Gleneden, is caught and thrown into prison. Another, M. Douglas, escapes up Gobelrins Glen.

Augusta, now grown up, marries Alexander of Elbë on the southern shores of Lake Elderno, in Angora. She intrigues against Rosina. Alexander is killed in battle by the side of Lake Elnor, in northern Gondal, and Augusta is imprisoned in the Dungeon Wall of the North College, which, with the Southern College, is at once the Palace of Instruction and the Gaol for political offenders.

When released, Augusta meets Fernando de Samara of Areon Hall in Gaaldine, a noted guitarist. He is imprisoned in Gaaldine, and is abandoned by Augusta. He kills himself. Arthur Gleneden, also released from prison, becomes another victim of Augusta.

Augusta then meets and loves her young uncle, Alfred

Sidonia, from Gaaldine, who has taken possession of Aspin Castle in Gondal. She marries him, and, on the death of Rosina, becomes Queen. Alfred dies while on a journey to England. The Republicans rise against the Royalists in Gondal. Augusta, hard pressed, retreats with her forces to Angora, and visits the grave of Alexander, where she is assassinated by Douglas, who is also killed. The Captain of her Guard, Lord Eldred W., discovers her body, and mourns her loss.

21   23   *Gaskell B* 124–5.

22   See *Harrison A* and *B* for an original and most valuable analysis of this influence.

23   *Gaskell B* 124; *Harrison B* and *C*; *O'Byrne*; *Shirley.*

CHAPTER IV

1   24   1792–1885; *S.H.I.* 84, Note 1.

2   25   Letter of 18 January 1856 from Mary Taylor to Mrs. Gaskell; *Gaskell B* 100–1; *S.H.I.* 89. See also *BST* Part LIV, 1944.

3   *Nussey*; *BST* Part X, 1899; *S.H.I.* 92–3.

4   Letter of 18 January 1846 from Mary Taylor to Mrs. Gaskell; *Gaskell B* 101; *S.H.I.* 89.

5   *Nussey; Gaskell B* 102; *S.H.I.* 90.

6   26   *Nussey; Gaskell B* 103; *S.H.I.* 90–1.

7   *Nussey; Gaskell B* 102; *S.H.I.* 90, 93, 95.

8   *Nussey; Gaskell B* 105; *S.H.I.* 94.

9   *Nussey; Gaskell B* 105; *S.H.I.* 92. See Charlotte's list, c. 1828–9, of the paintings she wished to see—including work by Titian, Raphael, Michael Angelo, Correggio, Leonardo da Vinci, Fra Bartolommeo, Vandyke, Rubens, Guido Reni, and Giulio Romano. *Gaskell B* 87.

10   27   *Gaskell B* 104–5; *Nussey*; *S.H.I.* 91, 97; III, 34.

11   *Gaskell B* 105; *S.H.I.* 91; *Shorter* I, 428–9.

12   *Nussey; Gaskell B* 106; *S.H.I.* 96.

13   *Nussey; Gaskell B* 108–18; *S.H.I.* 99.

14   *Nussey; Gaskell B* 108–18; *S.H.I.* 99. So vivid were Mr. Brontë's reminiscences, and so real his fear that further trouble was still to come that, when curate of Thornton, he alarmed Mr. Firth so much that he barred up the windows of his house. *Moore Smith; S.H.I.* 45.

15   28   *Nussey; Wroot B; BST* Part III; *Harrison B.*

16   One of the first times she made use of this material was in *The Twelve Adventurers,* 19–25.

17   Letter of 17 May 1831 to Branwell; *Gaskell B* 103–4; *S.H.I.* 87–8.

CHAPTER V

1   30   Letter of 21 July 1832; *Gaskell B* 120; *S.H.I.* 103.

CHAPTER VI

and contemplative men cling always to the discipline that they have cultivated as an enablement of their vision.' *Morgan.*

11   37   Reports of Mr. Brontë's peculiarities—the firing of the pistol, cutting up his wife's dress, sawing off the back of a chair in a fit of temper—are worthy of notice only because they emphasize the strong feelings he passed on to his children. *Nussey; Gaskell A* 1; *Gaskell B* 36–59; *Garrs; Century; Reid A; Dearden.*

12   *Harrison B* 133, 135.

13   38   Ibid.

14   39   *Misc. II,* 8, 12. See also *Corner Dishes*; Harvard U. Library.

15   *Misc.* II, 11–12.

16   40   *Agnes Grey,* Chapter 1.

17   Ibid.; books seen or read by the children, and now in the Brontë Museum, include: *A Grammar of General Geography for the use of Schools and Young Persons* by J. Goldsmith; the *Imitation of Christ; Modern Domestic Medicine* by T. J. Graham; a *Latin Homer; Horace; Historical and Miscellaneous Questions for the use of Young People, with a selection of British and General Geography* by Miss Ridmal Longall, 1813; *English Grammar* by Lindley Murray, 1818; *Sermons or Homilies appointed to be read in Churches in the time of Queen Elizabeth of famous memory* by W. Morgan, 1802; *Tales of a Grandfather and the Lay of the Last Minstrel* by Walter Scott; *History of British Birds* by T. Bewick, 1797; *The Doctrine of the Passions Explained and Improved; or, A Brief and Comprehensive Scheme of the Natural Affections of Mankind* by I. Watts, 1791; *Arithmetic in Whole and Broken Numbers, Digested After a New Method, and Chiefly Adapted to the Trade of Ireland* by Elias Voster, 1789.

18   Letter of 4 July 1834; *Gaskell B* 131; *S.H.I.* 122.

19   41   *Gaskell B* 86; *Misc.* I, 1.

20   *Gaskell B* 136; *S.H.I.* 128, 130.

21   *Gaskell B* 137; *S.H.I.* 129.

CHAPTER VII

1   42   *Gaskell B* 140; *S.H.I.* 136.

2   Charlotte's Memoir of Emily in the 1850 edition of *Wuthering Heights* and *Agnes Grey; PEA XXII.*

3   *Leyland A* I, 120.

4   43   Ibid. I, 117; *Searle; Chadwick A* 192.

5   *Leyland A* I, 144–5.

6   *Ratchford A* 114–15.

7   44   Letter of 7 December 1835; *Oliphant A.; S.H.I.* 133–4.

8   Letter of 8 April 1836; *Oliphant A.; S.H.I.* 135.

9   45   See, for instance, Charlotte's letter to Ellen in 1836; *Gaskell B* 144; *S.H.I.* 140.

Note	Page	
10	45	*Gaskell B* 153–5; *S.H.I.* 91. See also letter of 15 April 1839 from Charlotte to Ellen; *Gaskell B* 171; *S.H.I.* 176. See also *Methodist A* and *C*; *Wesley A* VI.
11		*Gaskell B* 140–1; *S.H.I.* 136.
12		*Gaskell B* 140–2; *S.H.I.* 136–7.
13	46	Diary Fragments, Bonnell Collection. 4 February 1836; *Misc.* II, 123. See also *PCB* 186, Note.
14	47	Diary Fragments, Bonnell Collection.
15	48	Diary Fragments, Bonnell Collection. 11 August to 14 October 1836; *Misc.* II, 255–6.
16		Diary Fragments, Bonnell Collection. *Misc.* II, 256–7.
17		Diary Fragments, Bonnell Collection.
18	49	Ibid.
19		Letter of 10 May 1836; *Gaskell B* 142–3; *S.H.I.* 139
20		Ibid.; *Shorter* I, 120.
21	50	Letter of 1836; *Gaskell B* 145; *S.H.I.* 141.
22		Ibid.; *Shorter* I, 122.
23		Letter of 1836; *Gaskell B* 143–4; *S.H.I.* 140.
24		Ibid.
25	51	Letter of 26 September 1836; *Gaskell B* 146 (part); *Shorter* I, 123; *S.H.I.* 146.
26		Ibid.
27		*Nussey*; *Gaskell B* 148–9 (part).
28	52	Letter of 1836; *Shorter* I, 142; *S.H.I.* 142–3.
29		Ibid.
30		*Gaskell B* 141–2; *S.H.I.* 137; *Harrison A* and *B*.
31		Ibid. See also Branwell's *Still and bright, in twilight shining*, 13 August 1836; *Gaskell A* I, 136 (part); *PCB* 291–300.
32	53	Letter of 6 December 1836; *Shorter* I, 141; *S.H.I.* 147–8.
33		Ibid. See Anne's poem to Cowper: *PEA* 216. Cf. *Chadwick A*.
34		Ibid.; *Shorter* I, 141; *S.H.I.* 147.

CHAPTER VIII

1	54	*Dowden.*
2		Ibid.
3	55	Letter of March 1837, *Southey* IV, 327; *Gaskell B* 155–7; *S.H.I.* 154–6.
4		*S.H.I.* 156.
5	57	Letter of 16 March 1837; *Gaskell B* 157–9 (part); *Shorter* I, 129–30; *S.H.I.* 157–8.
6		Letter of 22 March 1837; *Southey* IV; *Gaskell B* 159; *S.H.I.* 158–9.
7		*Dowden.*
8	58	Letter of 19 January 1837; *Gaskell B* 150–1; *S.H.I.* 151–2.
9		*Dowden.*
10	59	*Searle.*

CHAPTER IX

his wife a few months later. See Note in *Shorter* I, 150. This Note also deals with the resemblance between Nussey and St. John Rivers of *Jane Eyre*, and suggests the greater likelihood of the character emerging from Charlotte's reading of the life of Henry Martyn, the missionary. See also *Wroot A*, also Charlotte's reference to Henry Nussey as a missionary in her letter of November 1843 to Ellen, *Shorter* I, 273. And see letter of 4 February 1804 from Henry Martyn to W. Wilberforce; *S.H.I.* 2–3.

8	68	*Agnes Grey*, Chapter 1.
9	69	Letter of 15 April 1839; *Gaskell B* 170–1 (part); *Shorter* I, 155; *S.H.I.* 175; *Agnes Grey*.
10		*Wroot A* and *D*; *BST* Part III.
11		Letter of 8 June 1839; *Shorter* I, 158; *S.H.I.* 178.
12		Ibid.; *Gaskell B* 173; see also *Gaskell B* 171–2.
13		Ibid.; *Gaskell B* 174 (part); *Shorter* I, 159; *S.H.I.* 179.
14	70	Letter of 30 June 1839; *Gaskell B* 174–5 (part); *Shorter* I, 160–1; *S.H.I.* 180–1.
15		*ACB.*
16	71	*Wroot A* and *D.*
17	72	17 May 1839; *PEA* 87–8; *Hatfield* 36; *CWEB* 252. (No MS.)
18		Ellen Nussey footnote in *Turner*; *S.H.I.* 188.
19		The two girls spent a month at the farm of John Hudson at Easton, near Bridlington, and a week in lodgings at Bridlington. See *Wroot A* and *D*; *Lee B*; *BST* Part IV. See also *S.H.I.* 290–1.
20		Ellen Nussey footnote in *Turner*; *S.H.I.* 189.
21		Letter of 24 October 1839; *Gaskell B* 181; *S.H.I.* 191. See also Charlotte's letter of 4 August 1839 to Ellen; *Gaskell B* 178; *S.H.I.* 183.
22	73	October 1839, *PEA* 102; *Hatfield* 132; Berg Collection.
23		Letter of 10 January 1839 to the Rev. J. C. Franks; *S.H.I.* 168–9.
24		William Hodgson, 1837–8.
25		Letter of 4 August 1839; *Gaskell B* 179; *S.H.I.* 184.
26		Ibid.
27	74	Ibid.
28	75	1839, *Misc.* II, 403-4; Diary Fragment, Bonnell Collection.
29		They had also written smaller pieces before 1829.
30		At least, by W.T. and U.T.—We Two and Us Two, the combined signature of Charlotte and Branwell in the *Young Men's Magazine* and in other poems. See Note 7, Chapter 5.
31		The influence of one upon the other has been analysed fully in *Ratchford A*; although to some extent this can be no more than speculation.
32		For examples of this kind of tale, see *Miss Percy and Miss Thornton —in Yorkshire*, Bonnell Collection; and *Mr. Ashworth*, Widener Collection.

Note	Page	
33	75	Ibid.
34	76	Draft of letter of 1840 from Charlotte in reply to a letter from Wordsworth; *Gaskell B* 188–90; *S.H.I.* 211–12. See also Preface to *The Professor.*
35	77	Letter of 21 December 1839; *Gaskell B* 182, 315; *S.H.I.* 193–4.
36		Ibid. See also *Shorter* I, 416–18, 443.
37		Letter of 20 August 1840; *Gaskell B* 195 (part); *Leyland A* I, 270. *Shorter* I, 191; *S.H.I.* 215.
38		Although Charlotte later denied—but surely through a fault of memory—that she had read Balzac at this time. See letters of 17 October 1850 and 7 February 1853 to G. H. Lewes and George Smith; *S.H.III.* 172, 174.
39	78	*Robinson* 141, 285. Letter of 21 December 1839 from Charlotte to Ellen; *Gaskell B* 182.
40		*Nussey; Robinson* 51, 70 .
41		28 November 1839, *PEA* 104; *Hatfield* 135; Bonnell Collection.
42	79	Letters of 15 April 1839 and 24 January 1840 from Charlotte to Ellen; *Gaskell B* 188 (part); *Shorter* I, 155, 174; *S.H.I.* 175, 196; *Robinson* 156.
43		*Agnes Grey.*
44		Letter of 24 January 1840; *Gaskell B* 188; *S.H.I.* 196.
45		*Leyland A* I, 239–40; *Grundy A* 76.
46		*Leyland A* I, 176–7, 203–4.
47		*Leyland A* I. See, for example, *Caroline* poems, *PCB* 317–28. *Harrison C*, Chapters VIII and XI.
48	80	Letter of 28 December 1839 to Ellen; *Leyland A* I, 247–8; *S.H.I.* 194–5.
49		Letter of 20 April 1840 to Coleridge; *Shorter* I, 181–2; *S.H.I.* 204–5.
50		Letter of 27 June 1840; *Shorter* I, 182–3; *S.H.I.* 210–11.
51		See *Drinkwater; Misc.* II, 423–32.
52		Letter of 13 March 1840; *Leyland A* I, 255–9. Branwell had become a Freemason on 1 February 1836, and later became organist of the local Lodge; *Leyland A* I, 172–3.
53		*Leyland A* I, 264.
54	81	Ibid.

CHAPTER X

1	82	Weightman sent Ellen a brace of ducks and wrote a number of notes to her. See letters of 17 March, June, 14 July, and 20 August 1840 and 10 January 1842 from Charlotte to Ellen; *Gaskell B* 194; *Shorter* I, 185, 190; *S.H.I.* 201–2, 209, 212–14, 249.
2		It was whilst guarding Ellen from the attentions of Weightman during a walk that Emily first received the name of 'The Major'. Ellen Nussey footnote in *Turner; Robinson* 72; *S.H.II.* 274.

3   82   Letter of Ellen Nussey to Clement K. Shorter, *CKS B* 178–80; *S.H.*II. 274.

4   83   Ibid.

5   18 May 1840; *PEA* 112–13; *Hatfield* 144–5. Number 11 in Personal Poem Notebook (Law Collection). In the first line of the last stanza the word 'thee' has been added. It might be well, in this place, to set out the present writer's views on the Gondal and Angrian poems and stories, and on the widespread impression, with special reference to Emily, that because a poem is a Gondal poem it of necessity can have no bearing on Emily's own thoughts and feelings. This judgement betrays, in my view, a singular lack of imagination. It is necessary only to look at one's own work to see that even the most obviously objective writings carry within them the seed (the character, problems, views, hopes, feelings) of the one who wrote them. How much more so, the work of the four Brontës, which is subjective to an uncommon degree. Not a line did they write that cannot be referred directly to their own lives. The shell of Gondal and Angrian heroes and heroines, deeds and doings, is so thin that it cannot bear the weight of analysis. The distinction often drawn between Gondal and Angrian works and Brontë poems admittedly personal is, in my view, much too definite. The Brontës did what all young people of sensibility do—and not only young people; they projected themselves into characters who, in appearance, circumstance and action, were as far removed from their own lives as possible, but who, in thought and feeling, were the very imaginative spit of themselves. The slightest incident that broke the monotony of Haworth life, the reading of a new book, the arrival of a visitor, the sickness of a servant or animal, was enough to set their imaginations racing. So, in the present instance, Weightman could be and was made to fit, without difficulty, a dozen different roles to which Emily or Charlotte or Anne would react, in their Gondal or Angrian characters, exactly as they themselves would react in like circumstance. The classic example of this kind of criticism is perhaps Emily's poem 'How few of all the hearts that loved'. This was published by Charlotte in 1850, with the title *The Wanderer From the Fold*, and a sub-title, *On a Life Perverted*, and was afterwards generally taken to be Emily's lament for the death of Branwell, and a confession of her feeling for him. Many years later the poem was found to be a Gondal poem, written some four years before Branwell's death. The discovery caused a general reversal of views. The poem did not, after all, refer to Branwell, it appeared, as he was not really dead—and so the question of Emily's attitude to her brother must be revised. But this, I suggest, merely shows a lack of imagination in

making inadequate allowance for the imagination of Emily. The fact whether a person was or was not cold in the earth did not worry her so much as it has since worried some of her more literal-minded critics. See, for instance, *T.L.S.* 461, 1934.

6   83   Ellen Nussey footnote in *Turner; S.H.I.* 201, Note.

7   Ibid.; Charlotte's answering poem was written in the name of all. Weightman also sent Valentines to the girls the following year—see letter of 3 March 1841 from Charlotte to Ellen; *Shorter* I, 204; *S.H.I.* 227. The Valentine sent by Charlotte to Weightman in February 1840 is reprinted in *Shorter* I, 204–5 from the *Whitehaven News*, although Weightman's name is not mentioned; *A Roland for Your Oliver; PCB* 227–9.

8   Ellen Nussey footnote in *Turner; Gaskell B* 192.

9   Letter of June 1840, about the middle of the month, from Charlotte to Ellen; *S.H.I.* 209.

10   84   See Charlotte's letters to Ellen foll.; also letter of 21 March 1841; *Shorter* I, 206; *S.H.I.* 228.

11   Letter of Ellen Nussey to Clement K. Shorter; *CKS B.*

12   Letter of 17 March 1840; *Shorter* I, 175; *S.H.I.* 200–1.

13   85   Letter of June 1840; *S.H.I.* 209–10.

14   Letter of 7 April 1840; *Gaskell B* 192 (part); *Shorter* I, 178; *S.H.I.* 203.

15   Letter of 14 July 1840; *Shorter* I, 189; *S.H.I.* 213.

16   The youngest sister of Mrs. Brontë. She married her cousin, Joseph Branwell, on the day Maria married Patrick Brontë.

17   86   Baptist Wriothesley Noel, 1798–1873. See letter of 20 January 1842 from Charlotte to Ellen; *S.H.I.* 249.

18   Letter of 13 August 1840; *Shorter* I, 190; *S.H.I.* 214.

19   Letter of 29 September 1840; *Gaskell B* 197 (part); *Shorter* I, 192–3; *S.H.I.* 216–17.

20   87   Ibid.; *Gaskell B* 298 (part); *Shorter* I, 193; *S.H.I.* 217–18.

21   Letter of 14 July 1844 from Charlotte to M. Héger; *Times; S.H.II.* 9–13. See also *BST* Part L, 1940.

22   Letter of 20 August 1840 from Charlotte to Ellen; *Gaskell B* 195; *Leyland A* I, 270; *S.H.I.* 215.

CHAPTER XI

1   88   Letter of 24 January 1840 from Charlotte to Ellen; *Gaskell B* 188.

2   *Leyland A* I, 202.

3   Ibid. I, 264. Just before the line from Hebden Bridge to Normanton was opened.

4   Letter of 29 September 1840; *Gaskell B* 196 (part); *Shorter* I, 192; *S.H.I.* 216.

5   89   *Leyland A* I, 264.

6   See description by William Heaton in *Leyland A* I, 269.

Note	Page	
7	89	The contents of this note-book have been printed in *BST* Part XXXVII. Cf. *Harrison C* 215.
8		*Leyland A* I, 264. Grundy's father was the Rev. John Grundy, Unitarian Minister and colleague of the Rev. James Martineau, brother of Harriet Martineau.
9		The birthplace of Bishop Farrer.
10		*Grundy A; Harrison B* 23–30; *A* 120; *C* Chapter XIII; *Wesley* A V. Branwell visited Hebden Bridge and Hepstonstall, where there is a ruined church of Thomas-à-Becket; The Bridge, Todmorton; Wadsworth (dell of Crimsworth—name used by Charlotte in *The Professor*); the Jacobean Kershaw House; Haugh End, birthplace of Archbishop Tillotson; and Erringden, a Plantagenet Royal Deer Park—all within reach of Luddenden; *Leyland A* I, 285. See also *Wesley C* and *D*.
11		Ibid. *Myles; Grimshaw*.
12		Now Sowden's Farm.
13		*Harrison A, B* and *C; Newton; Myles; Hardy; Grimshaw; Laycock*.
14	90	To which he used to drive in a gig hired for the occasion. *Leyland A* I, 285.
15		*Grundy A* 84.
16		Ibid.; *Leyland A* I, 309.
17		*Harrison B* 32–3.
18		*Grundy A* 84; *Leyland A* I, 309. See, for instance, Branwell's poems, *Oh Thou, whose beams were most withdrawn*, 8 August 1841, and *The Triumph of Mind over Body; PCB* 372–81.
19		*Leyland A* I, 269.
20		*Harrison B* 23–30.
21	91	11 September 1840; *PEA* 113–14; *Hatfield* 146–7. Number 7 in Personal Poem Notebook (Law Collection).
22	92	1 March 1841; *Poems* by Currer, Ellis, and Acton Bell, 1846; *PEA* 30; *Hatfield* 163, Number 8 in Personal Poem Notebook (Law Collection). Emily gave this poem the title of *The Old Stoic*.
23		Letter of 3 March 1841 from Charlotte to Ellen; *Gaskell B* 203; *S.H.I.* 226.
24		Ibid.
25	93	Letter of 1 April 1841; *Shorter* I, 207; *S.H.I.* 228.
26		Letter of 21 March 1841 to Ellen; *Gaskell B* 204; *S.H.I.* 227.
27		Letter of 4 May 1841; *Shorter* I, 209; *S.H.I.* 230–1.
28		Letter of 3 March 1841; *Gaskell B* 204; *S.H.I.* 226. See also letter of Mrs. Strickland in the 'Westminster Gazette', May 1901; *S.H.I.* 225.
29	94	Letter of 4 May 1841 to Ellen; *Gaskell B* 201 (part); *S.H.I.* 231.
30		Letter of 21 March 1841; *Gaskell B* 204 (part); *S.H.I.* 227–8.
31		Letters of 10 June and 1 July 1841 to Ellen; *Shorter* I, 212–13; *S.H.I.* 234.
32		Letter of 10 June 1841; *Gaskell B* 205; *S.H.I.* 234.

CHAPTER XII

CHAPTER XIII

Note	Page	
8	114	*Robinson* 89.
9		Laetitia Wheelwright quoted in *Shorter* I, 232-3.
10	115	Ibid.; *Shorter* I, 232, 258.
11		Letter of 26 March 1842 from Charlotte to Ellen; *Shorter* I, 235-6; *S.H.I.* 258; *Gaskell B* 239.
12		Letter of May 1842; *Gaskell B* 230; *S.H.I.* 261.
13	116	Ibid.; *Gaskell B* 229; *S.H.I.* 260.
14	117	Ibid.; *Gaskell B* 229-30; *S.H.I.* 260-1.
15		Ibid.; *Gaskell B* 230; *S.H.I.* 261.
16	118	Ibid.; *Gaskell B* 228-9; *S.H.I.* 260.
17		*Gaskell B* 228.
18	119	Ibid.
19		Letter of May 1842 from Charlotte to Ellen; *Gaskell B* 230; *S.H.I.* 261.
20		*Gaskell B* 227-8.
21		Ibid. 227; see also Note 19 above.
22	120	Letter of July 1842 from Charlotte to Ellen; *Gaskell B* 238; *S.H.I.* 267.
23		Ibid.
24		Ibid.; *S.H.I.* 266-7.
25		Letter of 1 April 1843 from Charlotte to Ellen; *Gaskell B* 256; *S.H.I.* 295-6.
26		Letter of July 1842 from Charlotte to Ellen; *Gaskell B* 238; *S.H.I.* 267.
27	121	*Gaskell B* 242.
28		Weightman died on 6 September. Letters of 25 October 1842 from Branwell to F. H. Grundy; *Grundy A; S.H.I.* 272. See also *Gaskell B* 245.
29		Probably appendicitis.
30		Letter of 10 November 1842 from Charlotte to Ellen; *Gaskell B* 245; *S.H.I.* 282.
31		Ibid.
32		Letter of 30 October, 1 November 1842 from Mary Taylor to Ellen; *Shorter* I, 243-4; *S.H.I.* 274-5. See also references to Martha (Jessie Yorke) in *Shirley*; and to Charlotte's visit to the Brussels cemetery in *Villette*.
33	122	Letter of 10 November 1842 from Charlotte to Ellen; *Gaskell B* 245 (part); *Shorter* I, 246; *S.H.I.* 282. Also letter of 25 October 1842 from Branwell to F. H. Grundy; *Grundy A; S.H.I.* 273.

CHAPTER XIV

1	123	*Leyland A* I, 290-305.
2		See Anne's Birthday Note of 30 July 1841; *Gaskell B* 209.
3		*Harrison A.* See Note 18, Chapter XI.

Note	Page	
4	124	Letter of 22 May 1842 from Branwell to F. H. Grundy; *Grundy A* 84; *Leyland A* I, 309; *S.H.I.* 263–4.
5		*PCB* 390–2. See also *Gaskell B* 299–300.
6		Letter of 9 June 1842 from Branwell to F. H. Grundy; *Grundy A* 84; *Leyland A* I, 309; *Shorter* I, 242; *S.H.I.* 265.
7		Ibid.
8	125	Letter of 25 October 1842; *Grundy A; Shorter* I, 242; *S.H.I.* 272–3.
9		Letter of 29 October 1842; *Grundy A; Shorter* I, 242–3; *S.H.I.* 273.
10	126	Letter of 20 November 1842; *Shorter* I, 251; *S.H.I.* 283. See also *Gaskell B* 410.
11		Letter of 25 November 1842 from Charlotte to Ellen; *Shorter* I, 251; *S.H.I.* 283.
12		Ibid.; *S.H.I.* 284.
13		*Nussey; Gaskell B* 250–1.
14		Letter of 10 January 1843 from Charlotte to Ellen; *Shorter* I, 253; *S.H.I.* 284.
15		*Leyland A; S.H.I.* 284.
16		Letters of 10 and 15 January 1843; *Shorter* I, 252–3; *S.H.I.* 284–5.
17	127	Letter of 16 February 1843 from Mary Taylor to Ellen; *Shorter* I, 261; *S.H.I.* 292.
18	128	Letter of 5 November 1842; *Gaskell B* 248–50; *S.H.I.* 278–81.
19	129	Letter of July 1842 from Charlotte to Ellen; *Gaskell B* 238; *S.H.I.* 267; *Nussey;* Ellen Nussey's letter to Clement K. Shorter in *CKS B.*
20		Letter of 2 June 1843 from Charlotte to Mr. Brontë; *Gaskell B* 258.
21		Ibid. See also letter of 29 May 1843 from Charlotte to Emily; *Gaskell B* 258; *CKS B; S.H.I.* 299–300.
22		*Reid A;* confirmed by Ellen Nussey and A. B. Nicholls. *S.H.I.* 287.
23		Letter of 14 October 1846 from Charlotte to Ellen; *S.H.II.* 115.
24		Letter of 15 November 1843 from Charlotte to Ellen; *Gaskell B* 268; *S.H.I.* 309.
25		Letter of 1 April 1843 from Charlotte to Ellen; *Gaskell B* 256; *S.H.I.* 295.
26		Letter of 30 January 1843 from Charlotte to Ellen; *S.H.I.* 291.
27	130	Letter of 1 April 1843 from Charlotte to Ellen; *Gaskell B* 256; *S.H.I.* 295–6.

CHAPTER XV

1	131	*Gaskell B* 252–3; *Villette.*
2	132	Laetitia Wheelwright quoted in *Shorter* I, 256–8; letters of 30 January and 6 March 1843 from Charlotte to Ellen; *Gaskell B* 254; *Shorter* I, 260, 263; *S.H.I.* 291–4.
3		Letter of 6 August 1843 to Ellen; *Shorter* I, 269; *S.H.I.* 302.

Note	Page	
4	132	Letter of 18 February 1843; *Shorter* I, 262; *S.H.I.* 293.
5		Letter of 6 March 1843; *Gaskell B* 253; *S.H.I.* 293.
6		Ibid.; *Gaskell B* 254; *S.H.I.* 294.
7	133	Letter of 1 May 1843; *Shorter* I, 266; *S.H.I.* 297.
8		Letter of 29 May 1843; *Gaskell B* 257; *CKS B; S.H.I.* 298–9.
9		Letter of 1 May 1843 from Charlotte to Branwell; *Shorter* I, 267; *S.H.I.* 297.
10		Letter of 1 April 1843; *Gaskell B* 257; *S.H.I.* 295.
11	134	Letter of 1 May 1843; *Shorter* I, 267; *S.H.I.* 297.
12		Letters of 6 March and 15 November 1843 from Charlotte to Ellen; *Gaskell B* 254; *Shorter* I, 263, 273; *S.H.I.* 294, 308.
13		Letter of 13 October 1843 from Charlotte to Ellen; *Gaskell B* 267; *S.H.I.* 306.
14		Letter of 1 April 1843 from Charlotte to Ellen; *Gaskell B* 257; *S.H.I.* 296.
15		Letter of 6 March 1843 to Ellen; *Gaskell B* 254; *S.H.I.* 294.
16		Letter of 1 May 1843 to Branwell; *Shorter* I, 266–7; *S.H.I.* 297.
17		Ibid.; *Shorter* I, 267; *S.H.I.* 298. See Charlotte's list of the books given to her by Héger; Note 48, Chapter XVI.
18	135	*PCB* 231–5.
19		Letter of 29 May 1843 to Emily; *Gaskell B* 258; *CKS B; S.H.I.* 299.
20		Letter of 13 October 1848 to Ellen; *Shorter* I, 272; *S.H.I.* 306.
21	136	Letter of 29 May 1843; *Gaskell B* 258; *CKS B; S.H.I.* 299.
22		Letter of 1 May 1843 to Branwell; *Shorter* I, 266; *S.H.I.* 297–8.
23		Letters of 6 March and 29 May 1843 from Charlotte to Emily; *Gaskell B* 253, 257; *S.H.I.* 293, 299.
24		Letter of 6 March 1843 from Charlotte to Ellen; *Gaskell B* 253–4; *S.H.I.* 293.
25	137	*Villette; The Professor.*
26		Ibid.; *Gaskell B* 264; letter of 1 May 1843 from Charlotte to Branwell; *Shorter* I, 267; *S.H.I.* 297.
27		Letters of 1 April and 15 November from Charlotte to Ellen; *Gaskell B* 256, 267–8; *S.H.I.* 295, 309.
28		*Villette; The Professor;* letter of 6 August 1843 from Charlotte to Ellen; *Gaskell B* 263–4; *S.H.I.* 301–2.
29		Ibid.
30		Ibid.; also letter of 15 November 1843 from Charlotte to Ellen; *Gaskell B* 268; *S.H.I.* 308.
31		Letter of 2 September 1843 from Charlotte to Emily; *Gaskell B* 265–6; *S.H.I.* 303.
32	138	*Villette; The Professor; Gaskell B* 264; letter of *c.* Oct.–Nov. 1846 from Charlotte to Miss Wooler; *S.H.II.* 116–17.
33		Letters of 1 May, 6 August, 2 September, 13 October, and 15 November 1843 from Charlotte to Branwell, Emily, and Ellen; *Gaskell B* 263–4, 265, 267, 268; *Shorter* I, 267; *S.H.I.* 297, 301–2, 303, 306–9.

Note Page

34 139 Letter of 2 September 1843; *Gaskell B* 265-6; *S.H.I.* 303-4. Also
         see *Villette*.
35   Ibid.; *Gaskell B* 266; *S.H.I.* 304.
36   *Villette*.
37   Letter of 2 September 1843; *Gaskell B* 266; *S.H.I.* 304.
38 140 Ibid.; *Gaskell B* 265; *S.H.I.* 303.
39   Letter of 1 October 1843; *S.H.I.* 304-5.
40   Ibid.
41 141 Ibid.
42   Letter of 13 October 1843 from Charlotte to Ellen; *Gaskell B*
         267; *S.H.I.* 306.
43   Ibid.; *S.H.I.* 306-7.
44   In *Russell's General Atlas of Modern Geography*, Brontë Museum;
         S.H.I. 307.
45   Ibid.; 'We have as yet no fires here and suffer much from cold,'
         writes Charlotte to Ellen in her letter of 13 October 1843;
         Gaskell B 267; *S.H.I.* 307.
46   Ibid.; *Gaskell B* 267; *S.H.I.* 306. But see letter from Mary Taylor
         to Mrs. Gaskell in *Shorter*.
47 142 Letter of 15 November 1843; *Gaskell B* 268; *S.H.I.* 309.
48   Ibid.
49   Letter of 5 November 1842 from Monsieur Héger to Mr.
         Brontë; *Gaskell B* 248-50; *S.H.I.* 278-81.
50   Letter of 19 December 1843 from Charlotte to Emily; *Shorter* I,
         274; *S.H.I.* 309-10.

CHAPTER XVI

1   143 *Gaskell B* 216.
2   Letter of 1 May 1843 from Charlotte to Branwell; *Shorter* I, 266;
         S.H.I. 296. See also Letters of 23 January and 25 March 1844
         from Charlotte to Ellen; *Shorter* I, 277; *S.H.II.* 3, 5.
3   *S.H.II.* 7, Note 1.
4   Letter of 23 January 1844; *Shorter* I, 277; *S.H.II.* 3.
5   Ibid.; *Shorter* I, 276-7.
6   144 Ibid.; *Shorter* I, 277.
7   Ibid.
8   Ibid.; *Shorter* I, 276-7.
9   Letter of 24 July 1844 from Charlotte to M. Héger; *Times;*
         S.H.II. 10, 12. The post was worth £100 per annum.
10 145 Letter of 7 April 1844 from Charlotte to Ellen; *Gaskell B* 277;
         S.H.II. 5.
11   Letter of 25 March 1844; *Gaskell B* 273; *S.H.II.* 5.
12   Ibid.
13   *Gaskell B* 274; *Cautley; Robinson* 65, 107, 142; *Wilson* 122.
14 146 *Gaskell B* 275-6.

Note	Page	
15	146	*Shirley; Gaskell B* 274.
16		Ibid.
17		*Gaskell B* 276.
18		*Shirley; Gaskell B* 274; letter of Ellen Nussey to Clement K. Shorter; *CKS B* 178–80; *S.H.II.* 274.
19		*Robinson* 45.
20		Ibid. 49.
21		Letter of 1 October 1843; *Gaskell B* 270; *S.H.I.* 305.
22		Letters of 29 May 1843 to Emily, and 2 June 1843 to Mr. Brontë; *Gaskell B* 257–9. Martha Brown had also gone home for a time, leaving Emily without help. See Emily's Birthday Note of 31 July 1845.
23		*Gaskell B* 139; *Robinson* 106–7; *Chadwick A.*
24	147	*PEA* 169–70; *Hatfield* 35–6. CWEB 282. n.d. MS. missing.
25		*Wuthering Heights.*
26	149	14 April 1845; *Poems by Currer, Ellis, and Acton Bell,* 1846; *PEA* 3–4; *Hatfield* 225–7. Number 28 in Personal Poem Notebook (Law Collection).
27		*PEA* 180; *Hatfield* 255–6. Hatfield suggests that this poem was written by Charlotte. This is purely conjectural, and I am unable to accept it. The poem first appeared in 1850, and the present whereabouts of the manuscript is not known—but as Mr. Hatfield has accepted as genuine other poems (first printed in CWEB) for which there is also no manuscript evidence, his argument seems unconvincing. The only evidence, apart from the missing MS., that Emily may not have written the poem, rests in the appearance in it of one or two words—such as 'vexes'—that Emily rarely used. These words may well have been substituted by Charlotte, who doubtless altered this, as she altered other of Emily's poems, before publication. But there is not a shred of evidence, in the poems admittedly written by Charlotte, that she was capable of writing such a poem as this. And I do not feel that Charlotte was capable, in another sense, of writing this or any other poem and of passing it off publicly as her sister's.
28	150	Introduction to *Gondal.*
29		Letters of 20 and 24 July 1844 from Charlotte to Ellen and M. Héger; *Times; S.H.II.* 8, 10, 12.
30		See Miss Branwell's Will; *Shorter* I, 244–6; *S.H.I.* 277–8.
31		Letter of 20 July 1844 from Charlotte to Ellen; *Shorter* I, 281; *S.H.II.* 8–9; *Gaskell B* 277.
32		The circular is reprinted in *Gaskell B* 279; *S.H.II.* 1.
33	151	Letters of 29 July, 15 August, 2 October 1844 from Charlotte to Ellen; *Gaskell B* 279; *Shorter* I, 282–5; *S.H.II.* 15–17.
34		4 July 1844; *Leyland A* 2.
35		Letter of 13 January 1845 from Charlotte to Ellen; *Shorter* I, 188–9; *S.H.II.* 25.

Note	Page	

36   151   Letter of 24 October 1844, to M. Héger; *Times; S.H.*II. 18–19.

37   Letter of 31 July 1845 from Charlotte to Ellen; *S.H.*II. 43; *Gaskell A* I, Chapter 13.

38   152   3 September 1844; *Poems by Currer, Ellis, and Acton Bell*, 1846; *PEA* 18–19; *Hatfield* 205–7. Number 25 in Personal Poem Notebook (Law Collection).

39   153   14 October 1844; Ibid.; *PEA* 21–2; *Hatfield* 208–9. Number 26 in Personal Poem Notebook (Law Collection).

40   154   See, for example, letters of 23 January 1844, 24 March 1845, and 14 October 1846 from Charlotte to Ellen; *Gaskell B* 273, 283, 318–19; *S.H.*II. 3, 28, 115.

41   Ibid.; also letter of 21 August 1846 from Charlotte to Ellen; *Gaskell B* 310; *S.H.*II. 107.

42   See *The Eyesight of the Brontës* by Mrs. C. Mabel Edgerley, *BST* Part XLI, 1931.

43   156   Laetitia Wheelwright quoted in *Shorter*; letter of 18 November 1845 from Charlotte to M. Héger; *Times; S.H.*II. 67, 69; *Spielmann*.

44   Letter of 24 July 1844; *Times; S.H.*II. 9–13.

45   Ibid.; *S.H.*II. 11, 13–14.

46   Joseph Taylor.

47   157   Mary Taylor.

48   Letter of 24 October 1844; *Times; S.H.*II. 17–19.

49   158   Ibid., *S.H.*II. 18, 19.

50   Letter of October 1845 to F. H. Grundy; *Grundy A* 87; *S.H.*II. 64.

CHAPTER XVII

1   159   Letter of 14 November 1844 from Charlotte to Ellen; *Shorter* I, 286; *S.H.*II. 20.

2   Ibid.; *Shorter* I, 286–7 (but without the 'bitch').

3   160   Letter of 13 January 1845 from Charlotte to Ellen; *Gaskell B* 280; *S.H.*II. 25.

4   Ibid.

5   Letter of 6 January 1845 from Charlotte to Ellen; *Shorter* I, 289; *S.H.*II. 21.

6   Letters of 16 September 1844, 24 March and 2 April 1845 from Charlotte to Ellen; *Gaskell B* 285; *Shorter* I, 284, 291–3; *S.H.*II. 17, 28, 30.

7   Letter of 16 September 1844 from Charlotte to Ellen; *Shorter* I, 284; *S.H.*II. 16.

8   161   Letter of 8 January 1845; *Times; S.H.*II. 21–4.

9   Anne's Birthday Note of 31 July 1845; *S.H.*II. 51. But see Note 16, Chapter XXI.

10   162   Letter of 24 March 1845 from Charlotte to Ellen; *Gaskell B* 283; *S.H.*II. 28.

Note	Page	
11	162	Letter of 20 February 1845 from Charlotte to Ellen; *Gaskell B* 281; *S.H.II.* 25.
12		Letter from Mary Taylor to Mrs. Gaskell; *Gaskell B* 282–3; *S.H.II.* 26.
13		Ibid.
14	163	Letter of September 1848 from Charlotte to W. S. Williams; *S.H.II.* 256.
15	164	*Swinburne B.*

CHAPTER XVIII

1	165	Letter of 23 April 1845; *S.H.II.* 32.
2		Letter of 26 May 1845 to Mrs. Rand; *S.H.II.* 35.
3		Letter of 18 November 1845 from Charlotte to M. Héger; *Times; S.H.II.* 68, 70.
4		Letter of 18 June 1845 from Charlotte to Ellen; *Shorter* I, 301; *S.H.II.* 39.
5		Letter of 24 June 1845 from Charlotte to Ellen; *S.H.II.* 41.
6	166	Letter of 18 June 1845 from Charlotte to Ellen; *Shorter* I, 301; *S.H.II.* 39.
7		Charlotte wrote again to Héger on 18 May 1845, but the letter has not been preserved. See her letter of 18 November 1845 to Héger; *Times; S.H.II.* 67, 69.
8		Letter of 1 June 1845 from Charlotte to Ellen; *S.H.II.* 36.
9		Letter of 18 June 1845 from Charlotte to Ellen; *Gaskell B* 287; *S.H.II* 39.
10		Ibid.
11		This was J. W. Smith, then curate of Keighley, but formerly (1842–4) curate of Haworth. He, like Weightman before him, had fallen victim to the charms of Ellen when she visited the parsonage. But, like Weightman, he too showed no sign of following the matter to a conclusion. Hence much correspondence between Charlotte and Ellen; see letters of 16 and 20 July, 15 August, and 16 September 1844 from Charlotte to Ellen; *S.H.II.* 7–9, 16–17. Smith, however, never achieved the popularity of Weightman. Charlotte says in her letter of 20 July 1844 of the 'Rev. Lothario Lovelace Smith . . . I am glad now he did not ask you to marry him—you are far too good for him—Mr. Weightman was worth 200 Mr. Smiths tied in a bunch.' *S.H.II.* 9. Smith was later to be pilloried as the Peter Augustus Malone of *Shirley; Wroot D; BST:* Part XLV.
12		Letter of 18 June 1845 from Charlotte to Ellen; *Gaskell B* 287; *S.H.II.* 39–40.
13	167	Letter of 24 June 1845 from Charlotte to Ellen; *Shorter* I, 302; *S.H.II.* 40.
14		Emily's Birthday Note for 31 July 1845; *Shorter* I, 304–5; *S.H.II.* 49–50.

CHAPTER XIX

S.H.II. 84. The suggestion has been made in *Wilson* that Emily intended her remark to refer to her brother as 'a being without hope'. Cf. *Robinson* 124–7; *Benson: E. F.* 185–7.

3   182   3 March 1845; *Gondal* 44; *Poems by Currer, Ellis, and Acton Bell,* 1846; *PEA* 6–7; *Hatfield* 222–3. Number 36 in Gondal Poem Notebook.

4   184   2 June 1845; *Poems by Currer, Ellis, and Acton Bell,* 1846; *PEA* 11–12; *Hatfield* 231–3. Number 30 in Personal Poem Notebook (Law Collection). Charlotte wrote on the MS. 'Never was better stuff penned.'

5   186   9 October 1845. Complete but for three verses, in *Gondal* 18–24. Number 43 in Gondal Poem Notebook. Part, entitled *The Prisoner*, in *Poems by Currer, Ellis, and Acton Bell,* 1846. *PEA* 12–15, 178; *Hatfield* 236–42. Another part printed by Charlotte in 1850 under the title of *The Visionary*. Of the second stanza, cf. Charles Wesley's *Traveller Unknown; Harrison A* 133.

6   187   Perhaps most clearly in this comparatively early poem of 6 July 1841; No. 9 in Personal Poem Notebook; *Hatfield* 165:

> *Aye there it is! It wakes to-night*
> *Sweet thoughts that will not die*
> *And feeling's fires flash all as bright*
> *As in the years gone by.*
>
> *And I can tell by thine altered cheek*
> *And by thy kindled gaze*
> *And by the words thou scarce dost speak*
> *How wildly fancy plays.*
>
> *Yes I could swear that glorious wind*
> *Has swept the world aside*
> *Has dashed its memory from thy mind*
> *Like foam-bells from the tide—*
>
> *And thou art now a spirit pouring*
> *Thy presence into all—*
> *The essence of the Tempest's roaring*
> *And of the Tempest's fall—*
>
> *A universal influence*
> *From Thine own influence Free—*
> *A principle of life intense*
> *Lost to mortality.*
>
> *Thus truly when that breast is cold*
> *Thy prisoned soul shall rise*
> *The dungeon mingle with the mould—*
> *The captive with the skies.*

CHAPTER XX

CHAPTER XXI

Note	Page	
14	201	Letter of 18 November 1845; *Times; S.H.*II. 69.
15		His attitude towards Charlotte is seen in the uses to which he put her letters. He had used them as laundry and shopping lists; *Times; Spielmann; Macdonald B.*
16		Laetitia Wheelwright quoted in *Shorter* I, 157. See also obituary notice of M. Héger (died 6 May 1896) in 'The Sketch', 5 June 1896 by M. Colin of 'L'Etoile Belge' revised by Dr. Héger, son of M. Héger.
17	202	Ibid. But see the suggestion in *Dimnet* that Mme. Héger was herself the author of the proposal—this being, in her view, the one certain method of putting an end to the embarrassing correspondence.
18		*Harrison A, B* and *C.*
19		*Shorter* I, 303; *S.H.*II. 52.
20		*Nussey; Gaskell B* 316–17.
21		Letter of 3 March 1846, also letters of 4 November and 31 December 1845; *Shorter* I, 311, 314, 321; *S.H.*II. 66, 75, 84.
22	203	Letter of 12 January 1835; *Shorter* I, 113; *S.H.*I. 126.
23	204	*Searle; Grundy A; Leyland A.*
24		*Gaskell A* I, Chapter 13; II, Chapter 2. There is also some reason to suppose that Mrs. Robinson supplied Branwell with money after he left Thorp Green; letters of January and 12 May 1847, from Branwell to J. B. Leyland and Charlotte to Ellen; *Leyland A* II; *S.H.*II. 121, 132; a suggestion has also been made that Branwell met Mrs. Robinson after leaving Thorp Green; *Leyland A* II, 110–11; *S.H.*IV. 217.
25		*Leyland A* II. Letter of June 1846 from Branwell to J. B. Leyland; *S.H.*II. 95.
26		Letter of October 1845; *Grundy A* 87; *S.H.*II. 64–5.
27		Letter of June or July 1846 to J. B. Leyland; *Leyland A* II.
28	205	*Gaskell A* I, 327–32. It may be said here that Mrs. Gaskell's formal retraction of statements made in these chapters on 26 May 1857, and subsequent alteration of the text, was made under duress, and is therefore not necessarily of any particular significance. Some statements made by Mrs. Gaskell were certainly incorrect, and her study of Mrs. Robinson and Branwell suffers from over emphasis. Nevertheless, in essentials, her account must stand. Nothing has since transpired seriously to falsify the broad picture she draws. See *Cross* I, 441.
29		Letters of 21 November 1847, 28 January, 28 July, and 18 August 1848 from Charlotte to Ellen; *Shorter* I, 370, 392; *S.H.*II. 185, 240, 247. See also *Agnes Grey.*
30	206	Letter of 17 June 1846; *Gaskell B* 305 (part); *Shorter* I, 331–2; *S.H.*II. 96–7. Also *Shorter* I, 392, 447.
31		See the Will of Edmund Robinson, proved on 11 September 1846 in the Prerogative Court of York.
32		The Venerable Charles Thorp and Henry Newton.

Note	Page	
Note	*Page*	
33	206	Letter of June 1846 to J. B. Leyland; *Leyland A* II, 144–5; *S.H.II.* 95–6. Also letter of the same date from Branwell to F. H. Grundy; *Grundy A* 89; *S.H.II.* 98.
34	207	*Leyland A* II, 144–5; *S.H.II.* 97.
35		Letter of June or July 1846; *Leyland A* II; *S.H.II.* 98.
36	208	Ibid.; *S.H.II.* 99.
37		*Leyland A* II.
38	209	Searle; Grundy; Dearden; Leyland; Benson E. F. 168–9.

CHAPTER XXII

1	210	*Poems by Currer, Ellis, and Acton Bell* (London: Aylott & Jones, 8 Paternoster Row, 1846). Charlotte had wanted the poems to be printed in an octavo volume of the same quality of paper and size of type as Moxon's last edition of Wordsworth's *Poems*; but she was asked to name another book as model because the poems took up fewer pages than she had reckoned. Letters of 31 January and 16 February 1846 from Charlotte to Aylott and Jones. The cost of publishing these poems was £36 10s. In addition, the sisters spent £12 in advertisements; letters of 3 March, 11 and 25 May, and 10 July 1846 from Charlotte to Aylott and Jones; *Shorter* I, 319, 326–7; *S.H.II.* 81–3, 93–4, 102.
2		Letter of 16 June 1847 from Charlotte to Thomas De Quincey; *Quincey; Tennyson; Lockhart; Wordsworth; Gaskell B* 308; *S.H.II.* 136.
3		In the 'Athenaeum', July 1846; 'Dublin University Magazine'; October 1846; 'Critic', July 1846; letters of October and 10 November 1847 from Charlotte to W. S. Williams; *Shorter* I, 361, 366; *S.H.II.* 147–8, 154. The 'Critic' spoke of the presence in the poems of 'more genius than it was supposed this utilitarian age had devoted to the loftier exercises of the intellect'. The 'Athenaeum' described Ellis (Emily) as possessing 'a fine quaint spirit . . . and an evident power of wing that may reach heights not here attempted'. Copies of the poems were sent at Charlotte's request to 'Colburn's New Monthly Magazine'; 'Bentley's Magazine'; 'Hood's Magazine'; 'Jerrold's Shilling Magazine'; 'Blackwood's Magazine'; 'The Edinburgh Review'; 'Tait's Edinburgh Magazine'; 'Dublin University Magazine'; 'Daily News'; 'Britannia'; 'Fraser's Magazine'; 'Chambers' Edinburgh Journal'; 'The Globe'; and 'The Examiner': with advertisements in all but the last four; but it seems that the 'Athenaeum', 'The Literary Gazette', 'Critic' and 'The Times' were substituted by the publishers for the first four on her list. Letters of 7 May and 10 July 1846 from Charlotte to Aylott and Jones; *Gaskell B* 303–4, 307; *S.H.II.* 93, 102.

Note	Page	

Note *Page*

4   210   Letters of 6 and 11 April 1846; *Gaskell B* 302–3; *S.H.II.* 87–8. See also letter from Mrs. Martyn, a daughter of Mr. Aylott; *Shorter* I, 320; *S.H.II.* 80–1.

5   The arrangement was that Emily and Anne should pay £50 to be repaid if the book sold well. Letter of 18 September 1850 from Charlotte to George Smith; *S.H.III.* 60.

6   *Shorter* I, 358; *S.H.II.* 139.

7   211   Letter of 10 July 1846; *Gaskell B* 307; *S.H.II.* 101. Charlotte was even more decided in her letter of 15 October 1847 to Ellen who saw, truly enough, the interest of one of the pair: 'I cannot for my life see those interesting germs of goodness in him you discovered; his narrowness of mind always strikes me chiefly.' *S.H.II.* 148.

8   211   He returned there for a short time in November, and again the next year; letters of 17 November 1846 and 29 June and 7 October 1847 from Charlotte to Ellen; *Shorter* I, 340; *S.H.II.* 116, 137, 147.

9   Letter of 9 August 1846 from Charlotte to Ellen; *S.H.II.* 105–6. Charlotte settled upon W. J. Wilson, M.R.C.S. See *Honorary Medical Staff of the Manchester Infirmary* by E. M. Brockbank, 1904. As to the protests of Mr. Brontë, even at this late hour, see Charlotte's letter of 12 April 1852 to Laetitia Wheelwright; *S.H.III.* 331.

10   Ibid.

11   Letter of 21 August 1846 from Charlotte to Ellen, addressed from 83 Mount Pleasant, Boundary Street, Oxford Road, Manchester; *Gaskell B* 310–11; *S.H.II.* 106–7. See also *BST* Part XX, 1910.

12   Letter of 29 September 1846 from Charlotte to Ellen; *Shorter* I, 338–9; *S.H.II.* 111.

13   She suffered from bad toothache, which prevented sleep. Letter of 31 August 1846 from Charlotte to Ellen; *Shorter* I, 337; *S.H.II.* 109. See also letter of 24 July 1846 from Charlotte to Ellen; *Shorter* I, 333; *S.H.II.* 104–5.

14   Letter of 26 August 1846 from Charlotte to Ellen; *Gaskell B* 311; *S.H.II.* 107–9.

15   The manuscript was actually returned to Charlotte whilst she was at Manchester, on the day of the operation; *Gaskell B* 313.

16   212   Letter of 14 October 1846; *Gaskell B* 318–19; *S.H.II.* 115.

17   Letter of *c.* Oct.-Nov. 1846 from Charlotte to Miss Wooler; *Shorter* I, 340–1; *S.H.II.* 116–17.

18   213   See Note 15 above.

19   *Gaskell B* 314.

20   Letter of 17 November 1846; *Shorter* I, 340; *S.H.II.* 116.

21   Letter of 15 December 1846 from Charlotte to Ellen; *Gaskell B* 319; *S.H.II.* 117. This refers to Anne's asthma. Emily, too, may

Note	Page	
		have been a victim; letter of 29 May 1843 from Charlotte to Emily; *Shorter* I, 268; *S.H.I.* 300.
22	213	Letter of 15 December 1846; *Shorter* I, 341; *S.H.*II. 117–18.
23		Ibid.; *S.H.*II. 118.
24		Ibid.
25		Letter of 1 March 1847 to Ellen; *Shorter* I, 347; *S.H.*II. 128. Charlotte goes on: 'Branwell has been conducting himself very badly lately. I expect from the extravagance of his behaviour, and the mysterious hints he drops (for he never will speak out plainly) that we shall be hearing of fresh debts contracted by him soon.'
26	214	See, for instance, the letter of October 1846 from Branwell to J. B. Leyland; *Leyland A* II; *S.H.*II. 113.
27		*Harrison A* and *B*.
28		Letter of 24 January 1847; *Leyland A* II, 173; *S.H.*II. 123.
29		Ibid.
30	215	Ibid.
31		*Gaskell A* I, Chapter 13; II, Chapter 2; letter of 18 August 1848 from Charlotte to Ellen; *S.H.*II. 247. Mrs. Robinson married Sir Edward Scott and played a prominent part in a certain section of London Society. See letter of 23 November 1848 from Charlotte to Ellen. 'Mrs. Robinson is now Lady Scott. Her daughters say she is in the highest spirits.' *S.H.*II. 288.
32		Letter of 24 January 1847 to J. B. Leyland; *Leyland A* II, 174; *S.H.*II. 123–4.
33	216	Ibid.; *S.H.*II. 124.
34		*Searle.*
35		Letter of 24 January 1847 to J. B. Leyland; *Leyland A* II, 175; *S.H.*II. 124.
36	217	Ibid.; *S.H.*II. 124–5.
37		Ibid.; *S.H.*II. 125.
38	218	Letter of 1 March 1847 to Ellen; *Shorter* I, 347; *S.H.*II. 128.
39		Ibid.
40		Letter of 12 May 1847; *Shorter* I, 350; *S.H.*II. 132.
41		Ibid.
42		Letter of 14 May 1847; *Shorter* I, 351; *S.H.*II. 133.
43		Letter of 17 May 1847; *Gaskell B* 324; *S.H.*II. 133.
44		Ibid.
45		Letter of 20 May 1847 from Charlotte to Ellen; *Gaskell B* 325; *S.H.*II. 134.
46	219	Letter of 7 October 1847 from Charlotte to Ellen; *S.H.*II. 147.
47		Letter of 24 March 1847 from Charlotte to Ellen; *Gaskell B* 323; *S.H.*II. 130.
48	220	See Note 2 above.

CHAPTER XXIII

Note	Page	
1	221	See Note 47, Chapter 22.
2		See Note 33, Chapter 22.
3		See Note 30, Chapter 22.
4		*Gaskell B* 291, 316–17.
5		Letter of 15 February 1848 from T. C. Newby; *S.H.*II. 188. See also letter of 7 December 1848 from Charlotte to W. S. Williams; *S.H.*II. 291; *Simpson* 180–3.
6	222	Charlotte's Biographical Notice to 1850 edition of *Wuthering Heights* and *Agnes Grey*. Cf. *Gaskell B* 341.
7		Ibid. See also letter of 2 November 1848 from Charlotte to W. S. Williams; *Shorter* I, 461; *S.H.*II. 269–70.
8		In Charlotte's contract with Smith Elder, *The Professor* was set aside; letter of 14 December 1847 from Charlotte to W. S. Williams; *Shorter* I, 374; *S.H.*II. 162.
9	223	Letter of 24 August 1847 from Charlotte to Smith Elder; *Shorter* I, 359; *S.H.*II. 141.
10		*Gaskell B* 338–40. See also *BST* Part LVIII, 1948.
11	225	*Jane Eyre*, 1847, Volume I, Chapters 1 and 2.
12	226	Ibid., Volume II, Chapter 9.
13		Ibid., Volume I, Chapter 14.
14		Ibid., Volume III, Chapter 11.
15	227	Ibid.
16		Ibid.
17	228	Ibid., Volume II, Chapter 8.
18		Ibid., Volume III, Chapter 11.
19		Ibid., Volume III, Chapter 12.
20	229	Letter of 28 October 1847 to W. S. Williams; *S.H.*II. 150.
21	230	Letter of 10 November 1847; *Shorter* I 366–7; *S.H.*II. 154. See also letter of 14 December 1847 from Charlotte to W. S. Williams; *Shorter* I, 375; *S.H.*II. 162.
22		Letter of 25 September 1847; *Gaskell B* 331; *S.H.*II. 143.
23		Letters of 10 January 1843 and 23 June 1844 from Charlotte to Ellen; *Shorter* I, 253, 282; *S.H.*I. 284; II, 6.

CHAPTER XXIV

1	231	Letter of 5 February 1848 from Charlotte to W. S. Williams; *Shorter* I, 395; *S.H.*II. 187. See also *BST* Part LVII, 1947.
2		Letters of 31 December 1847 and 22 January 1848 from Charlotte to W. S. Williams; *Gaskell B* 348; *Shorter* I 378, 389; *S.H.*II. 170, 181.
3		*Hoffman N.*
4	232	*Jack Sharp and the Walker Family: heard at Law Hill; Halifax; Hanson A.*

Note	Page	
5	232	*Nussey; Harrison A, B* and *C.*
6		*Nussey; Shorter* I, 101 *foll.*; *S.H.*I. 111–13; *CWEB* XXXVIII–XXXIX.
7	234	*Harrison A, B* and *C.*
8		Ibid.
9		*C.P.S.*
10		*Nussey; Gaskell B* 148–9, 186.
11	235	*The Professor,* Chapter 20.

12 Actually, with immediate reference to the maniac in *Jane Eyre.* Letter of 4 January 1848 from Charlotte to W. S. Williams; *Shorter* I, 383; *S.H.*II. 173–4.

13 It has been suggested—in *Moore*—that Heathcliff is, in fact, Emily herself—the 'melancholy boy' who turns into the 'iron man' of her poems. Heathcliff is certainly Emily in so far as every living character is created by its author. Into Heathcliff was poured much of Emily's own nature—her love of violence, her frustration, passion and sense of injustice. So much cannot be doubted. But that Heathcliff could have attained existence in Emily's mind without the constant sight and sound of Branwell about the house, is, to say the least, improbable. In *Moore,* Emily is also credited with a mythical lover, Louis Parensell—a misreading of the title (given by Charlotte) of Emily's poem, *Love's Farewell.*

14 236 Charlotte's Biographical Notice to the 1850 edition of *Wuthering Heights* and *Agnes Grey.*

15 Ibid.

16 237 Ibid.

17 238 Charlotte's *Memoir* of Emily in the 1850 edition of *Wuthering Heights* and *Agnes Grey; PEA* XXII.

18 Charlotte's *Memoir* of Anne in the 1850 edition of *Wuthering Heights* and *Agnes Grey; PEA* XXIV.

19 *Leyland A* II, 83–4, 158; *Grundy A* 80, 90; *Searle; Dearden; BST* Part XXXVII; Edward Sloane of Halifax, another witness, in *Leyland A* II, 188. See also *Shorter* I, 451; *Benson, E. F.* 169–79; *Willis A.* Nor has speculation ceased here. It has been suggested—in *Law A*—that Branwell wrote the entire book and that Emily passed it off as her own. And in *Dembleby* it is even argued that Charlotte is the real author of *Wuthering Heights.* But the evidence marshalled in *Willis A* may be regarded as decisive.

20 See, for instance, *PCB* 290, 300–2, 353.

21 *Willis A; Lamont.*

22 243 *Wuthering Heights,* Chapter 18.

23 247 Ibid., Chapter 21.

24 Ibid., Chapter 34.

25 Ibid., Chapter 12.

26 Ibid., Chapter 13.

Note	Page	
27	248	Ibid., Chapter 24.

CHAPTER XXV

1	250	Letter of 6 November 1847; *Gaskell B* 343; *S.H.II.* 152–3.
2		Ibid.; *Gaskell B.* 344; *S.H.* II, 153.
3	251	Letter of 12 January 1848; *Gaskell B* 351; *S.H.II* 179.
4		Ibid.; *S.H.II.* 179–180.
5		Letter of 18 January 1848; *Gaskell B* 352–3; *S.H.II.* 180.
6		Ibid.
7	252	Ibid.; *S.H.II.* 180–1. See also letter of 12 April 1850 from Charlotte to W. S. Williams; *S.H.III.* 99.
8		Letter of 28 January 1848; *Shorter* I, 390–1; *S.H.II.* 183–4.
9	253	Letter of 1 May 1848 to W. S. Williams; *Shorter* I, 413; *S.H.II.* 210.
10		Letter of 4 January 1848 to W. S. Williams; *Shorter* I, 383; *S.H.II.* 173.
11	254	Letter of 22 June 1848; *Shorter* I, 424–5; *S.H.II.* 224–5.
12		*Gaskell B* 356; letters of 4 October 1847 and 4 January 1848 from Anne to Ellen, and of 7 October 1847, from Charlotte to Ellen; *Shorter* I, 355–7, 385; *S.H.II.* 144, 146, 175.
13		Letter of January 1848 from Branwell to J. B. Leyland; *Leyland* I, 214–226; *S.H.II.* 177. See also letter of 17 June 1848 from Branwell to Leyland; *S.H.II.* 223.
14	255	Letter of 11 January 1848; *Gaskell B* 350; *S.H.II.* 178.
15		Letter of January 1848; *Leyland* I, 214–226; II, 144–5; *S.H.II.* 177.
16		*S.H.II.* 176.
17		Letter of 15 February 1848 to W. S. Williams; *Shorter* I, 396; *S.H.II.* 189.
18		Letter of 14 December 1847 from Charlotte to W. S. Williams; *Shorter* I, 374; *S.H.II.* 161–2.
19		Letter of 11 March 1848 from Charlotte to W. S. Williams; *Shorter* I, 401; *S.H.II.* 197.
20		Letter of 22 January 1848 from Charlotte to W. S. Williams; *Shorter* I, 389; *S.H.II.* 181–2.
21	256	*Gaskell B* 360; Charlotte's *Memoir* of Anne in 1850 edition of *Wuthering Heights* and *Agnes Grey*; Note 28 below.
22		Letter of 4 September 1848 from Charlotte to Mary Taylor; *Gaskell B* 365–6; *Shorter* I, 435–6; *S.H.II.* 250-1.
23		Ibid.; *Gaskell B* 366; *Shorter* I, 436; *S.H.II.* 251.
24	257	Ibid.; *Shorter* I, 436–7; *S.H.II.* 251–2.
25	258	Ibid.; *Gaskell B* 366–7; *Shorter* I, 437; *S.H.II*, 252–3.
26	259	Ibid.; *Gaskell B* 367–8; *Shorter* I, 438–9; *S.H.II*, 253–4. See also *George Smith C*.
27		*Gaskell B* 360–1; *S.H.II.* 229.
28		Letter of 31 July 1848; *Shorter* I, 442; *S.H.II.* 241.

NOTES

Note	Page	
29	260	Letter of 14 August 1848; *Shorter* I, 446; *S.H.II.* 244-5.

Letter of 31 July 1848; *Shorter* I, 442; *S.H.II.* 241. Emily's anger has seemed to many a proof that Branwell had collaborated in *Wuthering Heights*—hence her reluctance to be known as the sole author—but this seems an extreme view. Emily had not forgotten Charlotte's discovery of her poems. Here was another, similar, occasion for wrath.

31 — Letter of 20 April 1848; *S.H.II.* 204.

32 — *Gaskell B* 423.

33 — Ellen Nussey footnote to *Turner; S.H.II.* 228.

34 — Ibid.

35 262 Letter of 3 May 1848; *Gaskell B* 358-9; *S.H.II.* 211-12.

CHAPTER XXVI

1 264 Letter of June 1848; *Leyland A* II; *S.H.II.* 222-3. Signed *Northangerland*, Branwell's pen-name.

2 — Letter of 17 June 1848; *Leyland A* II; *S.H.II.* 223.

3 — *S.H.II.* 224.

4 — *Grundy A* 90; *Leyland A* II, 133, 144; *S.H.II.* 258.

5 265 Letter of 18 August 1848 to Ellen; *Shorter* I, 447; *S.H.II.* 247. See *Gaskell A* I, 327-32.

6 — Letter of 28 July 1848 to Ellen; *S.H.II.* 246.

7 — Ibid.; *Gaskell B* 371.

8 266 *Grundy A* 90; *Leyland A* II, 133, 144, 166-7; *S.H.II.* 258-9; *Gaskell A* II, Chapter 2.

9 — Letter of 9 October 1848 from Charlotte to Ellen; *Gaskell B* 373; *S.H.II.* 264. See *The Causes of Death in the Brontë Family* by Mrs. C. Mabel Edgerley, *BST* Part XLIV, 1934; see also *BST* Part LI, 1941.

10 — *Gaskell B* 374; *Chadwick A* 360, denied by John Brown.

11 — Letter of 14 October 1848 to Mercy Nussey; *Shorter* I, 457; *S.H.II.* 265.

12 — Ibid.

13 — Letter of 6 October 1848 from Charlotte to W. S. Williams; *Shorter* I, 455; *S.H.II.* 263.

14 — Letter of 25 June 1849 to W. S. Williams; *Shorter* II, 53-4; *S.H.II.* 348-9.

15 267 Letter of 2 October 1848; *S.H.II.* 261. See also letter of 29 September 1848 from Anne to W. S. Williams; *S.H.II.* 260-1.

16 — Letter of 6 October 1848 to W. S. Williams; *Shorter* I, 454; *S.H.II.* 262.

17 — Letter of 14 October 1848 to Mercy Nussey; *Shorter* I, 457; *S.H.II.* 265.

CHAPTER XXVII

Note	Page	
I	268	Letter of 9 October 1848; *Shorter* I, 456; *S.H.II.* 264.
2		Letter of 29 October 1848 to Ellen; *Gaskell B* 375-6; *S.H.II.* 268.
3	269	Letter of 2 November 1848; *Shorter* I, 461; *S.H.II.* 269.
4		Ibid.
5		Letter of 7 November 1848 from Charlotte to George Smith; *Gaskell B* 377; *S.H.II.* 271.
6		Letter of 22 November 1848; *Gaskell B* 378-9; *S.H.II.* 286-7.
7		Ibid.; *S.H.II.* 287.
8		Ibid.
9		From a parcel of books sent by Smith Elder in October: 'Emily was then beginning to be ill—the opening of the parcel and fascination of the books cheered her—their perusal occupied her for many a weary day.' Letter of 25 June 1849 from Charlotte to W. S. Williams; *S.H.II.* 350.
10	270	Letter of 22 November 1848; *Gaskell B* 378-9; *S.H.II.* 287.
11		Letter of 23 November 1848; *Gaskell B* 378; *S.H.II.* 288.
12		Charlotte's Biographical Notice to the 1850 edition of *Wuthering Heights* and *Agnes Grey*.
13	271	She refused to see one when he was actually in the house; *Gaskell B* 379; letter of 23 November 1848 from Charlotte to Ellen; *S.H.II.* 288. See also letter of 9 December 1848 from Charlotte to W. S. Williams; *S.H.II.* 291.
14		Letter of 30 January 1849 to Ellen; *S.H.II.* 290.
15		Letter of 7 December 1848 to W. S. Williams; *S.H.II* 290.
16		Letter of 29 October 1848 from Charlotte to Ellen; *Shorter* I, 460; *S.H.II.* 268.
17	272	Letter of 25 December 1848 to W. S. Williams; *Gaskell B* 378; *S.H.II.* 295.
18		See, for instance, letters of 4 and 13 June to W. S. Williams; *S.H.II.* 337-9.
19		See, for instance, letter of 13 June to W. S. Williams; *S.H.II.* 340; 'One by one I have watched them fall asleep on my arm—and closed their glazed eyes—I have seen them buried one by one—and—thus far—God has upheld me. From my heart I thank him.' But in, for example, her famous Memoir in the 1850 edition of *Wuthering Heights*, Charlotte writes with power and sincerity.
20	274	Letter of 27 November 1848; *Shorter* II, 8; *S.H.II.* 289.
21		Ibid.
22		Letter of 7 December 1848 from Charlotte to W. S. Williams; *Shorter* II, 9; *S.H.II.* 289-90.
23		Letter of 9 December 1848 from Charlotte to W. S. Williams; *S.H.II.* 291.
24		Letter of 7 December 1848; *Shorter* II, 9; *S.H.II.* 290.

Note	Page	
25	274	Letter of 10 December 1848 from Charlotte to Ellen; *Gaskell B* 380; *S.H.II.* 293.
26		Ibid.; also letter of 27 November 1848 from Charlotte to Ellen; *S.H.II.* 289.
27		Letter of 2 November 1848 from Charlotte to W. S. Williams; *S.H.II.* 269.
28		Ibid.
29	275	Letter of 10 December 1848 to Ellen; *Gaskell B* 380; *S.H.II.* 292-3.
30		Letter of 19 December 1848 from Charlotte to Ellen; *Gaskell B* 382; *S.H.II.* 293.
31		*Gaskell B* 382.
32		Letter of 19 December 1848; *Gaskell B* 382; *S.H.II.* 293.
33		*Gaskell B* 382.
34		Ibid.
35		Letter of 12 April 1849 to Ellen; *Shorter* II, 42; *S.H.II.* 324.
36		Letter of 4 June 1849 from Charlotte to W. S. Williams; *S.H.II.* 327.
37		Letter of 13 June 1849 from Charlotte to W. S. Williams; *S.H.II.* 339; *Gaskell B* 382.
38	276	2 January 1846; *PEA* 158-9; *Hatfield* 243-4; Number 31 in Personal Poem Notebook (Law Collection). This poem was never printed as written by Emily until 31 May 1934—in T.L.S. See letter from Mr. Hatfield in T.L.S., 21 June 1934, and cf. with poem as printed in *Hatfield*.

CHAPTER XXVIII

1	277	See, for instance, her poem *Dreams*, Spring 1845; *PEA* 241-2.
2	278	Letter of 10 December 1848 to Ellen; *Gaskell B* 380; *S.H.II.* 293.
3		*Nussey;* see also Note 4 below; *Gaskell B* 394.
4		Letter of 18 January 1849 to W. S. Williams; *Gaskell B* 390-1; *S.H.II.* 300-1. See also letter of 15 March 1849 from Charlotte to Laetitia Wheelwright; *S.H.II.* 316.
5	279	John Forbes, 1787-1861.
6		Letter of 22 January 1849 from Charlotte to George Smith; *Gaskell B* 381; *S.H.II.* 302.
7		Ibid. See also letter of 7 December 1848 from Charlotte to W. S. Williams; *S.H.II.* 290.
8		Letter of 22 January 1849 from Charlotte to George Smith; *Gaskell B* 381; *S.H.II.* 302-3.
9		Letters of 30 January 1849 from Charlotte to Ellen, and 1 February 1849 from Charlotte to W. S. Williams; *Gaskell B* 394, 401; *S.H.II.* 304-5.
10		Letter of 16 March 1849 from Charlotte to Ellen; *Gaskell B* 394; *S.H.II.* 316.
11		Letter of 24 March 1849 from Charlotte to Miss Wooler; *Gaskell B* 395; *S.H.II.* 317-18.

Note	Page	

12   Letter of 16 April 1849 from Charlotte to W. S. Williams; *Shorter* II, 44; *S.H.*II. 327.

13   Letter of 24 March 1849 to Miss Wooler; *Gaskell B* 395 (part); *Shorter* II, 35; *S.H.*II. 317.

14   Letter of 12 April 1849 to Ellen; *Gaskell B* 400; *S.H.*II. 324.

15   280   Letter of 30 January 1849 to Ellen; *Gaskell B* 401; *S.H.*II. 304.

16   Letter of 12 January 1849 to Ellen; *Gaskell B* 390; *S.H.*II. 299.

17   Letter of 15 January 1849 from Charlotte to Ellen; *Gaskell B* 392; *S.H.*II. 299. See also letter of 16 April 1849 from Charlotte to W. S. Williams who was suggesting homoeopathy; *S.H.*II. 325.

18   Letter of 16 February 1849 from Charlotte to Ellen; *Gaskell B* 393; *S.H.*II. 310.

19   Letter of 30 January 1849 to Ellen; *Gaskell B* 400–1; *S.H.*II. 304. See also letter of 16 February 1849 from Charlotte to Ellen; *Gaskell B* 393; *S.H.*II. 310.

20   Letter of 16 February 1849 to Ellen; *Gaskell B* 394; *S.H.*II. 310.

21   Letters of 1 and 4 February 1849 to W. S. Williams; *Gaskell B* 415; *S.H.*II. 305–6.

22   Letters of 29 March 1849 from Charlotte to Ellen, and 5 April 1849 from Anne to Ellen; *Gaskell B* 396–8; *S.H.*II. 318–21.

23   Anne had received £200 from her godmother, Miss Outhwaite, as well as her aunt's legacy. Letter of 12 May 1849 from Charlotte to Ellen; *Gaskell B* 402; *S.H.*II. 330. But *Moore Smith* says £100.

24   Letter of 5 April 1849 from Anne to Ellen; *S.H.*II. 320–1.

25   281   Letter of 29 March 1849; *S.H.*II. 318–19. See also letter of 12 April 1849 from Charlotte to Ellen; *Gaskell B* 400; *S.H.*II. 324–5.

26   See letter of 5 April 1849 from Anne to Ellen; *Gaskell B* 397; *S.H.*II. 320.

27   282   Ibid.; *Gaskell B* 397–8; *S.H.*II. 320–1.

28   Letter of 1 May 1849 from Charlotte to Ellen; *Gaskell B* 401; *S.H.*II. 328.

29   Ibid.; *Gaskell B.* 401–2; *S.H.*II. 327–8.

30   283   Ibid.; *Gaskell B* 402. See also letter of 16 May 1849 from Charlotte to Miss Wooler; *Gaskell B* 403; *S.H.*II. 331.

31   Letter of 25 December 1848 to W. S. Williams; *Gaskell B* 384; *S.H.*II. 295.

32   Letter of 5 April 1849 from Anne to Ellen; *Gaskell B* 398; *S.H.*II. 321.

33   Ibid.

34   At No. 2 Cliff (now part of the Grand Hotel). Letter of 12 May 1849 from Charlotte to Ellen, and 16 May 1849 from Charlotte to Miss Wooler; *Gaskell B* 402; *S.H.*II. 330–1.

35   Letter of 16 May 1849 from Charlotte to Ellen; *Gaskell B* 404; *S.H.*II. 332.

Note	Page	
36	283	Letter of 16 May 1849 to Miss Wooler; *Shorter* II, 49; *S.H.*II. 331.
37		*Gaskell B* 404; *Nussey*.
38		Ibid.
39		Ibid.
40	286	*Gaskell B.* 404–8; *S.H.*II. 333–6.
41		Letters of 30 May, 4 June, 13 June 1849 from Charlotte to W. S. Williams, and letter of 5 June 1849 from Charlotte to Martha Brown; *S.H.*II. 337–9.
42		Charlotte's Biographical Notice to the 1850 edition of *Wuthering Heights* and *Agnes Grey*.
43		*George Smith C.*
44	288	*PEA* 158–9; *Gaskell B* 398–9 (part).

EPILOGUE

1	289	*Gaskell B* 434; *S.H.*III. 94.
2	290	See, for instance, letters of 26 July and 13 September 1849 from Charlotte to W. S. Williams; *S.H.*III. 9, 20. See also letter of 18 July 1853 from Charlotte to the editor of the 'Christian Remembrancer': 'My father is now in his seventy-seventh year; his mind is clear as ever it was, and he is not infirm, but he suffers from partial privation and threatened loss of sight; and his general health is also delicate—he cannot be left often or long: my place consequently is at home.' This was in reply to a review of *Villette* in April 1843, in which the reviewer congratulated Charlotte on 'having gained both in amiability and propriety since she first presented herself to the world—soured, coarse, and grumbling; an alien, it might seem, from society, and amenable to none of its laws.' But Charlotte goes on: '. . . Were I bound by no such ties, it is very possible that seclusion might still appear to me, on the whole, more congenial than publicity; the brief and rare glimpses I have had of the world do not incline me to think I should seek its circles with very keen zest—nor can I consider such disinclination a just subject for reproach.' W. Robertson Nicoll in 'The Bookman', November 1899. But this was after some years alone at the parsonage. Earlier, after Anne's death, Charlotte had occasional almost irresistible cravings for the life symbolized by London. Thus, on 1 November 1849, she writes to G. H. Lewes, who had said that he intended to review *Shirley* in the 'Edinburgh Review': 'There have been intervals when I have ceased to care about literature and critics and fame . . . but now I want these things to come back vividly if possible'; *Gaskell B* 422. See also *Gaskell B* 409–11, 434.
3	291	Letter of 23 June 1849; *Gaskell B* 410–11; *S.H.*II. 347.
4		Letter of 25 June 1849; *Shorter* II, 53–4; *S.H.*II. 348–9.

Note	Page	
5	292	Ibid.; *S.H.*II. 349.
6		Letter of 14 July 1849 from Charlotte to Ellen; *Gaskell B* 411–12; *S.H.*III. 8.
7		Letter of 26 July 1849; *Shorter* II, 62; *S.H.*III. 9.
8		Ibid.
9		Letter of 29 August 1849; *Shorter* II, 67; *S.H.*III. 15. See also letter of 5 September 1850 from Charlotte to James Taylor; *S.H.*III. 154.
10	293	Letters of 2 March and 2 April 1849 from Charlotte to W. S. Williams; *S.H.*II. 313, 319–20; III, 90. Charlotte denied having taken anyone as model for Caroline; *Gaskell B* 444.
11	294	On 8 September. See Charlotte's letters of 3 September 1849 to James Taylor; 29 August 1849 to W. S. Williams; and 31 August 1849 to George Smith; *Gaskell B* 387–8; *S.H.*III. 17. For the background of *Shirley* see *Shirley Land* by Ernest Hobson, 'The Westminster Review', July 1906; *Shirley—Its Scenes and Characters* by J. J. Stead, 'The Heckmondwike Herald', 1897; *The Shirley Country* by the same author, *BST* Parts VII and XVII; and *The Economic Background of Shirley* by Herbert Heaton, *BST* Part XLII, 1932.
12		Letter of December 1849 to Ellen; *Shorter* II, 96; *S.H.*III. 53.
13		Letter of 19 November 1849 from Charlotte to George Smith; *Gaskell B* 425; *S.H.*III. 37–8. See also letter of 4 December 1849 from Charlotte to Ellen; *Gaskell B* 426; *S.H.*III. 53.
14		Letter of 4 December 1849 from Charlotte to Mr. Brontë; also letter of 9 December 1849 from Charlotte to Ellen; *Gaskell B* 428–9; *S.H.*III. 54, 56.
15		Letter of 18 December 1849 from Charlotte to Ellen; *Gaskell B* 434; *S.H.*III. 60.
16		Letter of 14 February 1850 from Charlotte to Miss Wooler; *S.H.*III. 76.
17	295	*Gaskell B* 429; *George Smith B.*
18		*Brookfield*; *S.H.*III.50.
19	297	*Ritchie B.*; *S.H.*III. 48–9; *George Smith C.*
20		*Martineau A* II; letter of 20 November 1849; *Gaskell B* 430; *S.H.*III. 40.
21		*Martineau A* II.
22	298	Letter of 21 December 1849 from Mrs. Gaskell to Ann Shaen; *S.H.*III. 57; *Haldane, E. S.*
23		Letter of 22 February 1850 from Charlotte to W. S. Williams; *Gaskell B* 437; *S.H.*III. 50.
24		Letter of 19 January 1850; *Shorter* II, 107; *S.H.*III. 69.
25		Ibid.; *Gaskell B* 437.
26		Letter of 28 January 1850 to Ellen; *Gaskell B* 437; *S.H.*III. 71.
27	299	Letter of 14 February 1850 to Miss Wooler; *S.H.*III. 75.
28		Letter of 28 January 1850 to Ellen; *Gaskell B* 437; *S.H.*III. 71.
29		Letters of 4 February 1850 from Charlotte to Ellen, and 19 March

Note	Page	
		1850 from Charlotte to W. S. Williams; *Gaskell B* 451; *S.H.III.* 73, 90.
30	299	Letter of 14 February 1850 to Miss Wooler; *S.H.III.* 75.
31		Letter of 22 May 1850 from Charlotte to James Taylor; *Gaskell B* 455; *S.H.III.* 111.
32		Letter of 16 February 1850 from Charlotte to Ellen; *S.H.III.* 77.
33	300	Letters of 5 March 1850 from Charlotte to Ellen, and 16 March 1850 from Charlotte to W. S. Williams; *Gaskell B* 445–6; *S.H.III.* 81–2.
34		Letters of 16 March 1850 from Charlotte to W. S. Williams, and 19 March 1850 from Charlotte to Ellen; *Gaskell B* 447; *S.H.III.* 82, 86–7.
35		Letters of 21 May 1850 from Charlotte to Ellen, and 25 May 1850 from Charlotte to Mrs. Smith; *Gaskell B* 457; *S.H.III.* 110–13.
36		Letters of 12 April and 3 June 1850 from Charlotte to Ellen, and 27 September 1850 from Charlotte to Miss Wooler; *Gaskell B* 453–4; *S.H.III.* 100, 115, 164.
37		Letters of 21 May 1850 from Charlotte to Ellen, and 22 May 1850 from Charlotte to James Taylor; *Gaskell B* 454; *S.H.III.* 110–111.
38		Letter of 12 June 1850 from Charlotte to Ellen; *Gaskell B* 458; *S.H.III.* 117–18; *Cory* 187.
39		*Gaskell B* 483. See also letter of 1 November 1849 from Charlotte to G. H. Lewes; *S.H.III.* 31.
40		In 'The Edinburgh Review', January 1850, under the heading 'Mental Equality of the Sexes?' *Lewes D.* See also *Lewes B.*
41		Letter of January 1850 to G. H. Lewes; *Gaskell B* 439; *S.H.III.* 67.
42		Letter of 19 January 1850 from Charlotte to G. H. Lewes; *Gaskell B* 439–40; *S.H.III.* 68.
43		*Gaskell B* 483.
44		Letters of 10 January and 22 February 1850 from Charlotte to W. S. Williams; *S.H.III.* 66, 79–80.
45	301	Letter of 12 June 1850 to Ellen; *Gaskell B* 458; *S.H.III.* 118.
46		*Cross, J. W.; S.H.III.* 118.
47		*George Smith D; S.H.III.* 52.
48		Letter of 21 June 1850 from Charlotte to Ellen; *S.H.III.* 121; *Villette.*
49		Letter of 21 June 1850 from Charlotte to Ellen; *S.H.III.* 121.
50	302	Letters of 27 June 1850 from Charlotte to George Smith, 28 June 1850 from Charlotte to Mrs. Smith, 5 July 1850 from Charlotte to Ellen, and 30 July 1850 from Charlotte to Laetitia Wheelwright; *Gaskell B* 462; *S.H.III.* 121–3, 128.
51		See, for instance, letter of 20 July 1850 from Charlotte to W. S. Williams; *Gaskell B* 460–1; *S.H.III.* 125.
52		Letters of 1 August 1850 from Charlotte to Ellen and to George Smith, and 2 August 1850 from Mr. Brontë to George Smith: *Gaskell B* 464–6; *S.H.III.* 129–31.

Note	Page	
53		Letter of 6 November 1849 from Charlotte to James Taylor; *Gaskell B* 476; *S.H.III.* 35.
54		Letter of 14 September 1850; *Shorter* II, 171; *S.H.III.* 158.
55		Ibid.
56		Letter of 16 August 1850 from Charlotte to Ellen; *Gaskell B* 469; *S.H.III.* 139.
57		Letter of 27 September 1850; *Gaskell B* 473; *S.H.III.* 163.
58		Ibid.
59		Letter of 26 August 1850 to Ellen; *S.H.III.* 148.
60	303	Letter of 25 August 1850 to Catherine Winkworth; *Gaskell B* 470; *S.H.III.* 142; *Haldane, E. S.*; *Shaen.*
61		Ibid.
62		Ibid.; *Arnold.*
63		Letter of 26 August 1850 to Ellen; *Gaskell B* 472; *S.H.III.* 148.
64		Letters of 15 January 1850 from Charlotte to George Smith, and 25 April 1850 from Charlotte to W. S. Williams; *Gaskell B* 444; *S.H.III.* 67, 103.
65	304	Letters of 5 September 1850 from Charlotte to James Taylor and W. S. Williams, and *c.* October 1850 from Charlotte to Harriet Martineau; *Gaskell B* 477; *S.H.III.* 154, 156, 170.
66		Letters of 5 and 13 September 1850 from Charlotte to W. S. Williams; *Gaskell B* 481; *S.H.III.* 156-7.
67		Letter of 5 September 1850 from Charlotte to W. S. Williams; *S.H.III.* 156.
68		Letters of September 1850 from Charlotte to Ellen, 25 October 1850 from Charlotte to W. S. Williams, and 12 January 1851 from Charlotte to Laetitia Wheelwright; *Gaskell B* 482, 489; *S.H.III.* 166, 175, 197.
69	305	Letter of 29 September 1850 from Charlotte to W. S. Williams; *Gaskell B* 481; *S.H.III.* 165.
70		Letter of 20 September 1850 from Charlotte to W. S. Williams; *S.H.III.* 161.
71		Letter of 8 December 1850 from Charlotte to Sydney Dobell; *Gaskell B* 495-6; *S.H.III.* 186-7; *Dobell B.*
72		Letter of March 1851; *S.H.III.* 218.
73		Ibid.; *S.H.III.* 219.
74		Letter of *c.* April 1851; *S.H.III.* 220.
75		Letter of 17 April 1851; *S.H.III.* 226.
76	306	Ibid.
77		Ibid.
78		Letter of 1 May 1851; *S.H.III.* 229-230.
79		Letter of 21 May 1851; *S.H.III.* 235-6.
80		Letter of 24 May 1851; *Gaskell B* 517-18; *S.H.III.* 236-7.
81		Letters of 19 March 1850 from Charlotte to Ellen and to W. S. Williams; *S.H.III.* 87-8.
82	307	Ibid.
83		Letter of 18 December 1850 from Charlotte to Ellen; *S.H.III.* 189.

Note	Page	
84	307	'My sister Emily had a particular love for them, and there is not a knoll of heather, not a branch of fern, not a young bilberry leaf, not a fluttering lark or linnet, but reminds me of her. The distant prospects were Anne's delight, and when I look round she is in the blue tints, the pale mists, the waves and shadows of the horizon.' Letter of 22 May 1850 from Charlotte to James Taylor; *Gaskell B* 455; *S.H.III.* 111.
85		Letter of 2 October 1850 from Charlotte to W. S. Williams; *S.H.III.* 166-7.
86	308	Letter of 23 October 1850; *Shorter* II, 178-9; *S.H.* III, 173-4.
87		Letter of 18 July 1850 from Charlotte to Ellen; *S.H.III.* 125.
88		Charlotte claimed nine rejections; but these included three by Smith Elder. Letter of 5 February 1851 from Charlotte to George Smith; *Gaskell B* 504-5; *S.H.III.* 206-7.
89		Letters of 8 and 22 September 1851 from Charlotte to George Smith; *Gaskell B* 542; *S.H.III.* 274-5, 279-80; II, 61.
90		*Martineau A* II; *Gaskell B* 497-501; letters of 15 December 1850 from Charlotte to Mr. Brontë, 18 December 1850 from Charlotte to Ellen, and 7 January 1851 from Charlotte to George Smith; *S.H.III.* 189, 196.
91	309	Letter of 19 April 1851; *S.H.III.* 127, 227, 279.
92		Letter of 20 January 1851; *Shorter* II, 194; *S.H.III.* 202.
93		Ibid.; also letters of 30 January, 5, 9, 12, 23 April, 5 and 21 May 1851 from Charlotte to Ellen; *Gaskell B* 517; *S.H.III.* 205, 220-3, 229, 231, 236.
94		Letter of 20 January 1851; *Shorter* II, 194; *S.H.III.* 202.
95	310	Letter of 30 January 1851; *Shorter* II 195-6; *S.H.III.* 205.
96		Letter of 5 April 1851 to Ellen; *Shorter* II, 201-2; *S.H.III.* 220-1.
97		Letters of 9, 12, 23 April and 5 May 1851 from Charlotte to Ellen; *Shorter* II, 203; *S.H.III.* 222-3, 229, 231.
98	311	Letters of 24 June 1851 from Charlotte to Ellen, and 26 June 1851 from Charlotte to Mr. Brontë; *Gaskell B* 523, 525; *S.H.III.* 251-2.
99		Letters of 2 June 1851 from Charlotte to Ellen, 7 and 11 June 1851 from Charlotte to Amelia Ringrose, June 1851 from Charlotte to Mrs. Gaskell, and 15 November 1851 from Charlotte to James Taylor; *Gaskell B* 518-22, 548; *S.H.III.* 240-1, 244-45, 248, 289-290; *Villette*, Chapter 27.
100		Letters of 7 and 11 June 1851 from Charlotte to Amelia Ringrose, June 1851 from Charlotte to Mrs. Gaskell, 24 June 1851 from Charlotte to Ellen, 28 June 1851 from Charlotte to Sydney Dobell, and 15 November 1851 from Charlotte to James Taylor; *Gaskell B* 523, 548; *S.H.III.* 244-5, 248, 251, 253, 289-90; *Villette*, Chapter 23.
101		Letters of 2 June 1851 from Charlotte to Ellen, and 15 November 1851 from Charlotte to James Taylor; *Gaskell B* 519-20, 548; *S.H.III.* 241, 289-90.

Note Page

102		Letters of 24 June 1851 from Charlotte to Ellen, 26 June 1851 from Charlotte to Mr. Brontë, and 15 November 1851 from Charlotte to James Taylor; *Gaskell B* 523–5, 548; *S.H.III.* 251–2, 289–90. Sir David Brewster accompanied her.
103		Letters of 11 June 1851 from Charlotte to Ellen, June 1851 from Charlotte to Mrs. Gaskell, and 4 August 1851 from Charlotte to George Smith; *Gaskell B* 535; *S.H.III.* 245–6, 248, 267.
104		Letter of 27 July 1851 to Ellen; *Shorter* II, 226; *S.H.III.* 265.
105		*Gaskell B* 542; letter of 30 October 1851 from Charlotte to Ellen; *S.H.III.* 285.
106		Letter of 1 September 1851 to Ellen; *Shorter* II, 230; *S.H.III.* 273.
107	312	Letter of 30 October 1851 to Ellen; *Shorter* II, 236; *S.H.III.* 285.
108		Ibid.; letters of 7 November 1851 from Charlotte to George Smith, 17 December 1851 and 11 May 1852 from Charlotte to Ellen; *Gaskell B* 551, 572; *S.H.III.* 287, 300, 333.
109	312	Letter of 6 November 1851 from Charlotte to Mrs. Gaskell; *Gaskell B* 545–6; *S.H.III.* 286–7.
110		Ibid.; *Gaskell B* 546.
111		Letter of 7 November 1851 from Charlotte to George Smith; *S.H.III.* 287.
112	313	Letter of 20 November 1851 from Charlotte to George Smith; *S.H.III.* 293.
113		Letter of 28 November 1851; *Gaskell B* 549, 554; *S.H.III.* 295.
114		Letter of 1851 from Charlotte to George Smith; *Gaskell B* 558; *S.H.III.* 292.
115		Letter of 29 October 1851 from Mrs. Gaskell to Mrs. James; *C.B.*; *Gaskell B* 314–17; *S.H.III.* 284, 292, 294.
116		Letters of 31 July, 9 August, 7, 20, 28 November, 19, 31 December 1851, 1, 19 January, and 11 March 1852 from Charlotte to George Smith, and 10 December 1851 from Charlotte to Harriet Martineau; *Gaskell B* 534–5, 538–9, 552, 555–8, 566; *S.H.III.* 265–6, 269–70, 287, 292–3, 295, 299, 301–3, 307, 322.
117	314	Letters of 20 November 1851, 14 February, and 21 March 1852 from Charlotte to George Smith; *Gaskell B* 553, 561–3, 566; *S.H.III.* 293, 314–15, 324.
118		Letter of 31 December 1851; *Gaskell B* 557; *S.H.III.* 302.
119		Letter of 1 January 1852 from Charlotte to George Smith; *Gaskell B* 559; *S.H.III.* 303.
120		Letter of December 1851 from Charlotte to Ellen; *Gaskell B* 550; *S.H.III.* 298; *Stores-Smith.*
121		*Gaskell B.* 551–2.
122		Letters of 29 January 1852 from Charlotte to Mrs. Smith, 6 February 1852 from Charlotte to Mrs. Gaskell, and 28 July 1852 from Charlotte to W. S. Williams; *Gaskell B* 559–60, 576; *S.H.III.* 311–12; IV, 2.
123	315	Letter of 16 February 1852 from Charlotte to Ellen; *S.H.III.* 315–16.

Note	Page	
Note	*Page*	
124		Letter of 12 April 1852 to Laetitia Wheelwright; *Gaskell B* 570; *S.H.III.* 330–1.
125		Letter of 29 January 1852 to George Smith; *Gaskell B* 560; *S.H.III* 310.
126		Ibid.
127		Letter of 21 March 1852; *S.H.III.* 324.
128		Letter of 12 March 1852 to Miss Wooler; *Shorter* II, 258; *S.H.III.* 323.
129		Letters of 6 and 16 June 1852 from Charlotte to Ellen; *Gaskell B* 573–4; *S.H.III.* 336–7.
130	316	Letters of 26 July, 3 and 13 August 1852 from Charlotte to Ellen, and 19 August 1852 from Charlotte to George Smith; *Gaskell B* 575–7; *S.H.IV.* 2–4.
131		Letter of 29 January 1852; *S.H.III.* 311.
132		Letter of 11 May 1852 from Charlotte to Ellen; *Gaskell B* 572; *S.H.III.* 333.
133		Letter of 9 October 1852 from Charlotte to Ellen; *Gaskell B* 578; *S.H.IV.* 10.
134		Letter of 21 October 1852; *Gaskell B* 578–9; *S.H.IV.* 12.
135		Letters of 30 October and 3 November 1852 from Charlotte to George Smith; *Gaskell B* 579–82; *S.H.IV.* 13, 16.
136		Letters of 20 November 1852 from Charlotte to George Smith, and 22 November 1852 from Charlotte to Ellen; *Gaskell B* 585; *S.H.IV.* 20–1.
137		Letters of 3 November 1852 from Charlotte to George Smith, and 6 November 1852 from Charlotte to W. S. Williams; *Gaskell B* 581–3; *S.H.IV.* 16–17.
138		Letters of 23 November 1852 from Charlotte to George Smith, and 25 November 1852 from Charlotte to Mrs. Smith; *Gaskell B* 585; *S.H.IV.* 21.
139		Letter of 6 December 1852 from Charlotte to George Smith; *Gaskell B* 586–7; *S.H.IV.* 22–3.
140	317	Ibid.
141		Letter of 4 November 1851 from Charlotte to Ellen; *S.H.III.* 285.
142		Ibid.
143		Letter of 15 November 1851; *S.H.III.* 288–90.
144		Letter of 4 March 1852; *Shorter* II, 255; *S.H.III.* 319.
145		Letter of 7 March 1852 to Ellen; *Shorter* II, 257; *S.H.III.* 321.
146	318	Letter of 1 July 1852; *Shorter* II, 271; *S.H.III.* 341.
147	319	Letter of 15 December 1852; *Gaskell B* 590 (part); *Shorter* II, 295–6; *S.H.IV.* 29.
148		Ibid.; *S.H.IV.* 30.
149		Letter of 18 December 1852 from Charlotte to Ellen; *Shorter* II, 297; *S.H.IV.* 30.
150		Ibid.
151		Ibid.
152		Ibid.

Note Page
153   320   Ibid.; *S.H.*IV. 30–1.
154   Letter of 2 January 1853 from Charlotte to Ellen; *Shorter* II, 298; *S.H.*IV. 32.
155   Ibid.
156   Ibid.
157   Ibid.; *S.H.*IV. 33.
158   Postponed a few days to avoid clashing with the publication of Mrs. Gaskell's new novel *Ruth*. See letter of 19 January 1853 from Charlotte to Ellen, and her reply to Mrs. Gaskell's request in letter of 12 January 1853; *S.H.*IV. 34, 36.
159   Letter of 12 January 1853 from Charlotte to Mrs. Gaskell; *S.H.*IV. 34.
160   Letters of 7 and 16 February 1853 from Charlotte to George Smith, 15 February 1853 from Charlotte to Ellen, and 13 April 1853 from Charlotte to Miss Wooler; *Gaskell B* 594–5, 605; *S.H.*IV. 44–6, 58.
161   323   *Villette*, 1853, Chapter 15.
162   Ibid., Chapter 35.
163   Ibid., Chapter 15.
164   324   Ibid., Chapters 25 and 26.
165   Letter of 12 January 1853 from Charlotte to Mrs. Gaskell; *Gaskell B* 591; *S.H.*IV. 34.
166   Letter of 19 January 1853 from Charlotte to Ellen; *Gaskell B* 592–3; *S.H.*IV. 35.
167   Letter of 11 January 1853 from Charlotte to Ellen; *S.H.*IV. 33.
168   Ibid., *S.H.*IV. 33–34.
169   With Ellen. See letter of 28 January 1853 from Charlotte to Martha Brown; *Gaskell B* 593; *S.H.*IV. 41.
170   325   Letter of 4 March 1853 from Charlotte to Ellen; *Shorter* II, 311–12; *S.H.*IV. 49–50.
171   326   Letter of 27 January 1853; *Gaskell B* 600–1; *S.H.*IV. 39. This was a noble resolution, but Charlotte deceived herself about the flight of friends. Harriet Martineau was in no danger of being abandoned. See *Martineau A* and *B*.
172   *Martineau A* II; letter of 21 January 1853 from Charlotte to Harriet Martineau; *Gaskell B* 597; *S.H.*IV. 38.
173   *Martineau A* II.
174   Ibid.; *Gaskell B* 597–8; *S.H.*IV. 41. Harriet Martineau also reviewed *Villette* in the 'Daily News' at this time and in the same sense.
175   Letter of January 1853 from Charlotte to Harriet Martineau; *Gaskell B* 598; *S.H.*IV. 42.
176   Letters of 26 March 1853 from Charlotte to George Smith and 18 April 1853 from Charlotte to Ellen; *Gaskell B* 596–8, 606–7; *S.H.*IV. 55; *Martineau A* II. This action of Charlotte did not prevent Harriet Martineau from writing a generous and loving obituary notice in the 'Daily News', April 1855; *S.H.*IV. 180–4.

Note	Page	
177	328	*Gaskell B* 607–9; *S.H.IV.* 61–3.
178		Letter of May 1853; *Gaskell B* 610; *S.H.IV.* 67.
179		Letter of 13 June 1853 from Charlotte to Ellen; *Gaskell B* 613; *S.H.IV.* 71.
180		Letter of 18 December 1852 from Charlotte to Ellen; *S.H.IV.* 30–1. Nicholls was at Kirk Smeaton near Pontefract.
181		Letters of 15 July 1850 and 21 May 1851 from Charlotte to Ellen; *S.H.III.* 124, 236. See also letter of 5 May 1851 from Charlotte to Ellen; *Shorter* II, 207; *S.H.III.* 231.
182	330	Letter of 27 May 1853 from Charlotte to Ellen; *S.H.IV.* 68–9.
183		Letters of 4 March, 6 April, 16 and 27 May 1853 from Charlotte to Ellen; *S.H.IV.* 50, 56–7, 65, 68–9.
184		Letters of 14 May and 7 June 1854 from Charlotte to Ellen; *S.H.IV.* 125, 129; letter of 8 May 1854 from Catherine Winkworth to Emma Shaen; *S.H.IV.* 124; *Haldane, E. S.*; *Shaen.*
185		Letters of 28 March and 11 April 1854 from Charlotte to Ellen; *S.H.IV.* 110, 112.
186		*Gaskell B* 623; *S.H.IV.* 96.
187		Letter of 11 April 1854 from Charlotte to Ellen; *Shorter* II, 354; *S.H.IV.* 112.
188		See Note 182 above.
189		Letter of 11 April 1854 from Charlotte to Ellen; *Shorter* II, 354; *S.H.IV.* 112.
190		Letter of 28 March 1854 from Charlotte to Ellen; *Shorter* II, 353; *S.H.IV.* 111.
191		Letter of 11 April 1854 from Charlotte to Ellen; *Shorter* II, 354; *S.H.IV.* 112.
192		Ibid.
193		Ibid.; letter of 12 April 1854 from Charlotte to Miss Wooler; *Gaskell B* 627–9; *S.H.IV.* 113.
194		Letter of 11 April 1854 from Charlotte to Ellen; *Shorter* II, 354; *S.H.IV.* 112–13.
195	331	Letters of 12 April 1854 from Charlotte to Miss Wooler, 18 April 1854 from Charlotte to Mrs. Gaskell, and 25 April 1854 from Charlotte to George Smith; *S.H.IV.* 114, 116, 119; letter of 23 April 1854 from Mrs. Gaskell to John Forster; *S.H.IV.* 117; *Haldane: E. S.*; *C.B.* Mrs. Gaskell had reason for her fears if the fragment *Emma* is a true example of Charlotte's writing after marriage.
196		Ibid.
197		Letter of 8 May 1854 from Catherine Winkworth to Emma Shaen; *S.H.IV.* 122–3; *Haldane, E. S.*; *Shaen.*
198		Letters of 12 April 1854 from Charlotte to Miss Wooler, 15 April 1854 from Charlotte to Ellen, and 25 April 1854 from Charlotte to George Smith; *Gaskell B* 629–30; *S.H.IV.* 113–15, 119.
199		Letters of 11 April 1854 from Charlotte to Ellen, and 12 April 1854 from Charlotte to Miss Wooler; *S.H.IV.* 113–14.

Note	Page	
Note	*Page*	
200		Gaskell B 633. But see letter of 16 June 1854 from Charlotte to Miss Wooler; *S.H.IV.* 131.
201		Gaskell B 633; *S.H.IV.* 133–43. See '*An Account of her Honeymoon*', by Charlotte Brontë. *In a letter to Miss Catherine Winkworth*, 1930.
202	332	Letter of 25 April 1854 from Charlotte to George Smith; *Gaskell B* 629–30; *S.H.IV.* 119.
203		See her sketch of the Rev. Macarthey (Nicholls) in *Shirley*; *Wroot A* and *D*.
204		Letter of 19 September 1854 from Charlotte to Miss Wooler; *Gaskell B* 635; *S.H.IV.* 152–3.
205		Letter of 9 August 1854; also letter of 22 August 1854 from Charlotte to Miss Wooler; *S.H.IV.* 145, 148.
206		Letter of 19 September 1854 from Charlotte to Miss Wooler; *S.H.IV.* 152–3; *Gaskell B* 634–5 and Note 1, 634. The best proof of the effect of her new life on Charlotte's work is to be seen in the little she did write.
207		Letters of 14 September and 11 October 1854 from Charlotte to Ellen; *S.H.IV.* 151, 154. See also *Reid B*.
208		Letter of 20 October 1854 from Charlotte to Ellen; *S.H.IV.* 155.
209		Letters of 20 October and 7 November 1854 from Charlotte to Ellen; *S.H.IV.* 156, 158.
210		Letter of 31 October 1854 from Charlotte to Ellen; *S.H.IV.* 156–7.
211		Letter of 15 November 1854; *S.H.IV.* 160.
212		But see *Gaskell B* 638.
213		Letter of 29 November 1854 from Charlotte to Ellen; *Gaskell B* 636–7; *S.H.IV.* 161–2.
214		Letter of 7 December 1854 from Charlotte to Ellen; *S.H.IV.* 164–5.
215		Letter of 19 January 1855 from Charlotte to Ellen; *S.H.IV.* 171.
216		Letter of 14 February 1855 from Nicholls to Ellen; *S.H.IV.* 174.
217		Letter of 21 February 1855; also letter of 15 February 1855 from Charlotte to Laetitia Wheelwright; *Gaskell B* 638; *S.H.IV.* 174–5.
218		Letter of February 1855 from Charlotte to Amelia Taylor (née Ringrose); *S.H.IV.* 176.
219		Letter of 31 March 1855 from Nicholls to Ellen; *S.H.IV.* 177–8. Tabby had died six weeks earlier; *Gaskell B* 638.

NOTES ON THE ILLUSTRATIONS

Frontispiece: THE FOUR BRONTËS

An engraving of the painting known as 'the gun group'. Ellen Nussey described this as 'a photograph of an oil painting by Branwell Brontë of himself and sisters when quite a boy'. She identified the figures, from left to right, as Emily, Charlotte, Branwell, and Anne. This group was presumably seen by her when she visited Haworth in the autumn of 1833, a month or two after Branwell's sixteenth birthday (p. 31).

This group is interesting because it is the only picture in existence of all the Brontë children; because it contains the only known full-face portrait of Branwell; because, though an immature piece of work, it foreshadows Branwell's ability to catch a likeness; and, finally, because there is good reason for thinking that it was a sketch for a more finished group. Of this later group, only the head and shoulders of Anne—now in the National Portrait Gallery in London—still remain. The similarity of Anne's pose in both portraits is marked; and on her right in the later portrait there is plainly to be seen an arm similar in position to the left arm of Branwell in the gun group.

Of the rest of the later group, the portraits of Charlotte and Branwell were destroyed by Nicholls because he did not think them good likenesses; and the portrait of Emily he gave to Martha Brown. This portrait was seen by Sir W. Robertson Nicoll in Martha's cottage in 1879, and is mentioned by him in *Nicoll B.* See also *Chadwick A; CKS D;* and a letter by the Rev. J. J. Sherrard in 'The Kings County Chronicle' in April 1914 in reply to correspondence in the 'Morning Post' in March 1914. In this correspondence Mrs. Chadwick contended that the single head and shoulders portrait in the National Portrait Gallery was of Anne and not of Emily as had hitherto been assumed—a contention which has since been fairly generally accepted.

The original of the gun group has not been found. A number of prints of the photograph reproduced here were owned by people in and around Haworth. The present photograph was printed in *Haworth;* and the copy on which Ellen Nussey wrote her comments was printed in *Simpson.* The photograph is reproduced by permission of the Brontë Society. It was taken by Walter Scott.

MR. BRONTË *(facing page 36)*

A photograph, taken late in his life, when his white cravat, which grew higher with the years, had all but covered his chin. But sufficient of the prominent chin remains visible to show that, in this at least, Mr. Brontë had left his mark on Charlotte. The original is now in the Haworth Parsonage Museum. Reproduced by permission of the Brontë Society. Photograph by Walter Scott.

HAWORTH PARSONAGE *(facing page 37)*

This is how the parsonage appeared in the time of the Brontës. An addition has since been made to the left-hand side of the house, next to the room occupied by Mr. Brontë. Photograph by Walter Scott.

THE YOUNG MEN'S MAGAZINE (*facing page 52*)
The title-page of No. 6 (Second Series) for December 1830, and a page of text of No. 3 (Second Series) for October 1830. Reproduced exact size. No. 3 was written on 23 August, and 'published' 25 August, just a year after Charlotte had taken over the editorship from Branwell (p. 20). In this October number of 1830 Charlotte assures her readers that the Second Series 'is conducted on like principles with the first; the same eminent authors are also engaged to contribute for it'. No. 6 was the second issue to appear in December. Now in the Brontë Parsonage Museum. Reproduced by permission of the Brontë Society. Photographs by Walter Scott.

ROE HEAD SCHOOL (*facing page 53*)
A pencil sketch by Charlotte when she was at school—probably during her first period there, 1831-2. Now in the Brontë Parsonage Museum. Reproduced by permission of the Brontë Society. Photograph by Walter Scott.

CHARLOTTE, EMILY, AND ANNE (*facing page 148*)
Painted by Branwell about 1834-5, and now in the National Portrait Gallery, London. The order, from left to right, is Anne, Emily and Charlotte. Although the execution is crude, Branwell has caught a good likeness of all three girls—the overhanging forehead, large mouth, prominent chin, and bright, intelligent eyes of Charlotte, and the prominent mouths and large, liquid eyes of Emily and Anne (pp. 35-6, 301, 303). Reproduced by permission of the Director of the National Portrait Gallery.

LAW HILL, SOUTHOWRAM, BETWEEN BRIGHOUSE AND HALIFAX (*facing page 149*)
Only the shell of this building now remains, but the front view, shown here, is much as Emily must have known it when she taught at the school in 1837 (pp. 60-1). Photograph by Walter Scott.

HAWORTH MOOR (*facing p. 164*)
The track on the right, which still exists, is the one taken by the Brontës on their walks to 'The Meeting of the Waters' (p. 36). The dip of the valley through which the beck runs can be seen in the centre background. Photograph by Walter Scott.

EMILY'S DOG, KEEPER (*facing p. 165*)
Emily made water-colour sketches of the hawk, Hero, and of Keeper, a cross between a mastiff and bulldog (pp. 78, 84, 145-6, 234). The originals of both are now in the Haworth Parsonage Museum. The sketch of Keeper is inscribed 'Keeper from Life, April 24th, 1838. Emily Jane Brontë'. Reproduced by permission of the Brontë Society. Photograph by Walter Scott.

THE PENSIONNAT HEGER (*facing p. 260*)
The garden of the *pensionnat* has been greatly altered since the Brontë sisters

were there in 1842; but the *berceau* on the left of the photograph still remains. It formed part of the *allée défendue* up and down which Charlotte and Emily paced slowly in their free hours, the younger sister leaning on Charlotte's arm (pp. 112–14). Photograph by Walter Scott.

BRANWELL (*facing p. 261*)

This is the medallion made by Leyland at Halifax in April 1846 (p. 196). It gives a good idea of Branwell's fine forehead and less impressive chin. Reproduced by permission of the Brontë Society. Photograph by Walter Scott.

A GONDAL POEM (*facing p. 276*)

Entitled 'R. Alcona to S. Brenzaida' and dated 3 March 1845, but better known as 'Cold in the earth'. It is one of Emily's finest love lyrics. Occupying part of two pages in the little notebook into which Emily transcribed all her best Gondal poems. Reproduced exact size. Now in the British Museum (Smith Bequest). In both notebooks—of Gondal and purely personal poems (p. 192)— Emily used this small and sometimes almost illegible script. Reproduced by permission of the Director of the British Museum. Photograph by R. B. Fleming.

ANNE (*facing p. 277*)

A water-colour sketch by Charlotte dated 17 June 1834, when Anne was fourteen, and when Charlotte was still fired with the hope of becoming an artist (p. 31). Original now in the Brontë Parsonage Museum. Reproduced by permission of the Brontë Society. Photograph by Walter Scott.

INDEX

Brontë, Charlotte—*cont.*

manuscript books, 21; early development of character in her Angrian stories, 23; she goes to school at Roe Head (1831), 24; meets Mary Taylor and Ellen Nussey, 25; they describe her, 25; her good general knowledge, 25; does not play games, 26; works hard, 26; talks much of her dead sisters, 26–7; soon becomes top of the school, 27; tells horrific tales in the dormitory, 27; hears about the Luddite riots, 27–8; leaves Roe Head (1832), 29; effect of the school on her, 29–30; begins teaching Emily and Anne, 30; persuades her father to let them all take drawing lessons, 30–1; hopes to earn money this way, but is disappointed, 31; encourages Branwell, and visits an art exhibition with him at Leeds, 31; is indulgent to Branwell, 32; letters to Ellen and Mary, 34; visits Ellen, 34–5; described by Ellen when she returns the visit (1833), 36; on the moors with her sisters and friend, 36; more letters to her friends, and more Angrian tales, 37; she describes Branwell (1834), 38–9; her view of herself and sisters as seen by Branwell, 39; reads a great deal, 40; recommends a course of reading to Ellen, 40; again visits her, 40–1; announces the future plans of the family, 41; returns to Roe Head as teacher, accompanied by Emily (1835), 42; her plans disappointed, 42; her sense of duty forbids frequent visits to her friends, 44–5; her Tory views roughly handled at Mary's home, 45; Mary's father increases her interest in French, 45; she becomes melancholy at school, 45–6; her diary entries, 46–9; her letters to Ellen, 49–51; temporary recovery of spirits during summer holidays

at home (1836), 51; another relapse, and more letters to Ellen, 51–3; she writes to Southey, enclosing some poems, 54; his reply (1837), 54–5; she writes again, 55–7; Southey's second letter, 57; still writing Angrian stories, 59; her unhappiness increases, and she again writes to Ellen, 59–60; the school moves to Dewsbury, 60; her longing for Ellen, 60; criticisms of Miss Wooler, 60; she upbraids her for neglect of Anne's health, 63; her own health fails, and she leaves the school (1838), 64; a happy time at the parsonage, 64–5; her fear of consumption, 65; she has an unexpected proposal of marriage, 66–8; goes to Stonegappe as governess (1839), 69; her dissatisfaction, 69–70; she returns home, 71; goes to Bridlington with Ellen, 72; the effect of the sea on her, 72; she has a second proposal of marriage, 73; stops writing Angrian stories, and begins a novel, 74–6; sends part of the novel to Wordsworth, he criticizes it, and she writes no more (1840), 76; reads French novels lent by Mary's father, 77; her fears for Branwell's future, 80; she is attracted by a new curate, William Weightman, 82–7; is still unsettled about her writing, 87; criticism of Branwell for working on the railway, 88; goes to Rawdon as governess (1841), 92; is again unhappy, 92–4; plans to open her own school, 100–1; becomes more ambitious, and thinks of studying abroad, 101–2, 106–7; broaches the subject to Miss Branwell, and asks for help, 107–8; Miss Branwell agrees, Charlotte is triumphant, 108–10; she leaves Rawdon, 110; Charlotte, Emily and Mr. Brontë leave for Brussels (1842), 111; Charlotte in London, 112; arrival at the *Pension-*

Brontë, Charlotte—*cont.*

192–3; is rebuked by Emily but wins her over, 193–4; writes to Chambers of Edinburgh, then to Aylott and Jones, who agree to publish at author's expense, 194; her own poetry pedestrian, with debased poetic vocabulary, 164, 219; more complaints about Branwell, 195; his state after she returns from short visit to Ellen, 195; her feeling for Emily grows, 197; friction between them over railway shares and about Héger, 197; she does not hear from Héger, spends a wretched summer (1845), 198; writes again to Héger, 198–201; he asks her to send future letters to the Athénée, 201; she breaks with him, 202; begins to write out her unhappiness in *The Professor*, 202; discusses novels with Emily and Anne, 202; gradual change in her relations with Ellen, 202–3; more complaints of Branwell, 203, 205–6; she hurts his feelings, 208–9; her responsibility for his decline, 209; the *Poems* published but fail (1846), 210; *The Professor* rejected, 210; she denies a rumour that she is to marry Nicholls, 210; goes with Emily to Manchester to find eye surgeon and lodgings, 211; returns with her father, who has operation for cataract, 211; her misery in the lodgings, 211–12; *The Professor* again rejected, and she begins *Jane Eyre*, 213; she is worried by Anne's health, 213; more complaints of Branwell, 213; asks Ellen to stay but is disappointed, 218; tells Ellen her youth has gone, and nothing to show for it, 219; her treatment of Emily's poems, 219–20; her letter to famous authors, enclosing a copy of the unsold *Poems*, 220; she tries to prevent Anne from writing *The Tenant of Wildfell Hall*, 221–2; The

Professor again rejected, but with an encouraging letter from Smith, Elder, 222; she finishes *Jane Eyre* and sends it to them, it is accepted and proves an instant success (1847), 222–3; she tells her father, 223; begins correspondence with Williams, the Smith Elder reader, 229–30; analysis of *Jane Eyre*, 223–9; comparison with *Wuthering Heights*, 232–3; she writes Branwell into Crimsworth of *The Professor*, 235; her lack of understanding of *Wuthering Heights*, 236–7; and of Emily, although she desires a closer relationship, 237–8, 293; her reaction to the success of *Jane Eyre*, 249; she corresponds with well-known authors, including G. H. Lewes, 249–50; he recommends Jane Austen's work as a model, but Charlotte is critical, 250–2; she dedicates second edition of *Jane Eyre* to Thackeray (1848), 252; it causes gossip, 252; her views of Rochester, the maniac, and Mirabeau, 253–4; more fears for Anne after all have had influenza, 254; more bad reports of Branwell, 254–5; she begins another novel, 255; a third edition of *Jane Eyre* carries her disclaimer of the authorship of *Wuthering Heights* and *Agnes Grey*, 255; she hears rumours that *The Tenant of Wildfell Hall* is also being attributed to her, 256; she and Anne at once visit London to prove their separate identities, 256–7; they meet Smith and Williams, 257; are taken to the Opera, 257–8; return home laden with books, 258; comparison by Charlotte of Rochester, Huntingdon and Heathcliff, 259–60; trouble with Emily about revelation of her name, 260–1; Charlotte also wants to be known by her pen name, 261; largely because of the use she has made of local people in

2D*